EL PERÚ-WAKA'

Maya Studies

UNIVERSITY PRESS OF FLORIDA

Florida A&M University, Tallahassee
Florida Atlantic University, Boca Raton
Florida Gulf Coast University, Ft. Myers
Florida International University, Miami
Florida State University, Tallahassee
New College of Florida, Sarasota
University of Central Florida, Orlando
University of Florida, Gainesville
University of North Florida, Jacksonville
University of South Florida, Tampa
University of West Florida, Pensacola

EL PERÚ-WAKA'
NEW ARCHAEOLOGICAL PERSPECTIVES
ON THE KINGDOM OF THE CENTIPEDE

Edited by Keith Eppich,
Damien B. Marken,
and David Freidel

Foreword by Diane Z. Chase
and Arlen F. Chase

UNIVERSITY PRESS OF FLORIDA

Gainesville/Tallahassee/Tampa/Boca Raton
Pensacola/Orlando/Miami/Jacksonville/Ft. Myers/Sarasota

29 28 27 26 25 24   6 5 4 3 2 1

Library of Congress Cataloging-in-Publication Data
Names: Eppich, Keith, 1971– editor. | Marken, Damien B., 1977– editor. |
    Freidel, David A., editor. | Chase, Diane, author of foreword. | Chase,
    Arlen F. (Arlen Frank), 1953– author of foreword.
Title: El Perú-Waka' : new archaeological perspectives on the kingdom of
    the centipede / edited by Keith Eppich, Damien B. Marken, and David
    Freidel ; foreword by Diane Z. Chase and Arlen F. Chase.
Other titles: Perú-Waka' : new archaeological perspectives on the kingdom
    of the centipede
Description: 1. | Gainesville : University Press of Florida, [2024] |
    Includes bibliographical references and index.
Identifiers: LCCN 2023042351 (print) | LCCN 2023042352 (ebook) | ISBN
    9780813069937 (hardback) | ISBN 9780813070698 (pdf) | ISBN 9780813073156
    (ebook)
Subjects: LCSH: Mayas—Guatemala—Petén (Department)—Antiquities. |
    Excavations (Archaeology)—Guatemala—Petén (Department) | Social
    archaeology—Guatemala—Petén (Department) | Perú Waka' Site
    (Guatemala)—Antiquities. | BISAC: SOCIAL SCIENCE / Archaeology | SOCIAL
    SCIENCE / Anthropology / Cultural & Social
Classification: LCC F1435.1.P46 P47 2024 (print) | LCC F1435.1.P46
    (ebook) | DDC 972.81/200909—dc23/eng/20231002
LC record available at https://lccn.loc.gov/2023042351
LC ebook record available at https://lccn.loc.gov/2023042352

The University Press of Florida is the scholarly publishing agency for the State University System of
Florida, comprising Florida A&M University, Florida Atlantic University, Florida Gulf Coast Univer-
sity, Florida International University, Florida State University, New College of Florida, University of
Central Florida, University of Florida, University of North Florida, University of South Florida, and
University of West Florida.

University Press of Florida
2046 NE Waldo Road
Suite 2100
Gainesville, FL 32609
http://upress.ufl.edu

CONTENTS

FIGURES

TABLES

FOREWORD

Archaeological excavation produces an abundance of material remains that are processed, interpreted, and then made available for others through publication. But how this has been accomplished has changed significantly over the course of the last century. This volume is an excellent example of how modern archaeology can incorporate both descriptive synthesis and interpretation in presenting the results of basic research.

It used to be that site reports, usually in the form of oversized monographs, were the gold standard for the final publication of archaeological investigations. The belief was that a site report would never go out of fashion and would always be useful to the field. Yet, what constituted a site report? Fifty years ago, it was essentially a straightforward description of each archaeological investigation carried out, detailing all the stratigraphic layers and features within an excavation and how they articulated with each other; the material remains and contextual units that were thought to be important were also described within the framework of the stratigraphic write-up. The basic goal was to present the archaeological materials in chronological order. There was little offered in the way of interpretation or synthetic interpretive statements outside of the site being investigated. Interpretations and descriptions of past lifeways generally were separately published in articles and were not woven together with descriptive analysis as in this tome.

Keith Eppich and his collaborators, Damien Marken and David Freidel, have produced here a volume on the archaeology of El Perú-Waka' (Guatemala) that provides data for fellow researchers along with wide-ranging interpretations and that attempts to bring the archaeological record alive. It places the Waka' archaeological data within the broader context of both the archaeological records of other sites and regions in Mesoamerica and the historical reconstruction of ancient Maya history through the use of epigraphy and iconography. This is accomplished through individual chapters that are cohesive, integrated, and well written. This volume builds on research carried out over twenty years, incorporating fifteen field seasons at the site between 2003 and 2023. It further builds upon an earlier summary of the Waka' investigations focused on ritual that was published as an edited book in 2014

(Olivia Navarro-Farr and Michelle Rich, eds., *Archaeology at El Perú-Waka':
Ancient Maya Performances of Ritual, Memory, and Power* [Tucson: University of Arizona Press, 2014]), better positioning the earlier research at Waka'
with the benefit of additional fieldwork. This book is not a dry summary of
archaeological materials and excavations but rather makes the interpretations
of archaeological investigations and the recovered archaeological data interesting for the reader. The volume is a stalwart example of what archaeologists
can do to showcase the value of their research projects to the broader public.

Half a century ago, Maya archaeological projects were generally considered to be long-term if researchers carried out three to five years of excavation
at a given site. The seventeen years of continuous investigations carried out at
Tikal (Guatemala) by the University of Pennsylvania were seen as an aberration. Today, however, this past long-term research effort is an aspiration for
many archaeologists, like those whose work is included in this volume, and
continuous work within a single site or region is one of the reasons that our
understanding of the ancient Maya past has progressed.

A major question in the field of Maya studies has always been about the
best way to publish archaeological data in a form that is usable to others. For
researcher specialists, only a small percentage of the potential audience, extensive description of the archaeological record, the detailed presentation of
archaeological artifactual materials, and the formalized illustrations remain
important. However, the oversized monograph presenting such materials is a
practice that has largely disappeared for a number of reasons, including both
the substantial costs of large publications with extensive illustrations and the
requirements of host countries for more immediate, annual field reports. Synthetic interpretive statements, like those found in this volume, are the new
publication currency for the interested professional and for the general public. Contextualizing the results of archaeological research in well-written and
interesting ways has become the new—and invaluable—site report.

Diane Z. Chase and Arlen F. Chase
Series Editors

I

El Perú-Waka' in the Maya World

1

Introduction to a Ruined City

KEITH EPPICH, DAMIEN B. MARKEN,
AND JUAN CARLOS PÉREZ

Just twenty years ago, the city was dead. About that, there can be no doubt. Her palaces lay in ruins, her temples crumbling or fallen. The tropical forest had overgrown abandoned buildings, empty plazas, unused streets, and whole neighborhoods. Still today, spider monkeys chitter where kings and queens once held court. Macaws in flight slowly circle tree-covered pyramids. Jaguars nightly pad through ancient homes. No people live here. The ruins of El Perú-Waka' in the Laguna del Tigre National Park of Guatemala (PNLDT) has not been a city for a long time.

This was not always so. The modern forest clearly covers an ancient city. Cut stone masonry litters erosional slopes. Trees fall, and their upturned roots hold broken ceramics and flaked lithics. The forest covers odd conical shapes and rectilinear mounds arranged around internal patios and oriented to large, level spaces. Looters' trenches, illegally placed, burrow into these bounds, revealing destroyed architecture and plundered, smashed graves. The city's people are long gone, but their material culture remains.

What did life look like when the city was alive? Is it possible to use the remains of this material culture to model the reality of the Maya who lived there? This is the attempt made here: to go beyond the archaeological record, to bring forth a simulacrum of the living city, to build arguments from the material culture about how the city looked when it lived. This involves not just the reconstruction of urban settlement patterns and household archaeology but an understanding of art, of life, of sustenance and vitality, of gods and ancestors, and an appreciation for the depth and complexity of ancient Maya culture. The starting point for this is evident: the extant material remains of the people and their lives in the city. Since 2003, members of the Proyecto Arqueológico Waka' (PAW) have documented these remains. From this archaeology has come an understanding of the city's occupational sequence, a broad outline of its political history, a deep appreciation of its stunning artistic traditions, and knowledge of its settlement patterns, showing both the original formation and the final dissolution of life inside the city.

Reaching El Perú-Waka' requires patience, hard work, sometimes luck, and a healthy budget. The ancient city is roughly 80 kilometers north-northwest of the modern town of Flores, deep in the remaining rainforests of the Department of the Petén, Guatemala (Figure 1.1). It lies in the southern portion of the Laguna del Tigre National Park of the Maya Biosphere Reserve. The roads from Flores are unpaved and become even less developed as one enters the Reserve. Once inside the park itself, the road to the archaeological site is little more than an uneven jungle path, challenging even the tough Mitsubishi pickups rented during field seasons. During the rainy season, the road becomes a stream of mud and water, virtually impassable. In such a case, a boat must be either rented from locals in Paso Caballos or borrowed from the National Council of Protected Areas (CONAP), the National Park Administrator, and a river journey must be taken to the southern edge of the ruins, followed by a three-kilometer hike.

The ruins themselves sprawl across a karstic escarpment, a roughly triangular tabletop, elevated 80 to 100 meters above the swampy savannas and riverine lowlands to the south and west (Figure 1.2). The tabletop looks down on the junction of two rivers, the sluggish, navigable Río San Pedro Mártir and the seasonal, muddy Río San Juan. The city core itself covers more than a single square kilometer and is densely packed with more than 1,000 structures, representing an urban density rare for the Classic Maya world (Figure 1.3, see Marken and Ricker, this volume). Outside this core, various outlying communities and satellite villages irregularly dot the limestone hills to the north and east. In total, the urban landscape covers a vast area (20 square kilometers at a minimum). The urban core centers on the broad rectangle of Plaza 1, an open space 280 meters long and 80 meters wide, canted 22 degrees east of north and running from the northwest to the southeast. Plaza 1 is paralleled to the south by the smaller Plaza 2, which is elevated 10 to 12 meters above it. Together, the two plazas form one of the largest open public spaces of any Maya city, rivaling even the massive plaza of Quirigua (Ashmore 1984, 1991, 2009). Crumbling pyramids and broken palaces frame these two open spaces, with the Royal Palace anchoring the northwest corner. Another large palace, the Chok Group, sits on the opposite, southeast, corner. On the southern side is the impressive Paal Group and, on the northeast side, the complex and largely unexplored Xucub Group. The city's two great pyramids, O14-02 and O14-04, stand on a natural ridge to the southeast, on the edge of the core and the escarpment. They form their own sacred precinct, termed

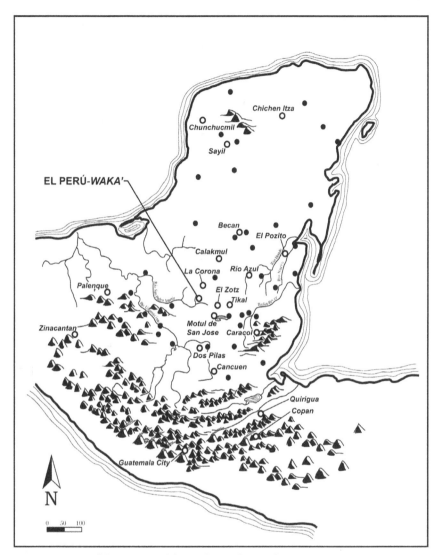

Figure 1.1. Map of the Maya world. Map by Keith Eppich.

the Mirador Group, a karstic rise encrusted with ritual architecture and an elevated causeway connecting to Plaza 2. The pyramids are 40 to 50 meters high
and offer, from their heights, a commanding view. On clear days, the tops of
the Sierra Lacandon become visible, almost 100 kilometers away to the west.
Certainly, every part of the old city, from its dense core to its hinterland communities, could have seen the large pyramids of the Mirador or, as termed by
David Freidel, the Oracle of Turtle Mountain.

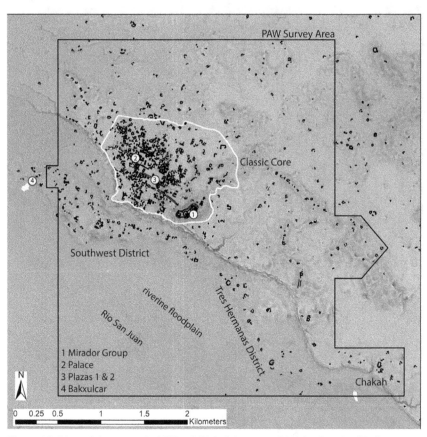

Figure 1.2. Map of the extended El Perú-Waka' cityscape. Map by Damien Marken, courtesy of Proyecto Arqueológico Waka'.

An Unfinished History, the Sequence of El Perú-Waka'

Current evidence gives only a partial and incomplete history of the city (Figure 1.4). It suggests that the Maya populated the area beginning in the Late Preclassic period, sometime during the centuries 300 BCE to 100 CE (Eppich, Marken, and Menéndez 2023). There was no city at that time, merely what appears to have been scattered farmsteads along the escarpment's edge. Even this early, the Mirador heights were sacred, possessing several hilltop shrines. This changes in the Protoclassic period, 100 to 250 CE, as the Maya constructed several ritual structures now interred beneath Plaza 2. These early structures remain poorly understood, as they lie below several meters of overburden. The Protoclassic settlement resembles less a big Classic city and more a small riverside town. The earliest neighborhoods were clustered along the riverine lowlands at the base of the escarpment, below the now-buried ritual center.

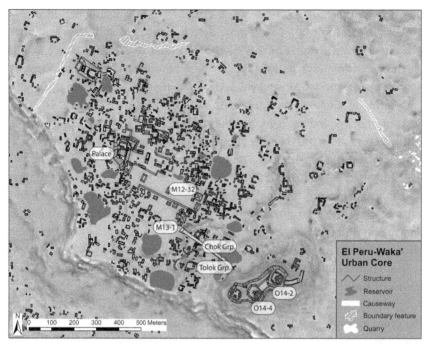

Figure 1.3. Map of the El Perú-Waka' urban core. Map by Damien Marken, courtesy of Proyecto Arqueológico Waka'.

The Maya then demolished this center to build the elevated open space of Plaza 2, which they oriented toward the city's civic temple, the impressive Structure M13-1 (Navarro-Farr 2016; Navarro-Farr, Pérez Robles, Menéndez, et al. 2020). The Early Classic period, 250 to 550, saw the development of Waka' into a true Maya city. This involved a low-density settlement straddling the escarpment and the areas around it, a pattern described as a "garden-city," with a managed mosaic of residences, temples, and palaces mixed in and among reservoirs, cornfields, garden plots, fallow brush, swampy low-lands, curated forests, and wholly wild tropical jungle (Chase and Chase 1998; Graham 1999; Fedick 1996; Fletcher 2012; Smith 2011; Isendahl 2012; Isendahl and Smith 2013; Marken 2011, 2015; Marken and Murtha 2017; Marken and Arnauld 2023). Despite periods of stasis and even decline, the Maya of Waka' continued to build and inhabit their city through the Late Classic period, 550–800, raising pyramid-temples to their full glory and boasting a high population in the outlying districts and dense neighborhoods in the urban core. The city began to falter in the 800s, experiencing a substantial shift as the Late Classic became the Terminal Classic period, 800–1050. Waka' seems to have convulsed and contracted and, with a complex series of movements that defies easy explanation, it appears to have mostly abandoned its outlying districts in favor of an even more densely nucleated core (Marken 2015; Marken, Ricker, Rivas, et al. 2019). The Terminal Classic city, concentrated on the defensible escarpment, appears as a pronounced departure from its earlier urban patterns. Most likely, such a settlement was not compatible with long-term sustainability in a tropical rainforest (compare Lentz et al. 2014; Scarborough and Valdez 2014; Scarborough, Chase, and Chase 2012). As the tenth century wore on, the Maya began to abandon parts of the core. Waka', in its last century, consisted of a ragged patchwork of ruins, households, and half-inhabited palace compounds. By 1050, even these evaporated, the final inhabitants departing, taking their belongings with them, and leaving behind votive deposits in the form of cumulative offerings in public spaces and other offerings positioned above the graves of their own ancestors (Eppich 2019; Navarro-Farr, Freidel, and Prera 2008; Navarro-Farr 2016).

The ruined landscape the Maya left behind contains the scattered fragments of the city's artistic traditions. It includes impressive ceramic works, now largely reduced to millions of broken sherds. This tradition possessed elaborate multislipped polychromes, the product of unique styles of palace-school workshops (see Reents-Budet et al. 1994). These lie alongside more commonplace ceramics, simple well-fashioned vessels for serving, storage, and cooking. The shifting styles and techniques of this potting tradition greatly aided the reconstruction of the occupational sequence described above (Eppich 2017). The city's artistic tradition also contains pieces of chert, obsidian, shell, and many other masterworks of both technical ability and quotidian utility. It includes crumbling pieces of architecture, a testament to the engineering ability of ancient architects. The archaeological remains yield evidence of weaving traditions, of a rich gastronomy culture, of elaborate political and religious rituals, and of narrative traditions of myth and history. A rich epigraphic history comes from the scribes who recorded the city's monumental history on some 51 known stelae (Guenter 2014; Kelly 2020). The surviving epigraphy details the city's history, from its third century founding to its fourth century embrace of Sihjay K'ahk' and his *entrada* (Freidel, Escobedo, and Guenter 2007). The scribes wrote of the city's position as the critical junior partner of the seventh-century Calakmul-Kaanul hegemony, and the stone-carvers depicted allied kings as companions in the famous Mesoamerican ballgame. They depicted the efforts of the city's final named king, in the ninth century, in his efforts to save the institution of Classic kingship. The Mayan glyphs even give the original name of the city, WAK-a', a toponym for the tropical centipede of Central America, *Scolopendra gigantea* (Guenter 2007, 2014). This impressive, venomous insect can reach 20 to 30 centimeters

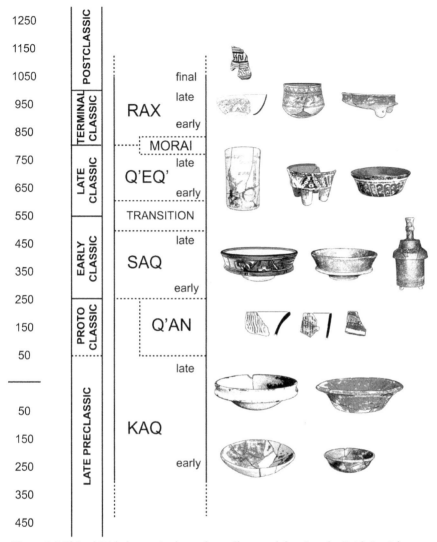

Figure 1.4. El Perú-Waka' ceramic chronology. Chart and drawings by Keith Eppich, courtesy of Proyecto Arqueológico Waka'.

in length and commonly preys on other insects, amphibians, and even small mammals. In the art of the Classic period, the centipede's prominent jaws served as a metaphor for the entrance to, or place of emergence from, the Underworld (Chinchilla 2017; Taube 2008:277). To modern Guatemala, this patch of ruins is El Perú, named for an unknown *chiclero*, or oil prospector, in the 1960s. To the ancient Maya, however, it was Waka', the "Kingdom of the Centipede."

Modern Scholarship in an Ancient City

Modern archaeology arrived at the ruined city in the early twenty-first century (Rich and Navarro-Farr 2014). Following several years of reconnaissance, the first of four major field seasons was launched in 2003 under the codirectorship of Héctor Escobedo and David Freidel (2004). Originally named the El Perú-Waka' Regional Archaeological Project, the research focused on the urban core, concentrating on the ceremonial and ritual contexts there in an effort to better understand the center's political history, occupational sequence, religious beliefs, and artistic traditions (Escobedo and Freidel 2004; Freidel and Escobedo 2014). This later transformed into its current incarnation, PAW (Proyecto Arqueológico Waka'). Then, as now, the project was a Guatemalan-administered project with multi-institutional involvement and support. This support includes scholars from Guatemala, the United States, Honduras, and Canada as well as participants who also conduct research in Honduras, El Salvador, and Belize. PAW project members represent a half-dozen colleges and universities across Guatemala and the United States. PAW has directed all subsequent field seasons and remains deeply embedded within the fabric of Guatemala and the local communities of the northern Petén, both providing and participating in employment, education, inclusion, and training.

The scholarly research conducted by PAW members has permitted reconstruction of the occupational sequence of the city, sketching out its Preclassic origin and its long Terminal Classic decline (Eppich 2015). PAW colleagues have rebuilt the political history, recorded votive and termination deposits, and reconstructed the artistic traditions present when the city was alive (Navarro-Farr and Rich 2014). PAW excavations and epigraphers have aided in the discovery of 11 stelae that have significantly expanded our working knowledge of the city's history, revealing previously unknown rulers and histories (Freidel, Escobedo, and Guenter 2007; Freidel, Masson, and Rich 2017; Guenter 2007; see also Kelly, Freidel, and Navarro-Farr, this volume). The PAW survey team has created one of the best-mapped Classic cities in the Petén, an effort that is now just bearing fruit, illuminating the ways in which the cityscape shifted through time (Eppich, Marken, and Menéndez 2023; Marken 2011, 2015; Marken, Pérez, Navarro-Farr, et al. 2019; Marken, Ricker, Rivas, et al. 2019; see also Marken and Ricker, this volume). Researchers have reconstructed the fluid economic patterns present in the city's extant material culture (Eppich and Freidel 2015; Eppich 2020; Freidel, Masson, and Rich 2017) and have demonstrated how buildings changed meaning and function over time (Navarro-Farr, Freidel, and Arroyave Prera 2008; Navarro-Farr

2016; see also Navarro-Farr, Pérez, and Pérez Robles, this volume). Research-ers have studied ancient acts of ritual and religious ceremony (Cagnato 2018; Eppich 2007, 2009; Freidel and Rich 2015, 2017; Fridberg, this volume) and conducted contextual analyses on eight prominent tombs that include five of the city's monarchs (Eppich and Navarro-Farr 2019; Freidel 2018; Freidel, Rich, and Reilly 2010; Navarro-Farr et al. 2020; Navarro-Farr, Robles, et al. 2020; Navarro-Farr, Pérez Robles, Pérez Calderón, et al. 2021; Rich 2017a, 2017b; Rich and Eppich 2020; Rich, Freidel, et al. 2010, Pérez Robles et al. 2018). These analyses have permitted a far more nuanced understanding of the city's rich dynastic and geopolitical history. Researchers have discussed and published on these findings in a score of dissertations, *licenciaturas*, con-ference presentations, working papers, book chapters, edited volumes, arti-cles, thoughtful dinner discussions, and fevered bar-side arguments. Through its first two decades, PAW has created knowledge about the deep antiquity of this one city and about the past of Guatemala and of the Maya people.

The heart of this research lies in the 19 Spanish-language archaeological reports produced by PAW at the request of the Guatemalan government. These reports, each written in the months following a field season, contain the raw data from the excavations in their purest and most unrefined state. Some of these reports even began as drafts while excavations still lay open. These reports, available online, are the wellspring from which all other PAW publications flow. As research on the old city continues, additional reports will follow. After the first four years of field research, while still under the auspices of the aforementioned El Perú-Waka' Regional Archaeological Proj-ect, Olivia Navarro-Farr and Michelle Rich organized a session at the Society for American Archaeology (SAA) meeting to review the already immense quantity of data highlighting the diverse manifestations of ritual behavior and displays of power within the city's political and monumental landscape. From this session came the best single publication yet produced on Waka', the 2014 volume, *Archaeology at El Perú-Waka': Ancient Maya Performances of Ritual, Memory, and Power*, edited by Olivia Navarro-Farr and Michelle Rich. That text contains all the major discoveries of the El Perú-Waka' Regional Archae-ological Project; a record of the epigraphic history; its termination deposits; the power of its ritual architecture and ceremonial narratives; its landscapes; its material culture; its honored dead; and the actions, thoughts, and nego-tiations of its ritual performance. The efforts of those first big field seasons flowered in that 2014 volume. As Patricia McAnany (2016:248) writes, the book "aptly characterizes the dynastic zeitgeist as it played out over 400 years of hieroglyphic texts, monumental constructions, and royal burials."

The Kingdom of the Centipede

The current volume serves as both an update and aspiring successor to that earlier, flowered text. The goal here is to gather the most recent scholarship on this ruined Classic center, examining the people who lived there and the city they built. This includes the organization of their settlement and the resources held by their landscape; their history and monumental art; their sacred architecture and their patron gods; the great tombs that held the bodies of their ancient rulers; and the patterns of everyday life inside the ancient, Native American city. From the contributions here, readers can obtain a detailed view of ancient life in a tropical biome, as explored through the reconstruction of the lives of the Classic Maya. For the ancient inhabitants, their city was a special and powerful place. It was *Waka'*, the sacred city and powerful kingdom of the giant centipede. It was their home.

The individual contributions here begin with Mary Kate Kelly, David Freidel, and Olivia Navarro-Farr's positioning of Waka' within the larger geopolitical landscape of the Classic Maya Lowlands and wider Mesoamerican world. Updating previous accounts of Waka's epigraphic history (e.g., Freidel, Escobedo, and Guenter 2007; Guenter 2014), Kelly and colleagues demonstrate the instrumental role of Waka' in the regional historical events of the Maya Lowlands throughout the Classic period, including the Early Classic Teotihuacan *entrada* (378 CE) and the Late Classic wars between the rulers of Tikal and the Kaan kingdom. Drawing from the inscriptions from three stelae recently discovered at Waka', each dating from a different era of the city's history, the authors not only flesh out the local dynastic history but also cement Waka's prominence in the political and ritual landscape of the Classic Lowlands.

Chapter 3, by Damien Marken and Matthew Ricker, introduces the reader to the Waka' urban core and its broader hinterlands. Combining more than a decade of traditional settlement surveys with recent lidar mapping and investigations of land-use patterns, they detail the occupational and physiographic contexts of the city and its environs. As they note, Waka' was both typical and unique as a lowland Maya city; it was a place molded to and molded by its local physiographic conditions and historical circumstances, resulting in a low-density city that was clearly Maya. This coupled natural and built environment served as the stage(s) where the city's inhabitants and its visitors both created and experienced the social relationships and interactions that gave the city life.

In Chapter 4, Keith Eppich examines Classic Maya social organization through an analysis of the architecture and artifacts of four residential groups at Waka'—one from the city hinterlands (Chakah) and three from the urban core (the Chok, Tolok, and Paal Groups). Eppich's detailed reconstruction of the settlement histories of these distinct household groups and their relations to Waka's wider social landscape indicates a heterogeneous urban society, one that exhibited features of multiple anthropological social models, varying dynamically through time and space.

Erin Patterson's Chapter 5 presents the current bioarchaeological data on the inhabitants of Waka', targeting variation in health and diet across age, sex, and class across the entire urban landscape, from the core to the near periphery and far periphery. Her analysis demonstrates the heterogeneity and hierarchical nature of the urban society of Waka', with clear health and dietary differences between men/women and elites/commoners, although urban core/periphery distinctions are less clear. Patterson's study, and others like it (e.g., Manzanilla 2017), demonstrate the vitality of bioarchaeological investigations in bringing the diversity of the lived experiences of past populations to life.

Chapters 6 through 11 of this volume focus on the monuments that dominated the Waka' urban built environment and on how those architectural constructions, and the rituals conducted within and around them, framed the lives of the city's inhabitants. The first of these contributions, Chapter 6, by Olivia Navarro-Farr, Juan Carlos Pérez, and Griselda Pérez Robles, discusses how the city's principal epicentral dynastic shrine, Structure M13-1, served as both the locus and symbol of dynastic authority throughout much of its history. In particular, Navarro-Farr and colleagues examine the role of royal women in shaping the Late Classic Maya political landscape through the history and interment of Lady K'abel—originally a foreigner from Kaanul—within Structure M13-1. In examining Lady K'abel's choice to be interred within Waka's most prominent dynastic monument, the authors demonstrate the ability and power of Maya royal women to not only actively direct political discourse during their lives but continue to impact the reigns of their successors, even after death.

Sarah Van Oss and Navarro-Farr delve deeper into the meaning and experience of Lady K'abel's reign in Chapter 7, through an in-depth analysis of the so-called Serpent Vessel recovered from her tomb excavation. Specifically, their analysis reveals that Lady K'abel's elevated social status—she held the supreme Classic Maya title of *kaloomte'*, while her husband was a mere *k'uhul ajaw* (holy lord) (Navarro-Farr, Kelly, et al. 2020)—was directly tied, at least in part, to her role as a recognized practitioner and leader of political rituals and divinations considered vital to the survival and success of the Waka' city and kingdom. The authors' comparative analysis not only further cements the prominence of this powerful woman in the city's history but elucidates a common source of political power for other royal Kaanul women.

Over the last few decades, archaeological theory has increasingly drawn from actor-network theory (e.g., Latour 2005) to examine how the use and symbolism of objects can imbue them with agency, transforming them from mere artifacts into cultural agents and intermediaries, able to influence and reconfigure human experience (e.g., Owens 2007). Michelle Rich and Keith Eppich add to this literature in Chapter 8, where they consider how the interment of individuals within Structure O14-04 of the Mirador Group at Waka' conferred a sense of "personhood" into one of the city's most visible pyramids. In asking, "Who is the pyramid?" the authors explore not only the individuals entombed within but their continuing active roles—through their embodiment in architecture—in shaping not only the history of the city but the daily lives of its urban residents.

In Chapter 9, Griselda Pérez Robles, Juan Carlos Pérez, David Freidel, and Elsa Damaris Menéndez describe the architectural and social history of the city's dynastic residential complex. The royal Waka' Palace is a massive monument in its own right; it is an architectural accretion that was built and rebuilt by a succession of royal sovereigns over nearly a millennium. While drawing upon the full catalog of PAW excavation data from the Palace, Pérez Robles and her fellow investigators focus on recent excavations in Structure L12-4, the complex's monumental façade and public access point, to create an architectural narrative of the city and its rulers, from their urban beginnings in the Late Preclassic period through centuries of shifting historical fortunes until its Terminal Classic end.

Diana Fridberg, in Chapter 10, provides an example of how localized ritual activities contributed to the fabric of Waka's sacred urban landscape. Her analysis of the zooarchaeological, artifactual, and architectural assemblage from the Cuartito, a small subterranean structure located behind the city's dynastic shrine of Structure M13-1, serves as a reminder that not all Maya rituals were monumental spectacles; private and semiprivate rituals and ritual spaces were integral activities in the creation and maintenance of civic and smaller-scale urban communities (see also Marken 2014).

In the final chapter of the volume, David Freidel returns to Waka's role in the larger Maya world, arguing that the city was widely recognized as a sacred place of ritual divination and political legitimization, Turtle Mountain. Weaving together epigraphic records with detailed comparative contextual and iconographic analyses of the grave furniture from multiple Waka' royal tombs, Freidel suggests that throughout its history Waka' was a place of unique sacral importance across the lowlands. Although not the largest Maya center, it was nevertheless an important cult center. It was a place with a long line of royal oracles over which the most powerful individuals in Classic Maya history continuously vied for influence and control. His contribution serves as an exclamation point with which to conclude the volume, which primarily focuses on the internal dynamics of Waka's population and history of Waka'. Not only is the archaeology of Waka' fascinating in its own right but the city was also a major ritual and political center for the entire Maya Lowlands.

Forests and Archaeology

As the following chapters demonstrate, the Classic Maya saw no hard dichotomies between the ancient past and the distant future, between history and myth, between city and country, or even between culture and nature. Rather, ideas of an integrated whole seem to have resided in their minds. The city appears to have reflected this, with towering pyramids beside humble shrines and richly ornamented palaces next to impoverished hovels. Most critical was the integration of the urban community and tropical rainforest. Dense urban settlement appears to have neighbored fecund outgrowths of nature, both wild forests and curated woodlands. Maya cities were cultivated gardens, not concrete jungles.

This integration lives on, even if the city itself does not. The ruins of Waka' lie within the Laguna del Tigre National Park (PNLDT), part of a series of protected national areas in northern Guatemala, collectively known as the Maya Biosphere Reserve (RBM). The RBM is the largest swath of tropical rainforest north of the Amazon, encompassing 2,083,498 hectares, and divided into 610 protected Biosphere Reserves as part of UNESCO's Humans and the Biosphere program. Within the RBM are two Ramsar sites that constitute the largest concentrations of wetlands in Mesoamerica. One of these areas is the PNLDT (CONAP 2006, 2015).

The PNLDT is a sanctuary of tropical marvels and is the largest reserve within the RBM, with 13 of the RBM's 16 distinct ecosystems represented inside its borders (CONAP 2006, 2008). The park itself contains thousands of tropical species, including highly endangered and spectacular ones. These include the brilliant *guacamayas*, the scarlet macaws that nest in the upper branches of trees, as well as the jaguars who silently trot in the shadows of the forest floor. The park is home to more than 200 bird species and more than 100 mammalian ones. Moreover, the PNLDT is invaluable to the development of local communities and the preservation of natural and cultural heritage, providing recreational, cultural, and spiritual benefits as well. In addition, protected areas such as the PNLDT provide environmental and ecosystem benefits such as CO_2 fixation, water regulation, biodiversity conservation, protection against disease and soil erosion, scenic beauty, food, resilience in the face of extreme climate events, and climate regulation (Mesa Nacional de Restauración del Paisaje Forestal de Guatemala 2018).

The PNLDT is a brilliant green jewel in Guatemala's richly ornamented crown of natural wonders. It is, however, a coveted jewel, and there are interests dedicated to prying it loose. Invaders and criminals have deforested almost a third of the park and annually threaten the remainder. Drug traffickers cut airfields from the jungle to refuel planes traveling north. Cattle barons slice off sections to feed their growing herds. Looters and smugglers raid the forest for illegal lumber, prohibited species, and stolen artifacts from the Maya past. Impoverished farmers, manipulated by these interests, seek the land of the park, thinking that small patches of cornfields will dramatically change their lot. Online searches for the Laguna del Tigre do not return results commenting on its stunning beauty, biological diversity, or the desirability of visiting it; instead, such searches return stories of fire, crime, "narco-jets," deforestation, cattle-smuggling, and cocaine.

The archaeological work at Waka', in the ruins of the City of the Centipede, aims to change this. PAW stands as one of several organizations dedicated to the preservation of the rainforest and to the continuance of the park. The efforts of the archaeologists in preserving the park have been noted, and PAW has received public and private accolades for these efforts (Radwin 2019). Archaeology hopes to move the narrative on the Laguna del Tigre away from fire, crime, and cocaine and toward natural beauty, conservation, and the wonders and details of the Americas' indigenous past. The city itself is dead, but the forest above it is very much alive; the study of the dead city may yet save the living forest.

References

Ashmore, Wendy

1984   Quirigua Archaeology and History Revisited. *Journal of Field Archaeology* 11(4):365–386.

1991   Site-Planning Principles and Concepts of Directionality among the Ancient Maya. *Latin American Antiquity* 2(3):199–226.

2009   Biographies of Place at Quirigua, Guatemala. In *The Archaeology of Meaningful Places*, edited by Brenda J. Bowser and Maria Nieves Zedeno, pp. 15–31. University of Utah Press, Salt Lake City.

Cagnato, Clarissa

2018   Shedding Light on the Nightshades (Solanaceae) Used by the Ancient Maya: A Review of Existing Data, and New Archeobotanical (Macro- and Microbotanical)

Evidence from Archeological Sites in Guatemala. *Economic Botany* 72(2):180–195.

Chase, Arlen F., and Diane Z. Chase

1998   Scale and Intensity in Classic Period Maya Agriculture: Terracing and Settlement at the "Garden City" of Caracol, Belize. *Culture and Agriculture* 20(2–3):60–77.

Chinchilla, Oswaldo

2017   *Art and Myth of the Ancient Maya*. Yale University Press, New Haven.

CONAP

2006   *Plan maestro 2007–2011, Parque Nacional Laguna del Tigre y Biotopo Laguna del Tigre-Río Escondido*. Consejo Nacional de Áreas Protegidas, Guatemala City.

2008   *Guatemala y su biodiversidad: Un enfoque histórico, cultural, biológico y económico*. Consejo Nacional de Áreas Protegidas, Oficina Técnica de Biodiversidad, Guatemala City.

2015   *Plan maestro Reserva de Biosfera Maya: Segunda actualización diciembre 2015, tomo I*. Documento técnico no. 20. Consejo Nacional de Áreas Protegidas, Guatemala City.

Eppich, Keith

2007   Death and Veneration at El Perú-Waka': Structure M14-15 as Ancestor Shrine. *PARI Journal* 8(1):1–16.

2009   Feast and Sacrifice at El Perú-Waka': The N14-2 Deposit as Dedication. *PARI Journal* 10(2):1–19.

2015   The Decline and Fall of the Classic Maya City. In *Archeology for the People: Joukowsky Institute Perspectives*, edited by John F. Cherry and Felipe Rojas, pp. 81–94. Oxbow Books, Oxford.

2017   Análisis cerámico, 2016: 1300 años de tradición cerámica de El Perú-Waka'. In *Proyecto Arqueológico El Perú-Waka': Informe no. 14, temporada 2016*, edited by Juan Carlos Pérez, pp. 288–385. Fundación de Investigación Arqueológica Waka', Guatemala City.

2019   WK13E, excavaciones en todo el Grupo Chok, concentradas principalmente en las secciones residenciales del norte, incluidas las Estructuras N13-2, N13-3, N13-9, N13-11, N13-12, N13-12, y N13-17. In *Proyecto Arqueológico El Perú-Waka': Informe no. 16, temporada 2018*, edited by Juan Carlos Pérez, Griselda Pérez, and Damien B. Marken, pp. 4–82. Fundación de Investigación Arqueológica Waka', Guatemala City.

2020   Commerce, Redistribution, Autarky, and Barter: The Multitiered Urban Economy of El Perú-Waka', Guatemala. In *The Real Business of Ancient Maya Economies: From Farmers' Fields to Rulers' Realms*, edited by Marilyn Masson, David A. Freidel, and Arthur A. Demarest, pp. 149–171. University Press of Florida, Gainesville.

Eppich, Keith, and David A. Freidel

2015   Markets and Marketing in the Classic Maya Lowlands. In *The Ancient Maya Marketplace: The Archaeology of Transient Space*, edited by Eleanor M. King, pp. 195–225. University of Arizona Press, Tucson.

Eppich, Keith, Damien Marken, and Elsa Damaris Menéndez

2023   A City in Flux: The Dynamic Urban Form and Function of El Perú-Waka'. In

Building an Archaeology of Maya Urbanism: Flexibility and Planning the American Tropics, edited by Damien Marken and M. Charlotte Arnauld, pp. 105–147. University Press of Colorado, Louisville.

Eppich, Keith, and Olivia Navarro-Farr
2019   The Curious Case of Lady K'abel's Snuff Bottle: The Functionality, Form, Context, and Distribution of Classic Maya Tobacco Flasks. In *Breath and Smoke: Tobacco Use among the Maya*, edited by Jennifer A. Loughmiller-Cardinal and Keith Eppich, pp. 203–326. University of New Mexico Press, Albuquerque.

Escobedo, Héctor L., and David A. Freidel
2004   Introducción: La primera temporada de campo del Proyecto Arqueológico El Perú-Waka'. In *Proyecto Arqueológico El Perú-Waka': Informe no. 1, temporada 2003*, edited by Héctor L Escobedo and David Freidel, pp. 1–6. Fundación de Investigación Arqueológica Waka', Guatemala City.

Fedick, Scott L., editor
1996   *The Managed Mosaic: Ancient Maya Agriculture and Resource Use*. University of Utah Press, Salt Lake City.

Fletcher, Roland
2012   Low-Density, Agrarian-Based Urbanism. In *The Comparative Archaeology of Complex Societies*, edited by Michael Smith, pp. 285–320. Cambridge University Press, Cambridge.

Freidel, David A.
2018   Maya and the Idea of Empire. In *Pathways to Complexity: A View from the Maya Lowlands*, edited by M. Kathryn Brown and George J. Bey, III, pp. 363–386. University Press of Florida, Gainesville.

Freidel, David A., and Héctor L. Escobedo
2014   Stelae, Buildings, and People: Reflections on Ritual in the Archaeological Record at El Perú-Waka'. In *Archaeology at El Perú-Waka': Ancient Maya Performances of Ritual, Memory, and Power*, edited by Olivia C. Navarro-Farr and Michelle Rich, pp. 18–33. University of Arizona Press, Tucson.

Freidel, David A., Héctor L. Escobedo, and Stanley P. Guenter
2007   A Crossroads of Conquerors: Waka' and Gordon Willey's "Rehearsal for the Collapse" Hypothesis. In *Gordon R. Willey and American Archaeology*, edited by Jeremy A. Sabloff and William L. Fash, pp. 187–208. University of Oklahoma Press, Norman.

Freidel, David A., Marilyn A. Masson, and Michelle Rich
2017   Imagining a Complex Maya Political Economy: Counting Tokens and Currencies in Image, Text and the Archaeological Record. *Cambridge Archaeological Journal* 27(1):29–54.

Freidel, David A., and Michelle M. Rich
2015   Pecked Circles and Divining Boards: Calculating Instruments in Ancient Mesoamerica. In *Cosmology, Calendars, and Horizon-Based Astronomy in Ancient Mesoamerica*, edited by Anne S. Dowd and Susan Milbrath, pp. 249–264. University Press of Colorado, Boulder.

2017 Maya Sacred Play: The View from El Perú-Waka'. In *Ritual, Play and Belief, in Evolution and Early Human Societies*, edited by Colin Renfrew, Iain Morley, and Michael Boyd, pp. 101–115. Cambridge University Press, Cambridge.

Freidel, David A., Michelle Rich, and F. Kent Reilly III

2010 Resurrecting the Maize King: Figurines from a Maya Tomb Bring a Royal Funeral to Life. *Archaeology* 63(5):42–45. https://archive.archaeology.org/1009/etc/maya .html.

Graham, Elizabeth

1999 Stone Cities, Green Cities. *Archaeological Papers of the American Anthropological Association* 9(1):185–194.

Guenter, Stanley P.

2007 On the Emblem Glyph of El Peru. *PARI Journal* 8(2):20–23.

2014 The Epigraphy of El Perú-Waka'. In *Archaeology at El Perú-Waka': Ancient Maya Performances of Ritual, Memory, and Power*, edited by Olivia C. Navarro-Farr and Michelle Rich, pp. 147–166. University of Arizona Press, Tucson.

Isendahl, Christian

2012 Agro-urban Landscapes: The Example of Maya Lowland Cities. *Antiquity* 86(334):1112–1125.

Isendahl, Christian, and Michael E. Smith

2013 Sustainable Agrarian Urbanism: The Low-Density Cities of the Mayas and Aztecs. *Cities* 31:132–143.

Kelly, Mary Kate

2020 Epigraphic Documentation during the 2019 Field Season at the Site of El Perú-Waka'. In *Proyecto Arqueológico El Perú-Waka': Informe no. 17, temporada 2019*, edited by Juan Carlos Pérez, Griselda Pérez Robles, and Damien B. Marken, pp. 272–290. Fundación de Investigación Arqueológica Waka', Guatemala City.

Latour, Bruno

2005 *Reassembling the Social: An Introduction to Actor-Network-Theory*. Oxford University Press, Oxford.

Lentz, David L., Nicholas P. Dunning, Vernon L. Scarborough, Kevin S. Magee, Kim M. Thompson, Eric Weaver, Christopher Carr, et al.

2014 Forests, Fields, and the Edge of Sustainability at the Ancient Maya City of Tikal. *Proceedings of the National Academy of Sciences* 111(52):18513–18518.

Manzanilla, Linda, editor

2017 *Multiethnicity and Migration at Teopancazco: Investigations of a Teotihuacan Neighborhood Center*. University Press of Florida, Gainesville.

Marken, Damien B.

2011 City and State: Urbanism, Rural Settlement, and Polity in the Classic Maya Lowlands. PhD dissertation, Department of Anthropolgy, Southern Methodist University, Dallas.

2014 *Sasamal* Performance: Variability in Ritual Contexts at El Perú-Waka'. In *Archaeology at El Perú-Waka': Performances of Ritual, Memory, and Power*, edited by Olivia Navarro-Farr and Michelle Rich, pp. 134–146. University of Arizona Press, Tucson.

2015   Conceptualizing the Spatial Dimensions of Classic Maya States: Polity and Urbanism at El Perú-Waka', Petén. In *Classic Maya Polities of the Southern Lowlands*, edited by Damien B. Marken and James Fitzsimmons, pp. 123–166. University Press of Colorado, Boulder.

Marken, Damien B., and M. Charlotte Arnauld

2023   Building an Archaeology of Maya Urbanism. In *Building an Archaeology of Maya Urbanism: Flexibility and Planning the American Tropics*, edited by Damien Marken and M. Charlotte Arnauld, pp. 5–52. University Press of Colorado, Louisville.

Marken, Damien B., and Timothy Murtha

2017   Maya Cities, People and Place: Comparative Perspectives from El Perú and Tikal. In *Research Reports in Belizean Archaeology, Papers of the 2016 Belize Archaeology Symposium, Architecture and Urban Design: Expressions of Kingly Power and Hegemony of the State*, edited by John Morris, Melissa Badillo, Sylvia Batty, and George Thompson, pp. 177–189. Institute of Archaeology, National Institute of Culture and History, Belmopan.

Marken, Damien B., Juan Carlos Pérez, Olivia Navarro-Farr, and Keith Eppich

2019   Ciudad de los Ciempiés: Urbanismo, fronteras y comunidad en El Perú-Waka', Petén, Guatemala. In *XXXII Simposio de Investigaciones Arqueológicas en Guatemala, 2018*, vol. 1, edited by Bárbara Arroyo, Luis Méndez Salinas, and Gloria Ají Álvarez, pp. 531–546. Ministerio de Cultura y Deportes, Instituto de Antropología e Historia, Guatemala City.

Marken, Damien B., Matthew Ricker, Alexander Rivas, and Erika Maxson

2019   Urbanismo de *Bajo* densidad en las tierras bajas Maya: El caso de El Perú-Waka', Petén, Guatemala. *Estudios de Cultura Maya* 54:11–42.

McAnany, Patricia

2016   Review of *Archaeology at El Perú-Waka': Ancient Maya Performances of Ritual, Memory, and Power*, edited by Olivia Navarro-Farr and Michelle Rich. *Journal of Anthropological Research* 72(2):248–249.

Mesa Nacional de Restauración del Paisaje Forestal de Guatemala

2018   *Oportunidades de restauración de Paisaje Forestal en Guatemala*. Instituto Nacional de Bosques, Guatemala City.

Navarro-Farr, Olivia C.

2016   Dynamic Transitions at El Perú-Waka'; Late Terminal Classic Ritual Repurposing of a Monumental Shrine. In *Ritual, Violence, and the Fall of Classic Maya Kings*, edited by Gyles Iannone, Brett A. Houk, and Sonja A. Schwake, pp. 243–269. University Press of Florida, Gainesville.

Navarro-Farr, Olivia C., Keith Eppich, David A. Freidel, and Griselda Pérez Robles

2020   Ancient Maya Queenship: Generations of Crafting State Politics and Alliance Building from Kaanul to Waka'. In *Approaches to Monumental Landscapes of the Ancient Maya*, edited by Brett A. Houk, Bárbara Arroyo, and Terry G. Powis, pp. 196–217. University Press of Florida, Gainesville.

Navarro-Farr, Olivia C., David A. Freidel, and Ana Lucía Arroyave Prera

2008   Manipulating Memory in the Wake of Dynastic Decline at El Perú-Waka: Termination Deposits at Abandoned Structure M13-1. In *Ruins of the Past: The Use and Perception of Abandoned Structures in the Maya Lowlands*, edited by Travis W. Stanton and Aline Magnoni, pp. 113–145. University Press of Colorado, Boulder.

Navarro-Farr, Olivia C., Mary Kate Kelly, Michelle Rich, and Griselda Pérez Robles
2020 Expanding the Canon: Lady K'abel the *Ix Kaloomte'* and the Political Narratives of Classic Maya Queens. *Feminist Anthropology* 1(1):38–55. https://doi.org/10.1002/fea2.12007.

Navarro-Farr, Olivia C., Griselda Pérez Robles, Damaris Menéndez, and Juan Carlos Pérez Calderón
2020 Forest of Queens: The Legacy of Royal Calakmul Women at El Perú-Waka's Civic-Ceremonial Temple. In *A Forest of History: The Maya after the Emergence of Divine Kingship*, edited by Travis W. Stanton and M. Kathryn Brown, pp. 67–87. University Press of Colorado, Louisville.

Navarro-Farr, Olivia C., Griselda Pérez Robles, Juan Carlos Pérez Calderón, Elsa Damaris Menéndez Bolaños, Erin Patterson, Keith Eppich, and Mary Kate Kelly
2021 Burial 61 at El Perú-Waka's Structure M13-1. *Latin American Antiquity* 32(1):188–200. https://doi.org/10.1017/laq.2020.99.

Navarro-Farr, Olivia C., and Michelle Rich, editors
2014 *Archaeology at El Perú-Waka': Ancient Maya Performances of Ritual, Memory, and Power*. University of Arizona Press, Tucson.

Owens, Erica
2007 Nonbiologic Objects as Actors. *Symbolic Interaction* 30(4):567–584.

Pérez Robles, Griselda, Juan Carlos Pérez, Damaris Menéndez y David Freidel
2018 Operación WK 18: Excavaciones en la acrópolis y el Palacio Real de Waka'. In *Proyecto Arqueológico El Perú-Waka': Informe no. 15, temporada 2017*, edited by Juan Carlos Pérez, Griselda Pérez Robles, and David Freidel, pp. 84–129. Fundación de Investigación Arqueológica Waka', Guatemala City.

Radwin, Max
2019 Fire, Cattle, Cocaine: Deforestation Spikes in Guatemalan National Park. *Mongabay*, June 21. https://news.mongabay.com/2019/06/invaders-cattle-cocaine-deforestation-spikes-in-guatemalan-national-park/.

Reents-Budet, Dorie, Joseph W. Ball, Ronald L. Bishop, Virginia M. Fields, and Barbara MacLeod
1994 *Painting the Maya Universe: Royal Ceramics of the Classic Period*. Duke University Press, Durham.

Rich, Michelle
2017a *Ancient Bodies: Archaeological Perspectives on Mesoamerican Figurines*, Exhibit at Los Angeles County Museum of Art (LACMA), July 1, 2017–February 4, 2018, Los Angeles County Museum of Art.
2017b Archaeology at El Perú-Waka': A Maya Ritual Resurrection Scene in Broader Perspective. *LACMA Unframed*, September 21. https://unframed.lacma.org/2017/09/21/archaeology-el-%C3%BA-waka%E2%80%99-maya-ritual-resurrection-scene-broader-perspective.

Rich, Michelle, and Keith Eppich
2020 Statecraft in the City of the Centipede: Burials 39, 38, and Internal Alliance Building at El Perú-Waka', Guatemala. In *A Forest of History: The Maya after the Emer-*

gence of Divine Kingship, edited by Travis W. Stanton and M. Kathryn Brown, pp. 88–106. University Press of Colorado, Louisville.

Rich, Michelle, David Freidel, F. Kent Reilly III, and Keith Eppich
2010   An Olmec Style Figurine from El Perú-Waka', Petén, Guatemala: A Preliminary Report. *Mexicon* 32(5):115–122.

Rich, Michelle, and Olivia C. Navarro-Farr
2014   Introduction: Ritual, Memory, and Power among the Maya and at Classic Period El Perú-Waka'. In *Archaeology at El Perú-Waka': Performances of Ritual, Memory, and Power*, edited by Olivia C. Navarro-Farr and Michelle Rich, pp. 3–17. University of Arizona Press, Tucson.

Scarborough, Vernon L., Arlen F. Chase, and Diane Z. Chase
2012   Low Density Urbanism, Sustainability, and IHOPE-Maya: Can the Past Provide More Than History? *UGEC Viewpoints* 8:20–24.

Scarborough, Vernon L., and Fred Valdez
2014   The Alternative Economy: Resilience in the Face of Complexity from the Eastern Lowlands. *Archaeological Papers of the American Anthropological Association* 24(1):124–141.

Smith, Michael E.
2011   Classic Maya Settlement Clusters as Urban Neighborhoods: A Comparative Perspective on Low-Density Urbanism. *Journal de la Société des américanistes* 91(1):51–73.

Taube, Karl
2008   The Classic Maya Gods. In *Maya: Divine Kings of the Rain Forest*, edited by Nikolai Grube, pp. 263–277. Könemann, Cologne.

2

Waka' on the International Stage

MARY KATE KELLY, DAVID FREIDEL,
AND OLIVIA C. NAVARRO-FARR

New epigraphic discoveries at Waka' enrich our perspective of the geopolitical position of the Classic Maya city. In this chapter, we provide our current
view of Waka' history, centered on the inscriptions and imagery provided by
the monuments, with a particular focus on a few recently discovered stelae.
We incorporate additional elements of the narrative as gleaned from contextual, artifactual, and comparative evidence. Our understanding of the city is
dominated by the sentiment that Waka' was profoundly connected to other
polities in the region and beyond—and the story told by the new monuments
continues to deepen this view. Waka' was internationally recognized as a
prominent center and played an important geopolitical role in notable Early
Classic interactions with Teotihuacan; and it continued to be a key player in
the Late Classic wars between the major centers of Tikal and the *kaan* (snake)
kings of Dzibanche and later Calakmul. These recent epigraphic findings imply an even greater ritual and commercial importance of the city with respect
to the broader region than previously recognized.

This chapter builds on, and serves as an update to, Stanley Guenter's work
(2014), albeit with an emphasis on three newly discovered monuments: Stelae
43, 44, and 51. Stela 43 was dedicated on 9.13.10.0.0 (January 27, 702 CE)[1]
and harks back to the era of Stela 44, carved on 9.6.10.0.0 (January 30, 564
CE). Stela 51 is earlier still, dedicated on 9.0.0.0.0 (December 12, 435 CE),
making it the second earliest dated monument at Waka'. All these monuments
were discovered during excavation at Structure M13-1 (see Figure 1.3 and
Navarro-Farr, Pérez, and Pérez Robles, this volume; Navarro-Farr and López
2020; Navarro-Farr, Pérez Robles, and Menéndez 2013; Pérez Robles and
Navarro-Farr 2013), and we explore the history that these stelae tell not only
of the city itself but also of their connections to the world beyond Waka'.

The Inscriptions of Waka'

Nearly all monuments currently known at Waka' bear evidence of intentional destruction: whether ancient, modern, or both. And all, including those few that escaped being chopped or sawn into pieces, were nevertheless subject to erosion. Ian Graham, as the first archaeologist to visit and document the site beginning in 1970,[2] noted the significant destruction caused by looting. He blamed "the great disaster that the sack of El Perú truly was" primarily on the oil company, Citgo (formerly Cities Service), which had first bulldozed a trail through the site in search for oil in the 1960s (Graham 2010:312). The result of this initial, unreported, discovery was evident by the time Graham got to the ruins—with many of the stelae sawn into pieces, the carved faces removed, and the blank limestone blocks left in heaps. In his visits, Graham photographed and sketched the monuments left on the surface, some 40 stelae and 3 altars, many of which bore carvings. He also identified and reconstituted several fragmented stelae, either those broken in antiquity or those damaged through looting; and in this work he recognized a handful of monuments or fragments from museums and private collections, which had come from Waka', and he matched them with the remaining pieces he located on-site (2010:310; see also Escobedo and Freidel 2004:3; Graham 1988:125). Two of the most delicately carved and best preserved of these are Stelae 33 and 34, housed at the Kimbell Art Museum and the Cleveland Museum of Art, respectively. When Graham found them, the blank white cubes of the sawed pieces of these stelae were scattered in Plaza 1, nicknamed the "tofu garden" by David Freidel. In subsequent visits, he remarked on the continued vandalism at the site (Graham 2010:303), a challenge that is still a concern today for the excavation and consolidation efforts of the Proyecto Arqueológico Waka' (PAW).

Since PAW began its research in 2003, continuing the city's epigraphic documentation has been a central objective (Escobedo and Freidel 2004:4). Guenter (2005, 2014) elaborated the history of the city, listing the known kings (Guenter 2005:Table 2; see also Guenter 2014:Figure 2) and detailing the evidence for deep-rooted connections to historical events in the broader region. Paramount among these are the post-*entrada* era of Teotihuacan influence in the Early Classic period and the wars between Tikal and the Kaan kings in the Late Classic. In piecing together the history of the region, including the many looted monuments now known to have come from Waka', other scholars have discussed the city's rich monumental texts (Guenter 2007; Martin 2000; Miller 1974; Wanyerka 1996).

Photogrammetric documentation of the monuments began in 2017, with the goal of producing 3D models and illustrations of the monuments (see Kelly 2019, 2020, 2023; Kelly and Paredes 2019). The first monuments addressed in this documentation process were the recently discovered stelae that are highlighted in this chapter: Stelae 43, 44, and 51. Some detailed discussions of these monuments and their contexts have been published elsewhere (Freidel, Navarro-Farr, et al. in press; Kelly 2019, 2020, 2023; Kelly et al. in press; Navarro-Farr, Kelly, et al. 2020; Navarro-Farr, Marken, et al. 2022; Navarro-Farr, Pérez and Pérez, this volume). The elements discussed in the current chapter are based on some preliminary readings, as well as on readings offered by others, and will be subject to a more thorough analysis of the city's monuments as the epigraphic documentation project progresses.

Current work includes a program to clean and protect the many monuments and monument fragments on the surface. New laminate roofs are currently being installed, replacing provisional thatched ones (Pérez Robles and Pérez Calderón 2019b). The laminate filters out the wavelengths of light necessary for photosynthesis, effectively preventing vegetal growth. In addition, platforms are being built to elevate the monuments off the forest floor, to keep the stelae dry. These efforts, in addition to the photographic and photogrammetric recording, are steps to preserve as much information as possible before further damage can deteriorate the monuments.

Establishment of Waka'

Ceramic and radiocarbon data suggest that at the time of the city's foundation in first or second century CE (Eppich and Marken, this volume), the civic design of Waka' consisted of the following: (1) a massive acropolis, named the Mirador Group, constructed atop the Mirador hill, rising 45 meters above the level of the city to the west of it (see Figure 1.3, Structure O14-2 and O14-4); (2) the Chok Group (see Figure 1.3; and Eppich, this volume); (3) Structure M13-1 (see Figure 1.3), which in the Late-to-Terminal Classic period, and likely earlier, can be identified as a fire shrine (see Navarro-Farr, Marken, et al. 2022); (4) a wide stone causeway that connects the Mirador Group, across the Chok Group, to Structure M13-1 at the southern end of the city (see Figure 1.3; Marken et al. 2019); and (5) a royal palace northwest of Structure M13-1 (see Figure 1.3; Pérez Robles and Pérez Calderón 2019a). This civic design is clearly discernible from both topographic and lidar surveys (Marken and Ricker, this volume) and shows that the temple of M13-1 was a focus at the time of the city's foundation, as was its connection to the Mirador Group, which Freidel (this volume) proposes was a monumental turtle effigy. The identification of the Mirador Group as a turtle may be related to a significant nominal feature that is discussed in this chapter, the frequent use of *ahk*, "turtle," in the names or titles of Waka' elite. The city is on an escarpment and the Mirador Group rises some 145 meters above the level of the Río San Juan that runs to the west of Waka' (Marken and Ricker, this volume). The pyramids atop the Mirador hill would have been observable from tens of kilometers to the west on the Río San Pedro Mártir, a major canoe transport route into and out of Petén (see Figure 1.1). Part of that canoe route continued up the Río San Juan to the floodtide port of El Achiotal (Acuña 2013; Acuña and Chiriboga 2019; Canuto and Barrientos 2020; Freidel, Acuña, et al. 2022; see also Figure 1.2) and on to the city of El Tintal in the Central Karstic Plateau.

Structure M13-1, the location where Stelae 43, 44, and 51 were excavated, was critically important to the people of Waka' from its earliest history on. That a Late Preclassic causeway would connect the most prominent location in the city, the Mirador Group, directly to Structure M13-1 reveals that this was a revered location from the time of the city's foundation. Structure M13-1 continued to be a focus for ritual activity up to the abandonment of the city (Navarro-Farr 2009). The ongoing excavations in this structure investigate the history of M13-1 and its relationship to the city as a whole (Navarro-Farr, Pérez, and Pérez Robles, this volume). In this chapter, we move outward from the texts discovered here to their implications for our understanding of the international connections harbored by Waka' elite.

Early Classic Connections to Teotihuacan

We begin our historical narrative in the Early Classic period, with the newly discovered Stela 51 (Figure 2.1; see Figure 6.8 for the 3D model of Stela 51) and its near contemporaries, Stelae 15 (Figure 2.2) and 16 (Figure 2.3). These earliest monuments at Waka' are impressive to behold not only in their sheer size (Stelae 15 and 16 are each over 3 vertical meters of carved surface, and Stela 51 is just under 3 meters) but also in the exceptional history and imagery they display: namely, a profound connection to the central Mexican highlands and the *entrada*-era figures Sihyaj K'ahk' and Spearthrower Owl (Freidel, Escobedo, et al. 2007; Guenter 2005, 2014; Stuart 2000).

The fully glyphic Stela 15 bears the dedication date of 8.19.0.0.0 (March 26, 416 CE) and twice gives the name of Sihyaj K'ahk' and his title, *kaloomte'*. The first of these instances of his name follows a glyph block discovered through excavation and recognized by Guenter (2005:366, Figure 4b) as **HUL-li-ya**, *hul-iiy*, "[he] had arrived,"[3] and associated with the date 8.17.1.4.4, 3 Kan 7

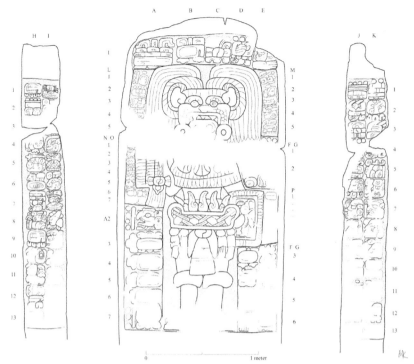

Figure 2.1. Stela 51. Illustration by Mary Kate Kelly, courtesy of Proyecto Arqueológico Waka'.

Figure 2.2. Stela 15 replica cast. Photograph by Mary Kate Kelly.

Figure 2.3. Stela 16 replica cast. Photograph by Mary Kate Kelly.

Mac (January 9, 378)—a mere 8 days before he is said to have arrived at Tikal (Guenter 2005; Stuart 2000:479–480). The arrival of Sihyaj K'ahk' in 378 sparks a cascade of events in the written history of the Maya Lowlands that highlights connections between Maya elites and Teotihuacan. This *entrada* may have been less an entrance of unfamiliar foreigners than an escalation or reinterpretation of established relationships between the Lowland Maya and Teotihuacan (Canuto, Auld-Thomas, et al. 2020). If, as proposed by Stuart (2000), Waka' was on the route taken by Sihyaj K'ahk' from Teotihuacan to Tikal, the city was likely chosen deliberately as a landing spot on that route. This may be due in part to the geographic location of the city; as mentioned above, Waka' was both prominently situated as a defensible city high on its escarpment, and conveniently located on important trade routes.

The term *hul-i*, "he/she/it arrived," is used in some contexts to refer to the establishment of governance or authority by some external entity as well as in the sense of the literal arrival of a person to a place (Martin 2020:122; Stuart 2000:477–478). Other historical events related to the arrival of Sihyaj K'ahk', as in the case of his arrival at Tikal, are directly correlated with "an intrusion by Teotihuacan that was dynastically disruptive and amounted to a political takeover" (Martin 2020:123). Waka' was likely already a pilgrimage center and important trade center by the end of the Late Preclassic period (Freidel, this volume; Rich 2011). In light of this possibility, the arrival of Sihyaj K'ahk' at Waka' in 378, eight days before his conquest of Tikal, was less a matter of his journey from west to east and more a matter of establishing or reinforcing a relationship with the elite of Waka' (Guenter 2005).

The Wak king K'inich Bahlam I appears in the historical narrative on Stela 15, just after the time of Sihyaj K'ahk's arrival. Two possible historical narratives can be drawn from this: either K'inich Bahlam was in power prior to 378 and welcomed the foreigners and the cultural and political shifts they instigated; or K'inich Bahlam, like Yax Nuun Ahiin of Tikal (Guenter 2014:51; see Stuart 2000:479), was placed on the throne by Sihyaj K'ahk' and, thus, helped to bring about the shift. As we do not yet know K'inich Bahlam's date of accession, either of these scenarios is possible. Archaeological data may provide clues as to the broader effects of this political alliance. Settlement patterns and household data suggest that in the Early Classic period the site population increased and densified (Eppich et al. 2023), though this is unlikely to be related to *entrada* events. However, a prominently located burial dated to just before the *entrada* suggests that the royals and elites were affected by Sihyaj K'ahk's arrival. On the summit of the Mirador Group, in a frontal platform of the pyramid in the middle of the three sacred localities (Structure O14-04), Rich discovered Burial 24, potentially a sacrificial offering of two young women, one pregnant, entombed with royal quality ceramics predating the *entrada* era (Rich, Piehl, and Matute 2006). The historically attested demise of Tikal's king, Chak Tok Ich'aak I, at the time of the arrival of Sihyaj K'ahk' coincides with the burial of high elite individuals believed to have been the royal family of the deceased in tombs in the eastern range of Tikal's Lost World Pyramid complex (Laporte and Fialko 1995:58–65). It is possible that the Waka' Burial 24 interments represent the elimination of the royal family of the Wak dynasty king preceding K'inich Bahlam I (cf., Rich and Eppich, this volume). What is certain is that the head of a larger-than-life stucco image of a Teotihuacan-style individual wearing goggles and buccal mask and a turban decorated with large goggles was discovered in the ruins of the seventh-century masonry shrine on this frontal platform (Figure 2.4). We take this to be a Late Classic commemoration of Sihyaj K'ahk's importance at Waka'.

As in the case of Tikal, this event was celebrated and commemorated. Sihyaj K'ahk' was remembered and revered nearly a century after the *entrada* at Waka', and he was mentioned by name and prominently portrayed on Stela 16 in 470 CE (Freidel, Escobedo, et al. 2007). The text to the right of his image states: **tz'a-pa-ja LAKAM-TUUN SIH-ja-*K'AHK'** . . . , *tz'a[h]paj lakamtuun sihyaj k'ahk'-Ø* . . . , "The stela was erected. [It is] Sihyaj K'ahk' . . ." The initial

Figure 2.4. Stucco head from Structure O14-04. Illustration by Sarah Sage (Rich 2011:Figure 6.46), courtesy of Proyecto Arqueológico Waka'.

verb of this phrase, *tz'ahpaj*, "was erected," is here derived in the passive voice. As a result, the subject of the sentence, the person responsible for erecting the monument, must be grammatically deleted or moved to a subordinate clause. Therefore, the name of Sihyaj K'ahk' immediately following the verb phrase cannot be referring to the individual who erected the stela (which we would also assume considering the century of removal in time); rather, he is the individual portrayed on the stela (see Stuart 1996). The lack of a possessive prefix on the term "stela" is somewhat unexpected. Had the term been written as **u-LAKAM-TUUN**, with the possessive *u-*, it would be read unambiguously as "Sihyaj K'ahk's stela." Rather, this instance of Sihyaj K'ahk's name more likely serves as a predicate noun, by which a null third person singular pronoun marker would (invisibly) inflect the name into the full verbal phrase "it is Sihyaj K'ahk."[4]

Another rather enigmatic figure associated with the influence of Teotihuacan in this historical moment is Spearthrower Owl. His name is often transcribed as Jatz'oom Kuy, "Owl Striker" (Grube and Schele 1994; Nielsen and Helmke 2008; Stuart 2000); however, the identification of the owl, and thus the reading of *kuy*, has recently been questioned (Stuart 2022). From Tikal Stela 31 we know he is the father of Yax Nuun Ahiin and the grandfather of Sihyaj Chan K'awiil, both kings of Tikal. Spearthrower Owl is said to have acceded as the *kaloomte'* of an unidentified place called 5 Cotton(?) Mountain (Tikal Marcador E1–E5; Nielsen and Helmke 2008:474n8; Stuart 2000; Stuart and Houston 2018). Significant aspects of this individual associate him with Teotihuacan: logographic versions of his name employ an *atlatl*, a highland Mexican projectile battle weapon (Schele and Freidel 1990:448n52); the front-facing bird also employed in his name hieroglyphs is in a stereotypically Teotihuacan position; and the 5 Cotton(?) Mountain place associated with Spearthrower Owl is also associated with the Teotihuacan War Serpent, Waxaklajuun Ubaah Chan (Tikal Marcador E1–E5). Spearthrower Owl does not appear to have been sovereign of Tikal, as the succession of kings at Tikal appears fully accounted for by others during his lifetime (he died in 438 CE, during the reign of his grandson, according to Tikal Stela 31). For these reasons, he has been proposed as a king of Teotihuacan (Stuart 2000, 2022). New evidence from Stela 51 of Waka' contributes to and complicates our understanding of the identity and political role of this individual.

Stela 51

Discovered in stages across three field seasons (2019, 2021, and 2022), Stela 51 (Figure 2.1) contributes to this early narrative connecting Waka' with Teotihuacan. The stela was found in two pieces: the bottom fragment excavated in 2019 and 2021, and the top fragment excavated in 2022. It was painted red and encased within a pen of roughly dressed stone and surrounded by the loose, unstable fill associated with the penultimate and final phases of Structure M13-1 (Navarro-Farr, Pérez, Pérez Robles, Freidel, et al. 2021). The monument was dedicated on the significant period ending of 9.0.0.0.0 (December 12, 435 CE). This date places its construction chronologically after Stela 15, but before Stela 16; it is therefore the second earliest dated monument at the city.

The archaeological context of this monument reveals that it was relocated in antiquity from its original, unknown position to the location from which it was excavated. It was repositioned in alignment with two other monuments: in east–west alignment with the flayed Stela 45 entombed inside M13-1 Sub III, and in north–south alignment with Stela 44. Navarro-Farr and colleagues (this volume) explore the significance of these alignments and consider how the associated archaeological data from this building narrate the connections between Waka' and the broader hegemonic structures throughout the Classic period. They discuss how Stela 51 was intentionally placed here to contribute to this narrative.

Its surface portrays a man standing, posed frontally, in full Teotihuacan regalia. The monument was broken at the level of the neck of the standing figure, effectively decapitating the ruler. As a result, much of the face is no longer visible; however, the traces of the Teotihuacan-style goggles can be discerned. He wears large earflares and a headdress with a feline wearing panaches of feathers over the ears, a motif dubbed by Freidel the "Feathered Feline of Teotihuacan," and the ruler's face emerges from this feline's open maw. He is wearing a short feather-ornamented cape that covers his shoulders, and a necklace of *Pecten* shells partly covers the cape. The arms emerge from the cape, with the ruler's right forearm lifted to display a feather-decorated scepter and his left arm displaying a rectangular feather-fringed shield (Navarro-Farr, Pérez, Pérez Robles, and Eppich 2022). The shield depicts an open-mouthed raptor that is likely an owl, given the tuft of feathers above the prominent round eye. The abdomen of the man displays an upturned crescent decorated with netting. This is a readily identifiable Teotihuacan motif, defined by Karl Taube as a mirror bowl, with this netted variant specifically associated with Spider Woman, Taube's definition of the Great Goddess associated particularly with the Moon Pyramid of Teotihuacan but also with the fire cult of the Sun Pyramid (1983, 2018 [1992]). Examples of the Teotihuacan mirror bowl given by Taube include one depicting a feather-fringed mirror upright on top of the crescent profile bowl, as in the case of the Esperanza Phase slate mirror back from Mound A at Kaminaljuyu (Kidder et al. 1946; Taube 1983). The Stela 51 mirror bowl has five prominent Teotihuacan-style flames/feathers on top of it, the middle three forming an in-line triad. As Taube has described in detail (2018 [1992]), Teotihuacan mirrors are, among other things, portals for deities and supernaturals. The mirror bowl depicted on Stela 51 demonstrates the individual's prominent role as a diviner.

We propose that this figure is wearing the names of the two prominent Teotihuacan-affiliated political figures of the *entrada* era: Sihyaj K'ahk' and Spearthrower Owl. The flames birthed from the mirror bowl womb of the Goddess on the ruler's abdomen may literally represent "Fire Born," as translates the name of Sihyaj K'ahk' (see Savkic Sebek and Velásquez García 2021:Figure 1e–f on "iconographic spelling"); and the raptor-decorated shield may represent the name of Spearthrower Owl. As such, this king of Waka', as we will discover thanks to the inscription, is wearing the names of his allies.

Some parallels can be seen in the costuming of Sihyaj K'ahk' on Stela 16. There, he wears a complex motif over the abdomen, with two rectilinear elements angled outward, flanking a center disc. The disc has two deep indentations that have the shape of eyes and rectilinear serrations on the rim. This motif has a resemblance to the *lechuzas y armas* motif defined by Hasso von Winning (1987), which depicts a medallion with an owl face framed by crossed weapons and often sits on the abdomen of warrior figures at Teotihuacan. While this might be a mirror or shield flanked by weapons, we suggest in this case that it is more specifically an example of the mirror bowl, as defined by Karl Taube (1983, 2018 [1992]), in which the feather-fringed mirror is shown upright in the divination bowl. While this section of Stela 16 is severely eroded, if we take the *lechuzas y armas* motif as an example, it may be the representation of an owl face. In a parallel with the shield on Stela 51, this would refer to Spearthrower Owl.

Returning to Stela 51, the hieroglyphic text surrounds the figure in three distinct registers. Read first are the large, low-relief glyphs starting in the upper left corner of the front face; one then reads down through the long count, then back to the line of lunar information across the top, and next, down the right side of the front face with a series of eroded glyph blocks. The text continues down the double-column of low-relief glyphs on the left face of the monument, then the right. The narrative continues to the larger of the incised glyphs on the front face of the monument, believed to have been originally five glyph blocks on either side of the headdress. And finally, one proceeds to the two sets of small, incised glyph blocks, one left of the scepter, and last, the nearly entirely eroded incised glyphs to the right of the shield. These last glyphs are difficult to decipher at the current stage and will not be highlighted in this discussion. The reading order of the inscription rotates four times from reader's left to right in a deliberate pattern. We suggest that the reader's experience would replicate the binding or bundling of the monument (Stuart 1996), and the ceremonial completion of creation and the 9th *baktun* (as celebrated on the monument), all done in emulation of the rotation of the Milky Way through the night sky (Freidel, Schele, and Parker 1993).

Text of Stela 51

The following discussion begins with an overview of the inscription recorded on Stela 51, with some elements of interest elaborated below. The opening date, while somewhat eroded, is unambiguously the ending of the 9th *baktun*. The *haab* date of 13 Ceh is no longer clearly visible; however, the three dots at the bottom right of the top fragment (glyph block G1) are most likely the dots for the number 13. Immediately following this (at F2-G2), we would anticipate the main verb of the sentence, and while the stela is broken, we can assume this was the ending of the 9th *baktun*. Nominal information likely follows, with the name of K'inich Bahlam visible at G3. It is unclear whether this is a new individual of that name or a parentage reference to K'inich Bahlam I who may have been the grandfather of the ruler portrayed on the monument.

The narrative picks back up at the top of the left face of the stela, with a rare, pluralized form of *yilajoob bolon tz'akbuul ajaw*, "they witnessed it the nine (or many) lords." This is followed by eight glyph blocks with nominal information, including K'uk' Ajaw, Bahlam Ajaw, and the "turtle" title, which will be discussed further below. The phrase ends with the declaration that this occurred *yichnal wiinte' naah ajaw* (before the Wiinte' Naah lord). Are these eight names and the Wiinte' Naah lord the nine who witnessed the erection of the monument? The syntax becomes a bit uncertain at this point, with additional nominal elements following the *wiinte' naah ajaw* title, including a second example of the "turtle" title, the name phrase Yajawte' K'inich, and what may be a name or title incorporating the severed head of the Maize God. If we anticipate only nine individuals present at this event (as suggested by the verbal phrase), are all these elements naming the Wiinte' Naah lord? Or are these separate individuals? The lack of conjunctions in the Maya inscriptions lends ambiguity to this. A discussion of this and other contexts of *wiinte' naah* in the inscriptions of Waka' will figure below. The end of this column becomes eroded, but it appears to name another witness to the event.

The narrative continues at the top of the right face of the stela with a distance number of 2 *k'atuns* and 19 *tuuns*, approximating a count back to the *entrada* event, given here as *huliiy sihyaj k'ahk' mut(al)*, "(since) Sihyaj K'ahk' arrived at Tikal." The count brings the narrative to the contemporaneous 9th *baktun* period ending, and while the monument is broken through these glyph blocks, the remaining details suggest that this event took place at **TI'-CHAN-na YAX-[T176]-NAL** (J5–K5). This location appears on Piedras Negras Altar 1 (M2–N2), Quirigua Stela C (B13–A14), Palenque Temple of the Cross Panel (D6–C7), Palenque Temple of the Sun Panel (F1–E2), and a carved jade mask in a private collection. In these other contexts, **TI'-CHAN-na YAX-[T176]-NAL** appears in mythological histories, and in some cases the event is conducted under the supervision of Itzamnaaj. Here, again, it appears that Itzamnaaj is responsible for the period-ending event, possibly in consort with other mythological beings, though in this context this event is associated with the contemporaneous date of 9.0.0.0.0 (December 12, 435 CE). This may imply that the location mentioned is indeed the physical location where the 9th *baktun* was celebrated.

Returning to the front of the monument, the accession of an individual is given with a distance number (L1–L5). We assume that this distance number is counting back from the ending of the 9th *baktun* period, though there is no calendar round to ascertain this assumption. This would give an accession date of 8.19.16.16.12, 5 Eb 0 Ceh (November 29, 432 CE). The name of the ruler who acceded is broken (L5) along the break that decapitated the stela. The text would have read from his name through the face of the portrayed ruler, to the incised text on the upper right. This strongly suggests that the ruler portrayed on the monument is none other than the individual whose accession date is given here. The phrase continues with a verb phrase **TZUTZ**-? 1-***PIH**-**K'UH**, *tzutz* ? *juun pih k'uh*, "it ended ? the 8,000 gods," the meaning of which remains opaque. The accession is said to have been witnessed by none other than Spearthrower Owl himself, *yilaaj jatz'[oom] ku[y](?)*. As an unprecedented surprise, Spearthrower Owl is given the Tikal emblem glyph (M4-M5).

Spearthrower Owl and Waka'

Stela 51 prominently mentions Spearthrower Owl, the enigmatic, *entrada*-related figure, as having witnessed the accession of the Wak king portrayed on the monument three years before the 9.0.0.0.0 period ending. Without explicit evidence to ascertain which is historically accurate, three scenarios are possible: first, the Wak king traveled to Teotihuacan to be invested in power; second, Spearthrower Owl "witnessed" the accession ritual from a distance; and third, and as we would suggest the most straightforward solution, Spearthrower Owl was present in the Maya Lowlands and orchestrated the accession of allies locally.

Further suggestion of Spearthrower Owl's deep connection to the Maya Lowlands comes in the form of his Tikal emblem glyph. As mentioned above, he never appears to be the sovereign of Tikal—Chak Tok Ich'aak I, Yax Nuun Ahiin, and Sihyaj Chan K'awiil follow one another as rulers of Tikal in succession, though not without the political upheaval and complex familial relations as we now understand from the political history of this time (Martin 2020; Stuart 2000). And yet, we now have evidence of his being given the Tikal lordly title. Was this in deference to his role as the father and grandfather of Tikal kings? Or does he receive this title due to his own family ties to the elite of this site (as suggested by Stuart 2022)? If so, what exactly was the nature of these family ties—by marriage or by descendancy?

We know that Spearthrower Owl died a little over three years after the 9.0.0.0.0 period ending (Tikal Stela 31:H24-H28; Stuart 2000:482, Figure 15.15). His reign lasted over 3 *k'atuns* and 6 *tuuns*, or approximately 65 years (Stuart 2000:483). Even if he had been a young boy when he acceded, he would have been an aged man when the events related on Stela 51 took place. Throughout his life, he held a role of pinnacle importance to the geopolitics of the Maya Lowlands, the details of which we are still discovering. Though provocative, this monument perhaps leaves us with more questions than answers with respect to Spearthrower Owl's position and role in this narrative.

Waka' and the Wiinte' Naah

We turn now to discuss three known instances in the inscriptions of Waka' that reference *wiinte' naah*, each in a different, frustratingly complicated context (Figure 2.5). This term is considered to refer to the name of a building (or "building-type" [Martin 2020:125]) also known in the literature as an "Origin House" (Stuart 2004:237–239), "House of New Fire" (Fash et al. 2009), or "House of Darts" (Bíró 2020). References to *wiinte' naah* occur in tandem with "Teotihuacan imagery as well as the themes of fire-making, calendar rituals, and the foundation of the new political order" (Tokovinine 2020:264). In the Early Classic period, the *wiinte' naah* was a pilgrimage destination and the location of important accession rituals believed to have been held at Teotihuacan itself, possibly at the Sun Pyramid (Fash et al. 2009; Stuart 2004). Other cities may have had their own *wiinte' naah*, such as discussed at Copan (Fash et al. 2009:210–212). Excavations at Structure M13-1 have revealed a monumental Late-to-Terminal Classic hearth indicative of revivalist fire ceremonies celebrated at this building (see Navarro-Farr, Marken, et al. 2022). This evidence demonstrates that at this very late time, there is a hearkening back to the city's Teotihuacan-influenced era, with an emphasis on rituals involving fire (Navarro-Farr, Marken, et al. 2022). The Early Classic use of the building has not been fully explored, though it is plausible that this late use was a continuation of an earlier identification of this building as a *wiinte' naah* itself.

One instance in the inscriptions at Waka' that obliquely refers to a *wiinte' naah* appears immediately following the crucial phrase announcing Sihyaj K'ahk's arrival on Stela 15 (Figure 2.5a). It occurs in a glyph block which bears the elements **wi** and **TE'**, as well as an eroded superfix bearing the double curves of "shininess." While this is not a traditional *wiinte' naah* glyphic compound, it is likely referring either to some *wiinte'* place, or to a *wiinte'* object, possibly a mirror. Despite the deviation from the standard form of the *wiinte' naah* glyph, it is possible that this is a reference to a Wiinte' Naah at Waka' as it occurs right after the arrival declaration. This has been described as Sihyaj K'ahk's establishment or recognition of a Wiinte' Naah at Waka' (Freidel, this volume; Freidel, Escobedo, et al. 2007; Guenter 2005).

A second example of what is clearly a full *wiinte' naah* compound appears as the final glyph of the inset text on the base of Stela 9 (Figure 2.5b); however, the context of this glyph is not clear because the preceding glyph blocks are quite eroded.

The most recently discovered example is the above-mentioned *wiinte' naah ajaw* on Stela 51 (Figure 2.5c). This occurs in the phrase describing the erection of the stela on the ending of the 9th *baktun*, as witnessed by the many

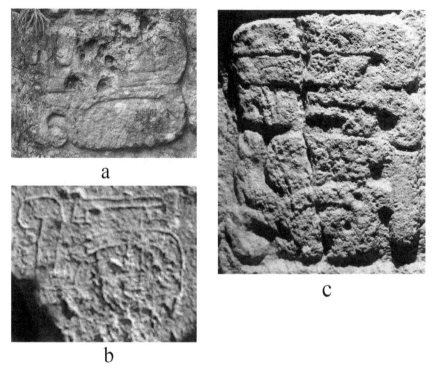

a

b

c

Figure 2.5. Examples of *wiinte' naah*: (*a*) wi-TE'-?, Stela 15; (*b*) wi-TE'-NAAH, Stela 9, incised caption; (*c*) yi-NAL-wi-TE'-NAAH-AJAW, Stela 51. Photographs 2.5a and 2.5c by Mary Kate Kelly; and photograph 2.5b by Phillip Hofstetter, courtesy of Proyecto Arqueológico Waka'.

lords, and *yichnal wiinte' naah ajaw*, "before the *wiinte' naah* lord." Estrada-Belli and Tokovinine (2016:Figure 7) collect five other known instances of this titular phrase. They note that "some could be foreign rulers; others were Maya lords who traveled to and derived legitimacy from *Wiin Te' Naah*" (Estrada-Belli and Tokovinine 2016:161). Martin (2020:245) proposed that one of these *wiinte' naah ajaw*, "Tajom Uk'ab Tuun [for Piedras Negras] fills much the same supervisory role as Sihyaj K'ahk' did at Tikal." Could Sihyaj K'ahk' have also received the *wiinte' naah ajaw* title? This is perhaps unlikely as we have little evidence of Sihyaj K'ahk's explicit actions this long after the *entrada*. Or, as might be suggested from this new context on Stela 51, could Spearthrower Owl be the *wiinte' naah ajaw*? He was alive until three years after this event, and if he was, indeed, in the Maya Lowlands at this time, the title could refer to him. A third possibility could be that the king of Waka' portrayed on Stela 51 bore this title, and thus he would be the individual before whom the 9th *baktun* events were carried out. If we read the following nominal information as part of his names and titles, the locally relevant "turtle" title may lend some weight to this last suggestion.

The "Turtle" Title

Recent research points to mounting evidence of turtles in the epigraphic and archaeological records of Waka'. Certainly, cosmic turtles are present in Maya royal iconography from the Late Preclassic period at least, and several realms had turtle titles and royal names. At Waka', kings' royal names include the **AHK,** "turtle," logogram, iconographic representations of turtles appear regularly, and archaeological evidence points to the identification of the Mirador Group as a terraformed pyramidal turtle mountain (see Freidel, this volume). The text of Stela 51 brings some of the epigraphic details of these turtle nominal elements into sharper focus.

There is an element present in many names of Wak dynasty kings in these early texts that has previously been parsed as [**CHAN**]**AHK,** "sky turtle" (Guenter 2005, 2014). These glyph blocks have been presumed to be names of kings, or elements of their names, and here we look at these examples as a set to note the diversity among them, and perhaps change our reading slightly.

The earliest king in the city's known history is "Leaf" Chan Ahk (alternatively, Hoja Chan Ahk, and Te' Chan Ahk), named on the left side of Stela 15 (Figure 2.6a). This individual may have been responsible for the 8.15.0.0.0 (May 20, 337 CE) period ending,[5] and is the earliest known ruler in the historical record of the city. His name is the first in the known history of this "turtle" title. K'inich Bahlam I is also sometimes given the "turtle" title, visible after his name on the left side of Stela 16 (Figure 2.6b)—though it is worth noting that on the right side of Stela 15, his name clearly does not have this element. There is an example of one of these "turtle" titles that may have been a part of the name of "Dragon Jaguar," listed on the right side of Stela 16 (Figure 2.6c), though the reading of this is not fully clear due to erosion and breakage. And finally, there is an individual provisionally named "Tapir" Chan Ahk (Figure 2.6d), whose name is a variant of this title, and his accession is given on Stela 16 as 9.1.3.0.17 (August 30, 458 CE) (Guenter 2014:153).

Stela 51 provides two new examples of "turtle" titles, both of which preserve new and interesting details. The first of these, at I5 (Figure 2.6e, detail of Figure 2.1), clearly shows a bird head sitting atop the turtle carapace. It has a curved, slightly open beak, a fan of feathers at the back of the head, and an unclear feature protruding from or resting on top of the forehead. This latter is reminiscent of the tassel often seen on the forehead of the Maize God. The turtle carapace in this case is simply **AHK,** and very clearly does not bear the "sky" markings that we might have anticipated should this have

Figure 2.6. AHK nominal glyphs: (a) "Leaf" Chan Ahk, Stela 15; (b) K'inich Bahlam Chan Ahk, Stela 16; (c) Chan Ahk "Dragon Jaguar," Stela 16; (d) "Tapir" Chan Ahk, Stela 16; (e) first example from Stela 51; (f) second example from Stela 51. Photographs 2.6a, 2.6e, and 2.6f by Mary Kate Kelly; and photographs 2.6b, 2.6c, and 2.6d by Phillip Hofstetter, courtesy of Proyecto Arqueológico Waka'.

read [**CHAN**]**AHK**. The "shiny" marker in the shell is characteristic of Early Classic examples of the **AHK** sign,[6] and likely refers to the shiny nature the Maya saw as inherent to turtle shells.[7] The "wavy reticulated pattern" typical of the **AHK** logogram (Zender 2006:3) is visible around the "shiny" marker as well as around the ventral plastron and the apertures. The second example of a "turtle" title appears four glyph blocks later, at I7 (Figure 2.6f, detail of Figure 2.1). A very similar bird head sits at the top, this time without the tassel element on its forehead. And between the bird and the turtle shell is a head with a large earflare, dark patches next to the eye and the mouth, and what appears to be a jeweled mohawk. The **AHK** logogram in this example also bears the "shiny" marker, the ventral plastron, and the apertures. The preservation of these two examples of the "turtle" title that do not seem to bear any diagnostic markings of the **CHAN,** "sky," logogram shifts our reading of the other examples of this title; we now no longer anticipate that these read as *chan ahk,* but rather that they end simply in *ahk.*

The bird element that is present in both examples from Stela 51 is certainly the same component as what had been called "Leaf" and was sometimes read as **TE',** in the Stela 15 example of "Leaf" Chan Ahk's name. The Stela 15 example has the same overall outline as the element in the Stela 51 example, which contains preserved details of the curved beak, the eye, and the feathers protruding from the back of the head. But what kind of bird this is and how it should be translated is unclear. Dmitri Beliaev pointed out to the first author[8] that the same bird appears at Rio Azul in the tomb mural as a part of a G6 glyph.

These two examples of the "turtle" title on the side of Stela 51, in quick succession but separated by two names (K'uk' Ajaw and Bahlam Ajaw) and the *yichnal wiinte' naah ajaw* phrase, appear to be naming two separate individuals. In the Early Classic period at Waka' there are six examples of names bearing the **AHK** logogram, as listed above: "Leaf" Chan Ahk; K'inich Bahlam (I) Chan Ahk (this being evidently optional on his name); possibly "Dragon Jaguar" (or someone contemporaneous to him and listed next to his name on Stela 16); "Tapir" Chan Ahk; and two individuals on Stela 51. The first three of this list—"Leaf" Chan Ahk, K'inich Bahlam I, and Dragon Jaguar (or his contemporary)—were all likely deceased prior to the accession of the king of Stela 51 and the 9th *baktun* period ending. As the name phrase appears twice within this list on Stela 51, it appears that two individuals are being referred to—both present for the 9th *baktun* ceremony. "Tapir" Chan Ahk (who acceded 20 or so years later) could possibly be the referent of one of these "turtle" phrases. This suggests either that the "turtle" element is a common part of names at this time among the Waka' elite, or that it is part of a shared title.

Additionally, these new data imply that we must significantly change our understanding of the name of the figure previously known only from Stela 15 as "Leaf" Chan Ahk. The initial element does not read **TE',** nor does it represent a leaf; rather, it appears to be some kind of bird. Also, there is no infixed **CHAN** logogram. Our new reading for the name shared by the individual on Stela 15 and the individual indicated by the first of the "turtle" titles on Stela 51 is ? Ahk. This may be the same name as the second instance of this title on Stela 51, with the intervening head representing an optional syllable, likely in that case giving the final consonant of the bird head logogram. Alternately, the head may be giving a slightly different name or title. Until we find dates attached to these individuals, a decipherment for glyphs of the bird head or the human head featured in the second example from Stela 51, or contexts that allow us to differentiate between individuals with more precision, these factors will remain a bit ambiguous.

Late Classic Connections to Kaan

In the Late Classic period, the rulers of Waka' became thoroughly enmeshed in the hegemonic power strategies of the Kaan regime. At least eight monuments at Waka' narrate the story of their alliance: Stelae 7, 20, 27, 33, 34, 43, and 44, and a block from Hieroglyphic Stairway 2.[9]

The apogee of the Wak-Kaan connection in the second half of the seventh century is famously depicted on the Kimbell Art Museum and Cleveland Museum of Art stelae, Stelae 33 and 34, respectively. K'inich Bahlam II's accession is carved on a fragment of Stela 33 and states the following:

CH'AM-wi[K'AWIIL]-K'INICH-BAHLAM-ma yi-chi-NAL-yu[ku]-no-ma[CH'EEN]
ch'am[aa]w k'awiil k'inich bahlam yichnal yu[h]noom ch'een
"K'inich Bahlam *k'awiil*-grasped (acceded) before Yuhknoom Ch'een."

K'inich Bahlam's accession took place *yichnal*, "before," Yuhknoom Ch'een, indicating his subordinate status to this great Kaan king. Though the exact date of his accession is unknown, we have some clues as to the timing. An incised slate plaque at the Princeton University Art Museum is carved with his birthdate of *9.*10.*4.*8.*5, 7 Chicchan 8 Xul (June 21, 637 CE) (Just 2007). At the time of the dedication of Stela 33 (692 CE), he would have been in his third *k'atun* of life, and indeed he is given the title of 3 *winikhaab ajaw* on this monument. We presume his accession took place before the carving of Stela 1, where K'inich Bahlam is portrayed celebrating the *ho'tuun*, "quarter-period ending," of 9.11.5.0.0 (September 19, 657 CE). This 20-year span, between his birth in 637 CE and his first known monument in 657 CE, falls toward the beginning of Yuhknoom Ch'een's lengthy reign.

Lady K'abel, the wife of K'inich Bahlam, strengthens the relationship between Wak and Kaan. Stela 34 portrays her; the stela was erected as the pair to Stela 33, but in quality and finesse of style it is the superior. Lady K'abel is of the Kaan line, given the titles *ix kaan ajaw* and *ix kaloomte'*, the latter announcing her superior status to that of K'inich Bahlam. Lady K'abel's role as a foreign emissary queen, military leader, and diviner engaged with the local patron gods can be seen through her depiction on Stela 34 and her elaborate royal tomb, Burial 61 (Navarro-Farr, Kelly, et al. 2020; Navarro-Farr, Pérez Robles, Pérez Calderón, et al. 2021).

Stelae 44 and 43

The discovery of Stela 44 (Figure 2.7) sheds light on much earlier historical ties between Wak and Kaan kings than have previously been known, stretching back at least to the mid-sixth century (Guenter, in Castañeda 2013:197–202; Kelly et al. in press). Though the only remaining element of the long count is the *haab* date of 13 Pax, the opening date can be securely identified as 9.6.10.0.0, 8 Ahau 13 Pax (January 30, 564 CE). The monument celebrates the accession of Wa'oom Uch'ab Ahk in 556 CE. Notably, his name echoes the Early Classic tradition to include a reference to turtles, as discussed above. In this case, his name can be translated as "he who stands up the turtle's offering." The monument posthumously depicts his father, named in part Chak Tok Ich'aak. Three lines of evidence bond Wa'oom Uch'ab Ahk to the early Kaan regime. The first and most explicit appears immediately following the announcement of his accession, in which he is called the *yajaw*, or vassal, of K'ahk' Ti' Ch'ich', the contemporaneous Kaan king (Martin and Beliaev 2017). The second is in an association through his father, who—in a fortuitous archaeological discovery excavated in the seasons of 2017 and 2018—was identified as the subject of La Corona Altar 5 (Stuart et al. 2018). This altar was dedicated in 544 CE and on it, Chak Tok Ich'aak received the title *sak wahyis*, a title held by rulers of La Corona and elsewhere who were subordinate to Kaan kings (Grube et al. 2012:22–23; Martin 2020:187). This suggests he was the ruler responsible for La Corona in 544 CE, but later, on Stela 44 at Waka', he is given the title of *wak ajaw*, leading us to believe that prior to his death in 556 CE, he was ruling at Waka'. Whether he was simultaneously or sequentially responsible for the two centers is yet to be determined, as is his place of origin (Kelly et al., in press; Stuart et al. 2018:11). Regardless, his intertwined relationship to La Corona and his title on La Corona Altar 5 as *sak wahyis* ground him firmly in his Kaan affiliation. The third, and perhaps most striking line of evidence for Wa'oom Uch'ab Ahk's relationship with the Kaan regime is in the identification of a woman whom we presume to be his mother, Ix Ikoom. Although the relationship glyph that would explicitly name her as his mother is lost to us (we expect it would have been on the effaced bottom section of the left side of the monument), the frequent naming order of first giving the father's name followed by the mother's name leads us to believe that the woman named at the top of the right side of the monument is Wa'oom Uch'ab Ahk's mother. She

Figure 2.7. Stela 44. Illustration by Mary Kate Kelly, courtesy of Proyecto Arqueológico Waka'.

bears the titles *ix sak wahyis* and *k'uhul* "cha" *tahn winik*, both of which are associated with Kaan (Grube et al. 2012; Velásquez García and García Barrios 2018). Our understanding of this woman comes to us, in part, from a much later monument that references back to her: Stela 43.

The severely fragmented Stela 43 (Figure 2.8) was discovered reset into the walls of M13-1's final Terminal Classic *adosada* terrace; it was a much later monument, dedicated in 702 CE. It refers to at least three 7 Ahau dates. The earliest is the 8.14.0.0.0, 7 Ahau 3 Xul period ending (September 2, 317 CE); the latest is the date of the dedication of the monument, 9.13.10.0.0, 7 Ahau 3 Cumku (January 27, 702 CE); and chronologically between these two events is a reference to 9.7.0.0.0, 7 Ahau 3 Kankin (December 8, 573 CE). We do not know what events took place on these 7 Ahau dates, but the name associated with the 573 CE date is a woman, Ix Ikoom, who is also given the *ix sak wahyis* title. Presumably her role on this date was significant as it is remembered and revered nearly 130 years later, as demonstrated by the carving of Stela 43.

We suggest that because this is only approximately ten years after the carving of Stela 44 and because the women named on Stelae 43 and 44 share the *ix sak wahyis* title, these two references are to the same woman. The alternative, that these references are to two different Kaan-affiliated women, may also be possible but seems less likely. Regardless, a Kaan-affiliated woman married into the royal line at Waka' and bore a son and heir to the throne. Freidel (this volume) suggests that this queen was the oracle of the city after the death of her husband. From both matriline and patriline, Wa'oom Uch'ab Ahk bears affiliation to Kaan, though whether either parent is a direct descendant of Kaan kings is not currently clear. Wa'oom Uch'ab Ahk's triad of Kaan connections leaves no doubt as to the status of Waka's vassalship in the mid-sixth century.

As a result of the discovery of Stela 44, it is apparent that Kaan kings considered Waka' to be a strategic ally early on in their empire-building efforts. We know that other centers in the Maya Lowlands began to have connections to Kaan—connections in which the Kaan rulers were always hierarchically superior—beginning in the transitional Middle Classic era. A retrospective monument at La Corona, Panel 6,[10] celebrates in text and imagery the arrival in 520 CE of Ix ? Naah Ek', a Kaan woman and daughter of Tuun K'ab Hix (Martin 2008). Naranjo's connection with Kaan is first apparent in 546 CE, when Aj Numsaaj Chan K'inich accedes under the same Kaan king, Tuun K'ab Hix (Naranjo Stela 47; Schele and Freidel 1990:175). And a Holmul king is named as the vassal of a Kaan king circa 580 CE (Holmul Stucco Frieze; Estrada-Belli and Tokovinine 2016; Martin 2020:248). Enveloping centers across the Lowlands into their political sphere was a strategy the Kaan kings employed in their campaign against Tikal.

Kaan Women

The dynamic that connected Waka' to Dzibanche and later to Calakmul relied fundamentally on the pivotal women who bridged the two elite houses: the two whom we recognize today are Ix Ikoom, in the mid-sixth century, and Lady K'abel, in the late seventh and early eighth centuries. This was a clear strategy employed by Kaan kings to impose bonds with the rulers of cities and centers across the Maya Lowlands. These two women, brought to Waka', have blended identities as outsiders who took on distinctly local responsibilities: they were diviners and caretakers of Waka' patron deities, they ushered in the new calendrical eras, they were emissaries of Kaan hegemonic strategies to their new homes, they were warriors, and, at least in some cases, they were generators of the future rulers of the city (Navarro-Farr, Kelly, et al. 2020; Navarro-Farr, Kelly, and Freidel, in press; Navarro-Farr, Pérez Robles,

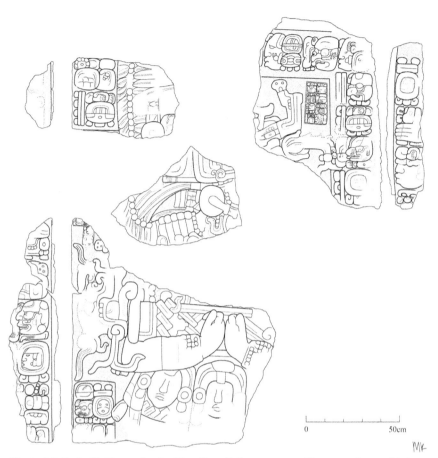

Figure 2.8. Stela 43. Illustration by Mary Kate Kelly, courtesy of Proyecto Arqueológico Waka'.

Menéndez, et al. 2020). These women were revered and celebrated both during their lifetimes and long after their passing. Lady K'abel's title, *ix kaloomte'*, demonstrates her role was hierarchically above that of her husband, who was given the Wak emblem glyph. Her tomb (Burial 61) and the building housing it (M13-1) were honored locations within the city, revisited and ceremonially embellished long after her passing (Navarro-Farr, Pérez, Pérez Robles, Freidel, et al. 2021). Ix Ikoom was responsible for an auspicious event on the 7 Ahau date in 573 CE, venerated, and likely emulated, nearly 130 years later (Kelly et al. in press). We understand the role of these women to have been more than that of mere "princesses" sent to produce offspring with Kaan bloodlines. We believe they were integral figures in their adoptive homes, with leadership roles spanning essentially comparable roles and responsibilities to their male counterparts (Navarro-Farr, Kelly, et al. 2020).

Additional Kaan Connections

Other textual references to Kaan kings are common at Waka'. Stela 20 gives Yuhknoom Ch'een's birthday, Stela 34 gives Yuhknoom Yich'aak K'ahk's accession date, and Stela 43 lists Yuhknoom ? Ti' K'awiil's accession date. The broken and reburied Stela 7 also bears a *kaan ajaw* title, and though the associated names and dates are lost, this may also refer to Yuhknoom ? Ti' K'awiil. And at some point, presumably between his accession in 686 CE and his defeat by Tikal in 695 CE, Yuhknoom Yich'aak K'ahk' is depicted playing ball on a block of Hieroglyphic Stairway 2.

The final reference to Kaan in the history of Waka' in our current understanding of the monuments comes from Stela 27, dedicated on 9.15.10.0.0 (July 1, 741 CE). It states that the accession of Bahlam Tz'am, which was likely circa 730 CE (Guenter 2014:160), was performed by Yuhknoom ? Ti' K'awiil (known at Calakmul as Yuhknoom Took' K'awiil), the contemporaneous Kaan king. Martin (2020:256) notes that this is the last recorded accession in which Calakmul bore some responsibility. Two years after the erection of Stela 27, this king of Waka' was captured in battle by Tikal, effectively ending Kaan influence in the region. Tikal Temple IV Lintel 3 celebrates the 743 CE defeat of Bahlam Tz'am and the capture of the Waka' patron god Akan Yaxaj (Martin and Grube 2008:49).

Their kings came to power under the authority of Kaan rulers, their queens married in from the Kaan bloodline, and Waka' was implicated in warfare with Tikal. The Waka' elite were a staunch ally, both early on when Kaan rulers based in Dzibanche began a campaign to ally with centers across the Maya Lowlands and well after the end of Calakmul's "golden age."

Conclusion

The new monuments discovered in Waka' Structure M13-1 have amplified our understanding of the depth and breadth of the international connections between Waka' and the political powerhouses of the Classic period. In pairing the monuments with their archaeological contexts, it becomes evident that the elite of Waka' saw Structure M13-1 as a place in which to celebrate their connections to the hegemonic powers of the region, both to Teotihuacan in the Early Classic period and to the Kaan kings of the Late Classic period. Stela 51 portrays a recently installed ruler who claims allegiance to Spearthrower Owl, and who prominently recalls the arrival of Sihyaj K'ahk', not to Waka', but to Tikal. He holds a shield that names the former and a belt that references the latter of these two pivotal *entrada*-era figures. From Stela 44 and the retrospective history of Stela 43 we learn of a Kaan-affiliated woman who marries into the royal line of Waka', establishing or reinforcing what would prove to be a long-lasting connection to the Kaan regime. Her importance in the historical memory of the city is clear in that she continues to be revered long after her time.

From these new monuments, we also glean insight into the local rulers at Waka': three new kings have been added to the city's list of kings, one from Stela 51 (though his name is broken), and two from Stela 44 (Chak Tok Ich'aak and Wa'oom Uch'ab Ahk) (see Table 2.1), as well as new details concerning the names and titles of Early Classic kings, and the enigmatic "turtle" title is gradually becoming clearer thanks to the preserved examples on Stela 51.

Waka' was a city whose international connectedness was rooted in its commercial and ritual importance. These aspects of the ancient city could only have been possible with relatively early and populous inhabitation—the folks who facilitated the movement of goods and people through the city. As population density estimates of the city increase (see Marken and Ricker, this volume) and its regional ritual importance becomes clearer (Freidel, this volume; Navarro-Farr, Pérez, and Pérez Robles, this volume), we are more fully witnessing the international prominence of the city. These new data contribute to our understanding of the city of Waka' and its interconnectedness to the broader Classic-era landscape and the truly international stage on which these political relationships played out.

Table 2.1. Known kings and queens of Waka', updated from Guenter (2014:Table 2)

Name	(also known as)	Date(s)	Mentioned on Monument(s)
KINGS			
? Ahk	"Leaf" Chan Ahk, Te' Chan Ahk	Prior to 357	Stela 15
"Snake Skull"		ca. 357	Stela 15
K'inich Bahlam I		ca. 378	Stelae 15, 16, Bagaces Mirror
"Dragon Jaguar"		5th century, son of K'inich Bahlam I	Stela 16
? (Name lost)		Accession: 432	Stela 51
"Tapir" Ahk		ca. 450	Stela 16
? Chan Yopaat		ca. 500	Stela 9
Chak Tok Ich'aak		Death: 556[a]	Stela 44
Wa'oom Uch'ab Ahk	Wa'oom Uch'ab Tz'ikin	Accession: 556	Stela 44

(continued)

Table 2.1—Continued

Name	(also known as)	Date(s)	Mentioned on Monument(s)
Muwaan Bahlam		ca. 550[b]	K8777
Bahlam Tz'am I		early 7th century[c]	Burial 39 Vessels
K'inich Bahlam II		Birth: 637[d] Death: 711 or later	Stelae 1, 33, Incised Belt Dangle
Chak Tz'i'ha' Ahk[e]	Chak "Animal-with-Fish" Ahk	8th century[f]	San Diego Museum of Man Vessel (20100010014)
Bahlam Tz'am II		Defeat by Tikal: 743	Tikal Temple IV Lintel 3, Waka' Stela 27
K'inich Bahlam III?		ca. 790	Stela 32
Aj Yax Chowpat		ca. 801	Stela 38
QUEENS			
Lady Wak To ?		Early Classic	Stela 16
Ix Ikoom		From before 556 to after 573[g]	Stelae 43 and 44
Ix Naah Chan[h]		ca. 682	Stela 18
Lady K'abel		ca. 692	Stela 34
Lady Pakal		ca. 771	Stela 32

[a] Presumed, as son accedes in 556, given on Stela 44.
[b] This is based on ceramic chronology (Guenter 2005:371).
[c] Rich and Matute (2014:74).
[d] Given on the Incised Belt Dangle (Just 2007).
[e] Not definite placement. See Looper and Polyukhovych (2016) for a discussion of the vessel bearing this king's name.
[f] Personal communication, Yuriy Polyukhovych, July 5, 2021.
[g] She performs some unknown event in this year as recorded on Stela 43.
[h] It is possible that this is the same individual we know as Lady K'abel.

Acknowledgments

This research would not have been possible without the expertise and efforts of the dedicated team of excavators, assistants, kitchen staff, truck drivers, and guards who support the PAW. The Instituto de Antropología e Historia, the Ministerio de Cultura y Deportes, and the Departamento de Monumentos Prehispánicos have generously granted us permission to conduct research at the site of Waka'.

Our sincere thanks to the thoughtful comments of Marc Zender, David Stuart, Stanley Guenter, Dmitri Beliaev, Simon Martin, and Yuriy Polyukhovych on the epigraphic elements of this conversation. Mark Willis was also an incredible collaborator and guide in creating the 3D photogrammetric model of Stela 51. We are also grateful for the comments of the reviewers whose insight helped to strengthen this chapter.

Notes

1 Calendrical conversions are given using the Martin and Skidmore (2012) conversion of 584286.
2 In May 1970, just before Graham's August 1970 visit to the site, archaeologist Sally Christie and her family were led to the site by Moisés Alpuch (who then also brought Graham). Her visit was short, according to her notes and as referenced by Graham (2010: 512, ch. 20, n2), and she and her family died soon after in a tragic airplane crash (Graham 2010:300; *New York Times* 1970), preventing her from formally reporting on the site or continuing to work on it.
3 Following epigraphic standards, we record Classic Maya transliterations in **BOLD University PressPERCASE**, transcriptions in *italicized lowercase*, and translations in "quotations."
4 Marc Zender (personal communication February 10, 2023) brought to my attention another example of a similar grammatical structure on Tikal Stela 16: *k'altuun-Ø ix? yax waay witz jasaw chan k'awiil-Ø*, "It was a stone raising at Ix? Yax Waay Witz. (He is) Jasaw Chan K'awiil."
5 If this date was given on Stela 15, it is on a section that is not visible today, as it was broken. The following three *k'atun* endings, however, are listed, each with a presiding ruler, and all following the instance of "Leaf" Chan Ahk's name. Because of this pattern, Guenter (2005, 2014) has suggested that the date we should associate with this earliest named ruler is 8.15.0.0.0 (May 20, 337 CE).
6 See Yaxchilan Lintel 37, A6; Yaxchilan Lintel 49, D6; Yaxchilan Lintel 60, A6 for examples of **AHK** with the "shiny" marker.
7 Personal communication, Marc Zender, July 14, 2021.
8 Personal communication, Dmitri Beliaev, November 14, 2019.
9 Additional monuments that are too eroded to list with absolute certainty but that in their original states likely also referred to the connection to Kaan, are Stelae 1, 11, 12, 29/31.
10 Previously known as the Dallas Altar; it is currently housed at the Dallas Art Museum.

References

Acuña, Mary Jane
2013   Art, Ideology, and Politics at El Achiotal: A Late Preclassic Frontier Site in Northwestern Petén, Guatemala. PhD dissertation, Department of Anthropology, Washington University in St. Louis.
Acuña, Mary Jane, and Carlos R. Chirigoba
2019   Water and the Preclassic Maya at El Tintal, Petén, Guatemala. *Open Rivers, Rethinking Water, Place and Community* 14:147–166. https://openrivers.lib.umn.edu/article/water-and-the-preclassic-maya/.

Bíró, Péter
2020   A Short Note on *Winte' Nah* as "House of Darts." *PARI Journal* 21(1): 14–16.
Canuto, Marcello A., Luke Auld-Thomas, and Ernesto Arredondo
2020   Teotihuacan and Lowland Maya Interactions: Characterizing a Mesoamerican Hegemony. In *Teotihuacan: The World Beyond the City*, edited by Kenn Hirth, David M. Carballo, and Bárbara Arroyo, pp. 365–401. Dumbarton Oaks Research Library and Collection, Washington, DC.
Canuto, Marcello A., and Tomás Barrientos Q.
2020   La Corona: Negotiating a Landscape of Power. In *Approaches to Monumental Landscapes of the Ancient Maya*, edited by Brett A. Houk, Bárbara Arroyo, and Terry G. Powis, pp. 171–195. University Press of Florida, Gainesville.
Castañeda, Francisco
2013   Monumentos del Perú-Waka': Nuevos hallazgos. In *Proyecto Regional Arqueológico El Perú-Waka': Informe no. 11, temporada 2013*, edited by Juan Carlos Pérez Calderón and David A. Freidel, pp. 192–207. Fundación de Investigación Arqueológica Waka', Guatemala City.
Eppich, Keith, Damien B. Marken, and Elsa Damaris Menéndez
2023   A City in Flux: The Dynamic Urban Form and Functions of El Perú-Waka', Guatemala. In *Building an Archaeology of Maya Urbanism: Flexibility and Planning in the American Tropics*, edited by Damien B. Marken and M. Charlotte Arnauld, pp. 105–147. University Press of Colorado, Denver.
Escobedo, Héctor L., and David A. Freidel
2004   Introducción: La primera temporada de campo del Proyecto Arqueológico El Perú-Waka'. In *Proyecto Arqueológico El Perú-Waka': Informe no. 1, temporada 2003*, edited by Héctor L. Escobedo and David Freidel, pp. 1–6. Fundación de Investigación Arqueológica Waka', Guatemala City.
Estrada-Belli, Francisco, and Alexandre Tokovinine
2016   A King's Apotheosis: Iconography, Text, and Politics from a Classic Maya Temple at Holmul. *Latin American Antiquity* 27(2):149–168.
Fash, William L., Alexandre Tokovinine, and Barbara W. Fash
2009   The House of New Fire at Teotihuacan and Its Legacy in Mesoamerica. In *The Art of Urbanism: How Mesoamerican Kingdoms Represented Themselves in Architecture and Imagery*, edited by William L. Fash and Leonardo López Luján, pp. 201–229. Dumbarton Oaks Research Library and Collection, Washington, DC.
Freidel, David A., Mary Jane Acuña, Carlos R. Chiriboga, and Michelle E. Rich
2022   Water Trails and Water Mountains: The View from Northwest Petén. In *Sustainability and Water Management in the Maya World and Beyond*, edited by Jean T. Larmon, Lisa J. Lucero, and Fred Valdez Jr., pp. 119–142. University Press of Colorado, Louisville.
Freidel, David A., Héctor L. Escobedo, David Lee, Stanley P. Guenter, and Juan Carlos Meléndez
2007   El Perú y la ruta terrestre de la Dinastía *Kan* hacia el Altiplano. In *XX Simposio de Investigaciones Arqueológicas en Guatemala, 2006*, edited by Juan Pedro Laporte, Bárbara Arroyo, and Héctor Mejía, pp. 59–76. Ministerio de Cultura y Deportes, Instituto de Antropología e Historia, Guatemala City.

Freidel, David, Olivia Navarro-Farr, Michelle Rich, Juan Carlos Meléndez, Juan Carlos Pérez, Griselda Pérez Robles, and Mary Kate Kelly

n.d.   Mirror Conjurors of Waka'. Manuscript accepted by *Ancient Mesoamerica*.

Freidel, David, Linda Schele, and Joyce Parker

1993   *Maya Cosmos: Three Thousand Years on the Shaman's Path*. William Morrow, New York.

Graham, Ian

1988   Homeless Hieroglyphs. *Antiquity* 62:122–126.

2010   *The Road to Ruins*. University of New Mexico Press, Albuquerque.

Grube, Nikolai, Kai Delvendahl, Nicolaus Seefeld, and Beniamino Volta

2012   Under the Rule of the Snake Kings: Uxul in the 7th and 8th centuries. *Estudios de Cultura Maya* 40:11–49.

Grube, Nikolai, and Linda Schele

1994   Kuy, the Owl of Omen and War. *Mexicon* 16(1):10–17.

Guenter, Stanley P.

2005   Informe preliminar de la epigrafía de El Perú. In *Proyecto Arqueológico El Perú-Waka': Informe no. 2, temporada 2004*, edited by Héctor L. Escobedo and David Freidel, pp. 359–400. Fundación de Investigación Arqueológica Waka', Guatemala City.

2007   On the Emblem Glyph of El Peru. *PARI Journal* 8(2):20–23.

2014   The Epigraphy of El Perú-Waka'. In *Archaeology at El Perú-Waka': Ancient Maya Performances of Ritual, Memory, and Power*, edited by Olivia Navarro-Farr and Michelle Rich, pp. 147–166. University of Arizona Press, Tucson.

Just, Bryan

2007   An Incised Slate Belt Plaque at the Princeton University Art Museum. *Mexicon* 29(3):62.

Kelly, Mary Kate

2019   Documentación epigráfica: Ilustración de inscripciones jeroglíficas de El Perú-Waka'. In *Proyecto Arqueológico Waka': Informe no. 16, temporada 2018*, edited by Juan Carlos Pérez Calderón, Griselda Pérez Robles, and Damien Marken, pp. 349–361. Fundación de Investigación Arqueológica Waka', Guatemala City.

2020   Documentación epigráfica durante la temporada de campo de 2019 al sitio El Perú-Waka'. In *Proyecto Arqueológico Waka': Informe no. 17, temporada 2019*, edited by Juan Carlos Pérez Calderón, Griselda Pérez Robles, and Damien Marken, pp. 282–301. Fundación de Investigación Arqueológica Waka', Guatemala City.

2023   Documentación fotogramétrica y epigráfica, Waka', 2022. In *Proyecto Arqueológico Waka': PAW, Informe no. 20, temporada 2022*, edited by Griselda Pérez Robles, Olivia Navarro-Farr, and Damien Marken, pp. 338–349. Fundación de Investigación Arqueológica Waka', Guatemala City. https://www.mesoweb.com/resources/informes/Waka2022.pdf.

Kelly, Mary Kate, Olivia C. Navarro-Farr, David A. Freidel, Juan Carlos Pérez Calderón, and Griselda Pérez Robles

in press Waka' Stela 44 and the Early Classic Kaan Hegemony. Manuscript accepted by *Ancient Mesoamerica*.

Kelly, Mary Kate, and Hannah Julia Paredes

2019   Documentación epigráfica: Fotogrametría. In *Proyecto Arqueológico Waka': Informe no. 16, temporada 2018*, edited by Juan Carlos Pérez Calderón, Griselda Pérez Robles, and Damien Marken, pp. 333–348. Fundación de Investigación Arqueológica Waka', Guatemala City.

Kidder, Alfred V., Jesse D. Jennings, and Edwin Shook; with technological notes by Anna O. Shepard

1946   *Excavations at Kaminaljuyu, Guatemala.* Publication 561. Carnegie Institution of Washington, Washington, DC.

Laporte, Juan Pedro, and Vilma Fialko

1995   Un reencuentro con Mundo Perdido, Tikal, Guatemala. *Ancient Mesoamerica* 6:41–94.

Looper, Matthew, and Yuriy Polyukhovych

2016   A Familial Relationship between Nobles of El Peru (Waka') and El Zotz (Pa'chan) as Recorded on a Polychrome Vessel. *Glyph Dwellers* 47:1–11.

Marken, Damien B., Juan Carlos Pérez, Olivia Navarro-Farr, and Keith Eppich

2019   Ciudad de los Ciempiés: Urbanismo, fronteras y comunidad en El Perú-Waka', Petén, Guatemala. In *XXXII Simposio de Investigaciones Arqueológicas en Guatemala, 2018*, vol. 1, edited by Bárbara Arroyo, Luis Méndez Salinas, and Gloria Ají Álvarez, pp. 531–546. Ministerio de Cultura y Deportes, Instituto de Antropología e Historia, Guatemala City.

Martin, Simon

2000   Nuevos datos epigráficos sobre la guerra Maya del clásico. In *La guerra entre los antiguos Mayas: Memoria de la primera mesa redonda de Palenque*, edited by Silvia Trejo, pp. 105–124. Instituto Nacional de Antropología e Historia, Mexico City.

2008   Wives and Daughters on the Dallas Altar. *Mesoweb*. https://www.mesoweb.com/articles/martin/Wives&Daughters.pdf.

2020   *Ancient Maya Politics: A Political Anthropology of the Classic Period 150–900 CE.* Cambridge University Press, Cambridge.

Martin, Simon, and Dmitri Beliaev

2017   K'ahk' Ti' Ch'ich': A New Snake King from the Early Classic Period. *PARI Journal* 17(3):1–7.

Martin, Simon, and Nikolai Grube

2008   *Chronicle of the Maya Kings and Queens: Deciphering the Dynasties of the Ancient Maya.* Thames and Hudson, London.

Martin, Simon, and Joel Skidmore

2012   Exploring the 584286 Correlation between the Maya and European Calendars. *PARI Journal* 13(2):3–16.

Miller, Jeffrey H.

1974   Notes on a Stelae Pair Probably from Calakmul, Campeche, Mexico. In *Primera Mesa Redonda de Palenque, Part I: A Conference on the Art, Iconography, and Dynastic History of Palenque*, edited by Merle Greene Robertson, pp. 149–162. Robert Louis Stevenson School, Pebble Beach, CA.

New York Times
1970   "Four Killed in Crash of Chartered Plane." May 27, 1970: 93. https://www.nytimes
        .com/1970/05/27/archives/four-killed-in-crash-of-chartered-plane.html.
Navarro-Farr, Olivia C.
2009   Ritual, Process, and Continuity in the Late to Terminal Classic Transition: Inves-
        tigations at Structure M13-1 in the Ancient Maya Site of El Perú-Waka', Petén,
        Guatemala. PhD dissertation, Department of Anthropology, Southern Methodist
        University, Dallas.
Navarro-Farr, Olivia C., Mary Kate Kelly, and David A. Freidel
in press Snake Queens and Political Consolidation: How Royal Women Helped Create
        Kaan—A View from Waka'. Accepted by *Ancient Mesoamerica*.
Navarro-Farr, Olivia C., Mary Kate Kelly, Michelle Rich, and Griselda Pérez Robles
2020   Expanding the Canon: Lady K'abel the *Ix Kaloomte'* and the Political Narratives of
        Classic Maya Queens. *Feminist Anthropology* 1(1): 38–55.
Navarro-Farr, Olivia C., and Rony López
2020   Operación WK01: Estructura M13-1. In *Proyecto Arqueológico Waka': PAW, In-
        forme no. 17, temporada 2019*, edited by Juan Carlos Pérez Calderón, Griselda
        Pérez Robles, and Damien Marken, pp. 13–36. Fundación de Investigación Arque-
        ológica Waka', Guatemala City.
Navarro-Farr, Olivia C., Damien Marken, Mary Kate Kelly, Keith Eppich, Griselda Pérez
        Robles, and Juan Carlos Pérez Calderón
2022   Queens and Statecraft: Royal Women in the Heart of the Fire Shrine at El Perú-
        Waka'. In *3,000 Years of War and Peace in the Maya Lowlands: Identity, Politics, and
        Violence*, edited by Geoffrey E. Braswell, pp. 159–183. Routledge, New York.
Navarro-Farr, Olivia, Juan Carlos Pérez, Griselda Pérez Robles, and Keith Eppich
2022   Researching the Past, Investing in the Present: Relationship Building and Com-
        munity Engaged Scholarship in Parque Nacional Laguna del Tigre, Petén, Gua-
        temala. Paper presented at the 87th Annual Meeting of the Society for American
        Archaeology, Chicago, March 30–April 3, 2022.
Navarro-Farr, Olivia, Juan Carlos Pérez, Griselda Pérez Robles, David Freidel, and Mary
        Kate Kelly
2021   Operación WK01: Estructura M13-1. In *Proyecto Regional Arqueológico El Perú-
        Waka': Informe no. 19, temporada 2021*, edited by Juan Carlos Pérez, Damien
        Marken, and Griselda Pérez Robles, pp. 11–33. Fundación de Investigación Ar-
        queológica Waka', Guatemala City.
Navarro-Farr, Olivia C., Griselda Pérez Robles, and Damaris Menéndez
2013   Operación WK-1: Excavaciones en la Estructura M13-1. In *Proyecto Regional Ar-
        queológico El Perú-Waka': Informe no. 10, temporada 2012*, edited by Juan Carlos
        Pérez Calderón, pp. 3–91. Fundación de Investigación Arqueológica Waka', Gua-
        temala City.
Navarro-Farr, Olivia C., Griselda Pérez Robles, Damaris Menéndez, and Juan Carlos Pérez
        Calderón
2020   Forest of Queens: The Legacy of Royal Calakmul Women at El Perú-Waka's Cen-
        tral Civic-Ceremonial Temple. In *A Forest of History: The Maya after the Emer-*

gence of Divine Kingship, edited by Travis W. Stanton and M. Kathryn Brown, pp. 67–87. University Press of Colorado, Louisville.

Navarro-Farr, Olivia C., Griselda Pérez Robles, Juan Carlos Pérez Calderón, Elsa Damaris Menéndez Bolaños, Erin E. Patterson, Keith Eppich, and Mary Kate Kelly
2021   Burial 61 at El Perú-Waka's Structure M13-1. *Latin American Antiquity* 32(1):188–200.

Nielsen, Jesper, and Christophe Helmke
2008   Spearthrower Owl Hill: A Toponym at Atetelco, Teotihuacan. *Latin American Antiquity* 19(4):459–474.

Pérez Robles, Griselda, and Olivia C. Navarro-Farr
2013   WK01: Excavaciones en M13-1 y el descubrimiento de la estela 44. In *Proyecto Regional Arqueológico El Perú-Waka': Informe no. 11, temporada 2013*, edited by Juan Carlos Pérez Calderón and David A. Freidel, pp. 3–26. Fundación de Investigación Arqueológica Waka', Guatemala City.

Pérez Robles, Griselda, and Juan Carlos Pérez Calderón
2019a   WK18: La acrópolis de Waka', el palacio real. In *Proyecto Arqueológico Waka': PAW, Informe no. 16, temporada 2018*, edited by Juan Carlos Pérez Calderón, Griselda Pérez Robles, and Damien Marken, pp. 83–126. Fundación de Investigación Arqueológica Waka', Guatemala City.
2019b   2018, Los monumentos de El Perú-Waka': Diagnóstico de deterioro. In *Proyecto Arqueológico Waka': PAW, Informe no. 16, temporada 2018*, edited by Juan Carlos Pérez Calderón, Griselda Pérez Robles, and Damien Marken, pp. 362–394. Fundación de Investigación Arqueológica Waka', Guatemala City.

Rich, Michelle E.
2011   Ritual, Royalty and Classic Period Politics: The Archaeology of the Mirador Group at El Perú-Waka', Petén, Guatemala. PhD dissertation, Department of Anthropology, Southern Methodist University, Dallas.

Rich, Michelle, and Varinia Matute
2014   The Power of the Past: Crafting Meaning at a Royal Funerary Pyramid. In *Archaeology at El Perú-Waka': Ancient Maya Performances of Ritual, Memory, and Power*, edited by Olivia Navarro-Farr and Michelle Rich, pp. 66–84. University of Arizona Press, Tucson.

Rich, Michelle E., Jennifer Piehl, and Varinia Matute
2006   WK-11A: Continuación de las excavaciones en el complejo El Mirador, Estructura O-14-04. In *Proyecto Arqueológico El Perú-Waka': Informe no. 3, temporada 2005*, edited by Héctor L. Escobedo and David Freidel, pp. 225–274. Fundación de Investigación Arqueológica Waka', Guatemala City.

Savkic Sebek, Sanja, and Erik Velásquez García
2021   Writing as Visual Art: The Maya Script. In *Motion: Transformation, 35th Congress of the International Committee of the History of Arts, Conference Proceedings*, edited by Marza Fiaetti and Gerhard Wolf, pp. 235–242. Bononia University Press, Bologna.

Schele, Linda, and David A. Freidel
1990   *A Forest of Kings: The Untold Story of the Ancient Maya*. William Morrow, New York.

Stuart, David

1996 Kings of Stone: A Consideration of Stelae in Ancient Maya Ritual and Representation. *Res: Anthropology and Aesthetics* 29/30:148–171.

2000 "The Arrival of Strangers:" Teotihuacan and Tollan in Classic Maya History. In *Mesoamerica's Classic Heritage: from Teotihuacan to the Aztecs*, edited by David Carrasco, Lindsay Jones, and Scott Sessions, pp. 465–514. University Press of Colorado, Boulder.

2004 The Beginnings of the Copan Dynasty: A Review of the Hieroglyphic and Historical Evidence. In *Understanding Early Classic Copan*, edited by Ellen E. Bell, Marcello A. Canuto, and Robert J. Sharer, pp. 215–248. University of Pennsylvania Museum of Archaeology and Anthropology, Philadelphia.

2022 Rulers from the West: Teotihuacan in Maya History and Politics. Paper presented at Dumbarton Oaks Research Library and Collection, Washington, DC, December 1, 2022. Hybrid in-person and virtual.

Stuart, David, Marcello A. Canuto, Tomás Barrientos, and Alejandro González

2018 A Preliminary Analysis of Altar 5 from La Corona. *PARI Journal* 19(2):1–13.

Stuart, David, and Stephen D. Houston

2018 Cotton, Snow, and Distant Wonders. *Maya Decipherment: Ideas on Maya Writing and Iconography*. https://mayadecipherment.com/2018/02/09/cotton-snow-and-distant-wonders/.

Taube, Karl A.

1983 The Teotihuacán Spider Woman. *Journal of Latin American Lore* 9(2): 107–189.

2018 [1992] The Iconography of Mirrors at Teotihuacan. In *Studies in Ancient Mesoamerican Art and Architecture: Selected Works by Karl Andreas Taube*, pp. 204–225. Precolumbia Mesoweb Press, San Francisco. https://www.mesoweb.com/publications/Works1/Taube[1992]2018a.pdf.

Tokovinine, Alexandre

2013 *Place and Identity in Classic Maya Narratives*. Dumbarton Oaks Research Library and Collection, Washington, DC.

2020 Distance and Power in Classic Maya Texts. In *Reshaping the World: Debates on Mesoamerican Cosmologies*, edited by Ana Díaz, pp. 251–281. University Press of Colorado, Louisville.

Velásquez García, Erik, and Ana García Barrios

2018 Devenir histórico y papel de los *Chatahn Winik* en la sociedad Maya clásica. *Mesoweb*. https://www.mesoweb.com/es/articulos/Velasquez-Garcia/Chatahn.pdf.

von Winning, Hasso

1987 *La iconografía de Teotihuacán: Los dioses y los signos*. Universidad Nacional Autónoma de México, Mexico City.

Wanyerka, Phil

1996 A Fresh Look at a Maya Masterpiece. *Cleveland Studies in the History of Art* 1:72–97.

Zender, Marc

2006 Teasing the Turtle from Its Shell: **AHK** and **MAHK** in Maya Writing. *PARI Journal* 6(3):1–14.

II

The Lived Urban Landscape

3

Fire, Earth, and Water

Settlement, Soils, and Hydrology at El Perú-Waka'

Damien B. Marken and Matthew C. Ricker

The last decade in Maya archaeology has witnessed a radical reconceptualization of Classic lowland centers as true urban places, cities with integrated, diverse populations and extensive infrastructural modifications of the landscape. This new disciplinary consensus represents a major advance for the study and interpretation of Maya civilization and culture history. Instead of accumulating data to simply assert the urban nature of Maya cities, investigators can now design research strategies to better explore the regional and local diversity of lowland urban form, life, meanings, and functions (e.g., Marken and Arnauld 2023). This chapter recognizes the Maya's "newfound" urbanity by summarizing more than a decade's worth of investigations of the El Perú-Waka' urban landscape, with a focus on describing its settlement and hydrological and agricultural contexts. In some ways, Waka' was typical of lowland Maya cities. An historically important Classic period capital (Kelly, Freidel, and Navarro-Farr, this volume; see also Freidel, Escobedo, and Guenter 2007), Waka' had a clear, monumental epicenter surrounded by residential zones, embedded within a more dispersed regional landscape. Yet in other ways, settlement distribution at Waka' is rather unique, the result of centuries of adaptive decisions to continuously evolving local circumstances.

Lowland Maya Urbanism and El Perú-Waka'

As currently recognized, lowland Maya cities fall firmly within Roland Fletcher's (2009, 2012) cross-cultural urban type of low-density, agrarian urbanism (see Isendahl 2012; Isendahl and Smith 2013; Marken, Ricker, Rivas, et al. 2019). Under this umbrella, however, Maya cities exhibit considerable local and regional variability. As a broad term, "low-density urbanism" itself masks localized variation in settlement distribution and land-use practices across an urbanized landscape; it is up to Mayanists to describe and define this variation and its potential roots.

As more fully described below, one of the more remarkable features of Waka' as a city is its compact urban core; it is one of the most densely occupied areas of the lowlands (Canuto et al. 2018; Marken 2015). Although the dense Waka' urban core is itself located in the southwest corner of the Petén Karst Plateau (Dunning, Beach, Farrell, et al. 1998), its hinterland settlement is distributed across a variety of physiographic zones (Figure 3.1). To the north and east is a continuous swath of broken, upland terrain, occasionally bisected by seasonal drainages created by erosion from the underlying limestone bedrock. To the west and south lie the extensive wetlands of the Laguna del Tigre National Park. The regional geology consists of sedimentary rocks derived from shallow marine sediments of Eocene age (56 to 33.9 million years old), primarily limestone, dolostone, and shale (Ramos 1975; Weyl 1980). The predominantly limestone bedrock in the Waka' region displays many karst landforms, including extensive dry cave systems, springs, disappearing streams, dry valleys, and unpredictable seasonal (deranged) surface hydrology (Hermitt et al. 2017; Marken, Cooper, et al. 2020). Soluble sulfur is present in many of the parent rocks, which results in the precipitation of secondary gypsum deposits (Ricker, Marken, Bauer, et al. 2019; Beach et al. 2019) and in high sulfate concentrations in surface water of the region (Luzzadder-Beach and Beach 2008). Quaternary sedimentary deposits consist of extensive alluvium and lacustrine deposits along the Ríos San Pedro and San Juan (see below) and colluvium derived from steep slopes near large sinkholes and escarpments. The soils formed in this region are typically shallow in erosional uplands, consisting mostly of topsoil over unweathered limestone rock (Rendolls in U.S. Soil Taxonomy; see Dunning et al. 2002). Shrink-swell soils (Vertisols and vertic Mollisols/Alfisols) are found in the lowlands (floodplains, wetlands, footslopes) that receive depositions of calcium and magnesium rich sediment necessary to form smectitic clays (Gunn et al. 2002; Dunning, Beach, and Luzzadder-Beach 2012; Ricker, Marken, Bauer, et al. 2019; Ricker, Marken, and Cooper 2018; Ricker, Marken, and Rivas 2017).

The karst plateau has minimal accessible groundwater resources, and regional hydrology is controlled by precipitation patterns. The majority of the Petén region is classified as tropical monsoon climate (Am) in the Köppen classification system. The area has distinct wet-dry seasons, typically rainy from May to October and dry from November to April. The seasonal precipitation dynamics were likely difficult for Maya urban management, with too

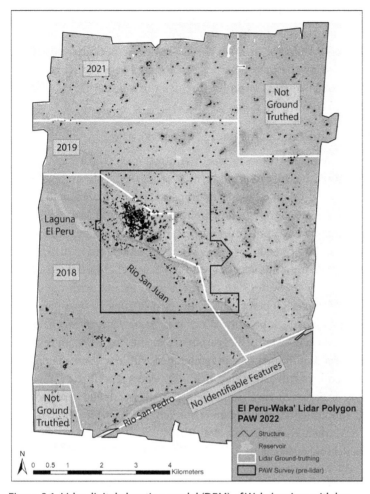

Figure 3.1. Lidar digital elevation model (DEM) of Waka' region, with hydrological features and survey areas. Lidar data provided by the National Center for Airborne Laser Mapping, courtesy of Fundación Patrimonio Cultural y Natural Maya. Map by Damien Marken, courtesy of Proyecto Arqueológico Waka'.

little water available in the dry season (Scarborough 1998; Dunning, Beach, Luzzadder-Beach, et al. 2012) and too much stormwater in the wet season.

With its urban core perched at the edge of the escarpment that forms the southern and western limits of the Petén Karst Plateau, the urban form of Waka' and its hinterlands are in many ways a product of its place as well as of its history. Its defensible location atop an 80-meter-high escarpment, and its advantageous position near the juncture of the Río San Pedro Mártir and its tributary, the Río San Juan, fostered the city's growth as a hub of both east–

west and north–south overland trade. This combination of geographic factors may also have contributed to the historical importance of the city as one of the first places visited by Sihyaj K'ahk' (in the Early Classic period), and whose shifting loyalty during the Late Classic often resulted in repeated conquest by the dynasties of Tikal and Calakmul (Freidel, this volume; Guenter 2014; Kelly, Freidel, and Navarro-Farr, this volume).

Settlement and Landscape Surveys at El Perú-Waka'

Since its initiation in 2003, the Proyecto Arqueológico Waka' (PAW) has maintained an intensive survey program that topographically mapped 98.8 hectares of the Waka' urban core and its transition to peripheral settlement with a total station (89,658 topographic points) (Marken and Maxson 2017). This was complemented by a full-coverage pedestrian survey of the surrounding hinterlands totaling 13.60 km² (see Figure 3.1; Marken 2011, 2015; Pérez and Marken 2017). Within this survey area, PAW researchers recorded a total of 2,111 structures, a majority (956) of which were located within a dense urban core (see Marken, Cooper, Gemberling, et al. 2020, for a summary). As stated above, when looked at broadly, Waka' is in some ways an excellent example of Classic Maya low-density, agrarian urbanism. The PAW survey data describe a mid-sized monumental core embedded within a dense residential matrix, enveloped by a still rather dense, multipurpose, "periurban" ring, all surrounded by a dispersed rural settlement dotted by satellite centers with smaller-scale monumental architecture (Marken 2011, 2015; Marken and Maxson 2017; Marken, Ricker, Rivas, et al. 2019).

Features reflecting patterns of land-use within the urban core identified during the PAW surveys were varied. Mapping recorded four public plazas; several large, monumental complexes; large-, medium-, and small-scale reservoirs; and several "natural" canals that diverted water to the urban peripheries (and to several interconnected basins that served as reservoirs and/or urban gardens along the way), integrating the city's immediate hinterlands into its urban fabric. Hinterland surveys identified quarries and additional household-scale reservoirs. The most striking aspect of the Waka' regional settlement pattern, however, is the packed nature of its "residential" surface remains within the urban core; few Classic Maya sites (Copan, Palenque) exhibit such a high structure density (Marken 2015; Marken and Maxson 2017; see also Canuto et al. 2018).

During the summer of 2016, a 91.2 km² Light Detection and Ranging (lidar) survey of the region—conducted by the National Center for Airborne Laser Mapping (NCALM) as part of the first phase of a multiproject lidar survey of over 2,100 km² of forested areas within the Maya Biosphere Reserve (RBM) of the northern Petén district of Guatemala—confirmed many of these findings (Canuto et al. 2018).[1] To better assess the preliminary visual analyses of the digital elevation model (DEM) produced by NCALM (Marken and Pérez 2018), ground verification of landscape and potential anthropogenic features within the larger lidar polygon began in earnest in 2018 and is approaching completion, with approximately 74 percent of the polygon having been ground-truthed by the end of the 2019 field season (Marken, Cooper, Gemberling, et al. 2020; Marken, Cooper, and Pérez 2019).[2]

While the lidar data largely confirm the settlement and landscape patterns and trends identified and/or suspected by previous PAW surveys, excavations, hydrological, and spectral analyses (e.g., Hermitt et al. 2017; Marken 2011, 2015; Marken, Pérez, et al. 2019; Marken, Ricker, Rivas, et al. 2019; Maxson and Marken 2018; Ricker, Marken, Bauer, et al. 2019; Ricker, Marken, and Cooper 2018; Ricker, Marken, and Rivas 2017), the DEM enables a detailed topographic view of the Waka' regional landscape for the first time. Whereas PAW mappers were able to compile high-resolution topographic maps, these were maps limited to the urban core and small areas of surrounding settlements. Conversely, the low resolution of earlier regional DEMs, such as ASTER and SRTM30, inhibited localized examination of the relationships between settlement and the natural geography. With the increased spatial accuracy in the relative distribution of natural and anthropogenic features provided by lidar, investigators can better map patterns of land-use decisions not only within the urban center but also between the center and its surrounding hinterlands.

Settlement Patterns

The Waka' urban core is indeed located atop the southwest corner of the escarpment that defines the southern edge of the Petén Karst Plateau. Just north and west of the urban core, the escarpment largely disappears, turning into a series of colluvial terraces watered by east–west drainages. Even though the escarpment provides natural southern and western boundaries to the core, its northern and, to a lesser degree, eastern limits have proven difficult and time-consuming to define prior to the lidar survey. The identification of a possible ditch, or "boundary feature," visible along its northwest corner in the lidar DEM, when combined with the fully mapped escarpment, however, define an estimated 1.38 km² urban core encompassing the ceremonial epicenter and the connected monumental Mirador Group (Figure 3.2).

Unfortunately, from the lidar DEM alone, it is difficult to fully confirm the presence, much less define the function, of the boundary feature as an

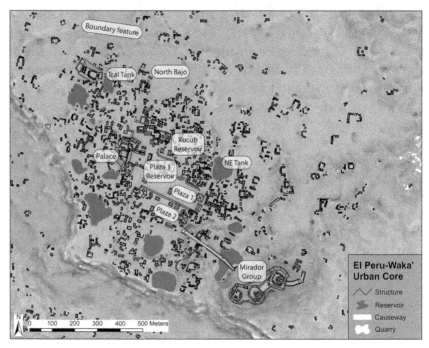

Figure 3.2. Red Relief Image Map (RRIM) of lidar DEM of the El Perú-Waka' urban core. Lidar DEM provided by National Center for Airborne Laser Mapping. Map by Damien Marken, courtesy of PAW.

entirely anthropogenic feature. While the western edge and northwest corner are well defined, and the northeast segment has been verified in the field, the central section is a tightly meandering channel section that may be the eroded remains of a constructed ditch, but may also be a relic natural channel, and thus will require a targeted excavation program to accurately evaluate it. If the boundary was indeed continuous, running 1969.5 meters from the edge of the escarpment on the west to a set of elevated ridges on the east, it would have represented a clear physical and probably symbolic delimitation that, along with the escarpment, perhaps defined "downtown" Waka'.[3]

This potential 1.38 km² "downtown," defined by the boundary feature, escarpment, and the Mirador hill, is significantly larger than the estimated 0.7 km² urban core suggested by PAW survey settlement density drop-offs (e.g., Marken and Maxson 2017). PAW and lidar surveys have identified 1,217 structures within the newly defined "downtown" urban core area, resulting in a core settlement density of 881 structures/km², a core density significantly lower than the last suggested by PAW surveys (Marken and Maxson 2017). This discrepancy is a result of the substantial area increase in the estimated urban core encompassed by the boundary feature, which includes extensive

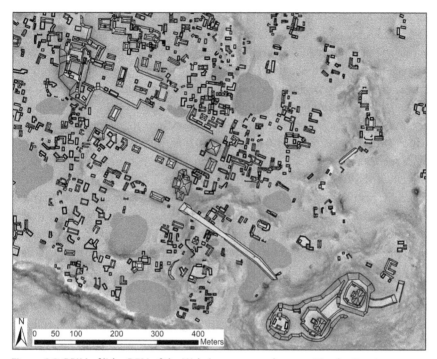

Figure 3.3. RRIM of lidar DEM of the Waka' monumental center. Map by Damien Marken, courtesy of Proyecto Arqueológico Waka'.

tracts of "vacant" terrain that previously marked the core limits. However, while these areas appear devoid of visible settlement, it would be a mistake to consider them as unoccupied (M. L. Smith 2008); some have been confirmed as large-scale water management features, while others were likely fields and gardens (see below).

Monumental Planning

Monumental architecture at Waka' is relatively centralized in its distribution within the urban core (Figure 3.3). The city's epicenter consists of two, offset, 250-meter-long rectangular platforms, Plazas 2 and 4, and the 350-meter-long, leveled rectangular space between them (Plaza 1). It is within this Epicenter that the majority of the city's ritual and civic architecture is located, including some of the most important dynastic structures, such as the Palace and the funerary buildings M13-1 and M12-32 (e.g., Navarro-Farr, Pérez, and Pérez Robles, this volume; Pérez Robles et al., this volume).

The second monumental sector of the city is the highly visible, but more restricted in terms of access, Mirador Group, situated on a high hilltop that forms the southeast edge of the urban core. The Mirador Group houses the largest pyramidal structures at Waka', namely Structures O14-02 and O14-04 (e.g., Rich and Eppich, this volume). Recovered ceramics from excavations across the urban core indicate that the general layout of this monumental core was established during the Late Preclassic period, 300 BCE to 250 CE (Marken, Pérez, et al. 2019). Besides the earliest construction phases of Plazas 1 and 2, the Palace and the platform underlying Structure O14-04, Late Preclassic ceramics were also recovered from excavations into the Mirador Causeway, which links Structures O14-04 and O14-02, as well as from the Epicenter–Mirador Causeway, which physically connects the two monumental loci of the city (Marken, Pérez, et al. 2019). This Late Preclassic configuration—adjacent, parallel plazas within the Epicenter connected via causeway to ritual locations atop the Mirador hill—appears to have remained important to the design of the city throughout its development, as it was maintained even as the Epicenter was modified by later monumental and domestic construction (Marken, Pérez, et al. 2019).

Later constructions increased the scale of monumentality within these sectors of the city (e.g., Rich and Eppich, this volume; Pérez Robles et al., this volume), while also significantly reorganizing the plaza spaces of the epicenter. Plaza 2, in particular, underwent a series of redesigns on its west end, with the establishment of residential patios beginning in the Early Classic period and its division into two plazas during the Late/Terminal Classic transition (ca. 770–820 CE) by the construction of Structure L13-12 (see Marken, Pérez, et al. 2019). Additionally, Plaza 4 witnessed considerable architectural reconfiguration during this same period (Marken, Pérez, et al. 2019).

Residential Settlement: Urban Core

As stated above, one of the rather unique characteristics of the Waka' urban core in its final form is the dense residential matrix within which the Maya embedded the "monumental scaffold" of their ritual architecture. With 1,217 identified structures, previous formulas for estimating populations (Marken 2011) provide an absolute population range of 2,738–4,564 inhabitants in the urban core at its Late Classic height. These populations occupied at least 51 residential groups in the city's final form that enveloped the public epicenter and elevated causeway linking it to the more restricted Mirador Group (Figure 3.4).

Structure groups were initially defined by PAW excavators based on preliminary sketches and maps combined with on-site impressions of settlement divisions (e.g., Tsesmeli 2004). While some of these early designations have been retained to maintain continuity in the spatial documentation of completed excavations, current group boundaries are defined by topographic and

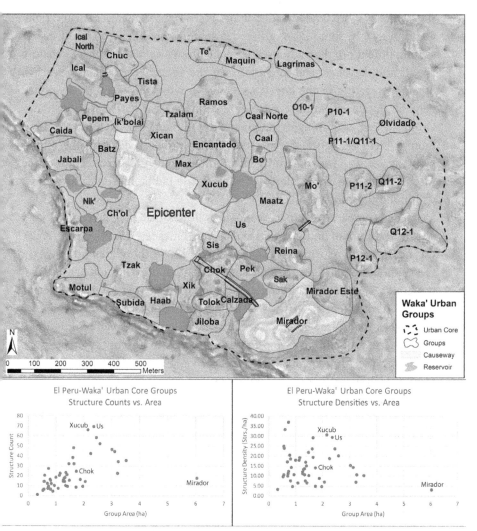

Figure 3.4. Map of Waka' urban core groups (*top*); Waka' urban core group structure count densities (*bottom left*); Waka' urban core group structure densities by area (*bottom right*). Map by Damien Marken, courtesy of Proyecto Arqueológico Waka'.

architectural features as well as by potential land-management features, as identified by total station and lidar surveys. The resulting wide range of variation between these "final" groups in area (0.3–3.5 hectares), structure count (1–69 structures), structure density (2.98–36.77 structures/ha), and land-use features highlights the etic nature of these definitions. This is further reflected in the variable patterning when comparing scatter plots of group area by structure counts (which is relatively linear) and group area by structure density (which is more randomly distributed) (see Figure 3.4, lower left and right, respectively). In some cases, group designations are likely too small, representing little more than a household. Still, groups with the highest structure counts and densities tend to cluster near the Epicenter as well as near each other, aggregating in the largest and most heavily built of the 17 identified neighborhoods within the core (Figure 3.5). The clear outlier is the Mirador Group, which is thoroughly dominated by monumental architecture. Even more evident at higher spatial orders (neighborhood, district), the monumentality, elevated topography, and minimal residential architecture of the Mirador sector marks it, along with the clearly public Epicenter, as distinct within the city core (Figure 3.6).

Recent comparative urban research indicates that neighborhoods are a universal feature of both modern and ancient cities (e.g., Smith 2010); Waka' was no different. As with settlement groups, neighborhood definition within the Waka' core is also primarily based on topographic continuity and spatial proximity. These designations are also supported by average nearest neighbor and kernel density analyses, although the high overall structure density across the urban core renders clear statistically significant neighborhood spatial clustering difficult to define empirically (see also Thompson et al. 2022). Excluding the Mirador area, the range of variation in neighborhood area (1.68–9.15 ha) and structure counts (23–133 structures) remains considerable, while the range in structure density (8.7–25.86 structures/ha) is reduced compared to that between groups. As expected, comparing plots of neighborhood area versus structure count, and neighborhood area versus structure density, demonstrates that smaller neighborhoods have higher structure densities than larger neighborhoods, with a median neighborhood size of approximately 5 hectares (Figure 3.5).

Looking at neighborhood distribution, the most heavily occupied core neighborhoods by structure count (Figure 3.5, lower left) ring the Epicenter, and those with the highest structure densities flank the northern and western sides of the Epicenter (Figure 3.5, lower right). This pattern of settlement aggregation around the monumental epicenter, with its imposing ceremonial/ political architecture and open public plazas, is the probable result of a combination of "push-pull" factors that simultaneously encouraged and required residents to settle in close proximity to the levers of dynastic power (e.g., Eppich, Marken, and Menéndez 2023; Hutson 2016). The Epicenter itself likely offered access to regionally unique economic, ceremonial, political, and/or administrative activities and opportunities. Over time, the neighborhoods themselves would have developed their own opportunities and services to attract further immigration and energize continued residency (e.g., Smith

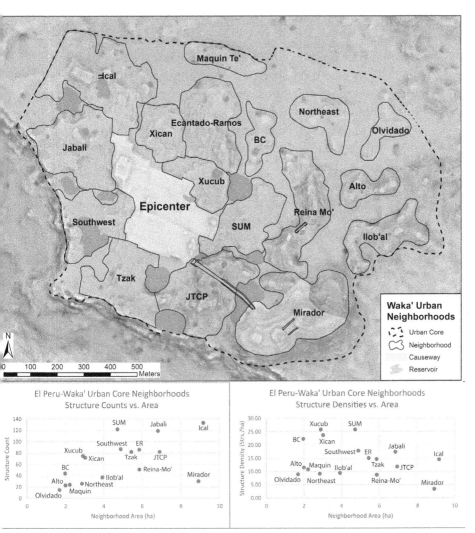

gure 3.5. Map of Waka' urban core neighborhoods (*top*); Waka' urban core neighborhood ructure count densities (*bottom left*); Waka' urban core neighborhood structure densities by area *ottom right*). Map by Damien Marken, courtesy of Proyecto Arqueológico Waka'.

2010). While a spatially comprehensive chronology of residential development across the urban core is beyond the current PAW data sets, testpit and household excavations indicate that the broad residential areas originate in the second and third centuries CE and possess a settlement pattern that shifts repeatedly throughout the Classic period (Eppich, Marken, and Menéndez 2023; Marken, Pérez, et al. 2019). Known early occupations, however, are deeply buried under later constructions, and the recovered ceramic assemblages may not be fully representative of the scale of Preclassic to Early Classic settlement.

Further examination of the topography and final phase architectural distribution also suggests that settlement within the urban core not only aggregated at the group and neighborhood levels but also formed possible higher-order residential communities, such as districts (e.g., Smith 2010). This preliminary assessment suggests that urban core settlement consisted of four major residential districts—the Central District, the Southern District, the Ical District, and the more dispersed Northeast District—and two districts that combined public and/or monumental spaces with residential components—the Mirador District and the Epicenter itself (Figure 3.6). While further data and comparative artifactual analyses are required to determine whether these spatial units coincided with shared community identities or administrative organization, their geographic and architectural separation is considerably more pronounced than either defined group or neighborhood boundaries.

Regional Population Estimates

Combined, the lidar survey and ground-truthing have identified and confirmed 3,599 structures within the ground-truthed 57.74 km^2 of PLI Polygon 12, resulting in a 62 structures/km^2 structure density across this area as of 2020. Plugging structure counts into the population estimation equations previously used for the PAW survey area (Marken 2010, 2011) results in an estimated absolute population range of 8,100–13,500 people (141–234 people/km^2) inhabiting this area during the region's Late Classic occupation peak. These data further indicate that an estimated 2,738–4,564 of these individuals, approximately 34 percent, resided within the 1.38 km^2 urban core (1,984–3,307 people/km^2). These absolute estimates are considerably higher than those reported previously by Marken (2011:Table 7.5 [structure counts], Table 7.8 [patio counts]) for the smaller PAW survey area, but they do bracket the Late Classic population index estimate of 12,956 reported by Canuto et al. (2018:Table 6) for the entire polygon based on preliminary analysis of the lidar DEM.

Compared to the low overall population densities assumed by earlier generations of scholars, the 141–234 people/km^2 for the verified area of the Waka' lidar polygon is rather high and would still be considered an overestimation by some scholars (e.g., Webster 2018). However, a classified kernel density analysis of structures in ArcMap 10.9.1 (14 classes) demonstrates that settlement is not evenly distributed across the polygon (Figure 3.7), with extensive zones of little (1–20 structures/km^2) to no occupation outside the dense urban core, punctuated by smaller settlement clusters.

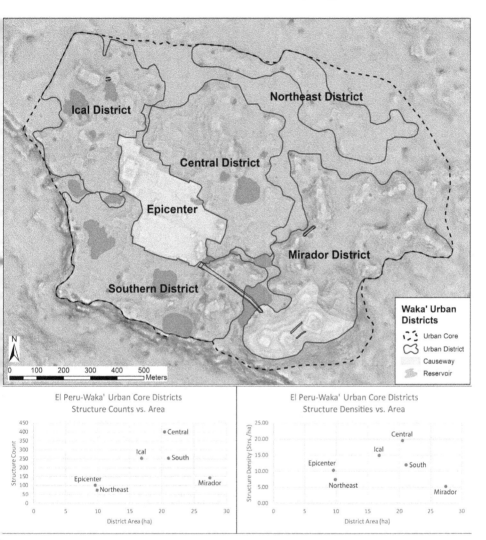

Figure 3.6. Map of Waka' urban core districts (*top*); Waka' urban core district structure count densities (*bottom left*); Waka' urban core district structure densities by area (*bottom right*). Map by Damien Marken, courtesy of Proyecto Arqueológico Waka'.

Looking specifically at the original PAW survey area, the lidar data and their verification provide an absolute population estimate range of 5,106–8,510 inhabitants, with an estimated population density range of 375–626 people/km^2 across its 13.6 km^2.[4] Even for this smaller area, these absolute estimations are 450–750 and 1,000–2,250 people higher than Marken's estimates based on structure counts (2011:Table 7.5) and patio counts (2011:Table 7.8), respectively. Since these lidar-based estimates are calculated using

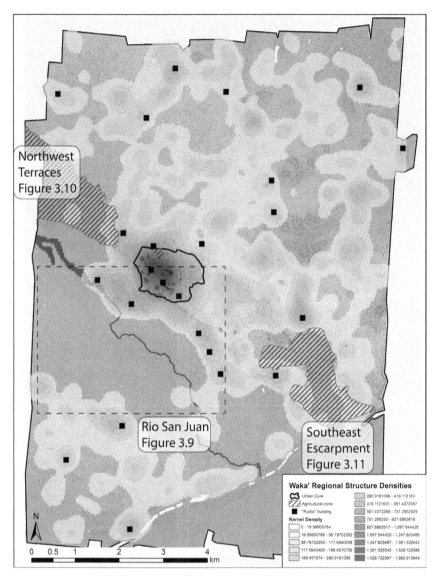

Figure 3.7. Kernel Density analysis of regional structure distribution showing potential agricultural zones. Lidar DEM provided by National Center for Airborne Laser Mapping (2017). Map by Damien Marken, courtesy of Proyecto Arqueológico Waka'.

structure counts, the significantly lower patio-based absolute estimates are unsurprising, as they consistently produce lower estimates than structure-based methods (Marken 2011; Murtha 2009). While ethnographic and ethnohistoric data suggest that the patio is the more appropriate demographic unit for estimating ancient Maya populations (Webster 2018), these data have yet to be generated for Waka' with the lidar data. This remains a goal of future DEM processing and analysis.

Such high population densities would likely have required at least some surplus foodstuffs to be either produced locally or imported (see below). Moreover, clear, localized landscape modifications relating to the storage and release of captured rainwater have been documented within the Waka' urban core (Marken, Cooper, and Ricker 2018; Marken, Austin, et al. 2019; Marken and Maxson 2017; Marken and Murtha 2017; Maxson and Marken 2018; Ricker, Marken, Bauer, et al. 2019; Ricker, Marken, and Cooper 2018; Ricker, Marken, and Rivas 2017).

Surface Hydrology and Reservoir Engineering

Access to potable water has frequently been cited as a potential limiting factor to large, dense urban aggregations in the tropical lowlands, one that the ancient Maya resolved, particularly in the central lowlands, by engineering their urban landscapes to direct rainfall runoff into specially designed water catchment and storage features, such as reservoirs, for dry-season consumption and agricultural use (e.g., Lucero 2006; Scarborough and Gallopin 1991; Scarborough, Dunning, et al. 2012). In other lowland areas, excess rainy season water was a primary concern (e.g., French, Duffy, and Bhatt 2012; Halperin et al. 2019). Additionally, continued investigations of regional resource distribution and management continue to indicate the adaptive benefit of a dispersed (and mobile) hinterland settlement pattern (e.g., Fedick 1996; Marken and Arnauld 2023; Murtha 2023). Water management practices at Waka' indicate a concern with all three of these: scarcity, excess, and distribution.

Over the years, flow analysis of the Waka' urban core and regional surface hydrology has been conducted using topographic data collected via multiple terrestrial and remote mapping instruments, including total station (core), lidar (core, PLI polygon), SRTM30 (region), and ASTER (PLI Polygon, region) data (Hermitt et al. 2018; Marken, Ricker, Rivas, et al. 2019; Maxson and Marken 2018). While water catchment was an adaptive practice within the Waka' urban core, exemplified by several large water-storage tanks, these features, along with much of the downtown landscape are also designed to direct excess rainwater outside the city center to prevent flooding and, in some cases, into potential agricultural zones (Figure 3.8; Marken and Ricker 2018; Marken, Ricker, and Austin 2022; Marken, Ricker, Rivas, et al. 2019; Maxson and Marken 2018).

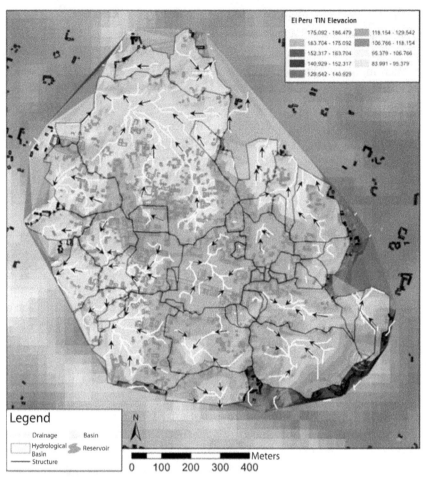

Figure 3.8. Flow map of the Waka' urban core hydrology. Map by Damien Marken and Erika Maxson, courtesy of Proyecto Arqueológico Waka'.

An overarching concern with flooding within the Waka' urban core is exemplified by Plazas 1 and 2 within the Epicenter, which were built canted to direct stormwater north into the Plaza 1 Reservoir (Freidel and Castañeda 2014; see below). The most densely settled northern residential sectors of the urban core intentionally followed local topography so that excess runoff was directed to two primary "channels" that flowed to the "vacant" North Bajo. Additional indicators of engineered flood control are the documented outlets built to release excess water from two of the largest water-storage features within the core (Marken, Austin, et al. 2019; Marken and Cooper 2018). In fact, visual analysis of the lidar DEM indicates that nearly all large potential reservoirs within the Waka' core had some sort of spillway that avoided residential areas.

Even with flooding a primary concern, residence atop the escarpment, far from natural potable water resources, nevertheless required active collection and storage of rainwater for human consumption. Recent analyses of reservoir capacities suggest that stored rainwater was rather abundant and potentially readily available within the Waka' urban core (Marken, Ricker, and Austin 2022), with the landscape adaptively managed by adjacent populations as local circumstances shifted. At present, based on terrestrial mapping and ground-truthed lidar survey data (Marken, Cooper, et al. 2020), four "classes" of water catchment features are identifiable across the Waka' urban core and hinterland: (1) community tanks, (2) residential reservoirs, (3) household reservoirs, and (4) domestic pools. The primary distinction between these four classes is size, in terms of both area and volume. Intensive geoarchaeological investigation of six of these features, however, provides further distinction between classes. These subsurface investigations also serve as invaluable comparisons for surface evaluation and verification.

(1) Community or district tanks are the largest water-storage features within the region, and range between 2,400 and 11,700 m² in area and between 1,180 and 10,175 m³ in estimated volume based on the lidar survey (see also Marken, Ricker, and Austin 2022). Several of these features form critical nodes within larger pond and drainage systems. Nine of these features have been identified within the Waka' urban core.

Extensive field surveys including 190 soil descriptions from dry cores and testpits have revealed varied construction, including extensive limestone floors, terraces, clay liners, and access platforms (Marken, Ricker, and Austin 2022; Ricker, Marken, and Rivas 2017, Ricker, Marken, and Cooper 2018; Ricker, Marken, Bauer, et al. 2019). Large community reservoirs (Ical and NE tanks, see Figure 3.2) had the most extensive construction engineering, with testpit and soil-core measured cut limestone blocks and fill that constituted reservoir floors and access terraces averaging 34–31 centimeters thick, respectively. Several urban tank-outlet constructions (cut outlets and spillways) were designed to release excess rainwater into potential agricultural zones at the periphery of the densely populated core. Terraces around the margins of these large, shared tanks would be useful to provide inhabitants with easy access to water during low-water periods associated with the dry season. Soil morphologies on edges of the community tanks suggest dredging of the *bajo* center to increase storage capacity, and clayey materials were moved locally to the edges of the *bajo* center. Soil data also suggest that these landscape features were likely naturally occurring sinkholes that were dredged to increase water-storage capacity and subsequently constructed around as central water features of the urban core.

(2) Residential reservoirs exhibit capacities ranging between 590 and 2,000 m^2 in area and between 215 and 690 m^3 in volume. Eight such features have been identified and are often spatially associated with elite groups or neighborhoods, although some functioned as parts of larger hydrological systems. Two residential reservoirs (Xucub and Plaza 1) have been evaluated with test-pits and dry soil cores (Figure 3.2). The smaller size of these modified natural *bajos* necessitated access platforms rather than the extensive terraces such as those of the larger community tanks; but overall, the engineering needs to maintain freshwater supplies in this reservoir were much less, with only dredged *bajo* clay liners added to hold adequate rainwater. The Xucub Reservoir outlet was cut into limestone bedrock to allow preferential flow outward during times of excess rainfall, thus constituting an important area for storm water management within the Waka' city core. The safe transmission of storm flow from the Xucub Group toward lower *bajos* and constructed canals would have been important during the rainy season to maintain dry conditions within the densely populated upland areas of the city core. In contrast, the Plaza 1 Reservoir shows very deep cultural fill/slope wash deposits. Depths to reach a solid rock or engineered surface are between 220 and 302 centimeters. The Plaza 1 Reservoir has no outlet indicating it was likely used for flood-control purposes. The reservoir would capture runoff from impervious surfaces associated with the city core and allow for slow infiltration through the groundwater rather than risk the potentially destructive flooding generated by urban runoff. The Plaza 1 Reservoir also has significantly different soil morphology and engineering as compared to the Xucub Reservoir. The discovery of rough-cut limestone riprap and stucco flooring at the base of the reservoir are unique to the urban water features of Waka' (Ricker, Marken, Bauer, et al. 2019).

(3) Household reservoirs are smaller depressions that are near ubiquitous in residential groups within the urban core and across the surveyed hinterlands. These have small sizes and capacities, ranging between 55 and 530 m^2 in area and between 10 and 150 m^3 in volume, and many appear to have originated as borrow pits for household construction or as natural karstic sinkhole depressions that were subsequently modified with access terraces and platforms. Some of these may have functioned as silting pools, as hypothesized by Vernon Scarborough, Nicholas Dunning, and colleagues (2012) at Tikal, as many often ring the edges of larger basins and/or pocket *bajos*. Small household reservoirs (Trista and Chuc) show little evidence of active water

management activities (see Ricker, Marken, and Cooper 2018). Subsurface soil morphologies suggest these were natural sinkholes on the landscape that were built up around for short-term water storage. There is no evidence of construction floors within the reservoirs, further suggesting that minimal engineering was needed to maintain water in these features. Extensive slope wash deposits have filled these areas since the Waka' core was abandoned; thus, the Maya likely managed these systems periodically through dredging to maintain adequate surface water–storage capacity to meet local water needs.

(4) The smallest water catchment features are domestic pools, five of which have been identified, defined by their small size and capacity; all are less than 40 m^2 in area and less than 10 m^3 in estimated volume. To date only one such small-scale water feature has been excavated at Waka' (Pérez Robles et al. 2019).

The extensive and intensive field investigations of Waka' urban water catchment features have shown how extremely complex the various surface water systems were within the city core. All the reservoirs evaluated have varied soil properties, engineering structures, and water management purposes. The use of a particular reservoir seems to have been tied to intrinsic properties of the natural sinkholes that were modified by the Maya. The complexity of the Petén region's surficial geology, groundwater quality, and freshwater accessibility necessitated adaptive management techniques that employed the correct management and engineering strategies to overcome site-specific adverse environmental conditions. This adaptation is evident in the amount of construction engineering used in areas of problematic soils (Vertisols) and elevated groundwater sulfate versus areas with minimal engineering that lacked these underlying conditions. At Waka', local residential areas (neighborhoods) managed their water resources to fit the environmental conditions present and, thus, overarching conceptual models of centralized water management in the Maya region are likely unable to capture this local variability in natural resource management strategies.

Hinterland Water Management and Hydrology

Pedestrian and lidar surveys have identified several potential small residential reservoirs and a multitude of household reservoirs across the Waka' hinterlands (Marken 2011). Surface investigations of these features indicate that the majority match form, size, and surface characteristics of Tista and Chuc Reservoirs (Marken et al. 2020). While lidar ground-truthing and volumetric analysis are ongoing, nearly all hinterland patio groups are spatially associated with at least one small catchment feature, a pattern seen elsewhere across the Maya Lowlands (e.g., Brewer 2018; Chase 2016).

Regional hydrology is dominated by the Río San Pedro Mártir and the lagoon wetlands to the west, largely fed by runoff from the escarpment uplands (Hermitt et al. 2018). The upland terrain is highly broken, dotted by settled ridges and hilltops separated by a network of dry creeks, *quebradas*, gullies, and gorges that converge into narrow upland "valleys." Excess rainfall collects in these and flows off the escarpment into the wetland areas flanking the Río San Pedro and surrounding the lagoons. Sediments carried by this runoff also collect along the northern portion of the Río San Juan with a profound impact on hydrological analyses of modern surface models.

The lidar DEM confirms what PAW researchers have long suspected based on field surveys and the analysis of satellite imagery (Marken 2011): today the Río San Juan seeps underground at multiple points along its route to the Río San Pedro, largely due to colluvial infilling from water flowing off the escarpment, particularly the large gorge just southeast of the Mirador Group (Figure 3.9). When considering traditional evidence for agricultural intensification in the region (see below), it is possible that this infilling has obscured Classic-era modifications of the Río San Juan and its adjacent wetlands.

Beyond subsistence concerns, regional hydrology and Waka's role as a market center (Eppich 2020; Eppich and Freidel 2015) suggest the potential that inhabitants within the region also employed the Ríos San Juan and San Pedro to establish and maintain connections with peoples across the lowlands. The hinterland settlement patterns along both rivers suggest this, with several settlements placed at what appear to be strategic locations along the river courses. In 2017, excavations and ground-truthing along the shoreline of the El Perú Lagoon uncovered the remains of what might have been a built waterfront adjacent to the settlement of Bakxulcar (Rivas 2018). A cluster of settlements border the middle portion of the Río San Juan, one of which is suggestive of an administrative control point along its course. While the lidar data indicate that tracts of the modern Río San Juan floodplain have been covered by colluvial soils, forcing the river underground at various points, this may not have been the case in the Preclassic or Classic periods. If the Río San Juan was navigable (or maintained) when Waka' was occupied, it would suggest that water transport via canoe may have been a vital means of communication and trade along the western margins of Petén, particularly during the rainy season (Freidel, Acuña, et al. 2022). North of Waka', the Río San Juan ultimately connects with the canal and relic lake recently identified in the Tintal region (Chiriboga et al. 2017).

Ground-truthing by Dúglas Pérez and Alex Rivas in 2017 identified a potential built waterfront along the northern shore of the Laguna El Perú

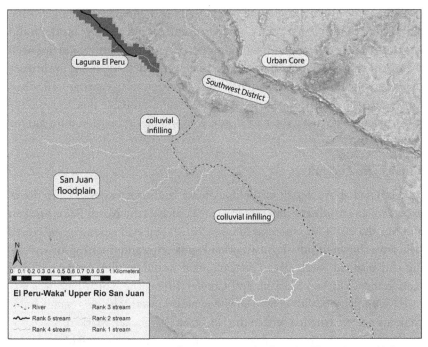

Figure 3.9. The upper Río San Juan showing areas of colluvial infilling. RRIM of lidar DEM. Map by Damien Marken, courtesy of Proyecto Arqueológico Waka'.

in the vicinity of Bakxulcar (Rivas 2018). The linear nature of the southern end of the Laguna's north shore suggests that this waterfront may be much longer than previously guessed (Marken and Pérez 2018:Figure 30). When considering subsistence resources within the region, the two lagoons and the surrounding wetlands represent an important potential food source (Eppich, Marken, and Menéndez 2023), possibly augmented by canoe-carried agricultural imports to the waterfront.

Agriculture

Current visual analyses of the lidar DEM have thus far failed to identify any traditional features associated with Maya agricultural intensification—raised fields, terraces, or irrigation canals—which may hint that those methods of intensification were limited in the region. Aside from Waka' itself, settlement is relatively dispersed across the remainder of the landscape. Nevertheless, there are several potential, if not mutually exclusive, explanations for this apparent absence of large-scale agricultural features.

Perhaps the overall population was indeed lower compared to neighboring parts of the central Petén (e.g., Canuto et al. 2018), and perhaps residents did not construct large-scale agricultural works because they simply did not need them. The ridges, hilltops, and narrow drainages that characterize the broken uplands of the northeastern half of the lidar polygon would appear well suited for terracing, but none is present. Instead, it seems probable that regional rural populations focused their subsistence efforts on drainage bottom and/or upland areas.

Urban Core Agriculture

As discussed above, much of the downtown landscape is designed to direct excess water outside the city center to areas such as the North Bajo (Marken and Murtha 2017; Maxson and Marken 2018). Soil evaluations in the North Bajo have shown minimal construction engineering and thick topsoil overlying native shrink-swell clays (Vertisols) that would be ideal for agricultural management (Ricker, Marken, and Cooper 2018). The North Bajo was terraced from the southern upland edge downward toward the *bajo* center, but it contains no construction within the *bajo* itself (see Ricker, Marken, and Cooper 2018). This area receives drainage from the northern section of the Waka' core and may have been used as an area for lowland agriculture. The *bajo* contained extensive wetland soils, as indicated by redoximorphic features and organic matter buildup on the soil surface. Therefore, this landscape would have held abundant moisture to support agriculture during the dry season. In addition, multiple periods of sedimentation and subsequent stabilization are evident in the soils from buried surfaces (Ab horizons), which is typical of *bajos* used for wetland agriculture in the region (Dunning, Luzzadder-Beach, et al. 2002). Soil morphologies suggest this *bajo* received high rates of water inflow, possibly from directed stormwater carrying eroded sediment off the urban center during the wet season. Although soil cores are useful to identify potential uses of this *bajo*, it is difficult to discern the exact management of such a broad area without the use of soil testpits and trenches. Similar geomorphic areas in the hinterlands of the city core (Figure 3.7) would have been areas of potential agricultural production as well, due to the lack of structures, high surface water inflow, adequate drainage, and predominantly flat land (less than 3% slope). Future efforts should be undertaken to further understand the management of this area using larger excavations and soil sampling.

Hinterland Agriculture

Although there are no visible lidar signatures of engineered agricultural districts around the dense core of Waka', there are naturally occurring river terraces and low-lying valleys to the northwest and southeast of the city that would have received stormwater flow from the surrounding uplands. Multiple natural strath terrace scarps are visible on lidar, with few structures built upon these high areas above the Río San Juan (Figure 3.10). In addition, there is a visible dug north–south canal that would have diverted water from the natural hydrologic flow to areas in the center of these natural terraces, further emphasizing the importance of water in this area that is relatively devoid of structures. The effort required to dig such canals would have been immense, which suggests large-scale production of agricultural commodities in this area. The large local alluvial valleys southeast of the core atop the escarpment would also have provided ideal conditions for large-scale agricultural production (Figure 3.11). All these potential agrarian landscapes on the Waka' core periphery would have been ideal for crop production because of the combination of abundant water supply directed from surrounding uplands (as suggested by flow paths into them), the fertile alluvial soils that formed in these landscapes (Alfisols and Mollisols), and the naturally flat topography (less than 3% average slope) that would have slowed down water flow and minimized topsoil erosion.

In addition, erosion and overland flow emanating from the surrounding uplands would have been predictably high in nutrients like nitrogen and phosphorus, providing excess fertilization to cultivated crops planted in these areas. Studies within the Waka' regional watersheds (particularly the Northeast Tank) show precipitating gypsum within the soils, suggesting supersaturated sulfate in the regional groundwater (Ricker, Marken, and Rivas 2017; Ricker, Marken, Bauer, et al. 2019). The local geology is composed of oceanic sedimentary deposits (limestone/dolostone) that contain reduced sulfur in the form of pyrite. In the Maya region, sulfate concentrations tend to increase in surface water at lower elevations (Luzzadder-Beach and Beach 2008) and can impair the quality of a potable water source (WHO 2011).

Precipitating gypsum, however, can provide improvement for maize agriculture by increasing soil aggregation and structure, which allows for deeper plant rooting, increased water holding capacity, and decreased penetration resistance (compaction) in clayey soils (Seidel et al. 2016). Thus, gypsum can provide beneficial alterations to soil's physical properties that allow maize to better survive periods of drought and that increase annual yield. Although the flat strath terraces of the Río San Juan and local alluvial valleys would be ideal areas for agriculture, the periodic flooding and poor water quality of this area could explain the lack of large-scale residential construction in these peripheral areas. While there are many likely benefits of using natural river terraces or alluvial valleys for agriculture in the region, further extensive geo-

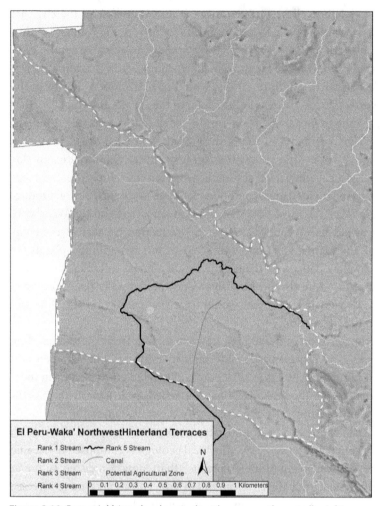

Figure 3.10. Potential hinterland agricultural zone: northwest alluvial terraces. RRIM of lidar DEM. Map by Damien Marken, courtesy of Proyecto Arqueológico Waka'.

archaeology research is needed to confirm physical and chemical soil properties indicative of agricultural production.

While generally lower overall population density in the western Petén, compared to the eastern Petén (Canuto et al. 2018), could explain the absence of overt features of agricultural intensification within the Waka' region, such an assumption becomes more tenuous when local physiographic and settlement patterns and adaptive potentials (challenges and opportunities) are considered, specifically the Waka' urban core and its periurban ring. Such a

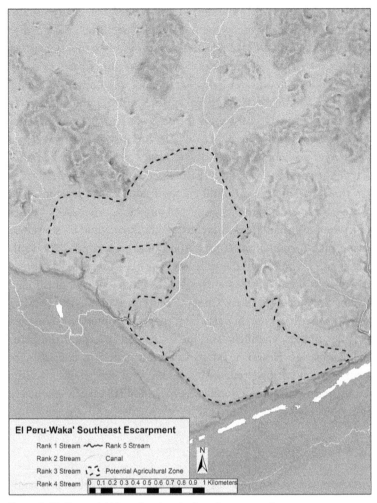

Figure 3.11. Potential hinterland agricultural zone: southeast escarpment. RRIM of lidar DEM. Map by Damien Marken, courtesy of Proyecto Arqueológico Waka'.

highly aggregated population would likely have required at least some surplus foodstuffs to be either produced locally or imported.

Setting external imports and trade aside for the moment to focus on strategies of agricultural intensification, extrapolation from the clear urban engineering practice of directing water to designated collection points (reservoirs and tanks) to be stored and from which its release could be controlled (see above), it is possible that, at least in the periurban suburbs, farmers collected and stored rainwater not only in small household reservoirs for personal consumption (e.g., Marken 2011; Marken, Ricker, Rivas, et al. 2019) but also in larger, less archaeologically recognizable features specifically designed to slow and control water flow to take advantage of, or improve upon, existing drainage systems for irrigation purposes. Such "store and release" systems, sometimes referred to as floodwater irrigation, are not uncommon across the Maya Lowlands (e.g., Dunning, Griffin, et al. 2015; Scarborough, Dunning, et al. 2012), although they are typically more formally constructed and/or better preserved than those proposed here for Waka'. In contrast to canal or terrace systems, however, archaeological traces of floodwater irrigation can be rather ephemeral, quickly washing away if not maintained.

Several of these potential floodwater storage features were located along the base of the eastern side of the Mirador hill and along the bases of other steep slopes in the periurban area, where horizontal flow could be slowed or released during high precipitation events. Additional hinterland upland valleys and pocket *bajos* within the lidar polygon have been identified as potential examples of such floodwater systems, all with settlement well positioned to control water flow rates (Marken, Cooper, and Pérez 2019). The DEM of the area north of the urban core, in particular, suggests a potentially complex network of tanks, outlets, channels, and fields adapted to exploit the natural hydrologic landscape. However, extensive ground-truthing, consisting of pedestrian survey, soil coring, trench excavations, and soil analysis will be needed to confirm the presence of floodwater irrigation at Waka' or elsewhere in the Petén.

Conclusion

The recent widespread recognition of Maya centers as true urbanized landscapes, even if they still carry a "low-density" caveat (e.g., Fletcher 2009, 2012), is a welcome development. Yet prevailing cross-cultural characterizations of lowland cities—their form, social organization and structure, meaning, and stability—tend to overgeneralize their similarities and to stress their limitations in a manner that often obscures the long-term adaptive successes of Maya urbanism across a massive and highly variable tropical landscape. Hundreds of Maya cities flourished across the lowlands for more than two thousand years. Like all ancient cities, they were eventually abandoned, but this reality does not negate their ability to have continuously transformed their environments to meet evolving socio-ecological circumstances.

While the data in this chapter are primarily presented from a synchronic perspective, the Waka' urban landscape was anything but static (see Eppich,

Marken, and Menéndez 2023; Marken, Pérez, et al. 2019; see also Eppich, this volume). The above interpretations of settlement distribution, population estimates, surface hydrology, and agricultural potential and their intersections are thus best viewed as "maximal" assessments of critical physiographic and settlement factors underlying the culmination of Waka' urbanization until its regional abandonment around 1050 CE. Synthesis and comparison of these data provide fundamental parameters to better contextualize the city's economic and political histories (e.g., Kelly, Friedel, and Navarro-Farr, this volume; Navarro-Farr, Pérez, and Pérez Robles, this volume; Pérez Robles et al., this volume; Rich and Eppich, this volume; Freidel, this volume). They also serve as a vital point of reference for employing subsurface and artifact assemblage data to better understand diachronic changes in settlement decisions and resource management practices.

Notes

1 The lidar survey was funded by the Fundación de Patrimonio Cultural y Natural Maya (PACUNAM) as part of the PACUNAM Lidar Initiative (PLI). The collected point cloud data were subsequently processed by NCALM and converted into a 1 m × 1 m pixel digital elevation model (DEM) for each survey area. Ground-truthing of the PLI DEM described here has been funded by the GeoOntological Development Society of San Francisco.

2 This percentage includes the 29.85 square kilometers and the 28.15 square kilometers ground-truthed by PAW investigators in 2018 and 2019, respectively, as well as the 9.69 square kilometers south of the Río San Pedro Martír, where no structures or other potential anthropogenic features have been identified in the lidar DEM. This total area also encompasses the original 13.6 square-kilometer PAW survey area that was reexamined in 2018 and 2019.

3 Another possibility is that the ditch was a defensive feature, although there are currently no indications of an inner rampart, which often accompanies lowland defensive ditches (e.g., Puleston and Callendar 1967; Webster 1976). Additional evidence further suggests that defense was not the feature's primary function. Both field observations and elevation profiles confirm that along the central east–west segment of the feature, the exterior elevation is significantly higher than the interior, "defensive," side, rendering it an ineffective defensive measure. This, and the absence of an inner rampart, however, does not negate the possibility that the boundary feature segments did have some defensive capability. Previous hydrological analyses of the PAW urban core topographic data (Maxson and Marken 2018) indicate that during large rainfall events, surface water from much of the northern half of the urban core is directed toward the central segment, where it accumulates before flowing west along its course.

References

Beach, Timothy, Sheryl Luzzadder-Beach, Samantha Krause, Tom Guderjan, Fred Valdez
Jr., Juan Carlos Fernandez-Diaz, Sara Eshleman, and Colin Doyle
2019   Ancient Maya Wetland Fields Revealed under Tropical Forest Canopy from Laser
        Scanning and Multiproxy Evidence. *Proceedings of the National Academy of Sci-
        ences* 116:21469–21477.
Brewer, Jeffery L.
2018   Householders as Water Managers: A Comparison of Domestic-Scale Water Man-
        agement Practices from Two Central Maya Lowland Sites. *Ancient Mesoamerica*
        29:197–217.
Canuto, Marcello A., Francisco Estrada-Belli, Thomas Garrison, Stephen D. Houston,
Mary Jane Acuña, Milan Kováč, Damien Marken, et al.
2018   Airborne Laser Scanning of Northern Guatemala: A Reckoning with Ancient
        Lowland Maya Complexity. *Science* 361:eaau0137. https://doi.org/10.1126/science
        .aau0137.
Chase, Adrian S. Z.
2016   Beyond Elite Control: Residential Reservoirs at Caracol, Belize. *WIREs Water*
        3:885–897.
Chiriboga, Carlos R., Mary Jane Acuña, and Varinia Matute
2017   Investigaciones recientes en El Tintal y su paisaje arqueológico. Paper presented at
        the XXXI Simposio de Investigaciones Arqueológicas en Guatemala, Guatemala
        City, July 17–21.
Dunning, Nicholas, Timothy Beach, Pat Farrell, and Sheryl Luzzadder-Beach
1998   Prehispanic Agrosystems and Adaptive Regions in the Maya Lowlands. *Culture
        and Agriculture* 20(2/3):87–101.
Dunning, Nicholas, Timothy Beach, and Sheryl Luzzadder-Beach
2012   Kax and Kol: Collapse and Resilience in Lowland Maya Civilization. *Proceedings
        of the National Academy of Sciences* 109(10):3652–3657.
Dunning, Nicholas P., Robert E. Griffin, John G. Jones, Richard E. Terry, Zachary Larsen,
and Christopher Carr
2015   Life on the Edge: Tikal in a *Bajo* Landscape. In *Tikal: Paleoecology of an Ancient
        Maya City*, edited by David L. Lentz, Nicholas P. Dunning, and Vernon L. Scarbor-
        ough, pp. 95–123. Cambridge University Press, New York.
Dunning, Nicholas P., Sheryl Luzzadder-Beach, Timothy Beach, John G. Jones, Vernon
Scarborough, and T. Patrick Culbert
2002   Arising from the *Bajos:* The Evolution of a Neotropical Landscape and the Rise of
        Maya Civilization. *Annals of the Association of American Geographers* 92:267–283.
Eppich, Keith
2020   Commerce, Redistribution, Autarky, and Barter: The Multitiered Urban Economy
        of El Perú-Waka', Guatemala. In *The Real Business of Ancient Maya Economies*,
        edited by Marilyn A. Masson, David A. Freidel, and Arthur A. Demarest, pp. 149–
        171. University Press of Florida, Gainesville.
Eppich, E. Keith, and David Freidel
2015   Markets and Marketing in the Classic Maya Lowlands: A Case Study from El Perú-

Waka'. In *The Ancient Maya Marketplace: The Archaeology of Transient Space*, edited by Eleanor M. King, pp. 195–225. University of Arizona Press, Tucson.

Eppich, Keith, Damien B. Marken, and Elsa Damaris Menéndez
2023   A City in Flux: The Dynamic Urban Form and Functions of El Perú-Waka', Guatemala. In *Building an Archaeology of Maya Urbanism: Flexibility and Planning in the American Tropics*, edited by Damien B. Marken and M. Charlotte Arnauld, pp. 105–147. University Press of Colorado, Denver.

Fedick, Scott L., editor
1996   *The Managed Mosaic: Ancient Maya Agriculture and Resource Use*. University of Utah Press, Salt Lake City.

Fletcher, Roland
2009   Low-Density, Agrarian-Based Urbanism: A Comparative View. *Insights* 2(4):2–19.
2012   Low-Density, Agrarian-Based Urbanism: Scale, Power, and Ecology. In *The Comparative Archaeology of Complex Societies*, edited by Michael E. Smith, pp. 285–320. Cambridge University Press, Cambridge.

Freidel, David A., Mary Jane Acuña, Carlos Chiriboga, and Michelle Rich
2022   Water Trails and Water Mountains: The View from Northwest Petén. In *Sustainability and Water Management in the Maya World and Beyond*, edited by Jean T. Larmon, Lisa J. Lucero, and Fred Valdez Jr., pp. 119–142. University Press of Colorado, Louisville.

Freidel, David A., and Francisco Castañeda
2014   Operación WK17: Excavaciones en la Plaza 2 y Estela 7. In *Proyecto Arqueológico El Perú-Waka': Informe no. 12, temporada 2014*, edited by Juan Carlos Pérez, Griselda Pérez, and David A. Freidel, pp. 85–103. Fundación de Investigación Arqueológica Waka', Guatemala City.

Freidel, David A., Héctor L. Escobedo, and Stanley Guenter
2007   A Crossroads of Conquerors: Waka' and Gordon Willey's "Rehearsal for the Collapse" Hypothesis. In *Gordon R. Willey and American Archaeology: Contemporary Perspectives*, edited by Jeremy A. Sabloff and William L. Fash, pp. 187–208. University of Oklahoma Press, Norman.

French, Kirk D., Christopher J. Duffy, and Gopal Bhatt
2012   The Hydroarchaeological Method: A Case Study at the Classic Maya Site of Palenque. *Latin American Antiquity* 23(1):29–50.

Guenter, Stanley
2014   The Epigraphy of El Perú-Waka'. In *Archaeology at El Perú-Waka': Performances of Ritual, Memory, and Power*, edited by Olivia Navarro-Farr and Michelle Rich, pp. 147–166. University of Arizona Press, Tucson.

Gunn, Joel D., John E. Foss, William J. Folan, Maria del Rosario Dominguez Carrasco, and Betty B. Faust
2002   *Bajo* Sediment and the Hydraulic System of Calakmul, Campeche, Mexico. *Ancient Mesoamerica* 13(2):297–315.

Halperin, Christina, Jean-Batiste LeMoine, and Enrique Pérez Zambrano
2019   Infrastructures of Moving Water at the Maya Site of Ucanal, Petén, Guatemala. *Journal of Anthropological Archaeology* 56:101102. https://doi.org/10.1016/j.jaa.2019.101102.

Hermitt, Elijah, Erika Maxson, Kirk D. French, Damien B. Marken, and Timothy Murtha
2017   Landform, Water, and Regional Analysis of Three Classic Maya Cities. Paper presented at 45th Computer Applications and Quantitative Methods in Archaeology (CAA) Conference, Atlanta, GA, March 14–16.

Hutson, Scott R.
2016   *The Ancient Urban Maya: Neighborhoods, Inequality, and Built Form.* University Press of Florida, Gainesville.

Isendahl, Christian
2012   Agro-urban Landscapes: The Example of Maya Lowland Cities. *Antiquity* 86:1112–1125.

Isendahl, Christian, and Michael E. Smith
2013   Sustainable Agrarian Urbanism: The Low-Density Cities of the Mayas and Aztecs. *Cities* 31:132–143.

Lucero, Lisa J.
2006   *Water and Ritual: The Rise and Fall of Classic Maya Rulers.* University of Texas Press, Austin.

Luzzadder-Beach, Sheryl, and Timothy Beach
2008   Water Chemistry Constraints and Possibilities for Ancient and Contemporary Maya Wetlands. *Journal of Ethnobiology* 28:211–230.

Marken, Damien B.
2011   City and State: Urbanism, Rural Settlement, and Polity in the Classic Maya Lowlands. PhD diss., Department of Anthropology, Southern Methodist University, Dallas.
2015   Conceptualizing the Spatial Dimensions of Classic Maya States: Polity and Urbanism at El Perú-Waka', Petén. In *Classic Maya Polities of the Southern Lowlands*, edited by Damien B. Marken and James Fitzsimmons, pp. 123–166. University Press of Colorado, Boulder.

Marken, Damien B., and M. Charlotte Arnauld, editors
2023   *Building an Archaeology of Maya Urbanism: Flexibility and Planning in the American Tropics.* University Press of Colorado, Boulder.

Marken, Damien B., Haley N. Austin, Hannah Bauer, and Matthew C. Ricker
2019   WK24: Excavaciones de rasgos de manejo de agua y estructuras residenciales en el sector noreste de El Perú-Waka'. In *Proyecto Arqueológico El Perú-Waka': Informe no. 16, temporada 2018*, edited by Juan Carlos Pérez, Griselda Pérez, and Damien B. Marken, pp. 185–248. Fundación de Investigación Arqueológica Waka', Guatemala City.

Marken, Damien B., and Zachary Cooper
2018   WK22: Excavaciones en estructuras residenciales asociadas con rasgos de manejo del agua en el Barrio Ical. In *Proyecto Arqueológico El Perú-Waka': Informe no. 15, temporada 2017*, edited by Juan Carlos Pérez, Griselda Pérez and David Freidel, pp. 196–254. Fundación de Investigación Arqueológica Waka', Guatemala City.

Marken, Damien B., Zachary J. Cooper, Bailey Gemberling, Dúglas Pérez, and Robert Austin
2020   Reconocimiento regional de El Perú-Waka', 2019: Verificación y análisis del suelo del DEM de LiDAR de PAW, meseta este y área de influencia al norte del núcleo

urbano. In *Proyecto Arqueológico El Perú-Waka': Informe no. 17, temporada 2019,* edited by Juan Carlos Pérez, Griselda Pérez Robles, and Damien B. Marken, pp. 161–270. Fundación de Investigación Arqueológica Waka', Guatemala City.

Marken, Damien B., Zachary J. Cooper, and Dúglas Pérez

2019   Reconocimiento regional de El Perú-Waka' 2018: Verificación sobre el terreno y análisis de datos de LiDAR del PAW; Las zonas de los *bajos* sur y el río. In *Proyecto Arqueológico El Perú-Waka': Informe no. 16, temporada 2018,* edited by Juan Carlos Pérez, Griselda Pérez, and Damien B. Marken, pp. 249–328. Fundación de Investigación Arqueológica Waka', Guatemala City.

Marken, Damien B., and Erika Maxson

2017   Rellenadno los agujeros: Mapeo topográfico del núcleo urbano de El Perú-Waka', 2016. In *Proyecto Arqueológico El Perú-Waka': Informe no. 14, temporada 2016,* edited by Juan Carlos Pérez, Griselda Pérez, and David A. Freidel, pp. 249–264. Fundación de Investigación Arqueológica Waka', Guatemala City.

Marken, Damien B., and Timothy Murtha

2017   Maya Cities, People and Place: Comparative Perspectives from El Perú and Tikal. In *Research Reports in Belizean Archaeology, Papers of the 2016 Belize Archaeology Symposium, Architecture and Urban Design: Expressions of Kingly Power and Hegemony of the State,* edited by John Morris, Melissa Badillo, Sylvia Batty, and George Thompson, pp. 177–189. Institute of Archaeology, National Institute of Culture and History, Belmopan.

Marken, Damien B., and Dúglas Pérez

2018   LiDAR en El Perú (Polígono 12): Análisis preliminar y comprobación sobre el terreno 2017. In *Proyecto Arqueológico El Perú-Waka': Informe no. 15, temporada 2017,* edited by Juan Carlos Pérez, Griselda Pérez, and David Freidel, pp. 273–317. Fundación de Investigación Arqueológica Waka', Guatemala City.

Marken, Damien B., Juan Carlos Pérez, Olivia Navarro-Farr, and Keith Eppich

2019   Ciudad del ciempiés: Urbanismo, límites y comunidad en El Perú-Waka', Petén, Guatemala. In *XXXII Simposio de Investigaciones Arqueológicas en Guatemala, 2018,* vol. 1, edited by Bárbara Arroyo, Luis Méndez Salinas, and Gloria Ajú Álvarez, pp. 531–546. Ministerio de Cultura y Deportes, Instituto de Antropología e Historia, Guatemala City.

Marken, Damien B., and Matthew C. Ricker

2018   *Living with Water: Classic Maya Pond Management at El Perú-Waka', Petén, Guatemala.* National Geographic Society Research Council Grant #HJ-100R-17, Final Report.

Marken, Damien B., Matthew C. Ricker, and Robert Austin

2022   Combining Survey, Soil Coring, and GIS Methods to Improve Lowland Maya Reservoir Capacity Estimates. *Advances in Archaeological Practice* 10(2):187–199.

Marken, Damien B., Matthew C. Ricker, Alex Rivas, and Erika Maxson

2019   Urbanismo de *Bajo* densidad en las tierras bajas Maya: El caso de El Perú-Waka', Petén, Guatemala. *Estudios de Cultura Maya* 54:11–42.

Maxson, Erika, and Damien B. Marken

2018   Análisis preliminar con SIG de la hidrología superficial en el núcleo urbano del sitio El Perú. In *Proyecto Arqueológico El Perú-Waka': Informe no. 15, temporada*

2017, edited by Juan Carlos Pérez, Griselda Pérez, and David Freidel, pp. 316–329. Fundación de Investigación Arqueológica Waka', Guatemala City.

Murtha, Timothy M., Jr.

2009 *Land and Labor, Classic Maya Terraced Agriculture: An Investigation of the Settlement Ecology and Intensive Agricultural Landscape of Caracol, Belize.* VDM Verlag Dr. Müller, Saarbrücken, Germany.

2023 The Living Landscape: Livelihoods and Opportunities in the City and Region of Ancient Tikal. In *Building an Archaeology of Maya Urbanism: Flexibility and Planning in the American Tropics*, edited by Damien B. Marken and M. Charlotte Arnauld, pp. 315–348. University Press of Colorado, Boulder.

Navarro-Farr, Olivia C., and Michelle Rich, editors

2014 *Archaeology at El Perú-Waka': Ancient Maya Performances of Ritual, Memory, and Power.* University of Arizona Press, Tucson.

Pérez, Dúglas, and Damien B. Marken

2017 Reconocimiento y mapeo en el periferia este de El Perú-Waka'. In *Proyecto Arqueológico El Perú-Waka': Informe no. 14, temporada 2016*, edited by Juan Carlos Pérez, Griselda Pérez, and David A. Freidel, pp. 265–278. Fundación de Investigación Arqueológica Waka', Guatemala City.

Pérez Robles, Griselda, Juan Carlos Pérez, Damaris Menéndez, and Claver Couoj

2019 WK18: La Acropolis de Waka', el Palacio Real. In *Proyecto Arqueológico El Perú-Waka': Informe no. 16, temporada 2018*, edited by Juan Carlos Pérez, Griselda Pérez Robles, and Damien B. Marken, pp. 83–126. Fundación de Investigación Arqueológica Waka', Guatemala City.

Puleston, Dennis E., and Donald W. Callender Jr.

1967 Defensive Earthworks at Tikal. *Expedition* 9(30):40–48.

Ramos, E. López

1975 Geological Summary of the Yucatan Peninsula. In *The Gulf of Mexico and the Caribbean*, edited by A. E. M. Nairn and F. G. Stehli, pp. 257–282. Springer, Boston.

Ricker, Matthew C., Damien B. Marken, Hannah Bauer, and Haley N. Austin

2019 WK21: Gestión del agua en el repertorio conectado a Xucub y en los sistemas hidrológicos del tanque noreste. In *Proyecto Arqueológico El Perú-Waka': Informe no. 16, temporada 2018*, edited by Juan Carlos Pérez, Griselda Pérez, and Damien B. Marken, pp. 127–184. Fundación de Investigación Arqueológica Waka', Guatemala City.

Ricker, Matthew C., Damien B. Marken, and Zachary Cooper

2018 Uso de descripciones de suelos para evaluar la gestión de aguas superficiales en el noroeste del centro urbano de El Perú-Waka'. In *Proyecto Arqueológico El Perú-Waka': Informe no. 15, temporada 2017*, edited by Juan Carlos Pérez, Griselda Pérez, and David Freidel, pp. 130–195. Fundación de Investigación Arqueológica Waka', Guatemala City.

Ricker, Matthew C., Damien B. Marken, and Alexander Rivas

2017 Transectos de bases de suelo en rasgos hidrológicos de la superficie: Los reservorios Xucub, Plaza 1, y el tanque noreste. In *Proyecto Arqueológico El Perú-Waka': Informe no. 14, temporada 2016*, edited by Juan Carlos Pérez, Griselda Pérez, and David A. Freidel, pp. 161–221. Fundación de Investigación Arqueológica Waka', Guatemala City.

Rivas, Alex

2018   Operación WK23: Grupo Bakxulcar. In *Proyecto Arqueológico El Perú-Waka': Informe no. 15, temporada 2017*, edited by Juan Carlos Pérez, Griselda Pérez, and David Freidel, pp. 255–272. Fundación de Investigación Arqueológica Waka', Guatemala City.

Scarborough, Vernon L.

1998   Ecology and Ritual: Water Management and the Maya. *Latin American Antiquity* 9:135–159.

Scarborough, Vernon L., Nicholas P. Dunning, Kenneth B. Tankersley, Christopher Carr, Eric Weaver, Liwy Grazioso, Brian Lane, et al.

2012   Water and Sustainable Land-Use at the Ancient Tropical City of Tikal, Guatemala. *Proceedings of the National Academy of Sciences* 109(31):12408–12413.

Scarborough, Vernon L., and Gary G. Gallopin

1991   A Water Storage Adaptation in the Maya Lowlands. *Science* 251(4994):658–662.

Seidel, Edleusa Pereira, William dos Reis, Marcos Cesar Mottin, Emerson Fey, Ana Paula Reck Schneider, and Monica Carolina Sustakowski

2016   Evaluation of Aggregate Distribution and Selected Soil Physical Properties under Maize–Jack Bean Intercropping and Gypsum Rates. *African Journal of Agricultural Research* 12:1209–1216.

Smith, Michael E.

2010   The Archaeological Study of Neighborhoods and Districts in Ancient Cities. *Journal of Anthropological Archaeology* 29:137–154.

Smith, Monica L.

2008   Urban Empty Spaces. Contentious Places for Consensus Building. *Archaeological Dialogues* 15(2):216–231.

Thompson, Amy E., John P. Walden, Adrian S.Z. Chase, Scott R. Hutson, Damien B. Marken, Bernadette Cap, Eric C. Fries, et al.

2022   Ancient Lowland Maya Neighborhoods: Average Nearest Neighbor Analysis and Kernel Density Models, Environments, and Urban Scale. *PLoS ONE* 17(11):e0275916. https://doi.org/10.1371/journal.pone.0275916.

Tsesmeli, Evangelia

2004   Reconociendo y levantando el mapa de El Perú-Waka' y Chakah. In *Proyecto Arqueológico El Perú-Waka': Informe no. 1, temporada 2003*, edited by Héctor L. Escobedo and David A. Freidel, pp. 339–354. Fundación de Investigación Arqueológica Waka', Guatemala City.

Webster, David

1976   *Defensive Earthworks at Becan, Campeche, Mexico: Implications for Maya Warfare.* MARI, Tulane University, New Orleans.

2018   *The Population of Tikal: Implications for Maya Demography.* Paris Monographs in American Archaeology 49. Archaeopress Access Archaeology, Paris.

Weyl, Richard

1980   *The Geology of Central America 2: Completely Revised Edition.* Gebrüder Borntraeger, Berlin.

World Health Organization (WHO)

2011   *Guidelines for Drinking-Water Quality*, 4th ed. WHO, Geneva, Switzerland.

4

Repeopling the Cityscape of El Perú-Waka'

Classic Maya Social Models in an Urban Context

KEITH EPPICH

Throughout the whole of Rome's history, one feature remained constant—
the family. The city grew to be an empire, the republic became an autoc-
racy, old-fashioned religion yielded to frenetic new cults from the East,
but, through it all, Roman society was based on the family, economic life
was built around it, and its many complex problems continued to provide
endless matter for debate among Roman lawyers.

—Lionel Casson, *Everyday Life in Ancient Rome* (1975:10)

Reconstructing the daily life of the Classic Maya people remains a principal, if elusive, challenge in Mayanist studies. From kings to commoners, the
tropical sun rose on the same world for them all, yet it is highly unlikely that
they proceeded to experience that world in the same manner. Today, scholars
vigorously debate the best way to describe that world, much less arrive at a
consensus of how individuals lived their lives within it. This is the goal of the
research presented here; it is an effort to create an understanding of the daily
realities of life in a Classic Maya city, as evidenced through the archaeological
record of El Perú-Waka'. This is a complicated procedure. First, a perspective on daily life requires a focus on the people themselves. It requires an
approach that takes extant material culture and uses it to "develop peopled
interpretations of an ancient society" (Robin 2003:309). This involves a focus
on household archaeology: the direct investigation of the domestic spaces of
everyday Maya, especially in relation to the overall urban settlement. Second, this necessarily includes an appreciation of the social units that inhabited those domestic spaces and the social contexts that surrounded them. To
understand everyday life in a Maya city, one must repeople it with meaningful social units, reconstructing social organization and its relationship to

the overall city. Taking a cue from the great classicist Lionel Casson, quoted above, this means addressing the ancient Maya family. However they chose to construct it, the family very likely stood as the most important social unit in everyday life. In more formal anthropological terms, this is a reconstruction of social organization, building models of the ancient society's internal parts, the conjugal units, lineages, houses, neighborhoods, and communities that physically constituted the old city. Next, such models are applied and measured against the documented archaeological record and tested for their veracity. Last, these can be assembled to create an image of urban society as it existed for the Classic period. Then, one has a novel perspective of everyday life in a Classic center. As the sun might have risen over the ancient cityscape, one finds it repeopled with families, lineages, houses, and individuals living their lives in relation to the people they cared about. It seems that, throughout the whole of the city's occupation, the society of Waka' was based on its families.

This chapter explores four residential groups, or a collection of groups in one case, and it examines the archaeology of each, making a case for the type of social unit present. For some, this seems to be an endogamous community, for others, a noble house. Overall, an image of social heterogeneity emerges from the archaeology of these residences, a social heterogeneity that likely covered the whole of the ancient city.

Repeopling the Past: Maya Household Archaeology

A more peopled perspective on ancient urban settlement involves an archaeology specifically tailored toward "getting at the people behind the artifacts" (Robin 2012: 7; see also Robin 2001). The ancient city was not inhabited by identical, anonymous beings, but instead consisted of individuals building and inhabiting a framework that made their lives fulfilling and meaningful. Clark Erickson (2006: 353) wrote that "peopling the past is a radical alternative to viewing farmers as faceless masses, the passive recipients of what the elite impose on them." Erickson's subject was agricultural intensification, but the same point can be made of urban settlement. While there may have been some degree of city planning, local inhabitants—the people themselves—took such plans and reshaped them for their own convenience. Indeed, the history of cities is replete with examples of local communities ignoring and overwriting the carefully planned aesthetics of urban designers (see Kostof 1991, 1992). Maya shaman-kings or priestly lords may have imagined their cities as vast cosmograms, but the actual inhabitants may not have had any compunction to follow such plans.

This necessarily begs the question of who, exactly, these inhabitants were and what manner of frameworks they created or imposed on the urban landscape. These individuals—actors in their own right—developed sets of dynamic associations with other individuals, collections of individuals, and the objects around them (Law 2009; Latour 2005; Hubbard 2006). Such dynamic associations are, of course, social, and the totality of these associations comprise human society. Social networks serve the collective and general interest of the individuals and the social units within them. They provide the structure for fulfilling and meaningful lives. Urban inhabitants create and sustain social frameworks in an urban landscape. To the extent that this conforms with urban planning, there is no contradiction. When the two differ, however, local actors feel little hesitation in imposing their own social priorities onto the city around them, reconfiguring whole neighborhoods to meet their social requirements. In short, settlement patterns and architectural configurations have a strong tendency to reflect the social organization of the people who live there (Chang 1958; Ensor 2013a, 2013b). Hence, a more peopled perspective on the ancient city must explicitly address social organization and its effects on an urban landscape.

The most basic unit of any settlement pattern is, of course, the household residence. Household archaeology remains the most direct way to access the lives of the people in that household and to open up the lives of the domestic residents. It reveals the social complexities within and between households and illuminates the articulation between individual households and broader society (Robin 2003; see also Hendon 1996; Lohse and Valdez 2004; Webster and Gonlin 1988; Wilk 1991; Wilk and Ashmore 1988; Wilk and Rathje 1982). This involves not just broad, horizontal excavations of residences and attached structures but also the archaeological investigation of the open spaces around the residence. Household archaeology seeks to document living spaces, activity areas, workplaces, middens, and any extant material culture left behind by the activities of everyday life.

This has been used with great effect at Chan, in west-central Belize. There, Cynthia Robin and her colleagues (2013; Robin, Wyatt, Kosakowsky, et al. 2012; see also Robin 2015, 2016; Robin, Wyatt, Meierhoff, et al. 2015) documented the everyday lives of Maya farmers in a largely self-contained community over the course of two thousand years. The Maya of Chan only ever numbered a few hundred individuals, the population surpassing a thousand only during their Late Classic apex. Yet, they possessed a great deal of agency and autonomy, wielding sources of wealth and power quite independent of any royal overlords. They focused on their own land and developed complex agricultural terracing, elaborate arboriculture, and hydraulic strategies on their own (Lentz et al. 2014; Wyatt 2012). The Maya interacted with the sacred through small, personal acts of ritual, punctuated by larger festivals at a central, sacred community center. They wore shell jewelry on their persons. They used chert bifaces in the cornfields, and both jewelry and tools were locally manufactured for parts of Chan's occupation. They had ceramic vessels of excellent quality, and they apparently possessed healthy bodies. They lived well. Robin recorded the remains of their daily lives, from their solid, well-built homes and open living places to their workshops and sacred spaces. Her research places farmers living in the middle of their own agricultural fields, raising corn, beans, and squash in substantial quantities. The work, Robin writes (2012:126), was "not overly and materially gendered female and male . . . farmwork becomes a collaborative family project involving men, women, and children."

Robin's work flatly contradicts the traditional view of rural Maya farmers as homogenous, conservative, and passive, divorced from their own means of production and reduced to the status of an exploited peasantry. The farmers of Chan do not fit the conventional narratives of accepted social science. They were people—actors in their own right—not especially powerful or wealthy, but people who possessed their own productive patch of earth. Robin's work serves as a case study in how to do household archaeology on the scale of a local community. It shows the importance of focusing on the everyday lives of ancient people. In her own words, "Grand narratives of human history do not just overlook everyday life, they trivialize it and make it invisible . . . denying and mystifying the things people do and the structural causes that develop through everyday actions" (Robin 2012:4).

Household archaeology is not without its flaws, however. Principal among them is a general reluctance to address the complexities of Maya social organization. Household archaeology can intensely study a residence in great detail, as well as the structures and activity areas around it, and reconstruct ancient life very accurately. But, lacking a sense of how the inhabitants organized themselves socially, any reconstruction based on archaeology will necessarily be incomplete. After all, a "household" is not technically a social unit at all, which is to say, households are not units of any larger society that would be culturally meaningful to the household inhabitants. Households are not lineages, or houses, or clans, or families at all, neither conjugal nor extended. A household is the physical residence; and the household group refers merely to the collection of individuals residing at that location (Ensor 2013b:39–43; Parkin 1997). Households are analytical units used to describe small-scale corporate activity groups (Ashmore and Wilk 1988:3–4). In one of the first approaches to household archaeology, Richard Wilk and William Rathje (1982) intentionally left the definition of household vague, in order to facilitate cross-cultural usage. They defined it simply as "the level at which social groups articulate directly with the economic and ecological process . . . the most common social component of subsistence" (Wilk and Rathje 1982:618). In the original formulation, the term "household" is not limited to any single expression of social organization. Even Robin (2003: 311) avoids a direct and social definition of the term, choosing simply to describe households as "socioeconomic groups fundamental to human societies." Sometimes households seem to refer to conjugal families, at other times they are cognatic lineages; sometimes they are "houses," and sometimes they are interpreted as just the social group attached to agricultural activity (Dunning 2004). There is an advantage in using such culturally neutral terms as methodological units, as this allows scholars to focus on the archaeology of the domestic residence, regardless of who inhabited it. However, as a way to understand the everyday life of the ancient Maya, and as part of an attempt to repeople the past, the neutrality of the term is a significant obstacle. The reluctance to specifically address social organization leads to a scholarship on Maya household archaeology in which ancient people inhabit vaguely defined collectives of potentially related persons (cf. Freter 2004; Rice 1988). Any attempt to repeople the past must address the cohesion of household groups; it must address social organization.

Classic Maya Social Organization: Models in Muddles

The reluctance to address social organization is understandable, given the complexities of the literature on Classic Maya kinship and society. That body of scholarship is large, dense, contradictory, and sometimes accompanied by an ugly polemic. It requires diving headfirst into the entangled literature and terminology of mid-twentieth-century anthropology, understanding cognatic and acognatic descent, and grasping the difference between patrilines, matrilines, bilateral descent, and locality systems as well as trying to parse out how all the above articulate with each other as well as with the documented kin-terminologies, Crow-Omaha, Iroquois, or even Kariera systems (Parkin 1997; Parkin and Stone 2004). This is in addition to the postmodern critiques of social anthropology and kinship and the questioning of whether midcentury anthropology actually documented anything real (Schneider 1984). This has led to one of the more remarkable aspects of Mayanist studies: after nearly two centuries of scholarship, there is no single, widely accepted model for Classic Maya society.

Instead, there are models in muddles. There exist many different models for Classic society, most of which are contradictory and could not have coexisted in antiquity (Watanabe 2004). It often seems as if there are more models for ancient Maya society than there are researchers interested in ancient Maya society. Each model is generally presented as an idealized societal form, with other models dismissed as false and inaccurate, or as fundamentally epistemologically flawed. Consensus appears unlikely. Despite the variety of social models, they can be roughly collected into three basic approaches, each centered on anthropological concepts of lineage, house, and class. What follows is not a comprehensive literature review on the subject, although those do exist (Ensor 2013a; Fowler and Hageman 2004; Johnson and Paul 2016, see also Shenk and Mattison 2011; Souvatzi 2014, 2017; Watanabe 2004). This is an attempt to operationalize these models, to examine how they can be applied to the archaeological record and potentially identified in the material remains of Waka'.

Most commonly, a lineage model has been applied to explain ancient Maya society. This posits that Classic society was mostly composed of patrilineal social units, lineages where the line of descent passes through the male line. The descent group is small enough for the links of kinship between all members to be known and traceable (Parkin 1997:17–18; see also Ensor 2013b:44–45, 120–123). Family names, property, titles, and ritual obligations pass from father to son. Usually, the social unit centers on the residence and personage of the eldest, most capable male, who makes critical decisions on economic, political, and social matters. The core workforce consists of adult men, usually brothers, working cooperatively in the cornfields owned by the lineage. The system is also usually described as patrilocal, with brides moving into the expansive residence group of their husbands. The women worked the domestic spaces collectively, raising children, grinding corn, and weaving cloth, affinely connected with one another and generally under the oversight of the wife of the leading male. As described by Jon Hageman (2004:64), Maya patrilineages possesses five main characteristics. As a descent group, they hold property in common, they have strong group identity, they are exogamous, they are internally ranked, and they claim descent from a common ancestor, whom they venerate.

The lineage model possesses significant advantages and one critical weakness. One advantage is that the model emerges from the ethnography and ethnohistory of the Maya people themselves. Many twentieth-century anthropologists described the people they studied as being organized around patrilineages (Eppich 2011). These lineages could be the nested domestic groups and *sna* described by Evan Vogt (1969) for the Tzotzil. They could be the *cah* and *chibal* of the Colonial Yucatec documented by Mathew Restall (1997), or the patriarchal "household clusters" of the Lacandon (Boremanse 1998), or even the extended families of the Quiché described by Ruth Bunzel (1952). This model suggests some degree of commonality among the known Maya societies, commonalities that have the potential to be projected backward to the Classic period. However, this is also the weakness of the lineage model, as it runs into well-known problems of direct-historical analogy (Ascher 1961; Ensor 2013a; Lamoureux-St-Hilaire 2020; Wobst 1978; Wylie 1985). It assumes that Maya society has changed little since the Classic period, as well as running the epistemological risk where the hypothesis becomes the observed interpretation (Wobst 1978). However, if viewed as a means to generate hypotheses, the lineage model excels. It possesses patterned behavior that can be turned into testable statements. Hageman (2004) has noted that patrilineages should live in close proximity to collectively owned agricultural fields, they should possess an emphasis on cognatic descent, and their ancestor veneration should result in large, centrally located ancestor shrines. The shrine itself should lie in close proximity to the home of the main patriarch, who should dwell in the largest and most elaborate residence. Ensor (2013a; 2013b) notes that patrilocal traditions produce highly uniform living arrangements, with aggregates of small residences, each holding a conjugal unit, arranged around a central plaza.

However, the lineage model came under heavy critique in the early 2000s. In a series of publications, Susan Gillespie (2000a, 2000b, 2000c) argued that the lineage model is incapable of explaining the significant degree of variation present in the ethnographic or archaeological record (see also Kuper 1982; A. Chase and D. Chase 1996b). Operating off postmodern concepts of kinship and descent, she contended that many forms of social organization operate as social-economic constructions, with biological relatedness playing a very limited role. The solution, she argued, was to replace lineage with "house" and to address these social units as acognatic, wholly cultural creations. Gillespie used the definition supplied by Claude Lévi-Strauss (1982) in his discussion of Native American societies of the Pacific Northwest. A house, wrote Lévi-Strauss (1982:175), is "a corporate body holding an estate made up of both material and immaterial wealth, which perpetuates itself through the transmission of its name, its goods, and its titles down a real or imaginary line, considered legitimate as long as this community can express itself in the language of kinship." In short, Maya society consisted of nested "houses," corporate entities that expressed themselves in the language of kinship but that did not limit themselves to biological relatedness. The model proved influential and was applied to a wide variety of Mayanist studies on social organization (Hendon 2010; Hendon and Joyce 2001; Hutson et al. 2004; Joyce 2007; Joyce and Gillespie 2000). It is advantageous in that the flexibility of the model allows it to be broadly applied and applied without being bogged down in the complications of proving specific rules of descent and affinal locality.

The disadvantages of the house model lie in the inability of scholars to prove the existence of "houses" at all as well as in the continuing epistemological debate about the definition of the "house" unit itself. Since the house model consists of socially constructed relations and as those relations cannot be directly observed, a "house" cannot be proven to exist solely using the archaeological record. Attempts to do so have run directly into well-known problems of negative evidence (Duncan and Hageman 2015; Johnson and Paul 2016; Weiss-Krejci 2011; see also Stone 1981; Wallach 2019). After all, how does one demonstrate the nonexistence of biological relatedness? The socially constructed nature of the house simply cannot be demonstrated using archaeology (Houston and McAnany 2003). Secondarily, the house model itself, as defined by Lévi-Strauss, is not purely an acognatic social unit. Rather, the houses described by Lévi-Strauss are bilocal residence groups combined with bilateral descent (Ensor 2013b:130–131; 2013a). Rather than being purely social constructs, individuals in house societies make decisions about locality and descent based on biological relatedness. This is a decision informed by the social status of each marriage partner, with the lower-ranked spouse taking on the name of the higher-ranked partner and moving into the higher-ranked partner's house, and with children claiming dual descent but emphasizing the higher-ranked parent. This is why Lévi-Strauss compared such systems to the nobility of medieval Europe, where lower-ranked nobles were accepted into higher-ranked houses, regardless of gender (Lévi-Strauss 1982:174–178).

Next, there is the class model. This model organized Maya society into an internally ranked hierarchy of socioeconomic classes (see Willey 1956). These classes strongly resemble those from the past and present of the industrialized West. Often these models have slaves, commoners, nobles, and royals, with a prosperous "middle class" wedged somewhere in between (Chase 1992; see also Palka 1997). Alternatively, there is a simple two-class system of commoners and elites, again, sometimes with a commercialized "middle class" (Chase 1992; A. Chase and D. Chase 1996a). The chief difficulty with class models is that the presence of class structures is often assumed rather than demonstrated, and the concept of "class" is rarely defined. Scholars usually just presuppose the universality of class structures within human society. This is an unsubstantiated assumption, particularly since the fluidity of class has been demonstrated among the Maya (Masson and Peraza Lope 2004). Modern Maya social units, including lineages, cut across economic classes (Masson and Peraza Lope 2004:199). Bradley Ensor (2013a) has particularly focused on the concept of class, seeking to delineate the class structures present in ancient Maya society. He defines class as the commonly held relationship between people and their means of production. People can either possess it, that is, own the means of production for others, or they lack it entirely; and this relationship determines their social class. This model has the advantage that such economic relationships can be reconstructed using the archaeological record; but there are dangers in assuming that such relationships were important or meaningful to ancient people. Quite simply, we do not know. We do not even know that class structures are universal at all, or whether they can be projected backward into antiquity.

Last, there is the question of whether any of this matters. Postmodern critiques of kinship studies emerged in the early 1980s and argued that kinship and social organization exist as somewhat informal traditions, written down by Western anthropologists and then projected onto studied peoples as normative rules (Ensor 2013b:13–15). This view was pioneered by David Schneider in a series of articles and his influential 1984 volume (see also Beck 2007; Joyce 2000, 2007; Schneider 1968). The argument was that kinship was mostly, if not entirely, subjective. The kinship models developed in midcentury anthropology were largely created by anthropologists and reflected not indigenous practices but Western concepts and obsessions on blood and biology. This leads to a question: Do people actually practice their professed kinship rules? That is a question that can be evaluated objectively. Biological and genetic research has clearly shown that genetic relatedness follows kinship structure (see Chaix, Austerlitz, et al. 2004, 2007; King and Jobling 2009). Scientific evidence has established that cultures do practice their professed kinship rules and produce the social structures those rules dictate (Ensor 2011). Schneider, it seems, was simply wrong in his critique. The focus on kinship and social structure matters because it forms the basis of how people construct the society around them. To repeople the ancient cityscape of Waka', there must be a focus on the emic social units that the Maya built and maintained during the centuries they lived there.

Classic Maya Social Dynamism

A chief difficulty in modeling Classic Maya society is that there may not have been a uniform template for the totality of Classic society. Rather, it is much more likely that multiple social structures existed across the geography and chronology of Classic civilization. Tikal may have possessed one set of social relations while Copan possessed another, and these social systems transformed over time. At Tikal, William Haviland long ago argued that the system of kinship and social organization shifted significantly as composite families broke apart in the face of a powerful, centralized state, transforming from extended lineages to a dependent class of urban poor (Haviland 1968, 1992, 2003). At Copan, Julia Hendon argued that the humbler homes of the urban inhabitants indicated their own dependence on the powerful noble families that dominated the city's core (Hendon 1991, 1992, 2000, 2010). This took place as royal authority at Copan apparently faltered following the defeat and sacrifice of Waxaklajuun Ubaah K'awiil, likely at the hands of his own nobles (see Fash 2005; Fash and Stuart 1991; Sharer and Traxler 2006). At Postclassic Mayapán, widespread economic activity and apparent prosperity created an urban society characterized by significant variation and social mobility (Masson and Peraza Lope 2004, 2014; Hare et al. 2014). Any class differences seem to have blurred with this affluence, and elites seem to have been defined less by their economic status than by their relationship with ritual features. These models are not exclusive of one another. An understanding of and appreciation for variability is key in proposing a reconstruction of Classic society (see Inomata 2004). This was emphasized by Ensor (2013a:62), who writes that "kinship systems are both internally dynamic . . . and manipulated by political economic histories" (see also Ensor 2011, 2013b).

Models for Classic Maya society must possess two characteristics: multiplicity and dynamism. There simply is not a single model for Classic Maya society that can be applied from Mayapán to Copan. Any social model must include how the society changed over time, as dictated by their own internal logic as well as by external political and social events. Indeed, it seems best to picture the social organizations present among the Classic Maya not as a singular and rigid social order but as a social dynamic, with its own structure and internal components shifting with time and changing circumstances (Eppich 2011; see also D. Chase and A. Chase 2004). The next step is to take these social models, with an appreciation for their own dynamism, and to apply them to the archaeological record of Waka'. This is to be done in the

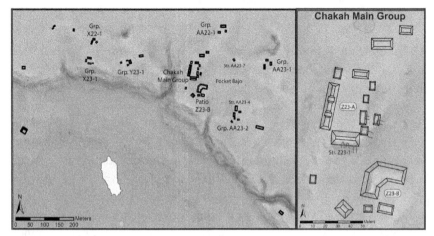

Figure 4.1. Map of Chakah, with detail of Chakah main group. Maps by Damien Marken, courtesy of Proyecto Arqueológico Waka'.

context of several urban communities studied by the Proyecto Arqueológico Waka' (PAW) and by evaluating which model best fits the recovered material evidence.

The Chakah Groups: An Endogamous Community of Exogamous Lineages

Chakah is a term applied to a loose cluster of household compounds lying 3.5 kilometers southeast of the Waka' urban core. It is one of a number of similar clusters that surround the urban center. These communities cover the broken karstic terrain to the north and east as well as the riverine lowlands to the south and west. Collectively, these clusters constitute the city's hinterland urban settlement, and Chakah is the best-studied among them. It lies on the southern edge of the limestone escarpment, beside the riverine lowlands of the Río San Pedro Mártir. Chakah itself consists of eight patio groups arranged around a large compound and adjacent *bajo* (Figure 4.1). This central compound, designated the Chakah main group, contains a mix of ritual and residential architecture formally arranged around a rectilinear plaza. Together, the Chakah groups can be seen as a single, distinct community. Indeed, it would be fair to characterize it as a kind of "*bajo* community," an agricultural settlement taking advantage of the rich alluvial soils in the swampy lowlands (Kunen et al. 2000; Kunen 2004). This characterization is supported by the quantity of chert tools uncovered by the excavators. Together with the proximity of the prime agricultural land, this argues for an agricultural focus for Chakah.

PAW investigated Chakah due to the heavy looting that occurred in the area. Chakah's architecture lies adjacent to the river and is thus easily accessible, allowing opportunistic looters to heavily damage Chakah's architecture, breaking open at least one rich burial, described below. Excavations took place there between 2003 and 2006 by a team led by Fabiola Quiroa Flores and Griselda Pérez Robles (Quiroa Flores 2004, 2008; Quiroa Flores and Pérez Robles 2005; Quiroa Flores and Guillot Vassaux 2006). Investigations focused on the main group but included excavations and testpits at many of the other patio groups.

The architecture consists of low earthen mounds for the patio groups and masonry platforms for the main group, foundations for perishable structures of wood or thatch. Investigations revealed that the Chakah groups existed as a purely Late Classic phenomenon (Eppich 2011). The main group shows initial occupation in the early seventh century with the construction of the masonry foundations. The remainder of the groups are then settled during the seventh century and are fully occupied through the eighth century. Some of the groups took advantage of long-abandoned structures from the Late Preclassic, likely old farmsteads from that period.

The Chakah main group is the earliest, most elaborate, and largest of the groups in the area. An additional patio group, Patio Z23-B, lies to the south and is likely a residential portion of the main group. Patio Z23-B is constructed on top of one of the old Late Preclassic farmsteads. The main group's placement adjacent to the *bajo* and its formal layout suggest a planned settlement. The most elaborate structure is the large and heavily looted Structure Z23-1. It possesses a large masonry platform standing 2.4 meters tall, with stone walls but a perishable roof. Structure Z23-1 has only a single construction episode, with the ceramics from the construction fill dating it to the earliest portions of the seventh century or even the final years of the sixth century. This is similar to all the platforms of the main group, which also display a single construction phase dating to the seventh century with later eighth-century modification. The pattern supports the idea that the Maya planned the settlement of Chakah, or at least the settlement of its main group. Additionally, Structure Z23-1 once held a very elaborate burial. Looters tore through the center of the masonry platform and ripped it open, but investigators were able to document the remains and reconstruct the funerary ceramics. The burial contained at least two polychrome ceramic vessels, a ceramic figurine, and a large number of chert and obsidian flakes. Excavators recovered only fragments of bone and portions of a cranium (Quiroa Flores and Pérez Robles 2005). One of the ceramic vessels was a royal polychrome that contained a glyphic band identifying it as the drinking vessel to a "fiery lord of El Zotz"

(Eppich 2011; see also Looper and Polyukhovych 2016). This indicates some connection between the interred individual and the highest levels of Maya society. The depth and placement of the burial strongly supports that its occupant was an honored ancestor, the first large burial at Chakah, and possibly even a lineage founder (see McAnany 1995).

The image that emerges is of Chakah as a planned settlement located southeast of the urban core and established to place the area under cultivation. Throughout the Late Classic, additional patio groups spread out from the main group. Their dispersed settlement suggests an emphasis on agriculture, and the settlement even resembles the farming community of Chan (Robin 2012, 2013). The groups of Chakah possess little evidence of craft production. The settlement lasts only until the end of the eighth century, when the whole of Chakah is abandoned, apparently all at once, likely as a result of increasing threats from outside (see Eppich, Marken, and Menéndez 2022; Dunning, Beach, and Rue 1997; Dunning, Beach, and Luzzadder-Beach 2012; O'Mansky and Dunning 2004).

Overall, the settlement pattern of Chakah strongly resembles the patterns identified for patrilineal descent groups (Ensor 2013a:76–77, 2013b:156–160). This consists of aggregates of small dwellings arranged around a central plaza. In this formulation, conjugal groups established new residences within the larger area claimed by the extended patrilineage. Chakah possessed a large, centrally located residence with an ancestor shrine containing the rich burial of the likely founder, one with royal connections. The entire community rose and fell as a single unit, although the archaeology reveals internal disparity among its inhabitants. Chakah perfectly fits the patterns expressed by Hageman (2004), Eppich (2011), and Ensor (2013a). Almost certainly, Chakah was a community inhabited either by a single exceptionally large lineage or by a cluster of lineages organized around principles of patrilineality and patrilocality. This, however, begs an additional question. What exactly was an ancient Maya community?

Multiscalar Urban Communities

A community is traditionally defined as a coresidential collection of households characterized by day-to-day interactions, shared experiences, and a common culture (Murdock 1949). Building from this, Jason Yaeger and Marcello Canuto (2000) stress the internally interactive nature of local communities and the manner in which they create a socially constituted institution. To exist, communities rely on the interaction between their internal elements, both individuals and households. Communities are created by social action, and the archaeological evidence of a community lies in the material remains of such actions. Thus, communities "represent a contextual, contingent, and temporally circumscribed materialization of people's thoughts concerning community identity" (Yaeger and Canuto 2000:9). For example, Yaeger (2000) himself argues that the remains of communal feasting events and collective ritual represent just such materializations.

A community exists then as a collection of households; it is an intermediate stage within a settlement hierarchy. As such, the concept strongly resembles the definition for neighborhoods used in the literature of urban settlement (Arnauld 2012; Smith and Novic 2012; Smith et al. 2015). Michael Smith (2010:139) defines the neighborhood as one tier of a complex urban settlement, "a residential zone that has considerable face-to-face interaction and is distinctive on the basis of physical and/or social characteristics." In Smith's (2010) design, neighborhoods serve as the internal components of large urban districts. In essence, neighborhoods are urban communities, possessing much the same social functionality and place within the settlement hierarchy.

As Joyce Marcus (2000) shows, often communities themselves are organized around the concept of kinship. She argues for the application of indigenous models of community onto settlement patterns, arriving at the conclusion that Maya societies possess a multiscalar nature. Household groups are organized into communities, which are arranged as hamlets or villages, as required. This is quite common among ethnographically or ethnohistorically known Maya societies (Eppich 2011; see also Boremanse 1998; Fox and Cook 1996; Restall 1997; Vogt 1969). For the Quiché of Chichicastenango, Bunzel's (1952:110–113) description is quite explicit. While the patrilineage practices a strict exogamy, spouses are sought out among nearby households of the same neighborhood. Studying the Yucatec Maya of the seventeenth century, John Weeks (1988) comes to a similar conclusion. The Maya he studied self-organized into exogamous patrilineal households nested inside large, endogamous local groups, or communities (see also Annereau-Fulbert 2012). While the individual lineages were organized around consanguineal relations between male relatives, the larger communities were organized around the affinal relations between female relatives.

What would be the archaeological manifestations of such a community? Despite considerable disparity between constituent lineages, the entire community should experience the same set of economic fortunes over time (cf. Freter 2004). Some lineages may be poorer and others more affluent, yet if they are all affinely related, the wealth should be distributed along the lines of kinship, especially during times of need. This could even be done during community ritual or through local community festivals (see Annis 1987). Connected through marriage, the whole community should rise and fall together, roughly experiencing the same occupational sequence. This is precisely the pattern demonstrated among the Chakah groups. While their occupation began in the early seventh century, the succeeding generations spread out along the southern edge of the escarpment above the riverine lowlands, either fissioning into a series of patrilineal households or attracting poorer ones over time. Finally, the end came before the year 800 CE, and the entire population left at once, as would be expected in an affinal community. From the current evidence, it seems that Chakah was an endogamous community in the near periphery of the ancient city, composed of exogamous patrilineal households. The people lived on the farmsteads above the river, the men living in or near the home of their fathers, surrounded by the families of their brothers. The women married into neighboring lineages but were never far from their place of birth, having sisters, mothers, and daughters in the lineages around them.

The Chok Group: A Maya Noble House

The Chok Group is considerably different from the farmsteads of Chakah. It is centrally located in the southeast corner of Waka's epicenter. It is immediately adjacent to the main urban temple, M13-1, and it straddles a processional causeway leading from the east end of Plaza 2 to the ritual district of the Mirador. Chok is a sprawling palace compound, covering 13,500 square meters (Figure 4.2). Only the Royal Palace itself, located in the northwest corner of the urban core, is larger and more elaborate. The entire compound of Chok is angled at 18 degrees east of north, approximately the orientation of Maya North (see Aveni 2001). It is elevated 16 meters above the surrounding terrain on an artificially shaped hill. The main entrance is to the west, with a long, ramped staircase. The Maya built the entire palace on top of the preexisting causeway, incorporating the road into the compound.

The Chok Group's size and location prompted considerable archaeological interest. A team led by the author investigated the group over several extended field seasons, excavating the ritual, political, and domestic structures (Eppich 2007b, 2019; Eppich and Quán Cuyán 2015; Eppich and Mixter 2014; Eppich and Haney 2018). The compound itself consists of 28 ruined structures organized around a central plaza and four private patios. On the southern end of the compound rests Structure M13-12, a 12-meter pyramid that contained one of the city's famous tombs, Burial 38 (see Rich and Eppich, this volume). A second funerary structure, N13-9, lies on the north side of the central plaza and contains multiple burials and a long and complex construction history. Facing the entrance is Structure N13-6, a masonry

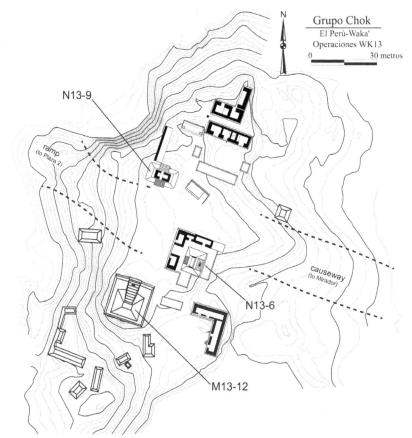

Figure 4.2. Map of Chok Group. Map by Keith Eppich, courtesy of Proyecto Arqueológico Waka'.

residential complex converted into an elevated audiencia, or open-air throne room and audience chamber. The domestic residences were located on either side of the audiencia, each with its own internal patio, although the northern structures were larger and more elaborate. This palace possesses three stelae, all blank, one each located in front of M13-12 and N13-9, and one buried inside Structure N13-6. The architecture included masonry structures with vaulted stone roofs. All have fallen since the city's abandonment, yet investigators observed fine-line carved elements on some of the structural collapse. The smaller structures lacked such rubble, indicating that the buildings of the Chok Group were a mixture of masonry and perishable architecture. Of particular interest were the large number of burials documented by investigators, 26 in total, almost a quarter of the known interments at Waka'. Investigators uncovered a complex occupational history. The oldest portion of the Chok Group is the causeway itself, which dates to the Late Preclassic, 300 BCE to 250 CE. Long before anyone lived there, the causeway ran up one side of the hill and down the other, connecting the ritual architecture of Plaza 2 to the sacred precinct of the Mirador Group. This changes in the early sixth century with the construction of masonry residences in the northern half of the Chok Group and the earliest stages of the N13-9 funerary structure. Even this early on, royal ceramics appear in the burials of Chok, indicating a close association with the ruling elite. The earliest known of the burials, the double interment of Burials 96 and 101, holds an incised bowl identical to those recovered from the royal tombs of Burials 8 and 37 (see Navarro-Farr et al. 2020; Freidel, this volume).

Over the next five centuries, the Chok Group expanded to the south, building ever larger and more elaborate architecture. This included large masonry residences and the 12-meter pyramid of Structure M13-12 with its own seventh-century tomb, holding yet more royal ceramics, in this case vessels identical to those recovered from the royal tomb of Burial 39 (Rich and Eppich, this volume). The Maya of the Chok Group incorporated the causeway into their palace, using it as their central plaza as well as their eastern and western entrances. A number of smaller structures were constructed south of M13-12, likely as residences for attached domestic servants or impoverished relations. A major shift occurs in or around the year 800. The Maya demolish one of their largest domestic residences, N13-6, and convert it to an audiencia, complete with elevated bench and vaulted gallery (compare Ball and Taschek 2001:200). Investigators have documented expansive feasting deposits associated with the usage of the new audiencia. At the same time, the northern domestic structures are systematically demolished and reconstructed in greatly enlarged and much more elaborate forms. This coincides with the diminution of royal authority at Waka', with the elite families of the city likely establishing themselves as principal political authorities.

Chok was likely inhabited by something resembling a cadet branch of the royal family of Waka'. Not rulers themselves, they nevertheless had regular contact with the highest echelons of Classic society, enough to possess palace ceramics and to practice royal funerary rites. They possessed sufficient authority that, as Classic kingship itself declined, the inhabitants of Chok were able to maintain themselves as a center of political power. With its clustered mass of large masonry residences, private patios, and impressive ritual-political structures, the architectural configuration of the Chok Group does not resemble the patterns identified for lineages. As the compound grew, additional members of the household moved in. The domestic space increases throughout the occupation of the compound, as likely did the number of people who inhabited it. This is not typical of the settlement patterns expected of patrilocal lineages. Indeed, large dwelling sizes and substantial domestic space are usually associated not with patrilocality but with some manner of matrilocal or bilocal tradition (Ember 1973; Ensor 2013a). Enlarged domestic spaces emphasize the product of female labor; in the Maya case, this is traditionally understood to be cooking, grinding corn, weaving, spinning, and perhaps even crafting and painting ceramics. Among the Maya, marketing itself is generally a female-gendered activity (Eppich and Freidel 2015; Kistler 2014; Halperin 2017; compare also Kovacevich 2016). Investigators recovered a large number of spindle whorls, including 109 from Burial 38, and more throughout the compound, suggesting spinning and possibly weaving as primary activities (and spindle whorls might also have been used as tokens in oracular casting). These are exactly the type of skills, feminine skills, one would expect to be valued among a highly competitive elite, activities that emphasized feasting and gifting in large quantities (see Eppich 2009, 2014; Houston and Stuart 2001; Inomata 2006; Inomata et al. 2002; LeCount 2001). To prosper in such an environment requires a flexible approach to resources, social units, and kin-relatedness. Bilateral descent would function as a distinct advantage in the context of elite competition (Ensor 2013b:293). Such bilateral households tend to self-organize into large corporate groups inhabiting sprawling residences. In short, they inhabit domestic spaces that would not be dissimilar to the palatial compound of the Chok Group.

Likely possessing bilocality and bilateral descent, the social unit in the Chok Group would necessarily be a "house," as defined by Lévi-Strauss (1982). There is considerable evidence, long noted, to support the existence of such a bilineal "noble house society" among the Maya (see Coe 1965:104; Haviland 1968:103–104; Marcus 1983:470). Ethnohistorically, Grant Jones (1998:80–81, 446n44) built a convincing argument that the royalty of the Petén Itza consisted of two noble lineages, male and female, each bestowing their patronym and matronym on the figure of the king (see also Fox and Cook 1996). Epigraphy similarly suggests bilateral descent, with royal genealogy prominently featuring male and female ancestors (Bricker 2002; Fox and Justeson 1986; Schele and Friedel 1990; Martin and Grube 2008:131). In its most striking manifestation, this appears on the Dallas Altar from the center of La Corona (see Figure 7.3). The epigraphy there mentions three royal women from Calakmul, their own parentage, and their noble husbands from La Corona, a striking and monumental display of the female contribution to the local noble line (Martin 2008; see also Canuto and Barrientos 2020; Navarro-Farr, Pérez, and Pérez Robles, this volume).

These ideas are supported by the distinct burial practices of the Chok

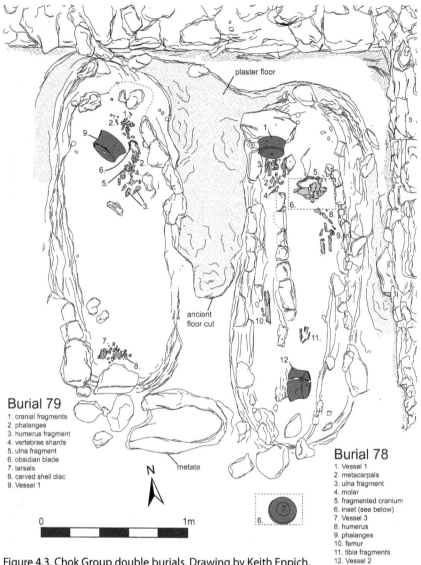

Burial 79
1. cranial fragments
2. phalanges
3. humerus fragment
4. vertebrae shards
5. ulna fragment
6. obsidian blade
7. tarsals
8. carved shell disc
9. Vessel 1

Burial 78
1. Vessel 1
2. metacarpals
3. ulna fragment
4. molar
5. fragmented cranium
6. inset (see below)
7. Vessel 3
8. humerus
9. phalanges
10. femur
11. tibia fragments
12. Vessel 2

plaster floor

ancient
floor cut

metate

N

0   1m

Figure 4.3. Chok Group double burials. Drawing by Keith Eppich, courtesy of Proyecto Arqueológico Waka'.

Group itself. Of the 26 burials documented from the Chok Group, twelve, almost half, consist of double burials. These are a paired set of adult interments directly associated in the archaeological record and deposited at the same time. When sex determination is possible, these are male and female individuals, usually interred side by side underneath the same sealed floor (Figure 4.3). While uncommon, such paired male-female burials are documented in the Maya region (Welsh 1988:300–308, 334). It has even been proposed that such paired interments were married couples of elite status (Healy 1990; Healy et al. 1998). If the burial of ancestors in domestic spaces connected the living Maya to their honored ancestors, then the practice of paired burials suggests that the Maya were honoring both parents and thus descent from both parental lines. The double burials of the Chok Group, and possibly other instances of paired burials, are likely archaeological manifestations of bilateral descent.

Current evidence then suggests that the inhabitants of the Chok Group were a noble house. In the strictest anthropological sense, this equates to a bilocal group with bilateral descent. It possessed an elite status from the very beginning of its occupation. Indeed, the house was likely a cadet branch of the royal family. Its placement in the early sixth century, directly atop a sacred processional route can be no coincidence. The group expands to cover the whole of the artificial hill, even placing humbler domestic residences along its base, and appropriating some of the function of government after the ninth century. To date, the palace is one of last occupied residences in the city. In the eleventh century, with large portions of the city already deserted, the inhabitants of the Chok Group carefully prepared their old home for abandonment. They cleaned the domestic spaces, leaving only burnt offerings and broken jar necks positioned directly above the paired burials underneath domestic floors (Eppich 2019; Eppich and Haney 2018). If the paired burials contain the remains of married couples, as they departed, the Maya of Chok honored their bilateral descent as their final act in the now-abandoned palace.

The Tolok Group: A Noble House with Distant Ties

Just to the south of the Chok Group, and adjacent to it, lies the Tolok Group. Only a slight gully divides the two. While less than one-third the size of Chok, Tolok is elevated six meters above it, on its own artificially shaped hillock. It consists of five structures tightly arranged around a small, internal patio (Figure 4.4). One of the structures is N14-2, an extended platform that may have held multiple perishable buildings. The structures were all solid masonry foundations with masonry walls, but only the forward section of N14-2 possessed a stone-vaulted roof. Tolok's main entrance is to the south, with a gated entry and a steep staircase. Excavators documented masonry foundations for a wall surrounding the whole group; Tolok was a fortified compound. Although small, the group meets all the requirements for the identification of elite status. These criteria include large and elaborate architecture, a rich ma-

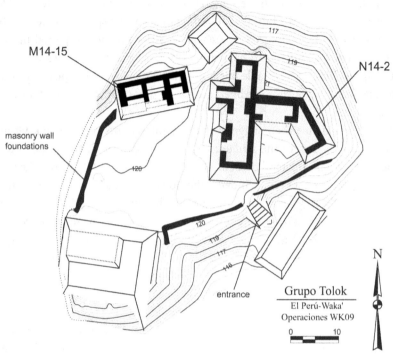

Figure 4.4. Map of Tolok Group. Map by Keith Eppich, courtesy of Proyecto Arqueológico Waka'.

terial assemblage, and a commanding viewshed (Guderjan et al. 2003; see also Haviland and Moholy-Nagy 1992).

Investigators have focused on two of the structures in the Tolok Group, Structures M14-15 and N14-2, with testpits and surface collections extending across the whole compound (Eppich 2006; Eppich and Matute 2007). The N14-2 excavations were limited to the northern portion of the structure, designed to acquire an architectural sequence. Instead, excavators uncovered a large dedicatory and feasting deposit under the building's north stairs. It features elaborate eighth-century polychrome pottery, broken chert points, ceramic drums, and burnt bones of turkey and deer all deposited beneath a pair of sacrificial victims (Eppich 2009). The M14-15 investigations documented a large residence converted into an ancestor shrine that contained five elite burials, four in directly associated pairs (Figure 4.5). The burials contained rich funerary materials, including decorated ceramic vessels and elaborate polychrome pottery (Eppich 2007a). One burial, in particular, contained highly unusual ceramics. Burial 21, the richest and earliest interment in Tolok, contained five vessels, including a full-figural Ik'-style polychrome cylinder vase

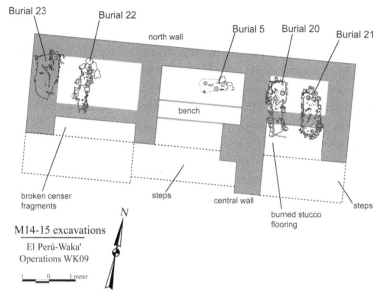

Figure 4.5. Structure M14-15, paired burials. Drawing by Keith Eppich, courtesy of Proyecto Arqueológico Waka'.

from the early eighth century (see Just 2012). The other ceramics of Burial 21 included three polychrome bowls and a cream-slipped tobacco flask (Eppich 2007a). They are not in the design corpus for the potting tradition at Waka'. They do, however, strongly resemble ceramics from Motul de San José, the city of Ik'a' (see Moriarty 2012). This suggests that the Burial 21 individual, whose sex could not be determined, either originated from Motul de San José or possessed especially strong ties to that city. The painted Ik'-style vase depicts a scene of a lord, a *bah ajaw* (first lord), kneeling in front of the king of Ik'a'. This may even be the Burial 21 individual; the depth, date, and quality of funeral goods also suggests that Burial 21 was the founder of the household group, with the M14-15 construction sequence detailing the conversion of his residence into an ancestor shrine. Over the next three generations, the Maya of Tolok placed three additional interments in the structure.

The Maya did not inhabit Tolok for very long. The entire group was constructed, occupied, and then abandoned in a single period between 770 and 850 CE (Eppich 2011). The arrangement of the structures, placed as they are in relation in an external wall, suggests a single design. Excavations in N14-2 and M14-15 show that they are single-phase constructions placed toward the end of the eighth century. The large feasting deposit of N14-2 aligns with the placement of Burial 21, making it quite likely that the Burial 21 and Burial 22 individuals were physically present at that dedicatory feast. Their successors only modified the existing architecture in the ninth century. Surface collections revealed scatters of mid- to late ninth-century ceramics lying on top of ruined architecture, placing the final abandonment of Tolok around the middle of that century. As with Chok, burned floors and cached offerings were placed above the paired burials.

The rich funerary materials and paired burials, which indicate elite status, suggest that the Tolok Group possessed the same manner of social structure as the Chok Group. This is likely a "noble house," a large kin-group with bilocality and bilateral descent. The ancestors were buried in pairs, most likely having been married couples, their descendants venerating both sides of their parentage. Like Chok, Tolok possesses an expansive domestic space and direct archaeological evidence of large-scale feasting events. Chok possesses ceramics linking its inhabitants to the ruling family of Waka'; Tolok possesses ceramics linking its inhabitants to royalty of the Ik'a' kingdom. At Ik'a', the late eighth century was a period of warfare and decline (Tokovinine and Zender 2012). It is possible that at least one noble of Motul de San José found it expedient to relocate, possibly even marrying into an elite lineage at Waka'. In short, the archaeology of the Tolok Group supports the concept of the "noble house society." In this model, a noble house occupied the compound, emphasized the descent of each parent, and participated in the competitive acts of gifting and feasting that characterized noble houses and the internal politics of a Classic Maya city.

The Paal Group: Social Mobility in an Urban Context

Among the studied residential compounds of Waka', the Paal Group stands out in its scale, occupational sequence, and apparent assertiveness on the cityscape. The Paal Group itself is a collection of structures on the western end of Plaza 2, in the southwestern area of the urban epicenter. The exact extent of the Paal Group is unknown, but it likely consisted of most of the buildings around Plaza 3. This would have been around twenty structures arranged around the central plaza space. The core of the group is constituted by eight structures on the southern side of the plaza, clustered around an internal patio (Figure 4.6). For the most part, these buildings consist of masonry platforms, some with terraced plaster floors and most with masonry walls. The absence of spring stones or vault stones argues for masonry buildings with thatched or wood roofs. The largest building is L13-21, a north-facing range structure 32 meters long and 12 meters wide. It held a series of open rooms and a plastered terrace on its northern front. It is flanked, to the west, by a pair of smaller residences, L13-16 and L13-53. On the northern side of the patio

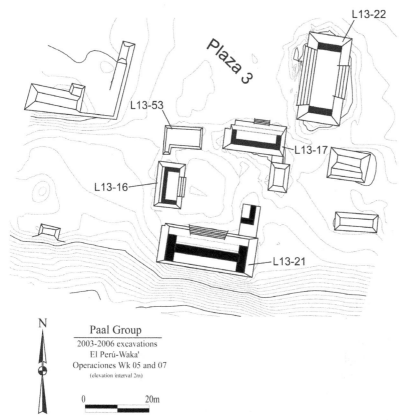

Figure 4.6. Map of Paal Group. Map by Keith Eppich, courtesy of Proyecto Arqueológico Waka'.

group is Structure L13-17, a low, range structure, open to the north with a series of broad, low steps leading down to the surface of Plaza 3. It possesses the remains of a bench or the foundation for a bench along its center. L13-17 is most likely an audiencia, a reception area for a seated lord to receive guests and supplicants (Ball and Taschek 2001: 200; Reents-Budet 2001). This assumption is supported by the monuments of the Paal Group, which are placed in front of and to the east of the building. The Paal Group possesses four fragmentary stelae placed to the north of L13-17 and in front of L13-22. These are the famous Stelae 14, 15, 16, and 17 bearing the Early Classic history of the city (Kelley, Freidel, and Navarro-Farr, this volume). However, they were placed there while in a fragmentary state, their original location unknown. Additional stelae fragments likely lie in the construction fill of L13-22. That building is a low masonry platform directly associated with the monuments of Plaza 3. L13-22 faces west, although it has a set of steps on its eastern side. It held a perishable structure, possibly nothing more elaborate than a thatched roof. It is associated with a large feasting deposit that covers the eastern steps.

Due to the historical importance of the Early Classic stelae (see Freidel et al. 2007), investigators conducted excavations across the Paal Group (Arroyave Prera 2006; Arroyave Prera, and Martínez 2004; Arroyave Prera and Matute 2005; Eppich and Mixter 2014; Guenter 2006; Guenter and Rich 2004). They recorded the architecture of the central residence of L13-21, documenting the domestic middens attached to the eastern side and to the rear of the structure as well as uncovering its complex architectural history. Part of this includes a cache of large, full-figural polychrome vases, royal ceramics in a dedicatory deposit for one of the building's later construction phases. As with Tolok and Chok, the eighth-century Maya of Paal possessed direct contact with the rulers of the city. These deposits are a pattern in the Paal Group (the Maya placed dedicatory deposits into buildings during substantial architectural modifications). These structures were substantially modified over the occupation of the group, often being transformed from small and simple platforms into large masonry structures. At the same time, additional single-phase structures were added as the compound grew larger. Investigations did not uncover a large number of burials, however, and the Paal Group lacks the paired burials described above. Indeed, the whole of the Paal Group yielded only seven interments in total, five of which were infant burials.

The most striking feature of the Paal Group is its complex architectural and occupational sequence. Prior to the Paal Group, some manner of Early Classic architecture occupied the space. The sixth-century Maya completely demolished these earlier buildings, using their rubble to create a large, level space. The Paal Group begins in the mid-sixth century as a series of perishable structures on low earthen and masonry platforms, the whole compound a humble patio group on the southern side of a broad public plaza. Throughout the next century, the Paal Group is undistinguished in any way, strongly resembling the outlier patio groups described for Chakah, above. This begins to change in the seventh century, when the Maya of Paal enlarge and substantially modify all the structures there. Low, earthen platforms are replaced with substantial masonry foundations, which are themselves enlarged in subsequent years. Stone architecture is added to those platforms. The Maya built additional patios and attached masonry rooms to the flanks of existing structures. The construction appears to be a steady drumbeat of enlargement, replacement, and elaboration from 600 to 900 CE rather than a series of distinct construction episodes. The main residence itself, L13-21 is substantially enlarged, experiencing five different architectural phases with multiple additions from 600 to 800 CE. Structure L13-17 is constructed as an audiencia, likely around 770 CE. As the architecture became more elaborate, the material culture of the group did as well. Polychrome ceramics become much more frequent, with royal ceramics occurring in the eighth century. Large eighth- and ninth-century middens appear on the flanks of the group, indicating large-scale food production and feasting events.

Toward the end of the eighth century, the Maya of Paal also extend their compound in two unusual ways. First, they constructed Structure L13-22, the platform that divides Plaza 2 from Plaza 3. They place the structure directly on top of the old plaza floor, cutting off the western end of Plaza 2 and creating the semiprivate Plaza 3, appropriating public space for their own private use. Second, they collect the shattered Early Classic stelae described above and assemble the pieces in front of the L13-22 and their audiencia of L13-17. In short, the architecture and material assemblage of the Paal Group appears to document considerable social mobility, as the inhabitants of the Paal Group rose from humble origins to elite status (Arroyave Prera and Matute 2005; Eppich 2011).

At its height, the Paal Group possessed the large domestic spaces of the noble houses that likely inhabited Chok and Tolok, yet it lacks any evidence of paired burials. Indeed, investigators did not discover any central ancestor shrine. In its earliest forms, Paal resembles the patterns identified for patrilineal groups: smaller dwellings arranged around a central plaza and main residence. Paal shares many similarities with the clusters of Chakah and probably their social organization as well. The social unit that built and occupied Paal seems to have been a patrilineal one, albeit one greatly transformed by its ascent within the society of Waka'. The Maya of Paal seem to resemble the "middlemen" described by Arlen Chase (1992) for the city of Caracol (A. Chase and D. Chase 1996). There, prosperous commoners adopted elements of elite status, notably glyphic texts and spacious tombs. Such mobility has also been noted at Postclassic Mayapán, where a vigorous economy created significant social fluidity (Masson and Peraza Lope 2004; Masson et al. 2014). Paal experienced similar social and economic mobility and adopted elements of elite status: high-quality ceramics and stelae fragments instead of the texts and tombs of Caracol. The social unit of Paal seems to have been part of a prosperous "middle class"; perhaps such prosperity is linked to the commercialism of the Late Classic and the proximity of the marketplace, which is suspected to have been at the western end of Plaza 1.

Perspectives on a Peopled Cityscape: Social Heterogeneity in an Urban Context

What seems to emerge from this survey is a heterogeneous society peopling an ancient cityscape. Different social structures occupied the households of Waka', each with its own history and idiosyncratic variation on kin-relations. Rather than a single social model, uniform and widely replicated, Waka' possessed different social structures that rose and fell individually through the city's long occupation. Chakah appears to have been an endogamous community consisting of exogamous lineages organized around patrilineality and patrilocality. This is a pattern well established for Postclassic and Colonial communities (see Annereau-Fulbert 2012). Much of the mapped and tested portions of the city's near periphery seem similar to Chakah. If Chakah can be held as broadly representative, then much of the city's hinterlands would have been occupied by numerous, similar communities. Certainly, endogamous communities of exogamous lineages would have served as the family units for a significant portion of the city's inhabitants. Their main occupation was likely agricultural, and such lineages may have even had a distinct advantage in cultivating tropical microclimates (Dunning 2004). However, Waka' society seems characterized by heterogeneity, so each of the districts and neighborhoods of the urban periphery held its own occupational history, its own individual set of political and economic relations, and its own unique variety of the social models described above.

The urban core seems to have had a different set of social relations. As demonstrated by the Maya of Chok and Tolok, there existed something of a noble house society. The core district includes large palace compounds with expansive domestic spaces. Perhaps they held social units of elite status, "noble houses" of bilateral descent and bilocal marriage traditions, broadly like those proposed for Chok and Tolok. These would been large social units, including not just the core members of the elite family itself, but likely a plethora of servants, slaves, poor relations, hangers-on, supplicants, clients, and hired hands. This would explain the smaller patio groups that cluster around the bases of the elevated palace compounds. Together, these noble houses would have constituted the main body of the royal court, peopling it with titled individuals who both needed and were needed by the kings and queens of the city (Houston and Stuart 2001; Inomata 2001). This is evidenced by elaborate architecture, including benches and audiencias, large feasting deposits, royal ceramics, and an evident tradition of paired burials.

Yet, not every elite compound will match the patterns from Chok and Tolok, and the existence of additional noble houses must be verified, not assumed. The Paal Group proves this. Paal was apparently the home for a large, highly prosperous lineage belonging to the "middlemen" of Waka' society. Such units possessed the fortune or grace to take advantage of the social fluidity present in the city, rising from humble origins to acquire elite status. Of course, it remains unknown if the pattern for Paal is exceptional or common.

Taken as a whole, Waka' seems to possess at least two different social strata, commoner lineages and noble houses. The former seem scattered across the city's hinterlands, the latter seem mostly concentrated in the core. In between the two are an unknown number of highly prosperous, socially mobile lineages. These two categories could be characterized as social classes, although exact economic relationships remain uncertain. The urban society was clearly heterogeneous, characterized by variety. Of all the social models proposed for Classic Maya society, they may not be as exclusive as modern scholars have argued. Different versions of each may have manifested in the many varied households of Classic civilization.

Only additional research, of course, can support, reject, or modify this image of the social cityscape of Waka'. Understanding these cities requires an approach that incorporates the tools and techniques of household archaeology, applied on an urban scale and incorporating a social dimension. Such work continues at Waka' and, in the coming years, the differences and commonalities of the groups discussed here will be apparent. Any perspective on a peopled cityscape grows more accurate with time and effort.

Conclusion: The Archaeology of the Family

For the Maya of Waka', daily life likely began before dawn. People rose before first light to start their day—to pick just one—perhaps 5 K'ib' 19 Yaxk'in, 9.17.8.4.18 of the Long Count, mid-March 780 CE by the reckoning of much later peoples. There were farmers in the outlying district of Chakah getting ready to work in the cornfields along the rivers. If the reconstruction proposed in this chapter is correct, this would have been a community organized around its patrilineages and likely with a single agricultural workforce of related men and a domestic workforce of related women. There were nobles in a palace later called Chok, preparing to address the complex internal politics of the city, likely still unsettled since the Tikal defeated Waka' in 743 CE. Part of their concerns would have involved the creation of artistic works, certainly richly woven cloth, among other items used in an economy of prestige gifting, patronage, and reputation. This work would have been done in the expansive domestic spaces of their palace, performed by a large collection of people in the orbit of a single noble family, one that traced their descent through both parents. A similar, though smaller, noble house would have been preoccupied with the construction of their own small palace at Tolok. This house would have possessed connections with the distant kingdom of Ik'a' or might have arrived from there recently. A very different social unit lived in their own palace near Plaza 3, later termed Paal. There a lineage with humble origins made their home, having transcended those origins, likely through affiliation with the highly commercialized economy. The sun likely shone on still other units, yet unknown within the archaeological record of Waka'.

All this contributes to the idea that there was not really a single Maya society. There were different social units, organized differently; a single, uniform model for Classic social organization simply cannot be imposed on the entirety of the Classic past (D. Chase and A. Chase 2004). It was a highly complex civilization with a highly complex society, possessing different internal social units. Classic Maya society was not composed solely of lineages nor was it composed only of houses, nor could it be easily reduced to economic class structures. Rather, it included different versions of all the above and likely more besides. This poses both a unique difficulty and distinct advantage for modern researchers. The difficulty lies in that social structure cannot be assumed for any archaeological site; instead, scholars must demonstrate the existence of any single social unit present in antiquity (Ensor 2011, 2013a, 2013b). The advantage is that the Maya likely tailored their social organization to fit local needs and demands. Thus, close study and identification of localized social organization opens novel perspectives on what those needs and demands likely were.

For instance, among the modern Maya of Chamelco, Ashley Kistler (2013) describes an unusual variation on kinship, a social unit emically termed the *junkab'al*. It consists of a wide circle of kinship that incorporates both consanguineous and fictive relations, both family and very close friends. It is clearly not a lineage and, contra Kistler, it does not really fit the definition of the house either. Rather it seems to be a social unit linked to the households deeply tied to the marketplace at Chamelco. Kistler (2013:101) writes, "market positions and the *derechos de vender*, literally 'rights to market,' or the right to sell and own a stall in the market, constitute a crucial part of the *junkab'al*." The social organization adapts to fit local needs and demands.

In the end, these are all families. There are, and were, different ways to organize and construct families, to be sure. The goal of the modern scholar studying ancient peoples is to demonstrate how ancient peoples organized and constructed their different families and to study how such organization and construction transformed through time. This is how one attempts to repeople the ancient past, to reconstruct not only the appearance of the physical landscape but also the composition of the social landscape. This necessarily includes the different kinds of families that lived there. Modern archaeology cannot directly address the vast majority of individuals in the ancient past, but it can model one of the great constants in their lives—their families.

References

Annereau-Fulbert, Marie
2012   Intermediate Settlement Units in Late Postclassic Maya Sites in the Highlands: An Assessment from Archaeology and Ethnohistory. In *The Neighborhood as a Social and Spatial Unit in Mesoamerican Cities*, edited by M. Charlotte Arnauld, Linda R. Manzanilla, and Michael E. Smith, pp. 261–285. University of Arizona Press, Tucson.

Annis, Sheldon
1987   *God and Production in a Guatemalan Town*. University of Texas Press, Austin.

Arnauld, M. Charlotte
2012   Neighborhoods and Intermediate Units of Spatial and Social Analysis in Ancient Mesoamerica. In *The Neighborhood as a Social and Spatial Unit in Mesoamerican Cities*, edited by M. Charlotte Arnauld, Linda R. Manzanilla, and Michael E. Smith, pp. 304–320. University of Arizona Press, Tucson.

Arroyave Prera, Ana Lucía
2006   WK-05: Última temporada de excavaciones en el Grupo Paal. In *Proyecto Arqueológico El Perú-Waka': Informe no. 2, temporada 2004*, edited by Héctor Escobedo and David Freidel, pp. 89–102. Fundación de Investigación Arqueológica Waka', Guatemala City.

Arroyave Prera, Ana Lucía, and Horacio Martínez
2004   WK-05: Excavaciones en las Estructuras L13-17 y L13-19. In *Proyecto Arqueológico El Perú-Waka': Informe no. 1, temporada 2003*, edited by Héctor Escobedo and David Freidel, pp. 119–144. Fundación de Investigación Arqueológica Waka', Guatemala City.

Arroyave Prera, Ana Lucía, and Varinia Matute Rodríguez
2005   WK-05: Excavaciones en un grupo habitacional al sur de la Plaza 3. In *Proyecto Arqueológico El Perú-Waka': Informe no. 2, temporada 2004*, edited by Héctor Escobedo and David Freidel, pp. 71–110. Fundación de Investigación Arqueológica Waka', Guatemala City.

Ascher, Robert
1961   Analogy in Archaeological Interpretation. *Southwestern Journal of Anthropology* 17(4):317–325.

Ashmore, Wendy, and Richard R. Wilk
1988   Household and Community in the Mesoamerican Past. In *Household and Community in the Mesoamerican Past*, edited by Richard R. Wilk and Wendy Ashmore, pp. 1–27. University of New Mexico Press, Albuquerque.

Aveni, Anthony F.
2001   Skywatchers: A Revised and Updated Version of Skywatchers of Ancient Mexico. University of Texas Press, Austin.

Ball, Joseph W., and Jennifer T. Taschek
2001   The Buenavista-Cahal Pech Royal Court: Multi-palace Court Mobility and Usage in a Petty Lowland Maya Kingdom. In Royal Courts of the Ancient Maya, Vol. 2: Data and Case Studies, edited by Takeshi Inomata and Stephen D. Houston, pp. 165–200. Westview Press, Boulder.

Beck, Robin A., editor
2007   The Durable House: House Society Models in Archaeology. Center for Archaeological Investigations, Southern Illinois University, Carbondale.

Boremanse, Didier
1998   Hach Winik: The Lacandon Maya of Chiapas, Southern Mexico. IMS Monographs, Vol. 11. Institute for Mesoamerican Studies, Albany.

Bricker, Victoria R.
2002   Evidencia de doble descendencia en las inscripciones de Yaxchilán y Piedras Negras. In La organización social entre los Mayas, edited by Vera Tiesler Blos, Rafael Cobos, and Merle Greene Robertson, pp. 125–146. Instituto Nacional de Antropología e Historia and Universidad Autónoma de Yucatán, Mexico City.

Bunzel, Ruth
1952   Chichicastenango: A Guatemalan Village. J. J. Augustin Publisher, Locust Valley.

Canuto, Marcello A., and Tomás Barrientos
2020   La Corona: Negotiating a Landscape of Power. In Approaches to Monumental Landscapes of the Ancient Maya, edited by Brett Houk, Bárbara Arroyo, and Terry G. Powis, pp. 171–195. University Press of Florida, Gainesville.

Casson, Lionel
1975   Everyday Life in Ancient Rome. Johns Hopkins University Press, Baltimore.

Chaix, Raphaëlle, Frédéric Austerlitz, Tatyana Khegay, Svetlana Jacquesson, Michael F. Hammer, Evelyne Heyer, and Lluís Quintana-Murci
2004   The Genetic or Mythical Ancestry of Descent Groups: Lessons from the Y Chromosome. American Journal of Human Genetics 75(6):1113–1116.

Chaix, Raphaëlle, Lluís Quintana-Murci, Tatyana Hegay, Michael F. Hammer, Zahra Mobasher, Frédéric Austerlitz, and Evelyne Heyer
2007   From Social to Genetic Structures in Central Asia. Current Biology 17(1):43–48.

Chang, Kwang-Chih
1958   Study of the Neolithic Social Grouping: Examples from the New World. American Anthropologist 60(2):298–334.

Chase, Arlen F.
1992   Elites and the Changing Organization of Classic Maya Society. In Mesoamerican Elites: An Archaeological Assessment, edited by Diane Z. Chase and Arlen F. Chase, pp. 30–49. University of Oklahoma Press, Norman.

Chase, Arlen F., and Diane Z. Chase
1996a   A Mighty Maya Nation: How Caracol Built an Empire by Cultivating Its Middle Class. Archaeology 49(5):66–72.

1996b   More Than Kin and King: Centralized Political Organization among the Ancient Maya. *Current Anthropology* 37(5):803–810.

Chase, Diane Z., and Arlen F. Chase

2004   Archaeological Perspectives on Classic Maya Social Organization from Caracol, Belize. *Ancient Mesoamerica* 15(1):139–147.

Coe, Michael D.

1965   A Model of Ancient Community Structure in the Maya Lowlands. *Southwestern Journal of Anthropology* 21(2):97–114.

Duncan, William N., and Jon B. Hageman

2015   House or Lineage? How Intracemetery Kinship Analysis Contributes to the Debate in the Maya Area. In *Archaeology and Bioarchaeology of Population Movement among the Prehispanic Maya*, edited by Andrea Cucina, pp. 133–142. Springer, New York.

Dunning, Nicholas

2004   Down on the Farm: Classic Maya "Homesteads" as "Farmsteads." In *Ancient Maya Commoners*, edited by Jon C. Lohse and Fred Valdez Jr., pp. 97–116. University of Texas Press, Austin.

Dunning, Nicholas P., Timothy P. Beach, and Sheryl Luzzadder-Beach

2012   Kax and Kol: Collapse and Resilience in Lowland Maya Civilization. *Proceedings of the National Academy of Sciences* 109(10):3652–3657.

Dunning, Nicholas, Timothy Beach, and David Rue

1997   The Paleoecology and Ancient Settlement of the Petexbatun Region, Guatemala. *Ancient Mesoamerica* 8(2):255–266.

Ember, Melvin

1973   An Archaeological Indicator of Matrilocal versus Patrilocal Residence. *American Antiquity* 38(2):177–182.

Ensor, Bradley E.

2011   Kinship Theory in Archaeology: From Critiques to the Study of Transformations. *American Antiquity* 76(2):203–227.

2013a   *Crafting Prehispanic Maya Kinship*. University of Alabama Press, Tuscaloosa.

2013b   *The Archaeology of Kinship, Advancing Interpretation and Contributions to Theory*. University of Arizona Press, Tucson.

Eppich, Keith

2006   WK-09: Excavaciones en el Grupo Tolok. In *Proyecto Arqueológico El Perú-Waka': Informe no. 3, temporada 2005*, edited by Héctor Escobedo and David Freidel, pp. 139–224. Fundación de Investigación Arqueológica Waka', Guatemala City.

2007a   Death and Veneration at El Perú-Waka': Structure M14-15 as Ancestor Shrine. *PARI Journal* 8(1):1–16.

2007b   WK-13: Excavaciones en el Grupo Chok. In *Proyecto Arqueológico El Perú-Waka': Informe no. 4, temporada 2006*, edited by Héctor Escobedo and David Freidel, pp. 259–316. Fundación de Investigación Arqueológica Waka', Guatemala City.

2009   Feast and Sacrifice at El Perú-Waka': The N14-2 Deposit as Dedication. *PARI Journal* 10(2):1–19.

2011   Lineage and State at El Perú-Waka': Ceramic and Architectural Perspectives on the Classic Maya Social Dynamic. PhD dissertation, Department of Anthropology, Southern Methodist University, Dallas.

2014   Ritual Narratives from El Perú-Waka': Ceremonial Deposits in Non-royal, Elite Contexts. In *Archaeology at El Perú-Waka': Ancient Maya Performances of Ritual, Memory, and Power*, edited by Olivia Navarro-Farr and Michelle Rich, pp. 112–133. University of Arizona Press, Tucson.

2019   WK13E, excavaciones en todo el Grupo Chok, concentradas principalmente en las secciones residenciales del norte, incluidas las Estructuras N13-2, N13-3, N13-9, N13-11, N13-12, N13-12, y N13-17. In *Proyecto Arqueológico El Perú-Waka': Informe no. 16, temporada 2018*, edited by Juan Carlos Pérez, Griselda Pérez, and Damien B. Marken, pp. 4–82. Fundación de Investigación Arqueológica Waka', Guatemala City.

Eppich, Keith, and David Freidel
2015   Markets and Marketing in the Classic Maya Lowlands: A Case Study from El Perú-Waka'. In *The Ancient Maya Marketplace: The Archaeology of Transient Space*, edited by Eleanor M. King, pp. 195–225. University of Arizona Press, Tucson.

Eppich, Keith, and Emily Haney
2017   Excavaciones en el Grupo Chok, Estructura N13-6. In *Proyecto Arqueológico El Perú-Waka': Informe no. 15, temporada 2017*, edited by Juan Carlos Pérez, Griselda Pérez Robles, and David Freidel, pp. 21–82. Fundación de Investigación Arqueológica Waka', Guatemala City.

Eppich, Keith, Damien B. Marken, and Elsa Damaris Menéndez
2023   A City in Flux: The Dynamic Urban Form and Functions of El Perú-Waka', Guatemala. In *Building an Archaeology of Maya Urbanism: Planning and Flexibility in the American Tropics*, edited by Damien B. Marken and M. Charlotte Arnauld, pp. 105–147. University Press of Colorado, Boulder.

Eppich, Keith, and Varinia Matute
2007   WK-09: Anexo a las excavaciones en el Grupo Tolok. In *Proyecto Arqueológico El Perú-Waka': Informe no. 4, temporada 2006*, edited by Héctor Escobedo and David Freidel, pp. 259–316. Fundación de Investigación Arqueológica Waka', Guatemala City.

Eppich, Keith, and David Mixter
2014   WKZ: Excavaciones en patios residenciales. In *Proyecto Arqueológico El Perú-Waka': Informe no. 11, temporada 2013*, edited by Juan Carlos Pérez and David Freidel, pp. 34–64. Fundación de Investigación Arqueológica Waka', Guatemala City.

Eppich, Keith, and María de los Ángeles Quán Cuyán
2015   Operación WK13B: Excavaciones en las estructuras N13-8, N13-9, y la función de la rampa del Grupo Chok. In *Proyecto Arqueológico El Perú-Waka': Informe no. 12, temporada 2014*, edited by Héctor Escobedo and David Freidel, pp. 36–84. Fundación de Investigación Arqueológica Waka', Guatemala City.

Erickson, Clark L.
2006   Intensification, Political Economy, and the Farming Community; in Defense of a Bottom-Up Perspective of the Past. In *Agricultural Strategies*, edited by Joyce

Marcus and Charles Standish, pp. 334–363. Cotsen Institute of Archaeology, University of California, Los Angeles.

Fash, William L.

2005   Toward a Social History of the Copan Valley. In *Copán: The History of an Ancient Maya Kingdom*, edited by E. Wyllys Andrews and William L. Fash, pp. 73–101. School of American Research Press, Santa Fe.

Fash, William L., and David S. Stuart

1991   Dynastic History and Cultural Evolution at Copan, Honduras. In *Classic Maya Political History: Hieroglyphic and Archaeological Evidence*, edited by T. Patrick Culbert, pp. 147–179. Cambridge University Press, Cambridge.

Fowler, William R., and Jon Hageman

2004   Introduction to Special Section: New Perspectives on Ancient Lowland Maya Social Organization. *Ancient Mesoamerica* 15(1): 61–62.

Fox, James A., and John S. Justeson

1986   Classic Maya Dynastic Alliance and Succession. In *Supplement to Handbook of Middle American Indians*, Vol. 4: *Ethnohistory*, edited by Victoria R. Bricker and Ronald Spores, pp. 7–34. University of Texas Press, Austin.

Fox, John W., and Garrett W. Cook

1996   Constructing Maya Communities: Ethnography for Archaeology. *Current Anthropology* 37:811–821.

Freidel, David A., Héctor Escobedo, and Stanley P. Guenter

2007   A Crossroads of Conquerors: Waka' and Gordon Willey's "Rehearsal for the Collapse" Hypothesis. In *Gordon R. Willey and American Archaeology: Contemporary Perspectives*, edited by Jeremy A. Sabloff and William L. Fash, pp. 187–208. University of Oklahoma Press, Norman.

Freter, AnnCorinne

2004   Multiscalar Model of Rural Households and Communities in Late Classic Copan Maya Society. *Ancient Mesoamerica* 15(1):93–106.

Gillespie, Susan D.

2000a   Beyond Kinship: An Introduction. In *Beyond Kinship, Social and Material Reproduction in House Societies*, edited by Rosemary A. Joyce and Susan D. Gillespie, pp. 1–21. University of Pennsylvania Press, Philadelphia.

2000b   Lévi-Strauss: *Maison* and *Société à Maisons*. In *Beyond Kinship, Social and Material Reproduction in House Societies*, edited by Rosemary A. Joyce and Susan D. Gillespie, pp. 22–52. University of Pennsylvania Press, Philadelphia.

2000c   Maya "Nested Houses": The Ritual Construction of Place. In *Beyond Kinship, Social and Material Reproduction in House Societies*, edited by Rosemary A. Joyce and Susan D. Gillespie, pp. 135–160. University of Pennsylvania Press, Philadelphia.

Guderjan, Thomas H., Robert J. Lichtenstein, and C. Colleen Hanratty

2003   Elite Residences at Blue Creek, Belize. In *Maya Palaces and Elite Residences: An Interdisciplinary Approach*, edited by Jessica Joyce Christie, pp. 13–45. University of Texas Press, Austin.

Guenter, Stanley P.
2006   WK-12 y WK-04B: Excavación de los monumentos esculpidos. In *Proyecto Arqueológico El Perú-Waka': Informe no. 3, temporada 2005*, edited by Héctor Escobedo and David Freidel, pp. 275–298. Informe Entregado a la Dirección General del Patrimonio Cultural y Natural de Guatemala, Guatemala.

Guenter, Stanley P., and Michelle Rich
2004   WK04: Excavaciones en la Estructura L13-22. In *Proyecto Arqueológico El Perú-Waka': Informe no. 1, temporada 2003*, edited by Héctor Escobedo and David Freidel, pp. 119–144. Fundación de Investigación Arqueológica Waka', Guatemala City.

Hageman, Jon B.
2004   The Lineage Model and Archaeological Data in Northwestern Belize. *Ancient Mesoamerica* 15(1):63–74. https://doi.org/10.1017/S0956536104151043.

Halperin, Christina T.
2017   Ancient Cosmopolitanism: Feminism and the Rethinking of Maya Inter-Regional Interactions During the Late Classic to Postclassic Periods (ca. 600–1521 CE). *Journal of Social Archaeology* 17(3):349–375.

Hare, Timothy, Marilyn Masson, and Bradley Russell
2014   High-Density LiDAR Mapping of the Ancient City of Mayapán. *Remote Sensing* 6:9064–9085.

Haviland, William A.
1968   Ancient Lowland Maya Social Organization. In *Archaeological Studies in Middle America*, pp. 93–117. Middle American Research Institute, Publication 26. Tulane University, New Orleans.
1992   Status and Power in Classic Maya Society: The View from Tikal. *American Anthropologist* 94(4):937–940.
2003   Settlement, Society, and Demography at Tikal. In *Tikal: Dynasties, Foreigners, and Affairs of State*, edited by Jeremy A. Sabloff, pp. 111–142. School of American Research Press, Santa Fe.

Haviland, William A., and Hattula Moholy-Nagy
1992   Distinguishing the High and Mighty from the Hoi Polloi at Tikal, Guatemala. In *Mesoamerican Elites: An Archaeological Assessment*, edited by Diane Z. Chase and Arlen F. Chase, pp. 50–60. University Press of Oklahoma, Norman.

Healy, Paul F.
1990   Excavations at Pacbitun, Belize: Preliminary Report on the 1986 and 1987 Investigations. *Journal of Field Archaeology* 17:247–262.

Healy, Paul F., Jamie J. Awe, and Hermann Helmuth
1998   An Ancient Maya Multiple Burial at Caledonia, Cayo District, Belize. *Journal of Field Archaeology* 25:261–274.

Hendon, Julia A.
1991   Status and Power in Classic Maya Society: An Archeological Study. *American Anthropologist* 93(4):894–918.
1992   Variation in Classic Maya Sociopolitical Organization. *American Anthropologist*, n.s., 94(4):940–941.

1996   Archaeological Approaches to the Organization of Domestic Labor: Household Practice and Domestic Relations. *Annual Review of Anthropology* 25:45–61.

2000   Having and Holding: Storage, Memory, Knowledge, and Social Relations. *American Anthropologist* 102: 42–53.

2010   *Houses in a Landscape: Memory and Everyday Life in Mesoamerica.* Duke University Press, Durham.

Hendon, Julia A., and Rosemary A. Joyce

2001   A Flexible Corporation: Classic Period House Societies in Eastern Mesoamerica. Paper presented at the 66th Annual Meeting of the Society for American Archaeology, New Orleans.

Houston, Stephen D., and Patricia A. McAnany

2003   Bodies and Blood: Critiquing Social Construction in Maya Archaeology. *Journal of Anthropological Archaeology* 22(1):26–41.

Houston, Stephen D., and David Stuart

2001   Peopling the Classic Maya Court. In *Royal Courts of the Ancient Maya*, Vol. 1: *Theory, Comparison, Synthesis*, edited by Takeshi Inomata and Stephen D. Houston, pp. 54–83. Westview Press, Boulder.

Hubbard, Phil

2006   *City.* Routledge Press, New York.

Hutson, Scott R., Aline Magnoni, and Travis W. Stanton

2004   House Rules? The Practice of Social Organization in Classic-Period Chunchucmil, Yucatan, Mexico. *Ancient Mesoamerica* 15(1):75–92.

Inomata, Takeshi

2001   King's People: Classic Maya Courtiers in a Comparative Perspective. In *Royal Courts of the Ancient Maya*, Vol. 1: *Theory, Comparison, Synthesis*, edited by Takeshi Inomata and Stephen D. Houston, pp. 27–53. Westview Press, Boulder.

2004   The Spatial Mobility of Non-elite Populations in Classic Maya Society and Its Political Implications. In *Ancient Maya Commoners*, edited by Jon C. Lohse and Fred Valdez Jr., pp. 175–196. University of Texas Press, Austin.

2006   Plazas, Performers, and Spectators: Political Theaters of the Classic Maya. *Current Anthropology* 47(5):805–842.

Inomata, Takeshi, Daniela Triadan, Erick Ponciano, Estela Pinto, Richard E. Terry, and Markus Eberl

2002   Domestic and Political Lives of Classic Maya Elites: The Excavation of Rapidly Abandoned Structures at Aguateca, Guatemala. *Latin American Antiquity* 13(3):305–330.

Johnson, Kent M., and Kathleen S. Paul

2016   Bioarchaeology and Kinship: Integrating Theory, Social Relatedness, and Biology in Ancient Family Research. *Journal of Archaeological Research* 24:75–123.

Jones, Grant

1998   *The Conquest of the Last Maya Kingdom.* Stanford University Press, Stanford.

Joyce, Rosemary

2000   Heirlooms and Houses. In *Beyond Kinship, Social and Material Reproduction in House Societies*, edited by Rosemary A. Joyce and Susan D. Gillespie, pp. 189–210. University of Pennsylvania Press, Philadelphia.

2007   Building Houses: The Materialization of Lasting Identity in Formative Mesoamerica. In *The Durable House: House Society Models in Archaeology*, edited by Robin A. Beck, pp. 53–72. Center for Archaeological Investigations, Southern Illinois University, Carbondale.

Joyce, Rosemary A., and Susan D. Gillespie, editors

2000   *Beyond Kinship, Social and Material Reproduction in House Societies*. University of Pennsylvania Press, Philadelphia.

Just, Bryan R.

2012   *Dancing into Dreams: Maya Vase Painting of the Ik' Kingdom*. Princeton University Art Museum, Princeton.

King, Turi E., and Mark A. Jobling

2009   What's in a Name? Y Chromosomes, Surnames and the Genetic Genealogy Revolution. *Trends in Genetics* 25(8):351–360.

Kistler, Ashley

2013   All in the Junkab'al: The House in Q'eqchi' Society. *Latin Americanist* 57(2):85–110.

Kostof, Spiro

1991   *The City Shaped: Urban Patterns and Meanings through History*. Bullfinch Press, Boston.

1992   *The City Assembled: The Elements of Urban Form through History*. Bullfinch Press, Boston.

Kovacevich, Brigitte

2016   Gender, Craft Production, and the State: Problems with "Workshops." In *Gendered Labor in Specialized Economies: Archeological Perspectives on Female and Male Work*, edited by Sophia E. Kelly and Traci Ardren, pp. 301–337. University Press of Colorado, Boulder.

Kunen, Julie L.

2004   *Ancient Maya Life in the Far West Bajo: Social and Environmental Change in the Wetlands of Belize*. Anthropological Papers of the University of Arizona, vol. 69. University of Arizona Press, Tucson.

Kunen, Julie L., T. Patrick Culbert, Vilma Fialko, Brian R. McKee, and Liwy Grazioso

2000   Bajo Communities: A Case Study from the Central Petén. *Culture and Agriculture* 22(3):15–31.

Kuper, Adam

1982   Lineage Theory: A Critical Retrospect. *Annual Review of Anthropology* 11:71–95.

Lamoureux-St-Hilaire, Maxime

2020   Comparative Approaches and Analogical Reasoning for Mayanists. *The SAA Archaeological Record* 20(1):8–13.

Latour, Bruno

2005   *Reassembling the Social: An Introduction to Actor-Network-Theory*. Oxford University Press, Oxford.

Law, John

2009   Actor Network Theory and Material Semiotics. In *The New Blackwell Companion to Social Theory*, edited by Bryan S. Turner, pp. 141–158. Wiley-Blackwell, Chichester.

LeCount, Lisa J.
2001   Like Water for Chocolate: Feasting and Political Ritual among the Late Classic Maya at Xunantunich, Belize. *American Anthropologist* 103(4):935–953.
Lentz, David L., Nicholas P. Dunning, Vernon L. Scarborough, Kevin S. Magee, Kim M. Thompson, Eric Weaver, Christopher Carr, et al.
2014   Forests, Fields, and the Edge of Sustainability at the Ancient Maya City of Tikal. *Proceedings of the National Academy of Sciences* 111(52):18513–18518.
Lévi-Strauss, Claude
1982   *The Way of the Masks.* University of Washington Press, Seattle.
Lohse, Jon C., and Fred Valdez Jr.
2004   Examining Ancient Maya Commoners Anew. In *Ancient Maya Commoners*, edited by Jon C. Lohse and Fred Valdez Jr., pp. 1–22. University of Texas Press, Austin.
Looper, Matthew, and Yuriy Polyukhovych
2016   A Familial Relationship between Nobles of El Peru (Waka') and El Zotz (Pa'chan) as Recorded on a Polychrome Vessel. *Glyph Dwellers* 47:1–11.
Marcus, Joyce
1983   Lowland Maya Archaeology at the Crossroads. *American Antiquity* 48:454–488.
2000   Toward an Archaeology of Communities. In *The Archaeology of Communities: A New World Perspective*, edited by Marcello Canuto and Jason Yaeger, pp. 231–242. Routledge, London.
Martin, Simon
2008   Wives and Daughters on the Dallas Altar. *Mesoweb*. https://www.mesoweb.com/articles/martin/Wives&Daughters.pdf.
Martin, Simon, and Nikolai Grube
2008   *Chronicle of the Maya Kings and Queens: Deciphering the Dynasties of the Ancient Maya*, 2nd ed. Thames and Hudson, London.
Masson, Marilyn A., and Carlos Peraza Lope
2004   Commoners in Postclassic Maya Society: Social versus Economic Class Constructs. In *Ancient Maya Commoners*, edited by Jon C. Lohse and Fred Valdez Jr., pp. 197–223. University of Texas Press, Austin.
Masson, Marilyn A., Timothy S. Hare, and Carlos Peraza Lope
2014   The Social Mosaic. In *Kukulcan's Realm: Urban Life at Ancient Mayapan*, edited by Marilyn A. Masson and Carlos Peraza Lope, pp. 193–268. University Press of Colorado, Boulder.
McAnany, Patricia A.
1995   *Living with the Ancestors: Kinship and Kingship in Ancient Maya Society.* University of Texas Press, Austin.
Moriarty, Matthew D.
2012   History, Politics, and Ceramics: The Ceramic Sequence of Trinidad de Nosotros, El Petén, Guatemala. In *Motul de San José: Politics, History, and Economy in a Classic Maya Polity*, edited by Antonia E. Foias and Kitty F. Emery, pp. 194–228. University Press of Florida, Gainesville.
Murdock, George Peter
1949   *Social Structure.* Macmillan, New York.

Navarro-Farr, Olivia, Griselda Pérez Robles, Damaris Menéndez, and Juan Carlos Pérez Calderón
2020   Forest of Queens: The Legacy of Royal Calakmul Women at El Perú-Waka's Central Civic-Ceremonial Temple. In *A Forest of History, the Maya after the Emergence of Divine Kingship*, edited by Travis W. Stanton and M. Kathryn Brown, pp. 67–87. University Press of Colorado, Boulder.

O'Mansky, Matt, and Nicholas P. Dunning
2004   Settlement and Late Classic Political Disintegration in the Petexbatun Region, Guatemala. In *The Terminal Classic in the Maya Lowlands: Collapse, Transition, and Transformation*, edited by Arthur Demarest, Prudence Rice, and Donald Rice, pp. 83–101. University Press of Colorado, Boulder.

Palka, Joel W.
1997   Reconstructing Classic Maya Socioeconomic Differentiation and the Collapse at Dos Pilas, Petén, Guatemala. *Ancient Mesoamerica* 8(2):293–306.

Parkin, Robert
1997   *Kinship: An Introduction to the Basic Concepts.* Blackwell, Malden, MA.

Parkin, Robert, and Linda Stone, editors
2004   *Kinship and Family: An Anthropological Reader.* Blackwell, Malden, MA.

Quiroa Flores, Fabiola
2004   CK-01 y CK-02: Excavaciones de sondeo en las Plazas 1 y 2. In *Proyecto Arqueológico El Perú-Waka': Informe no. 1, temporada 2003*, edited by Héctor Escobedo and David Freidel, pp. 299–338. Fundación de Investigación Arqueológica Waka', Guatemala City.
2007   Investigaciones en Chakah y reconocimientos en Yalá y Paso Caballos. In *Proyecto Arqueológico El Perú-Waka': Informe no. 5, temporada 2006*, edited by Héctor Escobedo and David Freidel, pp. 397–430. Fundación de Investigación Arqueológica Waka', Guatemala City.

Quiroa Flores, Fabiola, and Griselda Pérez Robles
2005   Investigaciones en Chakah: Reconocimineto de área, excavaciones de sondeo y registro de saqueos. In *Proyecto Arqueológico El Perú-Waka': Informe no. 2, temporada 2004*, edited by Héctor Escobedo and David Freidel, pp. 283–312. Fundación de Investigación Arqueológica Waka', Guatemala City.

Quiroa Flores, Fabiola, and Alejandro Guillot Vassaux
2006   Investigaciones en Chakah: Sondeo e intervenciones en las Estructuras J4-11, J4-12 y O3-35. In *Proyecto Arqueológico El Perú-Waka': Informe no. 3, temporada 2005*, edited by Héctor Escobedo and David Freidel, pp. 329–390. Fundación de Investigación Arqueológica Waka', Guatemala City.

Reents-Budet, Dorie
2001   Classic Maya Concepts of the Royal Court: An Analysis of Renderings on Pictorial Ceramics. In *Royal Courts of the Ancient Maya*, Vol. 1: *Theory, Comparison, and Synthesis*, edited by Takeshi Inomata and Stephen D. Houston, pp. 195–233. Westview Press, Oxford.

Restall, Matthew
1997   *The Maya World, Yucatec Culture and Society, 1550–1850.* Stanford University Press, Stanford.

Rice, Don S.
1988   Classic to Postclassic Household Transitions in the Central Petén, Guatemala. In *Household and Community in the Mesoamerican Past*, edited by Richard R. Wilk and Wendy Ashmore, pp. 227–248. University of New Mexico Press, Albuquerque.

Robin, Cynthia
2001   Peopling the Past: New Perspectives on the Ancient Maya. *Proceedings of the National Academy of Sciences of the United States of America* 98(1):18–21.
2003   New Directions in Classic Maya Household Archaeology. *Journal of Archaeological Research* 11:307–356.
2012   (editor). *Chan: An Ancient Maya Farming Community*. University Press of Florida, Gainesville.
2013   *Everyday Life Matters: Maya Farmers at Chan*. University Press of Florida, Gainesville.
2015   Of Earth and Stone: The Materiality of Maya Farmers' Everyday Lives at Chan, Belize. *Archeological Papers of the American Anthropological Association* 26(1):40–52.
2016   Neither Dopes nor Dupes: Maya Farmers and Ideology. *Ancient Mesoamerica* 27(1):221.

Robin, Cynthia, Andrew R. Wyatt, Laura J. Kosakowsky, Santiago Juarez, Ethan Kalosky, and Elise Enterkin
2012   A Changing Cultural Landscape: Settlement Survey and GIS at Chan. In *Chan: An Ancient Maya Farming Community*, edited by Cynthia Robin, pp. 19–41. University Press of Florida, Gainesville.

Robin, Cynthia, Andrew Wyatt, James Meierhoff, and Caleb Kestle
2015   Political Interaction: A View from the 2000 Year History of the Farming Community of Chan. In *Classic Maya Polities of the Southern Lowlands*, edited by Damien B. Marken and James Fitzsimmons, pp. 99–122. University Press of Colorado, Boulder.

Schele, Linda, and David A. Freidel
1990   *A Forest of Kings: The Untold Story of the Ancient Maya*. William Morrow, New York.

Schneider, David M.
1968   *American Kinship: A Cultural Account*. University of Chicago Press, Chicago.
1984   *A Critique of the Study of Kinship*. University of Michigan Press, Ann Arbor.

Sharer, Robert J., and Loa P. Traxler
2006   Copan and Quirigua: Shifting Destinies in the Southeastern Maya Lowlands. *Contributions in New World Archaeology* 4:139–156.

Shenk, Mark K., and Siobhán M. Mattison
2011   The Rebirth of Kinship: Evolutionary and Quantitative Approaches in the Revitalization of a Dying Field. *Human Nature* 22:1–15.

Smith, Michael E.
2010   The Archaeological Study of Neighborhoods and Districts in Ancient Cities. *Journal of Anthropological Archaeology* 29(2):137–154.

Smith, Michael E., and Juliana Novic
2012   Neighborhoods and Districts in Ancient Mesoamerica. In *The Neighborhood as a Social and Spatial Unit in Mesoamerican Cities*, edited by M. Charlotte Arnauld, Linda R. Manzanilla, and Michael E. Smith, pp. 1–26. University of Arizona Press, Tucson.

Smith, Michael E., Ashley Engquist, Cinthia Carvajal, Katrina Johnston-Zimmerman, Monica Algara, Bridgette Gilliland, Yui Kuznetsov, and Amanda Young
2015   Neighborhood Formation in Semi-urban Settlements. *Journal of Urbanism: International Research on Placemaking and Urban Sustainability* 8(2):173–198.

Souvatzi, Stella
2014   The Social Dynamics of Everyday Life. *Reviews in Anthropology* 43(4):238–259.
2017   Kinship and Social Archaeology. *Cross-Cultural Research* 51(2):172–195.

Stone, Glenn Davis
1981   The Interpretation of Negative Evidence in Archaeology. *Atlatl, Occasional Papers* 2:41–53. Department of Anthropology, University of Arizona, Tucson

Tokovinine, Alexander, and Marc Zender
2012   Lords of Windy Water: The Royal Court of Motul de San José in Classic Maya Inscriptions. In *Motul de San José: Politics, History and Economy in a Classic Maya Polity*, edited by Antonia E. Foias and Kitty F. Emery, pp. 30–66. University Press of Florida, Gainesville.

Vogt, Evon Z.
1969   *Zinacantan: A Maya Community in the Highlands of Chiapas*. Oxford University Press, London.

Wallach, Efraim
2019   Inference from Absence: The Case of Archaeology. *Palgrave Communications* 5(1):1–10.

Watanabe, John M.
2004   Some Models in a Muddle: Lineage and House in Classic Maya Social Organization. *Ancient Mesoamerica* 15(1):159–166.

Webster, David, and Nancy Gonlin
1988   Household Remains of the Humblest Maya. *Journal of Field Archaeology* 15(2):169–190.

Weeks, John M.
1988   Residential and Local Group Organization in the Maya Lowlands. In *Household and Community in the Mesoamerican Past*, edited by Richard R. Wilk and Wendy Ashmore, pp. 73–96. University of New Mexico Press, Albuquerque.

Weiss-Krejci, Estella
2011   The Formation of Mortuary Deposits, Implications for Understanding Mortuary Behavior of Past Populations. In *Social Bioarchaeology*, edited by Sabrina C. Agarwal and Bonnie A. Glencross, pp. 68–106. Blackwell, Malden, MA.

Welsh, W. Bruce M.
1988   *An Analysis of Classic Lowland Maya Burials*. International Series 409. BAR Publishing, Oxford.

Wilk, Richard R.
1991 *Household Ecology: Economic Change and Domestic Life among the Kekchi Maya in Belize*. University of Arizona Press, Tucson.
Wilk, Richard R., and Wendy Ashmore, editors
1988 *Household and Community in the Mesoamerican Past*. University of New Mexico Press, Albuquerque.
Wilk, Richard R., and William L. Rathje
1982 Household Archaeology. *American Behavioral Scientist* 25(6):617–639.
Willey, Gordon R.
1956 The Structure of Ancient Maya Society: Evidence from the Southern Lowlands. *American Anthropologist* 58(5):777–782.
Wobst, H. Martin
1978 The Archaeo-Ethnology of Hunter-Gatherers or the Tyranny of the Ethnographic Record in Archaeology. *American Antiquity* 43(2):303–309.
Wyatt, Andrew R.
2012 Agricultural Practices at Chan: Farming and Political Economy in an Ancient Maya Community. In *Chan: An Ancient Maya Farming Community*, edited by Cynthia Robin, pp. 71–88. University Press of Florida, Gainesville.
Wylie, Alison
1985 The Reaction against Analogy. In *Advances in Archaeological Method and Theory*, edited by Michael B. Schiffer, pp. 63–111. Academic Press, New York.
Yaeger, Jason
2000 The Social Construction of Communities in the Classic Maya Countryside: Strategies of Affiliation in Western Belize. In *The Archaeology of Communities: A New World Perspective*, edited by Marcello A. Canuto and Jason Yaeger, pp. 123–142. Routledge, London.
Yaeger, Jason, and Marcello Canuto
2000 Introducing an Archaeology of Communities. In *The Archaeology of Communities: A New World Perspective*, edited by Marcello A. Canuto and Jason Yaeger, pp. 1–15. Routledge, London.

5

The Ancient Inhabitants of Waka'

Osteology, Demography, and Pathology of the Burials and Ritual Deposits

ERIN E. PATTERSON

Over the last several decades, biological anthropologists have increasingly integrated osteological data with information from archaeology and adjacent disciplines to better understand the complex biological and social lives of ancient Mesoamerican people. This represents a shift from early studies of human skeletal remains that were primarily descriptions of a few elite individuals or inventories that ended up buried in site reports (Spence and White 2009). Age and sex estimation, one of the first steps in reconstructing identity, combined with the identification of pathological conditions, lay a solid foundation for investigating the role of gender and status in, for example, health outcomes or patterns of food consumption. The addition of modern analytical techniques like isotopic analysis has turned many poorly preserved remains into important sources of information about diet and mobility (Price et al. 2015; White et al. 2006). When combined with mortuary, epigraphic, and other sources of data, bioarchaeological studies can be used to answer big-picture questions about the nature of lowland Maya socioeconomic and political interactions.

At Waka', excavations have uncovered a relatively large burial sample, which allows for robust osteological and isotopic analyses. After 16 field seasons, the burial sample recovered at Waka' consists of 77 individuals from 72 interments (Table 5.1).[1] An additional 12 deposits with the partial remains of at least 17 individuals have been incorporated into the present study (Table 5.2). The funerary contexts range from the Late Preclassic to the Terminal Classic periods, with most dating to the Late Classic period. Excavators recovered both disarticulated, partial remains and primary interments from all

Burial No.	Age/Sex	Status/Class	Elements	Grave	Zone	Group/Structure	Date	Dental/Cranial modification	Linear enamel hypoplasia/Porotic hyperostosis/Periosteal reaction/Caries
WK1/2	S, S	C(1); C(1)		SC	UC	Paal/L13-17	LC	–/?;–/?	Y/Y/Y/–; N/Y/Y/–
WK3	S	C(0)		S/P	UC	Paal/L13-19	LC	–/Y	Y/?/?/N
WK5	MA, ?	C(1)		SC	UC	Tolok/M14-15	L-TC	?/?	N/?/?/N
WK6	YA, F	C(0)		SC	FP	Camp	?	D/?	N/?/?/N
WK7	S	C(0)		S/P	UC	Xucub/patio btw M12-21, 12-29	LC	–/Y	Y/?/?/N
WK8	Y-MA, F	RE(5)	FC, V, P, SS, B, M, PE, MO	EC/T	UC	NW Palace/L11-13	E-LC	N/?	Y/?/?/Y
WK9	S	C(0)		S/P	UC	Paal/L13-16 Sub1	LC	–/?	Y/Y/?/N
WK10	S	C(0)		S/P	UC	Paal/in front of L13-16	L-TC	–/?	N/Y/?/–
WK13	OA, F	C(0)		S/P	UC	Paal/L13-19	LC	?/?	Y/?/Y/Y
WK16	YA, F	C(1)		SC	UC	Paal/L13-21	E-LC	F/Y	Y/?/?/N
WK18	S	C(0)		S/P	UC	Tolok/off N14-2	L-TC	–/?	N/Y/?/N
WK19	MA, M	C(1)		SC	UC	Tolok/N14-2	L-TC	N/Y	?/?/?/–
WK20	A, ?	C(1)		SC	UC	Tolok/M14-15	L-TC	?/?	N/?/?/N
WK21	A, ?	NRE(2)	G	SC	UC	Tolok/M14-15	L-TC	F,D/?	N/?/?/N
WK22	A, ?	C(1)		SC	UC	Tolok/M14-15	L-TC	?/?	N/?/?/N
WK23	A, ?	C(1)		SC	UC	Tolok/M14-15	L-TC	?/?	N/?/?/N
WK24AB	YA, F; YA, F	RE; RE	FC, E, SS, P	EC/T	NP	Mirador/O14-4	EC	N/?; N/?	Y/?/?/N; N/Y/Y/N
WK25	OA, F	C(1)		C/CP	NP	Mirador/O14-4	EC	?/?	Y/?/?/Y
WK26	A, ?	C(1)		SC	UC	Xik/E of M14-6	LC	?/?	?/?/?/–

(continued)

Table 5.1—Continued

Burial No.	Age/Sex	Status/Class	Elements	Grave	Zone	Group/Structure	Date	Dental/Cranial modification	Linear enamel hypoplasia/Porotic hyperostosis/Periosteal reaction/Caries
WK27	A, ?	C(0)		S/P	UC	Epicenter/M13-1	TC	N/?	N/?/?/N
WK28	A, M	C(1)		C	UC	Xucub/MX5 patio btw M11-48,11-49,11-50	LC	?/Y	?/?/?/N
WK29	M-OA, ?	C(1)		S/P	UC	Epicenter/M13-1	L-TC	F/?	Y/?/?/Y
WK32	S	C(1)		S/P	UC	Encantado/patio btw M11-60, N11-26	EC	–/?	N/?/?/—
WK33	S	C(1)		C	UC	Encantado/patio of EC2	LC	–/?	N/Y/?/—
WK34	S	C(1)		C	UC	Encantado/patio of EC2	LC	–/Y	N/Y/?/N
WK36	MA, F	C(1)		S/P	UC	Epicenter/M13-1	L-TC	F/Y	N/?/?/N
WK37	M-OA, M	RE(4)	FC, P, E, B, G, MO	EC/T	UC	Epicenter/M12-32	E-LC	N/?	N/?/?/N
WK38	A, ?	RE(4)	FC, SS, G, O, MO	EC/T	UC	Chok/M13-12	E-LC	?/?	?/?/?/—
WK39AB	M-OA, ?; S	RE(5); ?	FC, V, P, E, SS, B, C, M, G, PE, O, MO	EC/T	NP	Mirador/O14-4	E-LC	?/?;–/?	N/?/?/N; Y/?/?/N
WK41AB	M-OA, M; A, M	C(1); C(1)		SC; C	FP	S5-1/patio S5-A	LPC	?/?; ?/?	?/?/?/—; ?/?/?/N
WK42AB	S; A, F	C(0); C(1)		SC	FP	U5-1/S patio of U6-A	LC	–/?; D/?	Y/?/?/N; Y/?/?/N
WK43	A, ?	C(1)		C	FP	I7-1/SE patio of I8-B	LC	D/?	Y/Y/?/N
WK44	S	C(0)		S/P	NP	H7-1/N patio of H7-1	LC	–/?	N/?/Y/N
WK45	A, M	C(1)		C	NP	J8-1/patio S of J9-C	LC	E,D/?	N/Y/?/Y
WK46	A, M	C(1)		SC	NP	J9-1/isolated platform in J9-B	LC	?/?	?/?/Y/—

WK50	A, M	C(1)		SC	FP	T12-1/patio U12-A	TC	?/?	N/Y/?/Y
WK51A	YA, M	C(0)		?	NP	P17-1	?	N//?	Y/Y/?/N
WK52	Y-MA, ?	C(1)		SC	NP	J9-2/patio J9-D	LC	E,D/?	Y/?/?/Y
WK54	A, ?	C(0)		H/PC	FP	P6-1/patio P6-A	?	F/?	?/?/?/—
WK55	YA, M	C(0)		S/P	UC	Xucub/M12-18	LC	F/Y	Y/?/?/N
WK57	A, ?	?		S/P	UC	Xucub/M12-18	LC	?/?	?/?/?/—
WK58/59	YA, M; S	C(1); C(0)		SC; C	NP	R9-1/patio N of R9-A	EC	F/Y;—/?	N/?/?/N; ?/?/?/—
WK60	A, ?	C(1)		C/CP	UC	Epicenter/M13-1	TC	F/?	N/?/?/N
WK61	M-OA, ?	RE(5)	FC, V, P, E, SS, B, M, G, PE, MO	EC/T	UC	Epicenter/M13-1	LC	D/?	N/?/?/Y
WK65AB	Y-MA, M; MA, M	C(1); C(0)		SC	UC	Payes/L11-54	?	?/?; N/N	N/Y/?/N; N/?/?/Y
WK66	S	C(0)		C	UC	Tista/L10-18 TTE	?	—/?	N/?/?/N
WK67	A, F	C(0)		SC	FP	Camp	?	F/Y	Y/?/?/Y
WK76	MA, F	?		EC/T	UC	Payes/K10-11	L-TC	?/?	N/?/?/N
WK77	Y-MA, ?	C(1)		SC	UC	Chok/N13-6	TC	?/?	N/?/?/N
WK80	Y-MA, M	RE(4)	FC, V, P, SS	EC/T	UC	NW Palace/L12-4	EC	D/?	N/Y/?/N
WK82	Y-MA, F	C(0)		H/PC	UC	Chok/N13-6	LC	F/N	N/?/?/Y
WK83	YA, F	C(1)		SC	UC	Chok/N13-6	LC	F/Y	Y/?/?/N
WK89	A, M	C(1)		C	UC	Chok/N13-13	TC	N/?	Y/?/?/N
WK99	Y-MA, M	C(1)		C	UC	Chok/N13-17	TC	N/?	N/?/?/N
WK100	Y-MA, F	C(1)		C	UC	Chok/N13-17	TC	N/?	Y/?/?/Y
WK101	A, F	C(1)		C	UC	Chok/N13-13	LC	F/?	N/?/?/N
WK102	A, ?	C(1)		C	UC	Chok/N13-9	LC	?/?	?/?/?/—
CK1	YA, ?	C(1)		SC	FP	CK Plaza 1/K6-2	LC	?/?	?/?/?/—
CK2	M-OA, M	C(1)		S/P	FP	CK Plaza 10/in front of C5-8	LPC	?/?	N/?/?/N

(continued)

Table 5.1—Continued

Burial No.	Age/Sex	Status/Class	Elements	Grave	Zone	Group/Structure	Date	Dental/Cranial modification	Linear enamel hypoplasia/Porotic hyperostosis/Periosteal reaction/Caries
CK3	M-OA, M	C(0)		S/P	FP	CK Plaza 7/in front of N6-45	LC	?/?	?/?/?/—
CK4	A, F	C(1)		H/PC	FP	CK Plaza 3/J4-12	LC	?/?	Y/?/?/N
CK5	A, ?	C(1)		C/CP	FP	CK Plaza 3/in front of J4-13	LC	N/?	N/?/?/N
CK6	M-OA, F	C(1)		SC	FP	Isolated mound M3-37	LC	?/?	?/?/?/—
CK7	A, ?	C(1)		SC	FP	CK Plaza 4/J3-53	LC	?/?	?/?/?/—
CK8	A, M	C(1)		SC	FP	CK Plaza 3/J4-58	LC	F;B/?	N/?/?/Y
CK9	Y-MA, F	C(1)		SC	FP	Isolated mound M3-37	LC	F/?	?/?/?/—
CK10	MA, M	C(1)		SC	FP	CK Plaza 10/C5-8	LC	F/Y	?/?/?/N
CK11	MA, ?	C(1)		SC	FP	CK Plaza 10/C5-8	LC	F/?	?/?/?/—
CK12	Y-MA, F	C(1)		SC	FP	CK Plaza 10/C5-8	LC	?/?	?/?/?/—

Notes: Burial No.: WK = Waka; CK = Chakah (satellite site in periphery)

Age: S = subadult; YA = young adult; Y-MA = young-middle adult; MA = middle adult; M-OA = middle-old adult; M-OA = middle adult; OA = old adult; A = unknown adult; ? = undetermined age

Sex: F = female; ? = undetermined sex; M = male

Status/Class (from Tiesler [1999]): status: C = commoner; NRE = non-royal elite; RE = royal elite; class: 0 = no offering; 1 = offering; 1 = offering, no element; 2 = 1 element; 3 = 2-3 elements; 4 = 4-6 elements; 5 = 7+ elements

Elements (from Tiesler [1999]): FC = funeral chamber (elaborate crypt/tomb); V = 14+ ceramic vessels; P = cinnabar/red pigment; E = earflares/earrings; SS = stingray spines; B = 21+ jadeite/shell beads; C = presence of companion/retainer burials; S = sarcophagus; M = mask; G = glyphs; PE = pearls; O = obsidian/chert objects; MO = mosaic

Grave (grave morphology): S/P = simple/pit; C/CP = cap/capped pit; C = cist; H/PC = head cist/partial cist; SC = simple crypt; EC/T = elaborate crypt/tomb; U = urn

Zone (settlement zone): UC = urban core; NP = near periphery; FP = far periphery

Group/Structure: group and building/patio/plaza name or number

Date (time period): LPC = Late Preclassic; EC = Early Classic; E-LC = Early-Late Classic; LC = Late Classic; L-TC = Late-Terminal Classic; TC = Terminal Classic; ? =undetermined

Dental/Cranial modification: F = filing; D = drilling; B = both filing and drilling on the same tooth; Y = yes; N = none/no; ? = undetermined;— = NA (subadult)

Linear enamel hypoplasia (LEH)/Porotic hyperostosis (PH)/Periosteal reaction (PR)/Caries: Y = yes; N = no; ? = undetermined;— = NA (no observable teeth)

Table 5.2. Summary of secondary deposits

Burial/Lot No.	Grave	Zone	Group/Structure	Date	Notes
WK30AB	S/P	UC	Xucub/MX5 patio	?	MNI=2: Y-MA M, MA F; evidence of burning
WK31	S/P	UC	Epicenter/M13-1	L-TC	on-floor deposit; skull burial, modified skull, filed teeth; MNI=1: MA, M
WK35	U	NP	Maquin/patio MQ-A	TC	termination deposit; MNI=1: A, F
WK40AB	S/P	FP	U5-1/patio U5-A	?	skull burial; MNI=2: A: Y-MA, M, B: MA, M; A: has modified skull, filed teeth; perimortem trauma on both
WK51B	?	NP	P17-1/unnamed? Platform	?	probable skull burial: A, ?; found with primary interment
WK56	S/P	UC	Xucub/M12-21	LC	placed in floor of vaulted room; MNI=2
WK63	U	UC	Chok/N13-9	L-TC	disturbed by looting; MNI=2, adult and subadult remains
WK64	U	UC	Chok/N13-9	L-TC	possible skull burial: MA, ?; filed teeth
WK01A-14-3-96,15-3-66,21--3-101	S/P	UC	Epicenter/in front of M13-1	L-TC	large, episodic, on-floor deposit
WK01L-84-6-446	?	UC	Epicenter/M12-44 (sunken room in patio)	LC	possible bone bundle; adult and subadult remains, MNI=2
WK09B-25-3-5	U	UC	Tolok/M14-15	L-TC	found above WK Burial 5, probable offering; MNI=1
WK10A-42-2-85	S/P	UC	Epicenter/Plaza 4, terrace btw L11-31,33	TC	large on-floor deposit next to hieroglyphic stairway

Notes: Burial/Lot No: WK = Waka'
Grave (grave morphology): S/P = simple/pit; C/CP = cap/capped pit; C = cist; H/PC = head cist/partial cist; SC = simple crypt; EC/T = elaborate crypt/tomb; U = urn
Zone (settlement zone): UC = urban core; NP = near periphery; FP = far periphery
Group/Structure: group and building/patio/plaza name or number
Date (time period): LPC = Late Preclassic; EC = Early Classic; E-LC = Early-Late Classic; LC = Late Classic; L-TC = Late-Terminal Classic; TC = Terminal Classic; ? =undetermined

three settlement zones identified by Damien Marken (2015; see also Marken and Ricker, this volume). The graves range from simple burials to vaulted tombs.

Overall, preservation of the osteological material is poor. Most bones are highly fragmented, and many also have significant erosion of the cortical surface. Rarely, intact long bones are preserved and can be measured for use in stature estimates. Teeth are generally much better preserved than bone, although tooth enamel is occasionally eroded as well. Despite their imperfect condition, however, the human remains found in the wet, acidic soils of the Maya Lowlands still give us valuable insight into the lives of past people.

The goal of this chapter is to summarize the bioarchaeological data available at Waka' to provide a comprehensive overview of all inhabitants of the city, both in the urban core and on the periphery. Osteological analysis in Navarro-Farr and Rich (2014) focused on elite interments, especially on the role of gender in health outcomes (Piehl et al. 2014). Here, by incorporating data from identifiable settlement zones and by using several osteological indicators (enamel hypoplasia, cranial porosity, periosteal reaction, and dental caries), the focus will be on exploring differences in health and diet as a consequence of differential access to food and resources not just between males and females but between individuals of different status groups. Finally, ongoing analysis and future avenues for research will be discussed.

Demography of the Waka' Burial Sample

Age and Sex

The burial sample consists of 77 individuals: 19 females, 20 males, 22 adults of undetermined sex, and 16 subadults. Infants and young children up to six or seven years of age are present in the sample, but older children and adolescents are absent. As it was often difficult to determine precise ages of the adults, to better enable comparison between groups, they were assigned to general age classes (young adult, middle adult, etc.). Given the challenges presented by poor preservation and incomplete remains, in many cases it was not possible to establish sex or even general age groups for many skeletons.

The individuals mentioned above refer to primary interments that represent complete or partial individuals with articulated skeletons that are largely in anatomical position.[2] This includes mostly articulated remains that are missing some elements due to selective removal in antiquity (extraction). They are considered separately from the clearly disarticulated, incomplete secondary deposits of human remains. This second category is diverse and includes previously interred remains (double funerals), bundle burials (reduction), or immediate postmortem processing (defleshing, dismemberment). Note that this category is intentionally inclusive, because determining the formation processes (and the intent behind them), especially in the Maya Lowlands, is challenging. Primary interments are the more common type in the city.

Body Modification

Intentional modification of the body has a long tradition in Mesoamerica. Two common practices that have long been of interest to researchers, in part because of their endurance in the archaeological record, are changes to the shape of the cranial vault and modification of the teeth. Cranial modification must be performed at a very young age and functions as a protective measure; it is a way to participate in shared customs and beliefs and a visible marker of group identity (Tiesler 2014). Dental modification, generally carried out on adolescents or adults, may also reflect family, community, and ideological ties, and it may incorporate personal choices of the individual as well (Spence and White 2009).

Due to poor preservation, fragmentation, or removal of the skull in antiquity or by looters, it was not possible to observe the presence or absence of intentional cranial modification in most cases of primary interments (63/77, or 81.8%). For the remaining individuals, 12 (15.6%) had modified skulls, and 2 (2.6%) had skulls that were not modified. The most common type of modification was tabular oblique. Among the secondary deposits, five crania come from "skull burials," ritual deposits in which an intact cranium or crania were interred with few or no postcranial remains (Figure 5.1). Two additional crania come from secondary deposits that contained larger numbers of postcranial bones. A total of two of these crania (2/7, or 28.6%) are modified, both from skull burials, while the others could not be assessed for the presence or absence of modification. Since cranial modification was detected only in very few individuals due to poor preservation, it is not possible to draw conclusions about the practice in the city. While it is present only in commoners in the Waka' sample, this is likely because so many crania could not be observed.

Dental modification, both drilling for inlays and filing, is common in the Waka' sample (Figure 5.2). The following data pertain to the permanent teeth of adults, as no modification was observed in the permanent dentition of

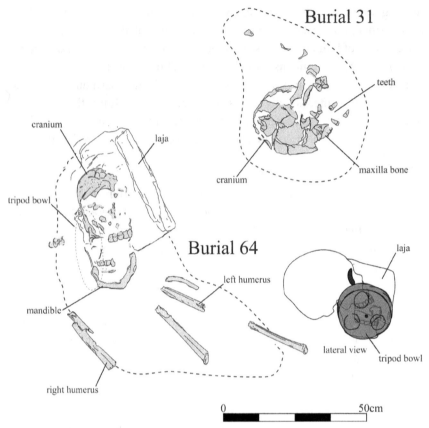

Figure 5.1. Skull burials: El Perú-Waka' Burials 31, 64, and 92. Drawings by Olivia Navarro-Farr and Keith Eppich, courtesy of Proyecto Arqueológico Waka'.

subadults. Twenty-three of 61 individuals (37.7%) have at least one modified tooth. Modification is absent in 12 individuals (19.7%) and could not be determined for the remaining 26 (42.6%). The majority of individuals have filed teeth, while relatively few have inlayed teeth or both types of modification. Among secondary deposits only filing was observed. Investigations at other Maya centers rarely show strong relationships between the frequency of dental modification and sex or status, though sometimes differences emerge when specific patterns of modification are considered (Tiesler 2011; Williams and White 2006). In the Waka' sample, dental modification is present among both elites and commoners as well as in males and females. No significant differences were observed in the type of modification between males and females. Elites were more likely to have dental inlays, while commoners were more likely to have filed teeth.

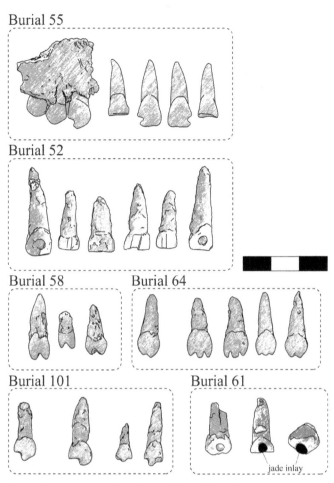

Figure 5.2. Dental modification at El Perú-Waka'. Drawing by Keith Eppich, courtesy of Proyecto Arqueológico Waka'.

Population Movement

Building on earlier work by Piehl (2009), a large-scale migration study has been carried out at Waka' and the nearby center of La Corona. Initial results of strontium stable isotope analysis identified relatively few migrants to the city (Patterson and Freiwald 2016a). The study includes isotope values for 45 individuals and 10 deposits that are part of the present discussion. Of these, 4 individuals (8.9%) have been identified through the use of strontium isotopes alone as migrants to the city. Preliminary analyses suggest that the addition of oxygen and carbon isotopes significantly enhances the ability to identify migrants in a skeletal sample (Patterson and Freiwald 2016b).

Burial Context

Grave Morphology and Interment Practices

Graves have been grouped into five categories developed following Lori Wright (2006), with modifications; in several instances two grave forms have been combined into a single type. Simple or pit burials lack architecture (Figure 5.3). Cap and capped pit graves are unlined pits covered by stones (Figure 5.4). In a head cist or partial cist, stones partially line the grave. A cist is a grave whose sides are completely encircled by stones; it is not covered by stones (Figure 5.5). A simple crypt is lined on the sides and covered by stones

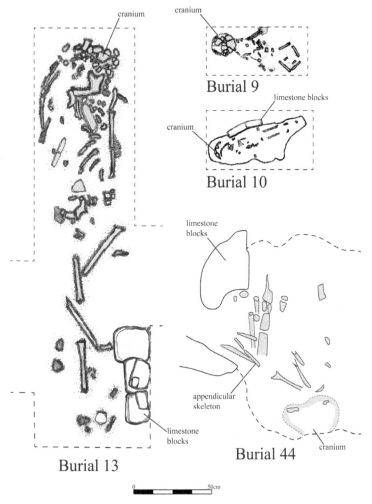

Figure 5.3. Pit burials: El Perú-Waka' Burials 9, 10, 13, and 44. Drawings by Ana Lucía Arroyave and Damaris Menéndez, courtesy of Proyecto Arqueológico Waka'.

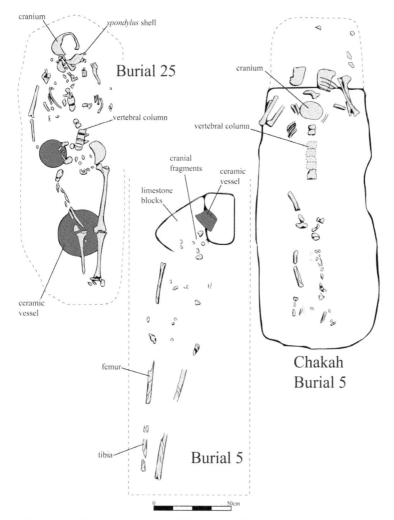

Figure 5.4. Cap and Capped pit graves: El Perú-Waka' Burials 5 and 25 and Chakah Burial 5. Drawings of Waka' Burials 5 and 25 by Arroyave, Rich, and Piehl; drawings of Chakah Burial 5 by Pérez Robles and Quiroa, courtesy of Proyecto Arqueológico Waka'.

(Figure 5.6). Elaborate crypts and tombs show a high degree of variability but are generally significantly larger than simple crypts. Simple crypts dominate the Waka' sample (31/76, or 40.8%), followed by simple/pit burials (15, or 19.7%), cists (13, or 17.1%), and elaborate crypts and tombs (10, or 13.2%) in roughly equal numbers. Cap/capped pit burials (4, or 5.3%) and head/partial cists (3, or 3.9%) are relatively uncommon.

Multiple burials are relatively rare at Waka'. When they do occur, they are double burials, either containing the remains of two primary (articulated) in-

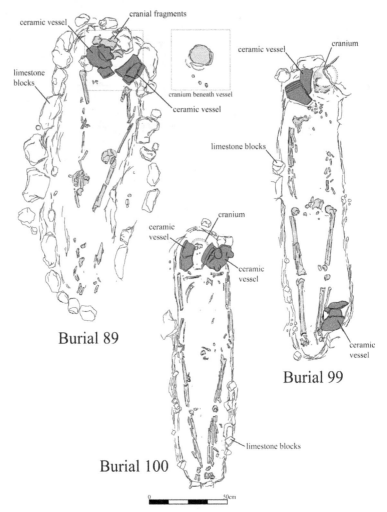

Figure 5.5. Cist burials: El Perú-Waka' Burials 89, 99, and 100. Drawings by Keith Eppich, courtesy of Proyecto Arqueológico Waka'.

dividuals or one primary individual and one or more sets of disarticulated remains. Graves containing large numbers of individuals, like those found at Kaminaljuyu, Lubaantun, and Tikal, have not been found in the city (Kidder et al. 1946; Hammond et al. 1975; Coe 1990).

In addition to the disarticulated remains found in graves with primary interments, secondary deposits at Waka' have been found in various ritual deposits. Some were cached inside inverted vessels. Following Wright (2006), this is an urn grave type, though W. B. M. Welsh (1988) calls this method for disposing of the dead a burial mode rather than a grave type. No primary

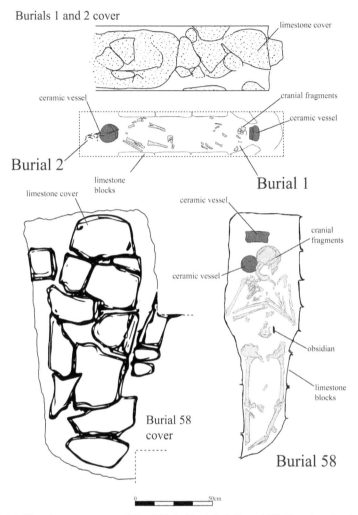

Figure 5.6. Simple crypt graves: El Perú-Waka' Burials 1, 2, and 58. Drawings by Juan Carlos Pérez and Ana Lucía Arroyave, courtesy of Proyecto Arqueológico Waka'.

interments in the city have been found in an urn. Several deposits take the form of large, scattered above-floor deposits created by repeated ritual activity over time (Navarro-Farr and Arroyave Prera 2014). Skull burials (discussed above) are common among secondary deposits. Ritual deposits at Waka' are not restricted to ceremonial spaces but are also found in residential sectors.

Grave Furniture

Grave goods in most interments, if there are any at all, usually consist of one or two ceramic vessels. Often one of the vessels is placed over the face of the individual. Elite graves, by contrast, are filled with a large number of items and variable assortment of prestige goods. For example, the vaulted tomb of Burial 39, arguably the most elaborate grave at Waka', contained 33 ceramic vessels, a cache of 23 ceramic figurines, a greenstone Olmec-style figurine, a jaguar pelt, a child companion burial, and the remains of several animals (Rich and Matute 2014; Rich and Eppich, this volume). Most other tomb and high-status burial contexts have also been reported elsewhere (e.g., Burial 8 [Lee and Piehl 2014]; Burials 24 and 25 [Rich and Matute 2014]; Burial 37 [Escobedo and Meléndez 2007]; Burial 38 [Eppich 2014]; Burial 61 [Navarro-Farr et al. 2021]; and Burial 80 [Pérez Robles et al. 2017]).

Burial Context and Social Status

Examination of the burial context can give important insight into social differentiation in a complex, hierarchical population such as that inhabiting an urban center like Waka'. While social status of individuals during life is not necessarily replicated in the treatment they receive after death (Gillespie 2001), burial customs generally "do reflect, even if in a somewhat encrypted form, the range of social differentiation and the degree of ritual elaboration" (McAnany et al. 1999:129). So, although the status groups used in this study are useful for getting a general sense of the distribution of status markers (grave goods) in burials across the city, they should not be interpreted as necessarily reflecting past social groups or classes. Based on the mortuary variables outlined above, primary burials were assigned a status level according to the criteria established by Vera Tiesler (1999), modified from Estella Krejci and T. Patrick Culbert (1995). In addition to grave furniture, Tiesler (1999) included a funeral chamber (in this study, an elaborate crypt or tomb), sarcophagus, and the presence of companion burials as elements in the scoring system that has a total of 13 elements. Individuals are assigned to one of six classes that correspond to three status levels (commoner, non-royal elite, royal elite) based on the number of elements present. The two higher status groups have been combined in this study due to the small sample size. A total of 65 individuals were classified as commoners, and seven were classified as elites.

Location of the Burials and Deposits

Marken (2015) identified three settlement zones of the city and its surrounding hinterlands: the urban core, the near periphery, and the far periphery (see also Marken and Ricker, this volume). Among primary interments, most individuals (43/77, or 55.8%) were recovered from the urban core, while 13

(16.9%) and 21 (27.3%) came from the near and far periphery, respectively. The distribution of the secondary deposits follows a similar pattern, with 9 (75%) located in the urban core, 2 (16.7%) in the near periphery, and 1 (8.3%) in the far periphery. The distribution of recovered burials and deposits reflects the excavation history and sampling strategies employed by project researchers and does not necessarily represent the true distribution of human remains in the city.

Osteological Indicators of Health and Diet

Pathological lesions of bones and teeth help us understand the impacts that social positions had on health outcomes. Here, enamel hypoplasia, porotic hyperostosis, periosteal reaction, and dental caries are examined for patterns that vary by sex, status, or settlement zone.

Enamel Hypoplasia

Enamel hypoplasia is a developmental defect that can take the form of lines, pits, or grooves on the surface of the tooth. These defects are most commonly seen on the anterior teeth and on the cervical and middle thirds of tooth crowns (Larsen 2015). While enamel hypoplasia has several causes, the correlation between the defects and nutritional status and illness during childhood has made them a useful measure of childhood stress (Goodman et al. 1984).

Twenty-two of 58 individuals (37.9%) have at least one enamel defect. Females are much more likely (10/16, or 62.5%) than males (3/13, or 23.1%) to be affected with the condition. Commoners (19/48, or 39.6%) are nearly twice as likely as elites (1/5, or 20%) to have at least one enamel hypoplasia. Settlement zone did not have much effect on the presence of the condition (urban core [12/37, or 32.4%], near periphery [5/11, or 45.5%], far periphery [4/9, or 44.4%]). Females, commoners, and perhaps those living outside the urban core appear to have been at greater risk of nutritional stress and illness during childhood than their counterparts.

Cranial Porosity

Porotic hyperostosis is a type of porous, pitted skeletal lesion of the bones of the cranial vault. This condition can be the result of the expansion of the spongy bone of the vault due to marrow hypertrophy in response to iron-deficiency anemia. Cranial porosity can also be caused by other anemias including megaloblastic anemia from vitamin B12 deficiency, scurvy, and rickets (Ortner 2003; Schultz 2001; Walker et al. 2009). Whatever the etiology, cranial porosity is useful as an indicator of chronic poor health. Today, the majority of active cases are found in children, especially those under five years of age (Larsen 2015).

Fifteen of 70 individuals (21.4%) with observable cranial material from primary interments exhibit cranial porosity. The presence or absence of the condition could not be determined for the remaining individuals because of fragmentation and poor preservation or because of removal of the skull in antiquity or by looters. It was observed in 5 males, 1 female, 13 commoners, 2 elites, 9 individuals from the urban core, 4 from the near periphery, and 2 from the far periphery. At least 25% of males and 5.6% of females had cranial lesions. Minimally, 21.3% of commoners and 28.6% of elites had porosity. Lesions were detected in at least 23.7%, 33.3%, and 10.5% of the urban core, near periphery, and far periphery samples, respectively. Cranial porosity is present in 5 of 7 (71.4%) crania from secondary deposits. It is difficult to draw conclusions about differences in prevalence of the condition based on sex, status, or settlement zone because of limited data due to poor preservation of the samples, but clearly it was not limited to a particular group.[3]

Periosteal Reaction

Periosteal reaction is the deposition of new, woven bone on the cortical surface that is eventually remodeled into lamellar bone. It occurs most frequently on the long bones, especially the tibial shaft (Weston 2012). Lesions involving multiple skeletal elements often indicate the presence of a systemic infection, while periosteal reaction that is limited may be the result of trauma or localized infection (Larsen 2015; DeWitte 2014). Periosteal lesions are useful as a general health indicator.

In the Waka' sample, systemic periosteal reaction was observed in six individuals. This group included 1 male, 2 females, 3 subadults, 5 commoners, 1 elite individual, 3 individuals from the urban core, and 3 from the near periphery. The reaction was active in the subadults and healed or a mix of active and healed in the adults. There was evidence for systemic infection in at least 5% of males, 10.5% of females, 7.7% of commoners, and 11.1% of elites. At least 7% of individuals in the urban core and 23.1% in the near periphery had extensive periosteal lesions; no systemic infections were detected in the far periphery sample. Poor bone preservation limits the conclusions that can be drawn about health outcomes in different groups within the Waka' sample.

Dental Caries

Caries is a bacteria-driven disease characterized by demineralization of dental enamel and other tooth structures. A variety of modifying factors that include tooth crown morphology, degree of attrition, enamel defects, and food processing techniques influence caries rates, but the consumption of carbohydrates is a major component of the disease (Larsen 2015). As such, caries rates in ancient populations are a popular way to study dietary patterns.

Caries rates for our sample population were calculated adjusting for the differential susceptibility of anterior and posterior teeth to carious lesions and accounting for antemortem tooth loss (Duyar and Erdal 2003; Erdal and Duyar 1999). Dental wear is generally low in the sample population and was probably not a major contributor to antemortem tooth loss. Thirteen individuals had at least one carious lesion. The caries rate for all primary interments is 9.2%. When just adults are considered, the caries rate is 10.2%. Carious lesions were less prevalent among males (7.6%) than females (11.6%). Commoners (11.9%) had higher rates of caries than elites (5.1%). Almost no difference in caries rates was detected between the settlement zones (urban core 8.7%, near periphery 7.3%, far periphery 9.7%). These differences suggest that males and elites may have consumed fewer carbohydrates than females and commoners.

For teeth from secondary deposits, the caries rate is 16.8%. The high caries rate in secondary deposits illustrates the importance of using methodologies that attempt to reflect the "real" caries rate by accounting for complicating factors like antemortem tooth loss. While only four lesions were observed in 96 teeth, an additional 14 teeth were lost antemortem, likely due to caries. However, just two crania from a skull burial account for 13 of the missing teeth, so the small sample size is also a factor.

Health and Diet at Waka'

Bones in the skeletal sample were generally fragmentary, and the cortical surface was often eroded, hampering observation of cranial porosity and periosteal reaction. While pathological conditions were noted where possible, some cases have likely been missed, and poor preservation made it difficult to determine when the conditions were absent. No patterns could be identified with regard to systemic periosteal lesions and sex, status, or settlement zone. For cranial porosity, the data suggest that the condition may have been less prevalent among females and in the far periphery. This could mean that individuals in these groups suffered less nutritional stress in childhood, patterns different from what is seen in the dental data, though these findings should be interpreted with extreme caution.

Dental data from the Waka' sample are more robust. Females were more than 2.5 times more likely to have at least one enamel hypoplasia than males. Commoners were almost twice as likely as elites to have an enamel defect. Individuals in the urban core were less likely to have an enamel hypoplasia than those from the other settlement zones. The groups with lower prevalence of the condition may have suffered fewer stress events during childhood.

Males have lower caries rates than females within the same status group, though the rate for male commoners (10%) is higher than for female elites (7.4%). So, while the data suggest sex-linked differences in diet at all levels of society, commoners probably consumed more carbohydrates than elites.

Conclusion

The Waka' skeletal sample is substantial and diverse, allowing us to explore the health and diet of the people of the city. Current research has revealed differences in skeletal and dental pathologies based on status and sex, though patterns involving settlement zones are less clear. These data suggest that males, elites, and perhaps those living in the urban core may have been more buffered from nutritional stress and infectious disease, and they may have consumed a more diverse diet with relatively fewer carbohydrates than their counterparts. These patterns reflect the heterogeneous, hierarchical society of Waka'.

Future work will reveal more exciting information. Final results of the analysis of strontium, carbon, and oxygen stable isotopes from tooth enamel will identify the migrant population of the city. Diet isotope data results will be available soon and will provide additional insights into past foodways at Waka'. A number of burials (n=32) from the 2016–2019 seasons have yet to be analyzed. The recent excavation of a significant number of burials from the Chok Group, an elite residential compound in the urban core (see Eppich, this volume), will give us the opportunity to explore a potential family group.

Through these types of analyses, we are working toward better integration of osteological and isotopic data with mortuary and other archaeological evidence to develop a better understanding of the lives of the people within the city. Skeletal remains have and will continue to play an important role in understanding the daily lives of the people of Waka'.

Notes

1 A further 32 individuals excavated during the 2016–2019 field seasons have yet to be analyzed.
2 A notable exception is Burial 38, which was reentered in antiquity and likely bundled (Eppich 2014). It has been grouped with primary interments because at least some of the skeleton remains in the grave, and the burial context gives clues to the original position of the body.

3 Individuals from this burial were excluded from status calculations due to the difficulty in assigning grave goods to a particular individual. However, this is clearly an elite context.

References

Coe, William R.
1990 *Excavations in the Great Plaza, North Terrace, and North Acropolis of Tikal.* Tikal Report No. 14. 6 vols. University Museum, University of Pennsylvania, Philadelphia.
DeWitte, Sharon N.
2014 Differential Survival among Individuals with Active and Healed Periosteal New Bone Formation. *International Journal of Paleopathology* 7:38–44.
Duyar, Izzet, and Yilmaz S. Erdal
2003 A New Approach for Calculating Dental Caries Frequency of Skeletal Remains. *Homo* 54:57–70.
Eppich, Keith
2014 Ritual Narratives from El Perú-Waka': Ceremonial Deposits in Non-royal, Elite Contexts. In *Archaeology at El Perú-Waka': Ancient Maya Performances of Ritual, Memory, and Power,* edited by Olivia C. Navarro-Farr and Michelle Rich, pp. 112–133. University of Arizona Press, Tucson.
Erdal, Yilmaz S., and Izzet Duyar
1999 Brief Communication: A New Correction Procedure for Calibrating Dental Caries Frequency. *American Journal of Physical Anthropology* 108:237–40.
Escobedo, Héctor L., and Juan Carlos Meléndez
2007 WK-03: Excavaciones en la Estructura M12-32. In *Proyecto Arqueológico El Perú-Waka': Informe no. 4, temporada 2006,* edited by Héctor L. Escobedo and David A. Freidel, pp. 89–124. Fundación de Investigación Arqueológica Waka', Guatemala City.
Gillespie, Susan D.
2001 Personhood, Agency, and Mortuary Ritual: A Case Study from the Ancient Maya. *Journal of Anthropological Archaeology* 20:73–112.
Goodman, Alan H., Debra L. Martin, George J. Armelagos, and George Clark
1984 Indications of Stress from Bones and Teeth. In *Paleopathology at the Origins of Agriculture,* edited by Mark N. Cohen and George J. Armelagos, pp. 13–49. Academic Press, Orlando.
Hammond, Norman, Kate Pretty, and Frank P. Saul
1975 A Classic Maya Family Tomb. *World Archaeology* 7:57–78.
Kidder, Alfred V., Jesse D. Jennings, and Edwin Shook; with technological notes by Anna O. Shepard
1946 *Excavations at Kaminaljuyu, Guatemala.* Publication 561. Carnegie Institution of Washington, Washington, DC.
Krejci, Estella, and T. Patrick Culbert
1995 Preclassic and Classic Burials and Caches in the Maya Lowlands. In *The Emer-*

gence of Lowland Maya Civilization, edited by Nikolai Grube, pp. 103–116. Anton Saurwein, Mockmuhl.

Larsen, Clark S.

2015   *Bioarchaeology: Interpreting Behavior from the Human Skeleton*. Cambridge University Press, Cambridge.

Lee, David F., and Jennifer C. Piehl

2014   Ritual and Remembrance at the Northwest Palace Complex, El Perú-Waka'. In *Archaeology at El Perú-Waka': Ancient Maya Performances of Ritual, Memory, and Power*, edited by Olivia C. Navarro-Farr and Michelle Rich, pp. 85–101. University of Arizona Press, Tucscon.

Marken, Damien B.

2015   Conceptualizing the Spatial Dimensions of Classic Maya States: Polity and Urbanism at El Perú-Waka', Petén. In *Classic Maya Polities of the Southern Lowlands*, edited by Damien B. Marken and James Fitzsimmons, pp. 123–166. University Press of Colorado, Boulder.

McAnany, Patricia A., Rebecca Storey, and Angela K. Lockard

1999   Mortuary Ritual and Family Politics at Formative and Early Classic K'axob, Belize. *Ancient Mesoamerica* 10(1):129–146.

Navarro-Farr, Olivia C., and Ana Lucía Arroyave Prera

2014   The Multilayered Meanings of Late-to-Terminal Classic Era, Above-Floor Deposits at Structure M13-1. In *Archaeology at El Perú-Waka': Ancient Maya Performances of Ritual, Memory, and Power*, edited by Olivia C. Navarro-Farr and Michelle Rich, pp. 34–52. University of Arizona Press, Tucson.

Navarro-Farr, Olivia C., Griselda Pérez Robles, Juan Carlos Pérez Calderón, Elsa Damaris Menéndez Bolaños, Erin E. Patterson, Keith Eppich, and Mary Kate Kelly

2021   Burial 61 at El Perú-Waka's Structure M13-1. *Latin American Antiquity* 32:188–200.

Navarro-Farr, Olivia C., and Michelle Rich, editors

2014   *Archaeology at El Perú-Waka': Ancient Maya Performances of Ritual, Memory, and Power*. University of Arizona Press, Tucson.

Ortner, Donald J.

2003   *Identification of Pathological Conditions in Human Skeletal Remains*. 2nd ed. Academic Press, London.

Patterson, Erin, and Carolyn Freiwald

2016a   Migraciones regionales en las tierras bajas centrales: Nuevos valores de isótopos de estroncio en La Corona y El Perú-Waka'. In *XXIX Simposio de Investigaciones Arqueológicas en Guatemala, 2015*, edited by Bárbara Arroyo, Luis Méndez Salinas, and Gloria Ajú Álvarez, pp. 797–807. Ministerio de Cultura y Deportes, Instituto de Antropología e Historia, Guatemala City.

2016b   Mobility in the Central Maya Lowlands: Strontium, Oxygen, and Carbon Isotope Values from La Corona and El Perú-Waka'. Paper presented at the 81st Annual Society for American Archaeology Meeting, Orlando.

Pérez Robles, Griselda, Juan Carlos Pérez, Damaris Menéndez, and David Freidel

2017   WK18: Excavaciones en la Acrópolis y el Palacio Real de Waka'. In *Proyecto Arqueológico Waka': Informe no. 4, temporada 2017*, edited by Juan Carlos Pérez,

Griselda Pérez Robles, and David Freidel, pp. 84–129. Fundación de Investigación Arqueológica Waka', Guatemala City.

Piehl, Jennifer

2009   Análisis de estroncio en muestras de fauna y restos óseos humanos: Informe de los materiales exportadas en marzo 2008. Report submitted to the Instituto de Antropología e Historia, Guatemala City.

Piehl, Jennifer C., David F. Lee, and Michelle Rich

2014   The Noblewomen of Waka': Mortuary and Osteological Insights into the Construction of Gender, Identity, and Power. In Archaeology at El Perú-Waka': Ancient Maya Performances of Ritual, Memory, and Power, edited by Olivia C. Navarro-Farr and Michelle Rich, pp. 184–202. University of Arizona Press, Tucson.

Price, T. Douglas, James H. Burton, Paul D. Fullagar, Lori E. Wright, Jane E. Buikstra, and Vera Tiesler

2015   Strontium Isotopes and the Study of Human Mobility among the Ancient Maya. In Archaeology and Bioarchaeology of Population Movement among the Prehispanic Maya, edited by Andrea Cucina, pp. 119–132. Springer Briefs in Archaeology. Springer, New York.

Rich, Michelle, and Varinia Matute

2014   The Power of the Past: Crafting Meaning at a Royal Funerary Pyramid. In Archaeology at El Perú-Waka': Ancient Maya Performances of Ritual, Memory, and Power, edited by Olivia C. Navarro-Farr and Michelle Rich, pp. 66–84. University of Arizona Press, Tucson.

Schultz, Michael

2001   Paleohistopathology of Bone: A New Approach to the Study of Ancient Diseases. Yearbook of Physical Anthropology 116:106–147.

Spence, Michael W., and Christine D. White

2009   Mesoamerican Bioarchaeology: Past and Future. Ancient Mesoamerica 20:233–240

Tiesler, Vera

1999   Rasgos bioculturales entre los antiguos Mayas: Aspectos arqueológicos y sociales. PhD dissertation, Facultad de Filosifía y Letras, Programa de Doctorado en Antropología, Universidad Nacional Autónoma de México, Mexico City.

2011   Decoraciones dentales. In Manual de antropología dental, edited by Andrea Cucina, pp. 183–206. Universidad Autónoma de Yucatán, Mérida.

Walker, Phillip L., Rhonda R. Bathurst, Rebecca Richman, Thor Gjerdrum, and Valerie A. Andrushko

2009   The Causes of Porotic Hyperostosis and Cribra Orbitalia: A Reappraisal of the Iron-Deficiency-Anemia Hypothesis. American Journal of Physical Anthropology 139:109–125.

Welsh, W. B. M.

1988   An Analysis of Classic Lowland Maya Burials. International Series 409. British Archaeological Reports, Oxford.

Weston, Darlene A.

2012   Nonspecific Infection in Paleopathology: Interpreting Periosteal Reactions. In

A Companion to Paleopathology, edited by Anne L. Grauer, pp. 492–512. Wiley-Blackwell, Chichester.

White, Christine D., Fred J. Longstaffe, and Henry Schwarcz
2006   Social Directions in the Isotopic Anthropology of Maize in the Maya Region. In *Histories of Maize*, edited by John Staller, Robert Tykot, and Bruce Benz, pp. 143–160. Elsevier, Amsterdam.

Williams, Jocelyn S., and Christine D. White
2006   Dental Modification in the Postclassic Population from Lamanai, Belize. *Ancient Mesoamerica* 17:139–151.

Wright, Lori E.
2006   *Diet, Health, and Status among the Pasión Maya: A Reappraisal of the Collapse.* Vanderbilt Institute of Mesoamerican Archaeology Series, Vol. 2. Vanderbilt University Press, Nashville.

III

Creating Monumental Landscapes and Experiences

6

Lady K'abel and the City's Temple

Reinforcing Cosmic Order through Sacred Architecture

OLIVIA C. NAVARRO-FARR, JUAN CARLOS PÉREZ,
AND GRISELDA PÉREZ ROBLES

The political dynamics of Classic Maya rulership and the manner in which such authority was established and maintained continues to fascinate scholars and provoke considerable debate. Research at Waka's Structure M13-1, the monumental public shrine situated in the city's epicenter (see Figure 1.2) and the locus of Waka' Burial 61, the tomb of Lady K'abel (Navarro-Farr, Pérez Robles, Pérez Calderón, et al. 2021; Navarro-Farr, Kelly, et al. 2020), permits a nuanced discussion of the significant and long overlooked role of women in such machinations. Critical to this is an appreciation of how the people of Waka' participated in and/or bore witness to the innovations and transformations accompanying the politics of dynastic succession. Because Waka' was a critical ally and vassal to the hegemonic Kaan regime, the Snake dynasts, during the Late Classic period, its role and that of its citizenry during these tumultuous times warrants deeper consideration. Specifically, it is becoming increasingly clear that the Late Classic (ca. 600–950 CE) Kaan dynasts elevated the political status of women to an unprecedented degree (see Reese-Taylor et al. 2009). These dynasts implemented this strategy to consolidate power through first-line access to trade routes and prowess in war. These goals were advanced in large part through the hypogamous marriages of royal Kaan women (Marcus 2001; Martin 2008; Teufel 2001) to politically subordinate male rulers of polities deemed important for Kaan. We now understand that royal women (see Chase and Chase 2017), including Lady K'abel of Kaan (Figure 6.1), had a pivotal part to play in these broader geopolitical schemes. Lady K'abel's actions anchored Waka' within the protective and lucrative Kaan fold. Her strategies are comparable to other Kaan queens whose political skills

Figure 6.1. El Perú-Waka' Stela 34, Lady K'abel. Limestone, 274.4 × 182.3 cm. Courtesy of the Cleveland Museum of Art, J. H. Wade Fund 1967.29.

included diplomatic savvy, ritual planning reliant on divination, and a willingness to deploy physical force. To this latter point, recent research (Wahl et al. 2019) attests to the efforts of Naranjo regent Lady Six Sky to raze the city of Witzna in "total war" (Martínez 2019). The influence and authority of the Kaan queens are also clearly manifest in the epigraphic and archaeological record (Martin 2020). How these political realities played out in terms of the lived experiences of Waka' citizenry are questions that remain under consideration.

In the present discussion, the goal is to contextualize Lady K'abel's decision to be interred in Waka's main civic-ceremonial building, Structure M13-1. Understanding that ancient Maya rulers commissioned monumental structures, the idea posited here is that they also had a hand in deciding where they would reside in a state of perpetual performance after their deaths. Therefore, with the intention of framing Lady K'abel's actions as informed and agential, and in keeping with a feminist approach (Navarro-Farr, Kelly, et al. 2020), the argument is that Lady K'abel herself chose to be interred in the city's most prominent civic-ceremonial shrine. This decision signaled her enduring role as a Waka' queen and reflects the planning in her political transition from Kaan princess to Waka' cosovereign. Because she understood her own narrative as part of that encoded in this building, by being interred therein, she effectively sealed the integration and became part of the collective memory. This move therefore reflects political agency on her part. Lady K'abel chose this location for her interment because of its ritual and cosmological significance.

Cosmology and Sacred Architecture

Cosmology refers here to the ordering and structure of the universe as conceived by the Classic Maya (see Freidel, Schele, and Parker 1993). Linda Schele talked about how people would "materialize belief," often in the form of sculpture commissioned on ancient monuments. To identify and interpret the materialization of cosmology, it is necessary to recognize that spatial elements are as intrinsic to this process as the consideration of the historical elements incised onto such monumental forms. That is, it is vital to consider the spatial and archaeological context for these monuments (in this case, stelae that appear differentially eroded or fragmentary when reerected into the construction phase of a monumental building) as well as for the historical texts they bear. Of course, the historical events known from epigraphic decipherment are also framed within a grander cosmological worldview. The physicality of cosmology at Structure M13-1 occurs in the form of various features deposited and/or incorporated into the Early, Late, and Late–Terminal Classic architectural phases that, in some instances, replicate elements of quadripartite spatial ordering.

Cosmological Features of the Late and Late–Terminal Classic Periods

The earliest research at M13-1 indicated the degree of its importance. Dense deposits blanketed nearly all surfaces. These deposits included material culture of the humblest variety, indicating that nonelite people enshrined the building with over a century's worth of cumulative offerings (Navarro-Farr 2009, 2016; see also Pérez Robles et al. this volume for more on similar activities at the Palace); recent identification of a Yucatan-style slate ware suggests that some items may even have come from considerable distances (Eppich, personal communication). Eventually it became clear that the building was designed, at least during the Late–Terminal Classic transition (ca. 750–880 CE), to function as a monumental fire shrine in a revival of Early Classic ceremonialism that hearkened back to historical affiliations between Waka' and Teotihuacan (Navarro-Farr, Marken, et al. 2022).

The Maya placed this fire shrine atop an *adosada*, a fronting platform attached to the main structure of M13-1 (Figure 6.2). The clear parallel of this feature with architecture of highland Teotihuacan has been discussed elsewhere (Navarro-Farr, Eppich, et al. 2020; Navarro-Farr, Marken, et al. 2022). Based on stratigraphic and ceramic evidence, this appears to be a Late–Terminal Classic–era feature. Investigations of the botanical elements recovered from the fire shrine indicate that weedy grasses typical of fallow fields were selected for burning (Cagnato 2016; see also Cagnato et al. 2017). Cagnato posits that the fire shrine was likely used during this transitional period for agricultural rituals. She also identified fragments of painted wooden objects that yielded Late Classic dates, suggesting the select ritual burning of relics. This constitutes clear evidence of fire ceremony that we interpret as a revival of New Fire Ceremonialism, a cult practice generally emblematic of Early Classic rulers (see Fash et al. 2009; Kelly et al., this volume; Freidel, this volume) and associated with an attached fronting platform identified as a *wiinte' naah*, which has been glossed as "Origin House" (Stuart 2004:237–239) and as "House of Darts" (Bíró 2020). The construction of a late-era revival of this feature suggests that the building may include an earlier version of a fire shrine dating to its Early Classic phase, a prospect we plan to test. The Late–Terminal Classic revival of the Early Classic fire ceremony and its continued reverence by the city's populace attest to its enduring significance (Navarro-Farr and Arroyave Prera 2014; Navarro-Farr, Marken, et al. 2022). Lady K'abel's decision to be

Figure 6.2. Late-Terminal Classic era Fire Shrine atop Structure M13-1. Photograph by Juan Carlos Pérez, with digital overlays by Olivia Navarro-Farr, courtesy of Proyecto Arqueológico Waka'.

buried within this ritually important structure was therefore distinctly political, an act key to her efforts at memory-making. Her efforts were not limited to this building. Another act that places her firmly within the city's political memory is the carved limestone masterpiece she commissioned at the height of her influence, Stela 34, which now resides in the Cleveland Museum of Art (Figure 6.1).

The building where Lady K'abel was interred was of such a public nature that the everyday citizen of Waka' likely identified it as central to the city's identity and, therefore, to their own. Its public position within the city was also amplified by its ritually and cosmologically charged character. The evidence for this includes not just the *adosada* and its monumental fire shrine but also the abundant surface deposits and Lady K'abel's tomb itself (Navarro-Farr 2009, 2016; Navarro-Farr, Eppich, et al. 2020; Navarro-Farr, Pérez Robles,

Pérez Calderón, et al. 2021). The longevity of its cosmological significance is attested to by more recent evidence including (1) the building's buried and painted Early Classic substructure (Sub III) featuring a six-tread staircase, and (2) numerous ritually (re)interred and cardinally aligned stelae. One of these monuments, Stela 45, was found interred within the building's Early Classic phase (Sub III). In addition, Stela 44 was found reerected within the penultimate Sub I construction phase, which was built immediately following the interment of Lady K'abel; Stela 51 was also ritually interred within what may be the penultimate or the final construction phase. The final phase also houses the fire shrine. We discuss each of these monuments further below.

Early Classic Significance: Preliminary Evidence

El Perú-Waka' Stelae 15 and 16 bear intriguing Early Classic texts referencing the political interactions between the Maya Lowlands and the central Mexican city of Teotihuacan. This includes, on Stela 16, one of the only known portraits of the enigmatic Sihyaj K'ahk'. Given these enticing links between Early Classic history and its commemoration in Late–Terminal Classic architecture atop this massive building, it became critical to investigate Structure M13-1's Early Classic significance and gauge its function during that time. Though understanding of M13-1 Sub III is preliminary, it appears reminiscent of analogous buried structures such as the Temple of the Night Sun within Structure F8-I of the El Diablo Group at El Zotz (Román et al. 2018) and the Structure 1 Complex at La Sufricaya (Tokovinine and Estrada-Belli 2015; Estrada-Belli and Tokovinine 2016). There are also striking architectural similarities in terms of the design of the masonry walls, featuring dramatic insets on front-facing walls and in corners on the Early Classic phases of this building, when compared to those from the same period at Waka's Palace (Pérez Robles et al. 2017; see also Pérez Robles et al., this volume). It may be that these architectural similarities between the Palace and Structure M13-1 also extend to the Preclassic era, but as excavations have not yet reached those levels, that question remains to be tested.

The centerline of Structure M13-1's Early Classic phase, dubbed Sub III, was located 1.5 meters east of, and beneath, M13-1 Sub II. Sub II's fronting staircase was the locus for Lady K'abel's masonry tomb chamber. The Sub II façade included two adjacent doorways. Each doorway was blocked—the northern by a dense ashy matrix and the southern by rubble. Though it was initially unclear whether the tomb chamber had been reentered, certain details like the associated burning, the ubiquitous knapped obsidian, and the way the interred was capped with flattish stones were discussed as potential indicators of a reentry event (Navarro-Farr et al. 2021). Indeed, the ash-filled north doorway of Sub II was posited as the potential point for a reentry. Subsequently, during the 2015 season, excavations revealed that the tread at the base of the rubble-filled southern doorway had been cut away. Excavations in the area of the removed tread exposed the sprung vault of a narrow masonry chamber. The chamber enclosed an entombed monument that had been deliberately flayed of its text and painted with red cinnabar. Designated Stela 45, this monument was discovered standing upright within the walled chamber (Figure 6.3). The chamber's sprung vault was a clear indicator that it had been reentered. The discovery of the entombed and reentered tomb of Stela 45, together with the missing riser from Sub II, indicated the entombed stela had been accessed along the same route as that of Burial 61, thus confirming that Burial 61 had indeed been reentered. Moreover, it had likely been reentered in the same episode as that of the flayed Stela 45.

In terms of the stratigraphy, Burial 61 corresponds to the Late Classic Sub II phase of Structure M13-1; and the tomb of Stela 45 was interred within the Early Classic phase, designated Sub III. Burial 61 is therefore situated northwest of the entombed Stela 45. The location of these two parallel tombs, Burial 61 holding Lady K'abel and the other containing Stela 45, emphasizes the role that memory played in the placement of each within successive subphases (Mills and Walker 1998). Specifically, it conveys the role of memory of place, of the memory of the defaced person once visible upon Stela 45, and the significance of the building as the locus where these important figures were situated for eternity. Together, this further underscores Lady K'abel's deliberate selection of this locale for her tomb as a place of political importance and symbolic power within the city's greater landscape.

The fact that Stela 45 was defaced in an earlier period significantly impacts our ability to interpret the monument. However, stylistic details offer some clues. First, the thickness of the stela resembles other monuments at Waka', while its steeply curved upper section is reminiscent of Middle Classic–era monuments at Tikal. Together, the evidence suggests that Stela 45 was Waka'-made but rendered in a style meant to imitate Tikal. This minor but important clue will reappear in the context of the discovery of a separate monument, discussed below.

Stela 45 is not in its original position but was reset upright in this location and positioned within a patch of flooring 61 centimeters above the floor associated with M13-1 Sub III (Figure 6.4). Rather than being in dedication to M13-1 Sub III, it was positioned flush with the doorway of its façade. Excavations revealed Stela 45 and its burial chamber were accommodated in that locale by ripping out Sub III's fronting staircase. The people of Waka' who

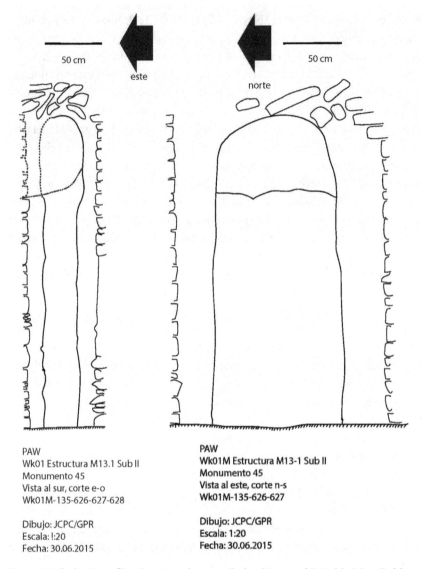

50 cm   este   norte   50 cm

PAW
Wk01 Estructura M13.1 Sub II
Monumento 45
Vista al sur, corte e-o
Wk01M-135-626-627-628

Dibujo: JCPC/GPR
Escala: !:20
Fecha: 30.06.2015

PAW
Wk01M Estructura M13-1 Sub II
Monumento 45
Vista al este, corte n-s
Wk01M-135-626-627

Dibujo: JCPC/GPR
Escala: 1:20
Fecha: 30.06.2015

Figure 6.3. Stela 45 profiles. Drawings by Juan Carlos Pérez and Griselda Pérez Robles, courtesy of Proyecto Arqueológico Waka'.

painted Stela 45 with red cinnabar and interred it into its funerary chamber clearly treated it as if it were a royal person. Its regal mortuary treatment suggests that it might have served as a proxy for the individual whose portrayal it once embodied. Moreover, great lengths were taken to inter it in its location, as the finely executed staircase of Sub III had to be destroyed to accommodate both the stela and its chamber. This action was closely followed by the infilling of the entire area and the construction of Sub II directly atop Sub

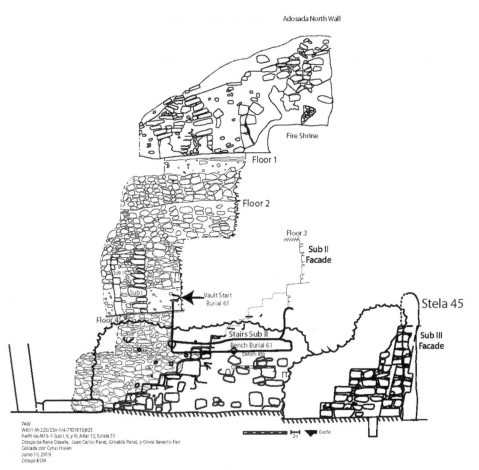

Figure 6.4. Structure M13-1, complete profile. Drawing by René Ozaeta, Juan Carlos Pérez, Griselda Pérez Robles, and Olivia Navarro-Farr; tracing by Cyrus Hulen, courtesy of Proyecto Arqueológico Waka'.

III. The stratigraphy demonstrates that Stela 45 was set into an Early Classic building at the point when the builders were transitioning into the Late Classic architectural phase. Therefore, the events associated with the monument's original commissioning, subsequent defacing, later healing, and ultimate entombment all must have occurred toward the end of the Early Classic period. Such events indicate the enduring significance of Structure M13-1. The stela's ritualized interment and its later reentry, mimic treatment of any royal ancestor. Such acts therefore suggest considerable reverence and may have served to heal or recommemorate the erased personage once depicted thereupon.

As noted, stylistic details indicate that the Early Classic version of this building is strikingly similar to the Early Classic phase of Waka's Palace (Pérez

Robles et al. 2017). Structure M13-1 Sub III features two inset corners with upper and lower tabular molding. The tabular moldings forming the second inset corner are slightly offset from each other. Remnants of specular hematite-infused red paint hint at how spectacular this building once was. The floor space associated with each inset corner has also been disrupted. The hole-like apertures were each infilled with sediment retained for flotation, and one included a large stone and a heavily burned greenstone bead. The other hole was filled with sediment containing carbonized flecks but no other discernible cultural material. Sub III's central staircase was composed of relatively few treads built with fine yellow limestone carved blocks. Because the stair risers were damaged, especially in their center where they were removed entirely, only about four of these risers are clearly visible in profile—but it seems likely there were once six in total. Each riser is notably high, possibly even two courses high, rendering each a steep step up and leading to what appears to be a single doorway into the superstructure that was Sub III (Figure 6.4). Suzanne Nolan (2015) identified six-step stairways as being symbolically representative of ball courts that, at Yaxchilan, refer to Creation Era sacrifices (see also Freidel, Schele, and Parker 1993). Again, most of the treads along with the central portion of the staircase were removed in antiquity and, in their place, a four-sided chamber with a vaulted roof was constructed to accommodate and entomb the reset Stela 45. The stela and its chamber were set into a patch of floor that appears to be "floating" above the floor level associated with Sub III.

Stela 44 and Stela 51

Continued investigation into construction episodes underlying Structure M13-1's *adosada* have demonstrated, time and again, that for generations, Waka's ruling elite, in concert with architects and builders, reerected some of its most important historical monuments within this building, dramatically interweaving the narratives of earlier history and living architecture. Stela 44, a historically pivotal monument, was discovered reerected within Structure M13-1's penultimate *adosada*, dubbed Sub I. Stela 44 is set into the floor of Plaza 2 and is positioned with its upper section slightly inclined toward a doorway that provides access to the Sub I superstructure, with the Sub I stairs built over the monument. Stela 44 was reset in this locale in antiquity. Additional excavation north of its current location revealed areas of heavy burning, a finely sifted yellow matrix, the existence of a containment platform, and the deposition of ritually charged objects, such as jade fragments, in the immediate vicinity (Navarro-Farr et al. 2017). Together this constitutes circumstantial evidence suggesting that some major feature was removed from this locale. Whether that may have been a stela or, indeed Stela 44, cannot be known, though resetting monuments was a frequent practice at Waka', and this stela is no exception. Stela 44 depicts the sixth-century Waka' ruler Chak Tok Ich'aak, who bears the same regnal name as two famous Tikal kings. That association has recently been interpreted by Simon Martin (2020) as evidence that Waka' had once been loyal to Tikal, an affiliation that dramatically shifted to Kaan as evidenced by this monument. This earlier Tikal loyalty is interesting because Stela 45 (discussed above), which bears few diagnostic clues to interpret, nevertheless features the steeply curved upper portion styled like other Middle Classic Tikal monuments. This constitutes a faint suggestion that Stela 45 may date to that earlier period when Waka' was presumably loyal to Tikal. The Stela 44 text states that the monument was dedicated by the ruler's son Wa'oom Uch'ab Ahk. This son also mentions his mother, a woman who bears the titles *ix sak wahyis* and *k'uhul* "cha"*tahn winik*, indicating she is a person of considerable pedigree (see Kelly et al. in press; Kelly et al., this volume). It is likely this woman is named Ix Ikoom, because she is named as such on a different monument, Stela 43. The Stelae 43 and 44 women likely refer to the same person, because on Stela 43 she is also referenced as living during the sixth century and because she also bears the *ix sak wahyis* title there. Interestingly, that monument was also found built into this building but on its final façade. It is therefore the position of these authors that the titled mother of Wa'oom Uch'ab Ahk, identified as such on Stela 44, is the same Ix Ikoom named on Stela 43.

Recent excavations also focused on continued exposure of a circular monument discovered in 2012, initially designated Altar 12 (Navarro-Farr, Pérez Robles, and Menéndez Bolaños 2013). These explorations began with a small investigatory tunnel oriented toward the plaza to the west and directly over where the monument was found. Once partially exposed, it seemed likely that the monument's surface was carved. However, as it was overlaid with a thick capping layer of lime mortar, details were obscured. The monument was also surrounded by layers of construction fill likely associated with the final *adosada*.

Continuing excavations westward revealed a previously unknown stela, designated Stela 51. It is located along the same north–south axis as that of Stela 44 and also faces west toward Plaza 2 (Figure 6.5). Strikingly, Stela 51 is also in line, on an east–west axis, with the defaced Stela 45. These arrangements therefore constitute a partial cardinally aligned cruciform pattern (Figure 6.6). Stela 44 was built into the penultimate Sub I phase. However, given that this is the least well-defined phase, it remains uncertain whether Stela

Figure 6.5. Altar 12, with rear of Stela 51 shown at discovery. Photograph by Rony López, courtesy of Proyecto Arqueológico Waka'.

51 was encased within the penultimate or the final phase. Nevertheless, we do know that the construction of Sub I over Sub II saw the movement of the building's east–west centerline axis farther north. This apparent preoccupation with cardinality is not limited to the placement of these monuments. We also see it in the orientation of the building itself. Structure M13-1 and the various phases of the *adosada* are also aligned along true north. Although this is certainly significant, there remains uncertainty about precisely how this significance may be understood, considering that the rest of Waka's monumental epicenter is oriented to Maya North, which is around 15 degrees east of true north. Perhaps its alignment follows the pathway of the sun; if so, it would more closely share cardinal alignments with buildings at Teotihuacan (Šprajc 2000).

Stela 51 (Figure 6.7) was discovered encased within a four-sided, roughly dressed pen or chamber that was itself surrounded by the same layers of fill surrounding the circular monument situated just behind (or east) of it. Excavations revealed that the face of Stela 51 was also painted red and that the

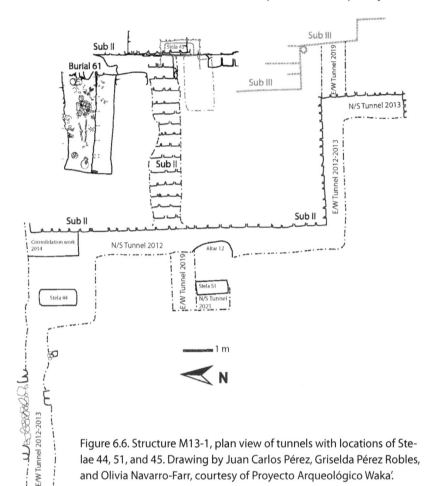

Figure 6.6. Structure M13-1, plan view of tunnels with locations of Stelae 44, 51, and 45. Drawing by Juan Carlos Pérez, Griselda Pérez Robles, and Olivia Navarro-Farr, courtesy of Proyecto Arqueológico Waka'.

base was likely cut off as it was interred only some 20 centimeters deep. The surrounding enclosure and the red-painted surface strongly suggest Stela 51 was deliberately interred in a similar way to Stela 45. The construction of the final *adosada* phase involved the use of dry-laid fill. The lack of mortar in this sector of construction fill greatly complicated the efforts to consolidate and stabilize the surrounding architecture and simultaneously record the archaeological context of Stela 51 and the monument to its east. The instability was even further challenged by the COVID-19 global pandemic. These obstacles extended the time required to complete recording and consolidation. Initially, only a small section of the lower right front Stela 51 was revealed (Navarro-Farr and López 2020). After a year's pause due to the pandemic, a smaller team reopened the investigation, working principally on consolidat-

Figure 6.7. El Perú-Waka' Stela 51, north side, as shown at Discovery. Photograph by Rony López, courtesy of Proyecto Arqueológico Waka'.

ing the surrounding architecture. As a result, much more of the monument was exposed and recorded in 2021. In 2022, the complete standing portion was revealed with its surrounding architecture consolidated. In addition, the circular fragment, believed initially to be an altar, was identified as the missing upper section, including the head of the standing figure with the continuation of associated texts on both lateral surfaces as well as the front. The following is an overview of preliminary details gleaned from this research. See Kelly and colleagues (this volume) for a more comprehensive treatment of the texts and iconography.

Stela 51 includes a well-preserved Long Count date of 9.0.0.0.0 8 Ahau 13 Ceh (December 12, 435 CE). This is 20 years after Stela 15 and 35 years before Stela 16, making this the second earliest securely dated monument in the city. The top of the monument is broken off, indicating an act of decapitation. The monument appears to be structured similarly to Stela 44, possessing a set of double columns on each side, and a figure on the front with a panel for text. The figure carries a feathered rectangular shield that includes an avian creature on it that is held in the figure's left hand; a feathered banner is held

Figure 6.8. Digital rendering of Stela 51. Photographs by Mary Kate Kelly and Mark Willis; digital rendering by Mark Willis, courtesy of Proyecto Arqueológico Waka'.

in the right hand. The figure's belt/toro is adorned with a bowl featuring an everted rim and adorned with trapeze motifs reminiscent of Karl Taube's (1983) "Spider Woman." The bowl contains five discernible flame/feather elements rising up from within. The figure wears tassels at the knees and has a pectoral decorated with bivalve shells (Figure 6.8). The regalia is unequivocally Teotihuacan-style garb (Fierer-Donaldson 2012). The figure's head, now known from the upper section, features a feathered jaguar headdress similar to that worn by Yax Nuun Ahiin on Tikal Stela 4. Moreover, although eroded by virtue of being at the locus of the decapitation/head removal, it is clear the figure bears goggles over the eyes. There are also texts that continue onto the upper section on both lateral surfaces and on the front on either side of the figure's face (for more on the texts and preliminary insights about them, see Kelly et al. this volume).

Again, the temporality of the monument and the imagery of the adorned figure bear the unmistakable emblems of power associated with Teotihuacan and clearly position Waka' as affiliated with that highland center in the Early

Classic era. This is unsurprising given the clear historical affiliations noted on Stelae 15 and 16. What is notable is (1) the interment of an Early Classic monument within the Late-Terminal Classic phase of this building, and (2) the placement of this monument both in direct east–west alignment with Stela 45, on the centerline of Sub III and in north–south alignment with Stela 44, which is itself on the centerline of Sub I and the fire shrine, constituting a partial cruciform pattern of buried monuments.

Discussion

The Late–Terminal Classic use of the building's *adosada* to support a fire shrine, paired with the significance of *wiinte' naah* ceremonialism indicate the enduring ritual significance of the public fire ceremony. Emphasis on agricultural ritual in such ceremonies, as suggested by Cagnato (2016), is also a point of interest as agricultural metaphors are also known to form the basis for the foundational associations of cruciform patterning (Zaro and Lohse 2005). It is therefore hypothesized that in its earliest iteration, Structure M13-1 represents a cardinally oriented, four-sided radial pattern, or quincunx, representative of a cruciform cosmogram. Moreover, based on the existence of the fire shrine and the associated revival of the cult of *wiinte' naah* ceremonialism, an earlier iteration of such a feature may be buried in a corresponding Early Classic phase. In our continued efforts to understand this building's Early Classic architecture, we now know that the Early Classic Sub III phase centerline, which featured a six-tread stairway, was dramatically removed to accommodate an interred stela that had been flayed before being ritually buried. Moreover, at some later point, likely during a reentry event into Lady K'abel's tomb, the vault on the entombed Stela 45 was sprung, and that tomb was also ritually reentered. Further examination of this feature and of the Sub III centerline itself will permit examination of the hypothesis regarding an earlier *entrada*-era fire shrine.

The replanting of stelae at different loci throughout the building was undertaken with the clear intent to align them cardinally. This results in a partial cruciform patterning pertaining to distinct architectural phases. The association of cruciform patterning and pan-Mesoamerican cosmological concepts has substantial support in the literature (Astor-Aguilera 2010; Freidel and Schele 1988; Mathews and Garber 2004; Zaro and Lohse 2005). The general form includes four-sided cardinal points forming a cross, intersected vertically through its core by a centering line or *axis mundi* (Coggins 1980; see also Freidel, Schele, Parker 1993; Smith 2005). The four sides or directions are horizontal and include multiple levels representing the multilayered form of the cosmos. Miguel Ángel Astor-Aguilera (2010) identifies cruciform patterning as a widely shared and long-enduring materialization of a key Indigenous American cosmological structuring principle. Cruciform patterns can therefore be understood to represent a materialization of Mesoamerican cosmic structure.

The resetting of these monuments in the locales where they were discovered resulted from careful planning and laborious physical execution. These actions reflect the pervasive importance, over generations, of meticulously planned efforts to shape the memories associated with them, their arrangements, their recorded (or erased) histories, and the building within which they are situated. This underscores the building's cosmological importance. It also demonstrates the ever-evolving role of social memory shaped both by the commissioners of these constructions and also, given the building's public face, by the city's collective consciousness (Mills and Walker 2008). Each of the previous architectural phases of M13-1 served as anchors for subsequent constructions. Memory was a key component of these plans because Stela 45 had long been buried when Stela 51 was reset in the aligning location where it was discovered. These earlier patterns were not only remembered by succeeding generations of Waka' rulers but also enhanced by each ruling generation. Each ruler left their individual mark on this built landscape, thus enhancing the ritual and cosmological significance of these built features. While this is not uncommon for Classic Maya rulers, far less discussion of this practice occurs in the context of female rulers because of characterizations of ruling women as commodities devoid of agency rather than as ruling cosovereigns. The argument here is that Lady K'abel contributed to Waka's ritual landscape identifiably in that she chose to be part of the ritual and cosmological significance of Structure M13-1, contributing to and commemorating that sacred space.

Conclusions

After nearly two decades of probing and plotting the life history of this monumental building, we are still very much scratching its surface. That said, taking a long view has been deeply rewarding. Understanding the later periods, which are complex, offers tantalizing insights into the long-term importance of this shrine for the city and the region. As hypothesizing about the building's earlier phases and its enduring cosmological significance continues, we will consider how politicians like Lady K'abel configured herself into the social memory of this living shrine. We see evidence that speaks strongly to an enduring legacy of influence and reverence for one of the city's greatest queens.

Acknowledgments

We thank the Instituto de Antropología e Historia de Guatemala (IDAEH), the Ministerio de Cultura y Deportes de Guatemala (MCDG), and the Departamento de Monumentos Prehispánicos (DEMOPRE) for their support and for their permission to conduct research. Thanks to Jerry Glick, the Waka' Foundation, and the Proyecto Arqueológico Waka' (PAW) team who supported and/or contributed to this research, including Damaris Menéndez, Francisco Castañeda, David Freidel, Stanley Guenter, Michelle Rich, Mary Kate Kelly, René Ozaeta, and Damien Marken. We acknowledge the editorial assistance of College of Wooster research assistant Alyssa Henss. This research was supported by the Fundación Patrimonio Cultural y Natural Maya (PACUNAM), the Alphawood Foundation, the University of New Mexico's Division for Equity and Inclusion and Department of Anthropology, a College of Wooster Henry Luce III Fund for Distinguished Scholarship, a College of Wooster Faculty Research Leave, the US Department of the Interior, the Hitz Foundation, and the GeoOntological Development Society.

References

Astor-Aguilera, Miguel Ángel
2010   *The Maya World of Communicating Objects: Quadripartite Crosses, Trees, and Stones.* University of New Mexico Press, Albuquerque.
Bíró, Péter
2020   A Short Note on *Winte' Nah* as "House of Darts." *PARI Journal* 21(1):14–16.
Cagnato, Clarissa
2016   A Paleoethnobotanical Study of Two Classic Maya Sites, El Perú-Waka' and La Corona. PhD dissertation, Department of Anthropology, Washington University in St. Louis.
Cagnato, Clarissa, Olivia Navarro-Farr, Griselda Pérez Robles, Juan Carlos Pérez Calderón, and Damaris Menéndez
2017   Feeding the Mountain: Plant Remains from Ritual Contexts on and around Structure M13-1 at El Perú-Waka'. Paper presented at the 82nd Annual Meeting of the Society for American Archaeology, Vancouver, British Columbia.
Chase, Diane Z., and Arlen F. Chase
2017   Caracol, Belize, and Changing Perceptions of Ancient Maya Society. *Journal of Archaeological Research* 25(3):185–249. https://doi.org/10.1007/s10814-016-9101 -z.
Coggins, Clemency
1980   The Shape of Time: Some Political Implications of a Four-Part Figure. *American Antiquity* 45(4):727–739.
Estrada-Belli, F., and Alexandre Tokovinine
2016   A King's Apotheosis: Iconography, Text, and Politics from a Classic Maya Temple

at Holmul. *Latin American Antiquity* 27(2):149–168. https://doi.org/10.7183/1045 -6635.27.2.149.

Fash, William L., Alexandre Tokovinine, and Barbara W. Fash

2009   The House of New Fire at Teotihuacan and Its Legacy in Mesoamerica. In *The Art of Urbanism, How Mesoamerican Kingdoms Represented Themselves in Architecture and Imagery*, edited by William L. Fash and Leonardo López Luján, pp. 201–229. Dumbarton Oaks Research Library and Collection, Washington, DC.

Fierer-Donaldson, Molly

2012   To Be Born an Ancestor: Death and the Afterlife among the Classic Period Royal Tombs of Copan, Honduras. PhD dissertation, Department of Anthropology, Harvard University.

Freidel, David, and Linda Schele

1988   Symbol and Power: A History of the Lowland Maya Cosmogram. In *Maya Iconography*, edited by Elizabeth P. Benson and Gillette Griffin, pp. 44–93. Princeton University Press, Princeton.

Freidel, David A., Linda Schele, and Joy Parker

1993   *Maya Cosmos: Three Thousand Years on the Shaman's Path*. William Morrow, New York.

Kelly, Mary Kate, Olivia Navarro-Farr, David Freidel, Juan Carlos Pérez Calderón, and Griselda Pérez Robles

in press Waka' Stela 44 and the Early Classic Kaan Hegemony. Manuscript accepted by *Ancient Mesoamerica*.

Marcus, Joyce

2001   Breaking the Glass Ceiling: The Strategies of Royal Women in Ancient States. In *Gender in Pre-Hispanic America*, edited by Celia Klein, pp. 305–340. Dumbarton Oaks Research Library and Collection, Washington, DC.

Martin, Simon

2008   Wives and Daughters on the Dallas Altar. *Mesoweb*. https://www.mesoweb.com/ articles/martin/Wives&Daughters.pdf.

2020   *Ancient Maya Politics: A Political Anthropology of the Classic Period 150–900 CE.* Cambridge University Press, Cambridge UK.

Martínez, Brenda

2019   Las guerras no causaron el colapso de la civilización Maya. *Prensa Libre*, August 13.   https://www.prensalibre.com/vida/escenario/las-guerras-no-causaron-el -colapso-de-la-civilizacion-maya/.

Mathews, Jennifer P., and James F. Garber

2004   Patterns of Cosmic Order: Physical Expression of Sacred Space among the Ancient Maya. *Ancient Mesoamerica* 15 (1):49–59. https://doi.org/10.1017/ S0956536104151031.

Mills, Barbara, and William Walker. editors

2008   *Memory Work: Archaeologies of Material Practices*. School of Advanced Research Press, Santa Fe.

Navarro-Farr, Olivia C.

2009   Ritual, Process, and Continuity in the Late to Terminal Classic Transition: Investigations at Structure M13-1 in the Ancient Maya Site of El Perú-Waka', Petén, Guatemala. PhD dissertation, Southern Methodist University, Dallas.

2016   Dynamic Transitions at El Perú-Waka': Late Terminal Classic Ritual Repurposing of a Monumental Shrine. In *Ritual, Violence, and the Fall of the Classic Maya Kings*, edited by Gyles Iannone, Brett A. Houk, and Sonja A. Schwake, pp. 243–269. University Press of Florida, Gainesville.

Navarro-Farr, Olivia C., and Ana Lucía Arroyave Prera
2014   A Palimpsest Effect: The Multi-layered Meanings of Late-to-Terminal Classic Era Above-Floor Deposits at Structure M13-1. In *Archaeology at El Perú-Waka': Performances of Ritual, Memory, and Power*, edited by Olivia C. Navarro-Farr and Michelle Rich, pp. 34–52. University of Arizona Press, Tucson.

Navarro-Farr, Olivia C., Keith Eppich, David A. Freidel, and Griselda Pérez Robles
2020   Ancient Maya Queenship: Generations of Crafting State Politics and Alliance Building from Kaanul to Waka'. In *Approaches to Monumental Landscapes of the Ancient Maya*, edited by Brett A. Houk, Bárbara Arroyo, and Terry G. Powis, pp. 196–217. University Press of Florida, Gainesville.

Navarro-Farr, Olivia, David Freidel, Griselda Pérez, and Danilo Hernández
2017   Excavaciones en la operación WK01 en la Estructura M13-1. In *Proyecto Arqueológico El Perú-Waka': Informe no. 14, temporada 2016*, edited by Juan Carlos Pérez, pp. 1–37. Fundación de Investigación Arqueológica Waka', Guatemala.

Navarro-Farr, Olivia C., Mary Kate Kelly, Michelle Rich, and Griselda Pérez Robles
2020   Expanding the Canon: Lady K'abel the *Ix Kaloomte'* and the Political Narratives of Classic Maya Queens. *Feminist Anthropology* 1(1):38–55. https://doi.org /10.1002/fea2.12007.

Navarro-Farr, Olivia C., and Rony López
2020   Operación WK01, Estructura M13-1. In *Proyecto Arqueológico El Perú-Waka': Informe no. 17, temporada 2019*, edited by Juan Carlos Pérez, Griselda Pérez Robles, and Damien Marken, pp. 13–36. Fundación de Investigación Arqueológica Waka', Guatemala City.

Navarro-Farr, Olivia C., Damien Marken, Mary Kate Kelly, Keith Eppich, Griselda Pérez Robles, and Juan Carlos Pérez
2022   Queens and Statecraft: Royal Women in the Heart of the Fire Shrine at El Perú-Waka'. In *3,000 Years of War and Peace in the Maya Lowlands: Identity, Politics, and Violence*, edited by Geoffrey E. Braswell, pp. 159–183. Routledge, London

Navarro-Farr, Olivia C., Griselda Pérez Robles, and Damaris Menéndez
2013   Operación WK-1: Excavaciones en la Estructura M13-1. In *Proyecto Regional Arqueológico El Perú-Waka': Informe no. 10, temporada 2012*, edited by Juan Carlos Pérez Calderón, pp. 3–91. Fundación de Investigación Arqueológica Waka', Guatemala City.

Navarro-Farr, Olivia C., Griselda Pérez Robles, Juan Carlos Pérez Calderón, Elsa Damaris Menéndez Bolaños, Erin Patterson, Keith Eppich, and Mary Kate Kelly
2021   Burial 61 at El Perú-Waka's Structure M13-1. *Latin American Antiquity* (1):188–200. https://doi.org/10.1017/laq.2020.99.

Nolan, Suzanne
2015   Late Classic Politics and Ideology: A Case Study of Hieroglyphic Stairway 2 at Yaxchilan, Chiapas, Mexico. Vol. I. PhD dissertation, University of Essex.

Pérez Robles, Griselda, Juan Carlos Pérez, Damaris Menéndez, and David Freidel
2017   Operación WK18: Excavaciones en la Acrópolis y el Palacio Real de Waka'. *Proyecto Arqueológico El Perú-Waka': Informe no. 10, temporada 2012*, edited by Juan Carlos Pérez Calderón, pp. 83–129. Fundación de Investigación Arqueológica Waka', Guatemala.

Reese-Taylor, Kathryn, Peter Mathews, Julia Guernsey, and Marlene Fritzler
2009   Warrior Queens among the Classic Maya. In *Blood and Beauty: Organized Violence in the Art and Archaeology of Mesoamerica and Central America*, edited by Heather Orr and Rex Koontz, pp. 39–72. Cotsen Institute of Archaeology, University of California, Los Angeles.

Román, Edwin, Thomas G. Garrison, and Stephen Houston
2018   Ruling through Defense: The Rise of an Early Classic Dynasty at El Zotz. In *An Inconstant Landscape: The Maya Kingdom of El Zotz, Guatemala*, edited by Thomas G. Garrison and Stephen Houston, pp. 70–92. University Press of Colorado, Louisville.

Smith, Michael E.
2005   Did the Maya Build Architectural Cosmograms? *Latin American Antiquity* 16(2):217–224.

Šprajc, Ivan
2000   Astronomical Alignments at Teotihuacan, Mexico. *Latin American Antiquity* 11(4):403–415.

Stuart, David
2004   The Beginnings of the Copan Dynasty: A Review of the Hieroglyphic and Historical Evidence. In *Understanding Early Classic Copan*, edited by Ellen E. Bell, Marcello A. Canuto, and Robert J. Sharer, pp. 265–296. University of Pennsylvania Museum of Archaeology and Anthropology, Philadelphia.

Taube, Karl
1983   The Teotihuacán Spider Woman. *Journal of Latin American Lore* 9(2):107–189.

Teufel, Stefanie
2001   Marriage Diplomacy—Women at the Royal Court. In *Maya: Divine Kings of the Rain Forest*, edited by Nikolai Grube, assisted by Eva Eggebrecht, and Matthias Seidel, pp. 172–173. Könemann Verlagsgesellschaft mbH, Cologne.

Tokovinine, Alexandre, and Francisco Estrada-Belli
2015   La Sufricaya: A Place in Classic Maya Politics. In *Classic Maya Polities of the Southern Lowlands: Integration, Interaction, Dissolution*, edited by Damien B. Marken and James L. Fitzsimmons, pp. 195–224. University Press of Colorado, Boulder.

Wahl, David, Lysanna Anderson, Francisco Estrada-Belli, and Alexandre Tokovinine
2019   Paleoenvironmental, Epigraphic and Archaeological Evidence of Total Warfare among the Classic Maya. *Nature Human Behavior* 3:1049–1054. https://doi.org/10.1038/s41562-019-0671-x.

Zaro, Gregory, and Jon C. Lohse
2005   Agricultural Rhythms and Rituals: Ancient Maya Solar Observation in Hinterland Blue Creek, Northwestern Belize. *Latin American Antiquity* 16(1):81–98.

7

Iconographic Analysis of a Royal Funerary Ceramic

Examining the Serpent Vessel from Burial 61

Sarah Van Oss
and Olivia C. Navarro-Farr

This chapter reviews the complex iconography pertaining to one of the artifacts from the mortuary assemblage of the tomb of Lady K'abel, El Perú-Waka' Burial 61 (Navarro-Farr et al. 2020). The iconographic depictions on this vessel tie Lady K'abel to broader patterns of ritual and political power that reflect associations with the Kaan dynasty and the women who acted as political agents within it. A study of the iconographic depiction reveals the presence of a Vision Serpent rising out of a sacrificial offering. By situating this representation within a regional understanding of Kaan women and their ritual associations with Vision Serpents, we propose that this vessel reflects Lady K'abel's role as a spiritual and political practitioner, as a woman of Kaan lineage, and as a ruler of Waka'.

Known as the Serpent Vessel, this plate possesses significant information regarding the political and religious role of the tomb's occupant (Figure 7.1). The Serpent Vessel represents a Palmar Polychrome type, possessing an orange base slip with red and black painted designs on the interior of the vessel (Eppich 2017). The exterior has no slip or decoration. The vessel remained intact despite the collapse of the tomb vault and did not require reconstruction. The shallow bowl shows no evidence of use-wear on its surfaces, suggesting that it may have been produced specifically for interment with the deceased ruler. Importantly the vessel was recovered from the west end of the burial chamber, at the feet of the interred.

Employing contextual and iconographic information, we examine the vessel's performative use as an implement in political ritual that has impor-

Figure 7.1. The Serpent Vessel. Drawing by René Ozaeta, courtesy of Proyecto Arqueológico Waka'.

tant associations with women of the Kaan lineage. We utilize comparative approaches drawn primarily from stone carvings of Kaan women from the centers of Saknikte' (La Corona) and Yaxchilan. In evaluating the different iterations of the Vision Serpent, we identify elements suggestive of its power to travel between spiritual realms. Lady K'abel and other Kaan women were important political and ritual leaders of their respective cities, and this is attested to in the frequent connection between Kaan women and Vision Serpents. The Serpent Vessel from Lady K'abel's interment reflects her role as a ritual specialist and political leader. Additionally, the vessel underscores Lady K'abel's association with the Kaan dynasty and connects her to widely understood symbols originating in Teotihuacan.

Vision Serpents, Transformation, and Transcendence

The iconographic elements present on the plate convey a zoomorphic creature comparable to others depicted from the region; it strongly resembles other snakelike creatures in Mesoamerican art. Vision Serpents take various forms, depending on the context of their appearance, while maintaining key characteristics indicative of an ability to travel between the spiritual and terrestrial realms (McDonald and Stross 2012; Miller and Taube 1997; Schele and Freidel 1992; Schele and Miller 1986; Taube 2004). The depiction of the zoomorph on the vessel includes elements of three creatures and represents transformation and the movement between worlds: the jaguar, the butterfly, and the snake. Although this Vision Serpent appears in Late Classic Maya contexts, its history can be traced through time to Teotihuacan and the influence of War Serpent iconography (Headrick 2003; Sugiyama 1989; Taube 2000, 2004).

The head of the zoomorph is positioned at the interior center of the plate. The jawless face looks to the left and supports a jaguar-spotted and feathered fan element that could represent a headdress or extensions of the creature's head. The squared, jawless mouth appears frequently in depictions of jaguars and jaguar-like creatures. Jaguars are perhaps the most well-known symbol of Maya political power and ritual transformation, as their spots, teeth, pelts, and claws appear in artifact assemblages and throughout representations of Classic kings (Bassie-Sweet 2021:129–133; Freidel and Guenter 2003; Schele and Miller 1986:51). Their hunting prowess on land, in water, or in the canopy associates them with physical power and the ability to transition between the underworld, terrestrial, and celestial realms (Miller and Taube 1997:102–104).

Atop the zoomorph's jaguar muzzle is a curled, serpentine nostril. Crowning the nostril and the head of the creature is a jaguar-spotted headdress with fanned elements. Feathered fans like these appear on serpents and serpentlike creatures throughout Maya artistic programs and draw on Feathered Serpent imagery from Teotihuacan (Headrick 2003; Schele and Miller 1986; Sugiyama 1989; Taube 2000). Like jaguars, snakes hunt and move among trees, water, and undergrowth, which makes them creatures who can also transition between symbolic and literal realms (Miller and Taube 1997:102). The ability of snakes to swallow prey whole and carry it away to digest likely contributes to the idea that serpentlike creatures can carry entire entities from one realm to another (Miller and Taube 1997:149–150; Schele and Freidel 1992). Serpents who open their mouths to reveal gods or spirits are common in Maya iconographic representations, such as on Yaxchilan Lintel 25, discussed below.

Elements associated with butterflies appear on this creature in the form of a feathered eyelid and a curling element extending from the mouth that likely represents a proboscis. Butterflies, too, represent transformations in the literal sense of metamorphosis from crawling caterpillars to flying insects.

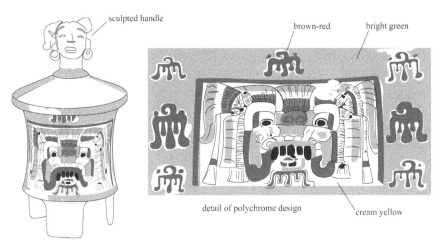

Figure 7.2. Vessel K6197 from a royal tomb at Copan. Drawing by Keith Eppich.

Additionally, butterflies are associated with Teotihuacan and the warrior cults there (Headrick 2003; Miller and Taube 1997; Taube 2000, 2004). Beneath the head of the creature is an overturned bowl-element reminiscent of Teotihuacan-style images of sacrificial offerings, again often associated with butterflies. Similar depictions are observed on the vessels found in a royal tomb at Copan (Figure 7.2; see also Guenter and Grube n.d.). This depiction suggests that the Serpent Vessel may bear an image of its own usage as a holder for sacrificial offerings.

From the curling proboscis drips the glyphic element *ak'bal*, or "darkness." This glyphic element is a kind of shortened version of what is often shown as a decorative element on gods or mythical figures associated with the underworld (Schele, Miller, Kerr, et al. 1992). The "darkness" signifier that drips from the creature suggests it comes from a dark and damp place, perhaps the underworld. Overall, the creature depicted on the Serpent Vessel represents an otherworldly, transcending Vision Serpent rising from the underworld on an overturned bowl containing a sacrificial offering. To further understand the importance of this creature within the mortuary context of Lady K'abel's tomb, we must examine the placement and significance of the bowl itself.

Serpents in Bowls

The Serpent Vessel, though it appears that it was unused at the time of interment, likely represented the kinds of practices Lady K'abel enacted during her lifetime. Other examples of sacrificial acts and Vision Serpents like the one observed on Yaxchilan Lintel 25 underscores the role of such vessels in ritual activity. The iconographic depiction of a sacrificial offering beneath a Vision Serpent associates it with ritual practices like bloodletting, autosacrifice, and conjuration (Navarro-Farr and Rich 2014; Schele, Miller, Kerr, et al. 1992; Schele and Miller 1986; Swenson 2015; see also Freidel, this volume). Following the interpretation presented by Linda Schele and Mary Ellen Miller (1986:194), the vessel served as a metaphorical portal for the Vision Serpent depicted on it. The Vision Serpent traveled from the underworld and the terrestrial realm, transitioning between a multilayered cosmos. The bowl could have even acted as a cave, connecting these layers through the person of the divine ruler (Taube 1986, 2004). The Maya often depicted the ruler as an *axis mundi*, situating them iconographically atop a sacred mountain (Schele and Freidel 1992). The presence of the sacred mountain is well known in Maya studies and tells the story of how humans emerged from a watery cave in the sacred mountain at the center of the world (Taube 1986, 2004). Caves can be understood as portals that connect the worlds and places from which living entities, human and nonhuman, emerged (Taube 1986). Therefore, the ruler acted as the connector of worlds and the conjurer of animate entities from the cave in the mountain. This interpretation is supported by the depiction of Lady K'abel on El Perú-Waka' Stela 34 (now located in the Cleveland Museum of Art; see Figure 6.1). Though the monument is missing its base, the stela's original base would have depicted Lady K'abel standing atop a *witz* monster, or mountain (Wanyerka 1996). If we compare this depiction with the layout of Lady K'abel's tomb, we can understand the Serpent Vessel as a cave/portal for the Vision Serpent, emerging from the mountain on which the ruler figuratively stands.

Taken as a whole, the combination of jaguar, snake, and butterfly elements on a single zoomorph indicates its otherworldliness and its ability to transition among the realms. The location of the vessel itself suggests that the Vision Serpent emerged from this vessel that acted as a cave through which spiritual entities emerge. This iconographic depiction and the significant location of the vessel reinforce the role of Lady K'abel as a diviner, summoning such entities in service to her city. In doing so, Lady K'abel acted in ways similar to other Kaan queens across the Southern Lowlands. These conjurer-queens used ritual means to communicate with supernatural messengers, ancestors, spirits, and even gods. The iconography of the Serpent Vessel reflects these rituals, likely enacted by Lady K'abel herself. She, and women like her, did so to facilitate political actions and even ritual warfare, making use of the Teotihuacan symbolism associated with warfare and conflict (Bassie-Sweet 2021).

Kaan Women

The appearances of Kaan women in the iconographic and epigraphic records reflect their roles and the political integration of the region (Freidel and Guenter 2003; Martin 2008; Navarro-Farr et al. 2020; Navarro-Farr and Rich 2014). Their marriages created vassal relationships between smaller polities like Waka', Saknikte' (La Corona), and Yaxchilan, among others, with the potent state of Calakmul. In examining the representations of the Kaan women at these centers, we situate the Vision Serpent vessel within a larger iconographic program associated with powerful women rulers. The Vision Serpent within Lady K'abel's mortuary tableau reinforces her role as a ritual specialist. Its iconography is comparable with two other examples of Kaan dynasty women of the time who also held the title *ix kaloomte'* and who appear with Vision Serpent–like creatures: Lady Ti' Kan of Saknikte', also known as La Corona, and Lady K'abal Xook of Yaxchilan.

Saknikte'

La Corona Panel 6 (Figure 7.3), now located in the Dallas Museum of Art, features three Kaan women who acted as political leaders and diplomats (Freidel and Guenter 2003; Martin 2008). This panel represents a ritual conducted to celebrate the ending of a *baktun* (20-year cycle) and discusses the "arrival" of three Kaan women in three different centuries. The image shows two women meeting face-to-face while standing on two elaborate battle palanquins. The woman on the viewer's left is identified by Martin (2008) as *ix ti' kanal ajaw*, Lady Ti' Kan in the literature, the contemporary ruler of the kingdom of Saknikte' and a daughter of the Kaan court. She holds the title *ix kaloomte'*, glossed as "Lady Emperor" by Martin (2008), and holds the Snake emblem glyph. The woman on the right is also identified as a Kaan woman known as Lady Nah Ek', but she arrived at Saknikte' over two centuries *before* the contemporary queen (Stuart 2013). A third Kaan woman is mentioned in the text but is not shown in the image.

Displayed alongside the women are mythical creatures like those observed on the Serpent Vessel. Over the queen on the left, a serpent writhes above the palanquin canopy. Though eroded, the serpent seems to tilt its jawless face toward the sky. On the right, behind the queen, a large jaguar-figure looms. Atop a bipedal "werejaguar" body is a head that resembles the head visible on the Serpent Vessel. Though not jawless, the head includes a similarly large eye, curled nostril, and feathered fans. Comparable circular elements in place of ears also appear on both creatures. The creatures also share an extended

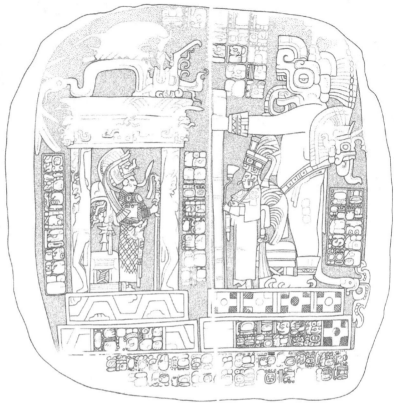

Figure 7.3. Dallas Panel 6 from La Corona. Drawing by David Stuart, courtesy of Proyecto Arqueológico Regional La Corona.

tongue, or proboscis-like feature, that lolls out of the mouth. Serpentine fans and curls also extend from the tail of the creature. Though not identical, this creature is an entity similar to that on the Serpent Vessel. The congruencies in the two creatures suggest that the Kaan women at both Saknikte' and Waka' employed Vision Serpents in their roles as *kaloomte'*.

Yaxchilan

At Yaxchilan, another Kaan woman appears in the carved stone lintels and monuments. In Lintel 25 (Figure 7.4), Lady K'abal Xook, who also possesses a *kaloomte'* title, summons a Vision Serpent from a sacrificial vessel at her feet (Schele, Miller, Kerr, et al. 1992:177). From the mouth of this serpent emerges a warrior holding a spear and shield. Lady K'abal Xook gazes up at the figure while holding a bowl with autosacrificial implements in one hand and reaching out with the other, her hand above the bowl at her knees. The Vision Serpent on Lintel 25 also possesses analogous characteristics to those

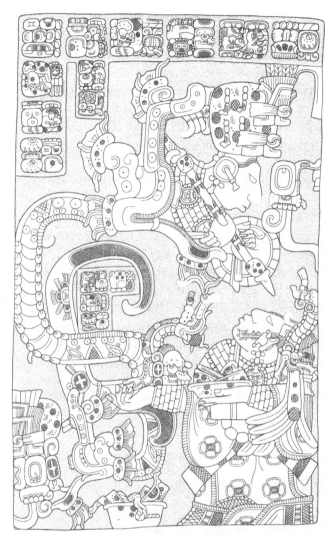

Figure 7.4. Yaxchilan Lintel 25. Drawing of Yaxchilan Lintel 25, underside, by Ian Graham. © President and Fellows of Harvard College, Peabody Museum of Archaeology and Ethnology, 2004.15.6.5.22.

observed on the Burial 61 Serpent Vessel from Waka'. Lady K'abal Xook's creature possesses jaguar and serpent elements, though butterfly aspects are not as apparent here. Nonetheless, the bared teeth that extend from a spotted and squared jaw support the idea that the Waka' and Yaxchilan creatures are of the same ilk. The jaguar-spotted headdresses and feathered fans that cap its eyes as well as the curled nostril also suggest that the Lintel 25 and the Serpent Vessel's creatures are similar, if they are not the same creature altogether. Although the body is not visible, the head of the Serpent on Lady K'abel's bowl can be understood to be in a state of emergence from the bowl, implying that its body will take on a serpentine form, like that shown on Lintel 25. Furthermore, implements typical of autosacrifice rest in the bowls in front and in the hand of Ix K'abal Xook, including bloodied paper (Schele and Miller 1986:177). The bowl on the ground is akin to that of the Serpent Vessel from Lady K'abel's tomb as the receptacle of sacrificial implements and a portal through which the Serpent emerges. The Serpent Vessel is likely a representation of the activities that Lady K'abel would have enacted in life, similar to Lady K'abal Xook's actions depicted on Lintel 25. These queens summoned supernatural entities through their ceramics.

Teotihuacan and Its Influence

Allusions to Teotihuacan can be seen within the iconography of the Serpent Vessel. The presence of a butterfly's proboscis alludes to imagery present in central Mexican representations of the Jaguar War Serpent (Taube 2000). Similar symbols also appear on another vessel, K8777, where the head of a Vision Serpent emerges, just like the zoomorph on the Waka' vessel (Figure 7.5). The serpent on K8777 possesses feathered eyes, a curled proboscis, and feathery wings as seen in Teotihuacan imagery (Headrick 2003; Sugiyama 1989; Taube 2000). The presence of Teotihuacan-style elements on the Vision Serpents that appear in conjunction with Lady K'abel and the other Kaan women suggests that the influence of Teotihuacan continued to play an important role in the construction of their political and ritual activities well into the Late Classic period.

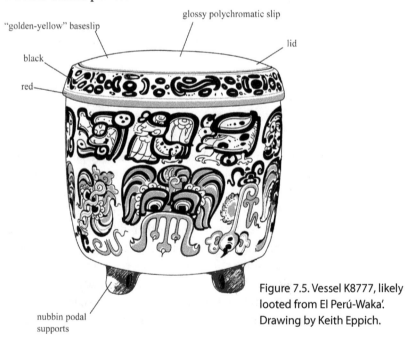

Figure 7.5. Vessel K8777, likely looted from El Perú-Waka'. Drawing by Keith Eppich.

Discussion

The different depictions of Vision Serpents and other supernatural creatures from Saknikte', Yaxchilan, and Waka' represent similar kinds of political and ritual power held by the women of the Kaan dynasty. That power demonstrates an ability to access ancestral and spiritual counsel in service to the political needs of their respective cities. The iconography we discuss here is a reiteration of political and ritual power held by Lady K'abel and other Kaan women in the region, and it signals their symbolic association with Teotihuacan.

The Serpent Vessel of Waka', La Corona Panel 6, and Yaxchilan Lintel 25 indicate the associations that Kaan women of the Late Classic had with martial activities. Martial associations are also apparent from the broader context of the Yaxchilan Lintel narratives, which convey conjuring as elemental in preparation for war. Specifically, at Yaxchilan, Lady K'abal Xook conjures the War Serpent of Teotihuacan, Waxaklajuun Ub'aah Kan, the god emerging from the open mouth of a Vision Serpent. The accompanying epigraphic inscription also describes her conjuring the "flint-shield" of another god, Aj K'ahk' O Chahk (Bassie-Sweet 2021). The women on La Corona Panel 6 arrive for their meeting on battle palanquins. For her part, Lady K'abel holds a mirror and shield on El Perú-Waka' Stela 34, and the Vision Serpent, depicted on the vessel described here, lies at her feet.

These three *ix kaloomte'* all engage Vision Serpents. The placement of the Serpent Vessel at the feet of K'abel conveys her role as war-priestess and supports our interpretation that Kaan women like her were not only charged with marriage diplomacy (Teufel 2001) but also played their part in the ritual preparations for war. The spirits they summon are combative and bear the martial icons of Teotihuacan (Bassie-Sweet 2021).

Conclusions

The Serpent Vessel's presence within the mortuary tableau of Lady K'abel speaks to her role as a ritual specialist who was able to rely on the Vision Serpent to connect her with ancestors and spirits from the spiritual realms through its transcendental nature. Additionally, the vessel's iconography ties Lady K'abel to other powerful women who similarly acted as marriage diplomats between the Kaan hegemony and its vassal polities. The presence of Vision Serpents, particularly their symbolic associations with Teotihuacan, in conjunction with three powerful women of the Kaan lineage, suggests that the political and ritual roles the women enacted included spiritual warfare. They employed symbols of the martial cult of Teotihuacan, war-priestesses of the Mesoamerican Rain God (Bassie-Sweet 2021). Lady K'abel's Serpent Vessel provides direct connections to broader iconographic and political programs throughout the region. By focusing on one element of the burial assemblage, we can situate the interred ruler within a larger regional narrative of Kaan influence in the Classic period Maya Lowlands and connect to even earlier influences of Teotihuacan on the Maya political system.

References

Bassie-Sweet, Karen
2021   *Maya Gods of War*. University Press of Colorado, Louisville.
Eppich, Keith
2017   Análisis cerámico, 2016: 1300 años de tradición cerámica de El Perú-Waka'. In *Proyecto Arqueológico El Perú-Waka': Informe no. 14, temporada 2016*, edited by Juan Carlos Pérez, pp. 288–385. Fundación de Investigación Arqueológica Waka', Guatemala City.
Freidel, David A., and Stanley P. Guenter
2003   Bearers of War and Creation. *Archaeology Magazine*, January 23. https://archive .archaeology.org/online/features/siteq2/.
Freidel, David A., and Linda Schele
1988   Kingship in the Late Preclassic Maya Lowlands: The Instruments and Places of Ritual Power. *American Anthropologist* 90(3):547–567.
Guenter, Stanley, and Nikolai Grube
n.d.   Comments on K8777. Maya Vase Database: An Archive of Rollout Photographs, Created by Justin Kerr. Accessed September 8, 2021. http://www.mayavase.com/ 8777/com8777.html.
Headrick, Annabeth
2003   Butterfly War at Teotihuacan. In *Ancient Mesoamerican Warfare*, edited by M. Kathryn Brown and Travis W. Stanton, pp. 140–170. Altamira Press, Walnut Creek.
Martin, Simon
2008   Wives and Daughters on the Dallas Altar. *Mesoweb*. https://www.mesoweb.com/ articles/martin/Wives&Daughters.pdf.
McDonald, J. Andrew, and Brian Stross
2012   Water Lily and Cosmic Serpent: Equivalent Conduits of the Maya Spirit Realm. *Journal of Ethnobiology* 32(1):74–107. https://doi.org/10.2993/0278-0771-32.1.74.
Miller, Mary Ellen, and Karl Taube
1997   *An Illustrated Dictionary of the Gods and Symbols of Ancient Mexico and the Maya*. Thames and Hudson, New York.
Navarro-Farr, Olivia C., Mary Kate Kelly, Michelle Rich, and Griselda Pérez Robles
2020   Expanding the Canon: Lady K'abel the *Ix Kaloomte'* and the Political Narratives of Classic Maya Queens. *Feminist Anthropology* 1(1):38–55. https://doi.org/10.1002/ fea2.12007.

Navarro-Farr, Olivia C., and Michelle E. Rich, editors
2014   *Archaeology at El Perú-Waka': Ancient Maya Performances of Ritual, Memory, and Power*. University of Arizona Press, Tucson.
Schele, Linda, and David A. Freidel
1992   *A Forest of Kings: The Untold Story of the Ancient Maya*. Quill/W. Morrow, New York.
Schele, Linda, and Mary Ellen Miller
1986   *The Blood of Kings: Dynasty and Ritual in Maya Art*. G. Braziller, New York, and Kimbell Art Museum, Fort Worth.
Schele, Linda, Mary Ellen Miller, Justin Kerr, Michael D. Coe, and Emily J. Sano
1992   *The Blood of Kings: Dynasty and Ritual in Maya Art*. Reprint edition. G Braziller, New York.
Stuart, David
2013   New Drawing of a La Corona Panel. Maya Decipherment, January 23. https://mayadecipherment.com/2013/01/23/new-drawing-of-a-la-corona-panel/.
Sugiyama, Saburo
1989   Iconographic Interpretation of the Temple of Quetzalcoatl at Teotihuacan. *Mexicon* 11(4):68–74.
Swenson, Edward
2015   The Archaeology of Ritual. *Annual Review of Anthropology* 44(1):329–345. https://doi.org/10.1146/annurev-anthro-102214-013838.
Taube, Karl
1986   The Teotihuacan Cave of Origin: The Iconography and Architecture of Emergence Mythology in Mesoamerica and the American Southwest. *Res: Anthropology and Aesthetics* 12:51–82.
2000   The Turquoise Hearth: Fire, Self-Sacrifice, and the Central Mexican Cult of War. In *Mesoamerica's Classic Heritage: From Teotihuacan to the Aztecs*, edited by David Carrasco, Lindsay Jones, and Scott Sessions, pp. 269–340. University Press of Colorado, Boulder.
2004   Flower Mountain: Concepts of Life, Beauty, and Paradise among the Classic Maya. *Res: Anthropology and Aesthetics* 45:69–98. https://doi.org/10.1086/RESv45n1ms20167622.
Teufel, Stephanie
2001   Marriage Diplomacy—Women at the Royal Court. In *Maya: Divine Kings of the Rain Forest*, edited by Nikolai Grube, pp. 172–173. Könemann, Cologne.
Wanyerka, Phil
1996   A Fresh Look at a Maya Masterpiece. *Cleveland Studies in the History of Art* 1:72–97.

8

Who Is the Pyramid?

The Maya Tombs of a Royal Ancestral Structure and the Personing of Architecture at El Perú-Waka'

MICHELLE RICH AND KEITH EPPICH

Structure O14-04 is one of two large pyramids that anchor the southeastern corner of the urban core of El Perú-Waka' (Figure 1.2). Both buildings are prominent features of the Mirador Group, a collection of structures that sprawl across a heavily modified, natural ridgeline. The elevation stands 38 meters higher than the nearest plaza, overlooking the city epicenter to the northwest. To the southeast, this overlook is even more pronounced. The ridgeline follows the edge of the karstic escarpment underlying the whole of the urban core. More than 80 vertical meters separate the Mirador Group from the escarpment's base. Moving south, the terrain sinks even further to the riverine floodplains of the Río San Juan and the perennial wetlands of the Río San Pedro Mártir. The ridgeline of the Mirador Group looms almost 100 meters above both rivers. The ancient Maya topped this natural feature with three significant structures. The most modest of these was a temple, Structure N14-12, flanked by two buildings. The other two are impressive pyramids, the aforementioned Structure O14-04 in the center, and Structure O14-02 to the east. These pyramids sit on a broad basal platform roughly 8 meters high, bringing their heights to 28 and 34 meters, respectively, which is a dizzying 150 meters above the two rivers. On a clear day, from the top of O14-04, one can discern the shadowy outlines of the Sierra Lacandon, some 80 kilometers to the southwest.

The Mirador Group was the focus of archaeological investigations for seven field seasons conducted between 2003 and 2016. During that time, Michelle Rich led teams that explored the smaller buildings on the western end of the group, situated atop a steep natural rise; the ritual structures at the base of that rise; Structure O14-04 itself; the platforms on which O14-04 and O14-02 sat; and the causeway connecting them (Rich 2011, 2012; Rich and Austin 2016; Rich, Freidel, and Matute 2011). Investigations at Structure O14-04 consisted of horizontal excavations to document surviving architecture as well as tunneling operations, during which three major funerary deposits were discovered and labeled Burials 24, 25, and 39. O14-04 was not just a prominent structure on an elevated landscape; it was the site of considerable ritual activity involving acts of interment and veneration for the individuals placed within these tombs.

Large, elaborate tombs are a highly visible aspect of Maya archaeology and have drawn considerable interest from both the scholarly community and the general public. These spaces, buried deep within pyramids and palaces, hold not only the earthly remains of Classic royalty but also the beautiful works of cultural and artistic significance that characterize the era. These works of art include carefully fashioned jades, carved shells, intricately flaked obsidian, and spectacular ceramic vessels among many other objects from the apex of Classic Maya art. That scores of such tombs remain undiscovered only adds to their allure.

Much of the scholarly literature about such tombs has tended to concentrate on two broad questions: *how* such tombs were incorporated into sacred architecture, and *why* the Maya buried their leaders with such pomp and ceremony (see D. Chase and A. Chase 1996; Fitzsimmons 2009; Houston, Newman, et al. 2015; Ruz Lhuillier 1965; Scherer 2015). Such studies have successfully constructed the "language" of royal funerary practices, rebuilding the historical narratives around individuals at the time of their death, and have even shown how their remains were placed within architectural programs in ways that reaffirmed the legitimacy and orthodoxy of Classic rulership. These remain laudable and impressive efforts, to be sure, yet there exists another, largely unasked question concerning those Maya entombed inside huge funerary structures, one that extends beyond political history or cultural functionality. The ancient Maya did not seem to approach these buildings either as concretized piles of collective memory or as instruments of political authority. The Classic Maya possessed a cosmology that included an animate landscape, with spirits contained within mountains and rivers and forests. This concept extended to architecture, where buildings possessed souls that needed to be succored and fed regularly (Freidel, Schele, and Parker 1993; Schele and Mathews 1999). To the ancient Maya, the placement of a royal ancestor within a structure involved more than the selection of a physical location to honor their memory; instead, it involved a transformation of that individual into something else entirely. Funerary acts transfigured the deceased, ensouling them within living structures of stone, plaster, and paint. To some extent, those entombed became the architecture that held their remains: the soul of the deceased became the spirit of the structure. A valid, largely unasked question of Maya funerary architecture is simply, *Who*. Who is the pyramid?

The focus of the current chapter is an exploration of the individuals entombed within Structure O14-04. This involves a review of the archaeology of the pyramid as well as its placement in the urban landscape. It includes a discussion of funerary contents and mortuary assemblages, with the goal of extrapolating the potential identities of the deceased, as best as that can be determined. The chapter concludes by examining the continuing role that these individuals may have played within the social and political fabric of Waka', even after they had ceased to be alive. This chapter takes the archaeology of Structure O14-04 and asks, "*Who?*" Who is the pyramid?

An Animate Landscape and the Personing of Architecture

In the study of human social systems, there is an awareness that agency extends beyond living persons. Humans attach meaning, memories, and motivations to nonhuman objects. People name mountains and rivers when simple letters or numbers would suffice. Indeed, spirited debates exist about the proper names for natural features. Is the highest peak in North America called Mount McKinley or Denali? Are people to refer to a prominent sandstone formation in central Australia as Ayers Rock or Uluru? Customarily, ships are named and even gendered. People interact with their environment in a social manner, even if the objects in their environment are not alive. By the attachment of identity and meaning, objects acquire agency; they become actors even though they may not be human, animate, or alive.

This idea of objects-as-actors, as actants, features prominently in the scholarship of Bruno Latour (1993, 2005), who noted that objects play a critical role in the human social collective. Humans form social ties with objects. They impose meanings upon them and inscribe symbols to communicate that meaning. A motorist interacts with an inanimate stop sign, obeying the symbol written upon it. "Objects," Latour writes (2005:79), "by the very nature of their connections with humans quickly shift from being mediators to being intermediaries, counting for one or nothing, no matter how internally complicated they might be." Objects influence the social actions around them and can play critical roles in those actions (see Owens 2007; Knappett 2002). After all, in a play on a stage in a theater, the lighting, the set, the costumes, the props, all these objects greatly influence, constrain, and enable performance (Mueller 2016). The objects do not need to be human. They do not need to be alive, even if they once were. Yorick's skull, after all, plays a critical role in *Hamlet*, even though the character died "three and twenty" years beforehand.

The concept of actants is especially relevant in a Maya context (see Vadala and Duffy 2020). It has long been noted that the modern Maya possess, and the ancient Maya possessed, a cosmology that includes an animate landscape in which active spirits live in forests and mountains, god-saints represent primordial forces of time and nature, and buildings hold souls of their own (Henderson and Woodfill in press; Woodfill and Henderson in press a, in press b). Akin to Latour, David Freidel, Linda Schele, and Joy Parker (1995) write extensively on the subject, describing how the modern Maya interact with this animate, ensouled landscape and then identifying parallels to these ritual acts in the Classic past. To the Maya, there exists an Earth Lord under the mountain, *santos* in the Church idols, and ritual specialists capable of speaking with them. Freidel, Schele, and Parker explain:

> Beginnings were important because of the way the Maya thought of the material world. They believed that places and things made by the gods during Creation were imbued with sacred force and an inner soul from the beginning of time. In contrast, places, buildings, and objects made by human beings had to have their inner souls, their *ch'ulel*, put in them during dedication ceremonies. As long as people used these objects, this power was safe, even though it grew through use. But when an object was no longer used, this living force could become dangerous. (1993:254)

Thus, objects in the natural world already possess active souls, but objects created by humans need to be gifted their own souls. This realization came from decades of ethnographic study of the living Maya, during which anthropologists documented the careful ensoulment of new construction and the periodic renewal of old. New homeowners, before occupying their houses, make small sacrifices in the presence of a shaman, giving the house food and drink, welcoming a propitious and friendly spirit into the home (Vogt 1969, 1970, 1976; see also Bunzel 1952; Christenson 2001, 2010; Tedlock 1997).

Linda Schele and Peter Mathews (1999) actively pursued this idea in their study of the royal and ritual architecture of the Classic cities, identifying dedicatory offerings found inside the monumental architecture as the remains of ensouling ceremonies (see also McAnany and Plank 2001). They developed this argument to explain the pageantry and imagery of the tombs, noting that the funeral ceremonies were not simply rituals of interment and remembrance. Such ceremonies involved the transfiguration of the dead, not only mourning their passing but also celebrating their rebirth, sometimes as flowery, symbolic trees hovering over the burial sites. The body lay in the earth, but the spirit remained. The Maya even constructed small passages, psychoducts, leading from the tomb to the outside world, thus allowing for continued communication with the transformed soul. The funerary rites transformed the deceased into a "living ancestor," their spirit contained in the structure holding their bones (see McAnany 1995, 1998; Stuart 1998).

The state of the newly transformed ancestor is visually depicted on one of the great artworks from the Classic period. The Dazzler Vase, a tripod cylinder recovered from deep inside the Copan Acropolis, bears an image of the deceased king of Copan, K'inich Yax K'uk' Mo'. The face of the king stares out from the structure that holds his tomb (Bell et al. 2003; see also Reents-Budet et al. 2004). The dead king appears to be wearing the funerary pyramid as his own body, and the structure holds his spiritual essence, which could be summoned through rituals of fire and smoke (Taube 2004; Fitzsimmons 2009:133). The Dazzler Vase leaves no doubt as to who looks out from the building holding the earthly remains of K'inich Yax K'uk' Mo'. It is the soul of the great king himself.

Returning to Waka', there remains the open question to be addressed here: Who is looking out from Structure O14-04?

The Mirador Group and Structure O14-04

At least six structures compose the ritual precinct of the Mirador (Figure 8.1). First, there are the two large pyramids, O14-04 and O14-02, situated on an extensive 8-meter-high basal platform connected by a broad causeway. Both pyramids are oriented toward specific locations inside the city. To the west lies a small group of buildings located on an artificially modified natural rise; these are a temple structure, N14-12, with two flanking buildings, Structures N14-13 and O14-07. Stelae are associated with all three locales: Stela 3 stands in the western group, Stela 2 is in front of O14-02, and Stela 1 is associated with Structure O14-04. A smaller building, O14-06, is in a plaza area between the basal platform of the pyramids and the natural rise of the western group. A number of small structures surround the base of the Mirador, including P13-05 to the north, a masonry structure built across a subterranean chamber. Excavations in and around N14-12 revealed that this western group was the locus of sustained ritual activity for the whole of the city's duration, as evidenced by offerings dating from the Late Preclassic to the Terminal Classic periods, including large numbers of broken censers (Rich 2011).

The major focus of investigations on the Mirador was, however, Structure O14-04. It is the second largest pyramid at Waka', surpassed only by the un-

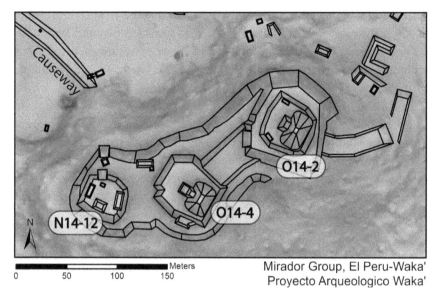

Mirador Group, El Peru-Waka'
Proyecto Arqueologico Waka'

Figure 8.1. The ritual precinct of the Mirador Group. Map by Damien Marken, courtesy of Proyecto Arqueológico Waka'.

excavated O14-02. Structure O14-04 is a composite pyramid comprising a frontal platform, the *adosada*, abutting the western face of the large, terraced pyramid. The *adosada* supports a shrine room, and at the summit of the pyramid are the ruins of another masonry shrine. The *adosada* is approximately 4-meters high, with the terraced pyramid behind it standing 12-meters high. The primary axis of O14-04 orients 20 degrees north of west—approximately W 290 degrees to E 110 degrees.

Excavations in, around, and across the pyramid revealed a complex and long history of construction, reconstruction, modification, and usage over at least nine centuries (see Rich 2011; Rich and Matute 2014). The structure possesses sloping talud-style walls adjacent to irregular staircases leading up to the basal platform. Only portions of architectural features remain intact, including a two- to three-course basal molding across the entirety of the excavated exterior, with only three to five courses of carved limestone blocks preserved above the intact molding. Based on the position of this wall in relation to the first terrace, it is estimated that a total of three terraces once led to the summit. Aspects of the architectural program speak to the attention lavished on this structure. For example, the base of the pyramid is curved; large vault stones found in the rubble indicate the presence of huge vaults; excavations along the front of the *adosada* revealed a poorly preserved staircase and cornering walls with several inset-outset elements that created a once-elaborate façade; and a tenoned stone head was recovered from the architectural rubble north of the *adosada*. O14-04 was not a smooth-sided pyramid leading to a single summit but rather a complex and ornate structure encrusted with sculpture, curved walls, vaulted chambers, offset staircases, and multiple shrine areas.

Fragments recovered in the architectural collapse in both the *adosada* and the summit shrines indicate they each supported a decorative program executed in stucco. The *adosada* shrine was partially demolished, likely following the reentry into Burial 39 described below. After this reentry, the portion of the shrine directly above the tomb chamber was never refloored, and the shrine room was filled with matrix. This suggests an intentional act, sealing off this room from any further use. A stucco sculptural head depicting Teotihuacan-style imagery was recovered just inside the doorjamb of the *adosada* shrine, lying cockeyed slightly above the level of the final floor. It portrays a male face sporting tasseled warrior goggles and a nose pendant (compare García-Des Lauriers 2017; Headrick 2007).

Excavation in three targeted locations on the *adosada* identified the shrine room atop it, a lateral stair bounded by short balustrades on its northern face, and the remnants of a poorly preserved outset stair at its front. Many of these areas exhibited ashy matrixes at the base of the collapse layer, above the floors or stairs that constitute the last architectural phase of Structure O14-04. So, in addition to the architectural and decorative complexity of O14-04, the pyramid would have had multiple small fires across its surface and thin columns of smoke rising into the sky. This evidence of fire seems indicative of efforts to summon and communicate with honored ancestors, just as described for Yax K'uk' Mo' above (Taube 2004). It is no surprise, then, that excavations into the *adosada* resulted in the discovery of three royal interments.

The remains of a staircase leading from the *adosada* to the summit of O14-04 were also recorded (Rich 2011; Rich and Matute 2014). Of the eleven stair treads identified, the first three appeared as lateral stairs at the southeastern edge of the *adosada* shrine. The remaining treads extended across the face of the pyramid, ascending to the summit platform. Originally, the first three identified treads likely also extended across the entire front face of the pyramid, but it seems the *adosada* shrine—as a later addition to the building—was constructed on top of those original stairs.

The fragmentary remains of Stela 1 were scattered in front of O14-04. It is a badly eroded monument bearing an image of a standing king with a jaguar-head in his headdress. No name glyph survives to be read on Stela 1, and the identity of the royal figure remains unknown, although a connection with Burial 39 is likely, given that it records a date of 657 (Guenter 2014; see Kelly,

Freidel, and Navarro-Farr, this volume). The area around Stela 1 was disturbed and the stela fragments were scattered around a pit, yet it was difficult to ascertain if this was ancient or modern, natural or human-caused destruction. In 2004, team members Hugo Martínez and Efraín Peralta reassembled as much of the stela as possible, laying it out horizontally to the east of the ground disturbance. It is tantalizing to imagine that had Stela 1 been intact, we may have been able to document the material remains of ritual activity as we did at Stela 3, adjacent to the small temple N14-12. There we identified an altar of fitted stone blocks on the south side of the stela as well as numerous offerings on and around the altar, including censer fragments, candeleros, concentrations of ceramic sherds, burned vessels, beads, greenstones, and a small chert eccentric. The disturbed context of Stela 1 notwithstanding, the story revealed at O14-04 seems to be consistent with acts of ancestor veneration clearly related to the six individuals documented inside the three mortuary contexts encountered in the *adosada*.

Burial 25

Burial 25 was the second interment encountered in the excavations at O14-04, yet it is likely the earliest of the three. Both radiometric and ceramic analysis propose a date for the burial between 250 and 350 CE. It is the least ornate of the three tombs in terms of form, funerary architecture, and mortuary assemblage. It contained the remains of an adult female of advanced age interred with very few grave goods.

The burial consists of a cist measuring 1.7 meters on the north–south axis and 0.55 meters on the east–west axis (Figure 8.2; see also Patterson, this volume). It is oriented slightly northeast–southwest, perpendicular to the primary axis of the pyramid. The floor of the cist is limestone ballast, and two intact stones in the southern portion of the chamber suggest a capping feature. Construction fill and burnt limestone rocks had collapsed on top of the burial. The limestones were smoke-blackened, indicating significant burning in or on the cist at the time of interment. The Maya placed the individual in the cist and in an extended supine position with the head to the north, oriented approximately 23 degrees east of north. Osteological analysis indicated a female of advanced age, with the histomorphology estimating an age between 68 and 73 years (see Tiesler et al. 2010). She possessed healed fractures on her left ribs as well as evidence of degenerative joint disease on her knees, ankles, feet, left hip, left shoulder, wrists, hands, rib, sternum, and the entire length of her spinal column (Piehl 2010; Rich 2011). The cranial fragments were covered in specular hematite, a dark red iron oxide, and a greenstone

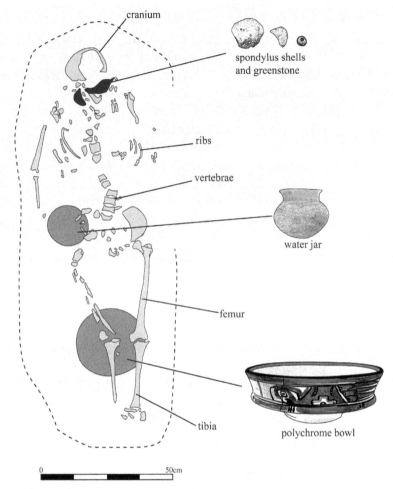

Figure 8.2. Burial 25 with grave goods. Drawing by Michelle Rich and Jennifer Piehl, courtesy of Proyecto Arqueológico Waka'.

bead was found near the area of her mouth. A *Spondylus* shell was associated with the cranium, possibly as part of a diadem or other piece of jewelry. The Maya buried her with two ceramic vessels, a striated water jar at her hip and a large macaw-emblazoned polychrome bowl below her knees.

Together, these materials argue for an individual of some prominence. Hematite occurs often with elaborate Maya burials and is thought to be associated with blood and spirit-force, *k'uhul*, linked to acts of death and rebirth (Fitzsimmons 2009:82–83; see also Houston, Stuart, and Taube 2006; Quintana et al. 2014). *Spondylus* shell is also commonly found in elite burials as well as in caches; it is linked to currency, royalty, shamanism, and a watery underworld (Freidel, Reese-Taylor, et al. 2002). The placement of a greenstone bead in the mouth is the quintessential example of the physical representation of precious breath (Coe 1988; Taube 2005). This can "mark some refined quality of royal and godly breath or allude to exalted status" (Houston, Stuart, and Taube 2006:142). Separately, none of these items would indicate a position at the top of ancient Maya society. Collectively, and combined with her interment inside the great pyramid, these artifacts indicate a very high status for the Burial 25 individual. Almost certainly, this was a royal woman.

Who was this woman? There is no text contained within the interment, so there is no known name. She was a woman of advanced age and of royal status, a queen or perhaps a queen mother, most likely from the early to midfourth century. At the time, Waka' was a new city, likely only a few generations removed from its Early Classic founding. She postdates one of the founder-kings discovered in Burial 81 by less than a century (see Pérez Robles and Pérez, et al., this volume). Indeed, given her advanced age, she might have known him. She was placed into the foundation of the *adosada* in a ceremony that celebrated her precious breath. She was coated with hematite, linked to rituals of rebirth, and she was covered with fire and smoke, part of her own rite of funerary transfiguration. Although unnamed, she could have been an elderly, honored, and much-respected founder-queen, mother to a subsequent line of kings, perhaps, and a shaman and ritual practitioner in her own right, possibly. In the last years of her life, her joints hurt, and her back was stiff, but she likely had a bright mind and a sharp wit, sharp enough to warrant a piece of greenstone on her tongue.

Burial 24

Burial 24 was the first interment to be discovered during the *adosada* excavations. It falls, chronologically, just after Burial 25 and centuries before Burial 39. Burial 24 was a small, intact tomb containing the remains of two young women, one of whom was pregnant, and an impressive array of mortuary offerings of high-quality ceramic vessels.

The tomb itself is located on the centerline of the *adosada*, at the base of stairs that represent earlier architecture encased within the bulk of later construction (Rich 2011; Rich and Matute 2014). The tomb was buried 4.5 meters below the current ruin of the *adosada* shrine. Indeed, the stratigraphic data surrounding the tomb suggest that the majority of the *adosada* was constructed on top, likely soon after the interment. The chamber had been intrusively inserted through the preexisting plaza floor and is partially cut into bedrock. The roughly rectangular chamber measures 2.6–2.7 meters long and 0.8–0.9 meters wide with a height of 1.2–1.4 meters (Figure 8.3). Flat capstones top

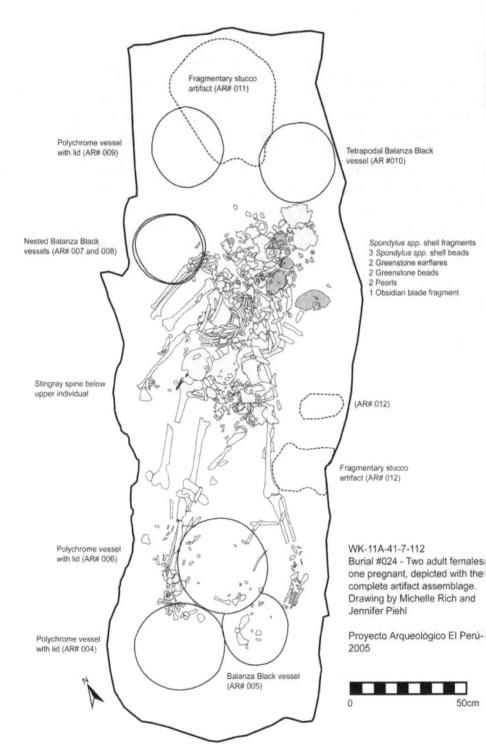

Figure 8.3. Burial 24 with grave goods. Drawing by Michelle Rich and Jennifer Piehl, courtesy of Proyecto Arqueológico Waka'.

a vault composed of large, unworked stones, predominantly limestones and large chert cobbles. The vault rests atop walls constructed of a mix of rough-cut stone and unshaped limestone boulders. The walls and vault were faced with mud, and the vaulted ceiling angled downward toward the northern end of the chamber. The chamber is oriented northeast–southwest, like Burial 25, perpendicular to the primary axis of the pyramid.

The tomb contained the remains of two females and an unborn fetus. The two females were stacked back-to-back in an extended position with their heads lying at the northern end of the chamber. The lower individual lay in the prone position and was pregnant at the time of death. Her fetus was approximately 5 to 6 months gestational age, indicating she was well into her second trimester of pregnancy. The upper individual lay atop the lower in a supine position. Both females were young adults, between the ages of 25 and 35 and show little evidence of skeletal pathology. Strontium analysis conducted on the dental enamel of the upper individual (0.707843) proved consistent with the range value of the local area (0.707807–0.707874). The upper individual possessed a degree of linear enamel hypoplasia, indicating an unknown insult to the individual's health around the age of three (Piehl 2010; Rich 2011). The lower individual possessed two fused lumbar vertebrae, suggesting possible ankylosing spondylitis. This is a rare condition, but one that has been documented among the elite population of Calakmul, where Vera Tiesler (2020) associated it with considerable endogamy among the urban elites.

The Maya adorned these women with modest but fine jewelry. Large *Spondylus* fragments and two greenstone earspools were recovered from around the crania. Two pearls, two additional greenstone beads, and three *Spondylus* beads were documented from the cranial and shoulder areas, all that remains of their funerary garb. Additionally, the tomb contained seven very fine, large, and well-preserved ceramic vessels representing the artistic height of the city's Early Classic potting tradition (Figure 8.4). Instrumental neutron activation analysis (INAA) indicated that the vessels were locally manufactured from similar paste recipes, suggesting that they were made by local potters sharing similar clay resources (Rich 2011; see Reents-Budet, Bishop, et al. 2011). Among the vessels are three brilliant and lustrous polychromes, portraying a complex mix of saurian and avian imagery, including a depiction of the Principal Bird Deity, the avian manifestation of the Creator God Itzamnaaj (Harrison-Buck 2015; Taube 1992). The four monochrome vessels bear designs incised into their dark, glossy slips: lizards; birds; and a repeated mat design, a symbol associated with royalty. One of the vessels held the remains of bobwhite quails, a known food resource. The vessels possess little to no use-wear, suggesting that most were crafted specifically for their inclusion

Figure 8.4. Ceramic vessels of Burial 24. Drawing by Keith Eppich, courtesy of PAW.

within the tomb and most likely contained sumptuous culinary offerings constituting a funeral feast to accompany the two young women. The form and iconography of the vessels are strongly indicative of the late fourth century, a date confirmed by radiometric dating.

The Maya placed additional artifacts in the tomb, including three painted organic objects composed of thin applications of stucco-paint over an organic substrate, such as gourds or wooden vessels. Over time, the perishable substrate decomposed, leaving a chaotic, jumbled mass of stucco flakes in the place of a finely crafted and painted object. One appears to have been a large plate with painted polychromatic designs of green, black, white, and three shades of pink. A second object exhibited polychrome painting and what appears to have been stucco modeled into multiple human faces painted green, as if to mimic jadeite. The third object seems likely to have been a stucco-painted lid paired to the object with the stucco faces.

Who were these women? Like Burial 25, there are no texts and hence, no names. The high-quality artifacts, specifically the ceramics, as well as their location in O14-04's *adosada* link the women to the city's royal elites. These were royal women, likely the spouses or daughters of royals. They lived in the late fourth century and died somewhere between 380 and 400 CE. They may have even been alive for the funeral of the potential founder-queen of Burial 25. They may have been her grandchildren, or her grandchildren's spouses. How did they die? There is no evidence of perimortem trauma on these well-preserved skeletal remains. One hypothesis is that the two young women were sacrificial offerings associated with a yet undiscovered interment deeper within the pyramid, an act potentially related to the Teotihuacan *entrada* (see Freidel, Escobedo, et al. 2007). Another hypothesis is simple tragedy: two royal women carried away by sickness, accident, or happenstance. Sacrifice or tragedy, we do not currently have further clarity. Regardless, the funeral ritual would have involved the entire royal court laying these women to rest, placing within the pyramid two young wives, or perhaps adored granddaughters. This may have even dictated the location of the tomb, near the burial of an aged and wise founder-queen, her presence easing the two women's own funerary transfigurations.

Burial 39

Burial 39 is the third interment discovered during the excavation of O14-04. It is the largest and most impressive tomb yet documented at Waka' and, indeed, remains one of the richest and most unique tombs ever recorded in the Classic Lowlands. The individual in this tomb was interred centuries after the previous two burials, and it is the only burial in the Mirador Group linked to a precise calendar date. The tomb chamber is intrusive into the core of the *adosada* and was later the focus of a dramatic reentry event in the late eighth century. It held the remains of two individuals, an elderly seventh-century ruler and a child sacrifice offered during the reentry event.

Burial 39 was placed deep within the *adosada*, directly beneath the shrine superstructure. The chamber rests atop earlier, red-painted stuccoed stair treads—part of the same staircase for which Burial 24 marked the base. It is possible that these stairs represent the front face of the main pyramid as it would have appeared prior to the construction episode in which the *adosada* was appended to it. If this is the case, these treads should be contiguous with those leading to the top of the pyramid. The tomb was intrusively inset into the *adosada*'s Early Classic construction and fashioned of cut stone blocks; it was vaulted and measured 3.3 meters north–south and 1.7 meters east–west (Figure 8.5). Like the previous two burials discussed, the chamber is oriented perpendicular to the primary axis of O14-04. It contains a bench that abuts the east wall of the chamber, measuring 1.1 to 1.2 meters wide. To the west, the bench borders a 30- to 40-centimeter-wide alley. During the reentry, the Maya cut through the floor of the shrine room and excavated through the construction fill to enter the tomb through its vaulted roof. Considerable evidence of burning and several sacrifices appear to be associated with this reentry activity. The sacrificial offerings included a seven-year-old child, laid out on top of the vessels in the northern portion of the alley, as well as several juvenile animals: a gray fox located on the northeast corner and an opossum positioned above the ceramic vessels in the alley area. The primary interment's remains were covered with carefully laid flat stones, likely reused from the partially dismantled roof vault. The large area of plaster floor that was removed to facilitate reentry was never repaired, nor was the tomb's roof restored. Indeed, the western side of the vault and the capstones appear to have been intentionally collapsed into the chamber, after which the Maya chose to infill the entire chamber with matrix and large pieces of stucco sculpture, faunal bone, chert, obsidian tools, obsidian debitage, broken ceramics, and partial vessels. Some of these ceramics hail from the late eighth century or early ninth century, corresponding with the later years of the calibrated AMS date of 670–880 CE from a carbon sample collected within the tomb fill. Finally, then, the *adosada* shrine room was also infilled, in an act akin to ritual termination, sealing it off from further use.

The primary interment in Burial 39 was an older adult laid in an extended supine position on the bench with the cranium again oriented to the north. Six distal phalanges from a jaguar were discovered on the bench, suggesting

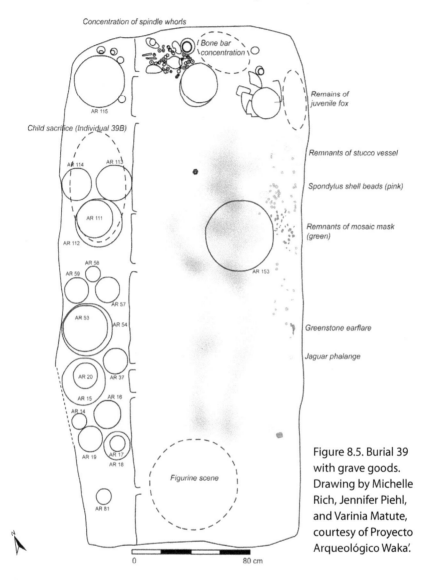

Concentration of spindle whorls

Bone bar concentration

Remains of juvenile fox

AR 115

Child sacrifice (Individual 39B)

Remnants of stucco vessel

AR 114   AR 113

Spondylus shell beads (pink)

AR 111

Remnants of mosaic mask (green)

AR 112

AR 58

AR 59

AR 57

AR 153

AR 53   AR 54

Greenstone earflare

AR 20   AR 37

Jaguar phalange

AR 15   AR 16

AR 14

AR 19   AR 17

AR 18

Figurine scene

AR 81

Figure 8.5. Burial 39 with grave goods. Drawing by Michelle Rich, Jennifer Piehl, and Varinia Matute, courtesy of Proyecto Arqueológico Waka'.

0   80 cm

that the individual was laid on top of, or covered by, a jaguar pelt. The skeletal remains were poorly preserved, and the sex was indeterminate. The individual was wrapped in a shroud of composite materials with a plain-woven textile on the interior and a hard leathery exterior layer. Only fragments of this textile survived, as did evidence of the reddish-pink pigments the Maya used to paint it. The paint even stained the skeletal remains, giving the fragmented bones a reddish tint. The individual possessed several bone pathologies, including minor infections in the legs, arms, and left ribs, indicating a susceptibility to infection (Piehl 2009; Rich 2011). Advanced age is inferred from the degree of degenerative joint disease present in the spinal column and in the right knee as well as in the ankles and feet. Vertebrae in all observed regions of the spinal column were affected. The osteology indicates a general gracility of muscle attachments, indicating limited activity during life, as may be expected for an individual of royal status and/or someone with chronic health threats. The right shoulder shows wear and slight degeneration at the articular margin of the scapular glenoid, a potential indicator of right-handedness.

Interestingly, strontium isotope analysis of dental enamel revealed that this individual did not appear to have spent their childhood at Waka'. The Burial 39 individual's strontium value of 0.707670 was outside of the local range of 0.707807–0.707874. This may indicate a number of different locations where the individual spent their adolescence, with Calakmul, Caracol, or Bonampak being possibilities. Given the politics of the late sixth century, Calakmul is the most likely of the three (see Kelly, Freidel, and Navarro-Farr, this volume).

Biological sex was indeterminate due to the poor condition of the skeletal remains. Discussion of the individual's sex has persisted as an open topic for some time. The general gracility of the extant bones seems to argue for a biological female, but this may also be consistent with a male possessing chronic illnesses. Burial 39 possesses an elaborate narrative figurine scene, discussed below, that portrays the resurrection of a kneeling male figure. Also among the mortuary assemblage are spindle whorls, bone needles and sticks, and other objects that suggest a weaving kit, which are more typically linked to women. The date of the interment is associated with the date on Stela 1, whose distressed surface seems to portray a male figure. Ultimately, the physical and circumstantial evidence is inconclusive—neither lends clarity to the biological sex of the individual, who could be either a king or a queen.

The individual's regal station, however, is undisputed. Royal status is apparent in the extremely large quantity of artifacts found on both the bench and in the alley, including ceramic vessels; three sets of greenstone ear flares; greenstone beads, plaques, and a pendant of a human figure carved in low relief found on the chest area under an inverted plate; the tesserae that formed the remains of a miniature greenstone mosaic mask; a number of painted organic objects; nine stingray spines clustered together underneath the aforementioned plate; an elaborate set of bone needles and sticks carved with images of faces, flowers, cacao pods, and hands; a number of carved *Spondylus* shell beads and other worked bivalve shells; an eroded square pyrite mirror; four miniature carved mosaic jewels, two of which portray monkey scribes, as well as a number of small carved shell flowers, stars, and intricately carved animals; and all this in addition to a royal jewel, a serpentine Olmec figure (Rich, Freidel, and Matute 2010; Rich 2011). This figure alone is sufficient to

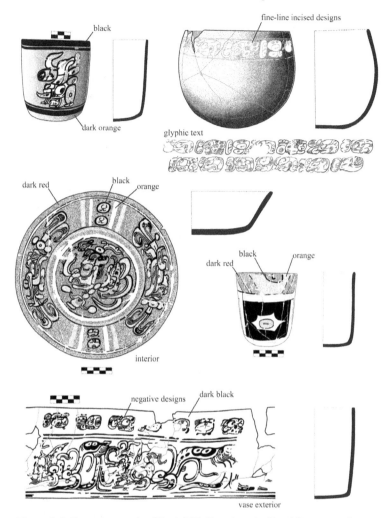

Figure 8.6. Ceramic vessels of Burial 39. Drawings by René Ozaeta and
Keith Eppich, courtesy of Proyecto Arqueológico Waka'.

establish a royal status for the individual. It is an ancient, Olmec-style heirloom, likely curated for centuries. The figurine depicts a young dancing boy,
wearing a deity mask and a shark-fin headdress. The mask holds the crown
of the Maize God and was itself a symbol of resurrection (Rich, Freidel, and
Matute 2010; Rich 2018).

Thirty-three whole and reconstructible vessels were documented from
the tomb, nine from the funerary bench and the remainder from the alley.
Many of the vessels were highly fragmented, and a team led by Griselda Pérez
Robles dedicated years to their careful reconstruction (Figure 8.6). They represent some of the finest vessels produced in the city's seventh-century ce-

ramic tradition, including multislipped polychromes with dazzling colors, intricately carved fine-line designs, and brilliant calligraphic iconography and hieroglyphs. The vessels are consistent with seventh-century ceramics documented elsewhere in the city. This includes examples of the city's own palace-school tradition of Miel Dorada vessels, where royally sponsored potters created a glossy and highly lustrous golden-honey baseslip (see Reents-Budet, Ball, et al. 1994). Three vessels, however, originate outside of the local ceramic traditions. These are of a type termed Chimbote Cream Polychrome, a ceramic associated with the central, southern, and western Yucatan (Ball 1977:77–78). This almost certainly signifies a connection to the Kaanul areas to the north. Few, if any, of the vessels possess use-wear on their interior or exterior surfaces, indicating that they were crafted specifically for the mortuary assemblage. The vessels are strikingly similar, if not identical, to another collection of funerary ceramics recovered from Burial 38, a tomb that seems, in many ways, to be a small-scale reproduction of Burial 39 (Rich and Eppich 2020). Again, the vessels date to the early to mid-seventh century. Taken together with the erection of Stela 1, this suggests that the stela and the burial are closely related. Thus, the most likely date for Burial 39 is on, or around, the Stela 1 date of 657 CE.

The most striking find of Burial 39 is the remarkable narrative figurine scene, already the subject of intense scholarship and featured in a number of museum exhibitions (Freidel and Rich 2017, 2021; Freidel, Rich, and Reilly 2010; Rich 2017; Rich and Freidel 2010; Rich, Sears, et al. 2019; see also Finamore and Houston 2010). The scene consists of 24 ceramic figurines, representing a "snapshot" of an ancient Maya royal court. The Maya placed it on the southwest corner of the bench, at the feet of the interred individual, purposefully arranging the figurines in a narrative scene comprising two concentric circles. The outer circle represented members of the royal court, including a king, queen, ballplayer, scribes, and female attendants. They share this circle with a kneeling king, who is attached to the same ceramic base as an anthropomorphic deer. The inner circle consisted of figurines of various dwarfs, a smoke-blackened frog figurine, a miniature vessel, and a seated figure with a hollow back containing a hematite-based substance. Each figurine is unique. Michelle Rich and David Freidel (2010:286) describe the scene as follows:

> This ritual tableau depicts the transformation by supernatural characters of a dead Maya king into a healed and reborn spirit. Members of the royal court, arranged in a circle surrounding the performance, witness the event. A portly male, arms crossed in the distinctive supplicant pose, represents the deceased king preparing for resurrection. An

anthropomorphic deer leans over him with "arms" outstretched and mouth open in chant or prayer . . . a frog, a hunchback scribe, and four dwarfs hold court with the shaman at the center of the tableau.

The figurine scene is one of funereal ritual, the transfiguration of a dead king into a new form, a rebirth following interment and transformation. It is a striking representation, executed in three dimensions, following the language of mortuary acts and the means by which the dead king becomes an honored ancestor. To some extent, much like Yax K'uk' Mo', the kneeling figurine ruler becomes the spirit in the pyramid. Examination via INAA revealed another remarkable aspect of the scene: the clay used to produce these figurines was consistent with clay recipes from Calakmul, another piece of evidence linking this individual to the capital of the Kaan polity (see Rich, Sears, et al. 2019).

Who was this person? Unlike the previous interments, Burial 39 possesses an embarrassment of glyphic texts. The funerary ceramics yield seven different texts and provide three different names. As translated by Stanley Guenter, one name is Bahlam Tz'am, the same name carried by a later eighth-century ruler of Waka'. Another vessel bears the partially preserved name "Bahlam . . . ," which may yet be another reference to Bahlam Tz'am. A third vessel bears the long name of a lord that incorporates the Early Classic version of the Waka' emblem glyph. Two others carry the untitled name Ak'ab Bahlam, a name otherwise unknown from the city's epigraphic record (Guenter 2014; Rich 2011). All, some, or none of these might be the name of the Burial 39 individual. By contrast, we have lines of evidence providing the names of some of the people who may have actually buried this individual.

Stela 1 was almost certainly raised by the most powerful monarchs of Waka', K'inich Bahlam II and the *ix kaloomte'* Lady K'abel (see Guenter 2014; Kelly, Freidel and Navarro-Farr, this volume). In fact, Navarro-Farr, Kelly, and colleagues (2020) built a convincing argument that the figurine scene portrays both K'inich Bahlam II and Lady K'abel. They are the monarchs witnessing the ritual transformation of the Burial 39 individual. Lady K'abel is known to have been a foreigner, one of the Snake queens from Calakmul (Navarro-Farr, Kelly, et al. 2020; see also Teufel 2008). Hence, the kneeling king represented in the scene is the likely predecessor and probable parent of K'inich Bahlam II. This would explain the political need for such a grand royal funeral: a young king and a queen boldly proclaiming their grasp on the city. This display seems especially true if the Burial 39 individual, potentially K'inich Bahlam's mother or father, was also foreign to Waka' or had spent an extended adolescence at Calakmul.

If this individual's death and funeral can be tied to 657, and if they were of advanced age, this would place their birth somewhere around 580. This person was either not a native of Waka' or had spent their formative years away from Waka', only arriving in the middle of the city's epigraphic hiatus, during a troubled sixth century (Freidel, Escobedo, et al. 2007; Guenter 2014; Kelly, Freidel, and Navarro-Farr, this volume). Evidence hints at a northern linkage, likely Calakmul again, as indicated by the strontium isotope analysis of the teeth and the quantity of Calakmul-style ceramics in the tomb. The individual may have even been a "stranger-king," an outside ruler invited or imposed on local Maya polities. Such rulers are well documented in Maya political history (A. Chase and D. Chase 2020; Marcus 2020; Price et al. 2014). Yet, the individual seems to have been sickly, plagued by infections and unused to, or incapable of, strenuous physical labor. Yet, if they were a ruler of Waka', they lived long enough to elevate the wealth and power of the city and to transfer such wealth and power to their successor and probable son. By that time, in the mid-seventh century, Waka' was sufficiently stable and wealthy to allow K'inich Bahlam to provide a lavish funeral honoring this individual and to supply the tomb with one of the finest mortuary assemblages in the Maya realm. In fact, the intrusive placement of this tomb may also speak to a certain degree of political insecurity and the need to firmly establish the right to rule. To a family that appears to largely hail from outside Waka', there is no better way to anchor itself to the city than to do so physically, by grafting their ancestor onto Structure O14-04 and ritually, through funerary transformation, ensouling their parent into one of the oldest and grandest pyramids of Waka'. And, inside that great structure, this ruler would not be alone.

Conclusion: A Plurality of Who

Within the architectural mass of Structure O14-04, there existed a plurality of *who*. There was no single ancestor looking out from the heights of the pyramid, but several. If the reconstructions here are accurate, there was an aged founder-queen from the very beginning of the royal dynasty. There were a pair of young, royal women, one with an unborn child, and both bearing the sadness of their demise, either in sacrifice or in tragedy. There was an elderly, possibly sickly ruler who bequeathed to their son a rich and powerful city. There was also a young child, sacrificed, with a fox and an opossum nearby, when the royal tomb was reentered. There may be others as well, interments and tombs buried deep within this massive building. Modern excavations can reach only so far and penetrated only the *adosada*, not the terraced pyramid beyond. The tunnels grew too unstable, the diggings too dangerous, and the excavations rapidly exceeded the modest budgets of such archaeological projects.

These individuals ensouled the structure; they became the persons in the architecture, at least from what can be understood from the Classic perspective. They remained actors on the social and political stage of Waka', even though they were no longer alive. They were living people, who died and then, transformed through funerary ritual, became honored ancestors inside the architecture. They were objects-as-actors, precisely as described by Freidel, Schele, and Parker (1993). This is portrayed perfectly in recent scholarship from Karen Bassie-Sweet (2021). She described a bench from Palenque's Temple XXI that portrays a ritual taking place between young lords, in which a grandfather, Pakal the Great, hands a ritual bloodletter to his grandson. However, as the date on the monument indicates, this ritual took place twenty-six years *after* the death of Pakal. This is even mirrored in an eroded monument from Waka'. Cast in front of the royal palace, El Perú-Waka' Altar 6 bears an image of K'inich Bahlam II, likely the same ruler from the figurine scene, sitting in the "heart of the turtle," a reference to his own buried tomb (Freidel, Schele, and Parker 1993:Figure 4.2). Carved almost a century after his death, K'inich Bahlam sits cross-legged, his right arm outstretched in offering. He is portrayed as neither a skull nor a pile of bones but as a living, entombed ruler, still active within the turtle shell of the earth's surface.

Understanding this "personing" of architecture allows for examinations of some of the more enigmatic aspects of Classic Maya monumental architecture at Waka'. For example, the orientation of structures and their place on a settled and crowded landscape appears patterned (Figure 8.7). From the Mirador, the western shrine group, centered on Structure N14-12, faces 18–20 degrees east of true north, the well-known orientation of Maya North (Aveni and Hartung 1986). This western group holds no burials at all and, based on its "rustic" architecture and the domestic quality of the ceramics in the votive deposits there, seems to have been a shrine used by the common people of the ancient city. It lies beside, but independent of, the great pyramids to its east. In contrast, Structure O14-04 faces to the north and west, toward M13-12 in the Chok Group, where the Maya placed Burial 38, a contemporaneous tomb likely mimicking Burial 39 (Rich and Eppich 2020). Beyond that lays Structure M13-1 and, even farther beyond, the royal palace. The unexcavated Structure O14-02 orients directly to a very prominent building, Structure M13-1, in which Burial 61, the tomb of Lady K'abel, was discovered (Navarro-Farr, Pérez Robles, et al. 2021; Navarro-Farr, Pérez, and Pérez Robles, this volume). Beyond M13-1 is, again, the direct center of the Waka' and the royal palace beyond that. This points to a tradition of contemporaneous, paired royal tombs at Waka'. Burial 39 is oriented to Burial 38. The tomb of Burial 37 in Structure M12-32 is oriented to Burial 8 in the royal palace (see Navarro-Farr, Eppich, et al. 2020). Structure O14-04 is oriented to Structure M13-1 and Burial 61. While speculative, these tombs may represent royal couples. The queen in Burial 8 may be facing her husband in Burial 37. The ruler in Burial 39 may be facing the individual entombed in Burial 38. If so, the husband of Lady K'abel should reside inside the unexcavated O14-02. If persons became the pyramids, then the cityscape of Waka' was crisscrossed with architectural monarchs, who are now spending centuries facing their partners in life, looking across the city they once ruled together.

The impact on the citizens of the city must have been substantial. Ordinary Maya would have had their own ancestral shrines in their own patio groups, but a glance upward would have taken in the adorned masses of the great pyramids on the horizon. The people of the city would have known that these structures held the souls of honored ancestral rulers, looking over and looming over the whole of the living city. Their spirits looked after the welfare of the city they once ruled. Even the living monarchs could not have been unaffected by this. K'inich Bahlam II, living in the royal palace during his long seventh-century reign, would have seen the sun rise, every morning, over the great pyramid where he buried his parent—the great pyramid that was his parent. But this pyramid was also a much-older founder-queen, and a pair of royal women, and a young child, and a fox and an opossum, and possibly more than that.

In recent scholarship on Maya monumental landscapes, Arlen Chase and Diane Chase (2020b) wrote of the manner in which the Classic Maya reshaped their landscape, creating anthropogenic terrains that directly reflected the aesthetic concepts of their own particular cosmology. The use of caves and the construction of underground spaces mirrored Maya concepts of a multilayered creation. Calendric architectural complexes like E-Groups represented their commitment to the agricultural cycles of their tropical calendar. *Bajos* and terraces, cornfields, and fallow forests, directly held the produce of that agricultural effort. Tombs and pyramids functioned in a similar way. They held the honored dead of past generations, their souls transformed into colossal architecture. The terrain was not just anthropogenic, it was anthropomorphized. Funerary ritual resulted in the personing of architecture, thus making the question, "*Who?*" one of the most important inquiries that modern scholars can ask of the ancient pyramids of the Classic Maya.

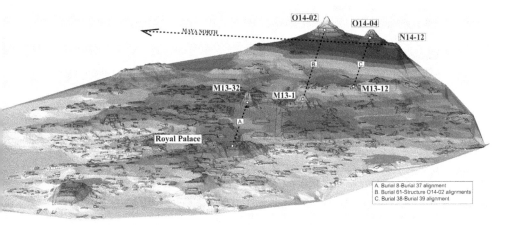

Figure 8.7. Architectural alignments at El Perú-Waka'. Map by Damien Marken, with modifications by Keith Eppich, courtesy of Proyecto Arqueológico Waka'.

References

Aveni, Anthony, and Horst Hartung
1986   *Maya City Planning and the Calendar.* Transactions of the American Philosophical Society, vol. 76, part 7. American Philosophical Society, Philadelphia.
Ball, Joseph W.
1977   *The Archaeological Ceramics of Becan, Campeche, Mexico*, Middle American Research Institute, Tulane University, New Orleans.
Bassie-Sweet, Karen
2021   *Maya Gods of War.* University Press of Colorado, Louisville.
Bell, Ellen E., Robert J. Sharer, Loa P. Traxler, David W. Sedat, Christine W. Carrelli, and Lynn A. Grant
2003   Tombs and Burials in the Early Classic Acropolis at Copan. In *Understanding Early Classic Copan*, edited by Ellen E. Bell, Marcello A. Canuto, and Robert J. Sharer, pp. 131–158. University of Pennsylvania Museum of Archaeology and Anthropology, Philadelphia.
Bunzel, Ruth
1952   *Chichicastenango, a Guatemalan Village.* J. J. Augustin Publisher, New York.
Chase, Arlen F., and Diane Z. Chase
2020a The Materialization of Classic Period Maya Warfare: Caracol Stranger-Kings at Tikal. In *A Forest of History: The Maya after the Emergence of Divine Kingship*, edited by Travis W. Stanton and M. Kathryn Brown, pp. 20–48. University Press of Colorado, Louisville.
2020b Monumental Landscapes of the Maya: Cogitating on a Past Built Environment. In *Approaches to Monumental Landscapes of the Ancient Maya*, edited by Brett A. Houk, Bárbara Arroyo, and Terry G. Powis, pp. 335–348. University Press of Florida, Gainesville.

Chase, Diane Z., and Arlen F. Chase
1996   Maya Multiples: Individuals, Entries, and Tombs in Structure A34 of Caracol, Belize. *Latin American Antiquity* 7(1):61–79.

Christenson, Allen J.
2001   *Art and Society in a Highland Maya Community: The Altarpiece of Santiago Atitlán.* University of Texas Press, Austin.
2010   Maize Was Their Flesh: Ritual Feasting in the Maya Highlands. In *Pre-Columbian Foodways: Interdisciplinary Approaches to Food, Culture, and Markets in Ancient Mesoamerica*, edited by John Staller and Michael Carrasco, pp. 577–600. Springer, New York.

Coe, Michael D.
1988   Ideology of the Maya Tomb. In *Maya Iconography*, edited by Elizabeth P. Benson and Gillett G. Griffin, pp. 222–235. Princeton University Press, Princeton.

Finamore, Daniel, and Stephen D. Houston
2010   *Fiery Pool: The Maya and the Mythic Sea.* Yale University Press, New Haven.

Fitzsimmons, James L.
2009   *Death and the Classic Maya Kings.* The University of Texas Press, Austin.

Freidel, David A., Héctor L. Escobedo, and Stanley P. Guenter
2007   A Crossroads of Conquerors: Waka' and Gordon Willey's "Rehearsal for the Collapse" Hypothesis. In *Gordon R. Willey and American Archaeology: Contemporary Perspectives*, edited by Jeremy A. Sabloff and William L. Fash, pp. 187–208. University of Oklahoma Press, Norman.

Freidel, David A., Kathryn Reese-Taylor, and David Mora-Marín
2002   The Origins of Maya Civilization: The Old Shell Game, Commodity, Treasure, and Kingship. In *Ancient Maya Political Economies*, edited by Marilyn A. Masson and David A. Freidel, pp. 41–86. Altamira Press, Walnut Creek, CA.

Freidel, David A., and Michelle Rich
2017   Maya Sacred Play: The View from El Perú-Waka'. In *Ritual, Play, and Belief in Evolution and Early Human Societies*, edited by Colin Renfrew, Iain Morley, and Michael Boyd, pp. 101–115. Cambridge University Press, New York.

Freidel, David A., Michelle Rich, and F. Kent Reilly III
2010   Resurrecting the Maize King. *Archaeology* 63(5). https://archive.archaeology.org/1009/etc/maya.html.

Freidel, David, Linda Schele, and Joy Parker
1993   *Maya Cosmos: Three Thousand Years on the Shaman's Path.* William Morrow, New York.

García-Des Lauriers, Claudia
2017   The Regalia of Sacred War: Costume and Militarism at Teotihuacan. *Americae: European Journal of Americanist Archaeology* 2: 83–98.

Guenter, Stanley
2014   The Epigraphy of El Perú-Waka'. In *Archaeology at El Perú-Waka': Ancient Maya Performances of Ritual, Memory, and Power*, edited by Olivia C. Navarro-Farr and Michelle Rich, pp. 147–166. University of Arizona Press, Tucson.

Harrison-Buck, Eleanor
2015   Maya Religion and Gods: Relevance and Relatedness in the Animic Cosmos. In

Tracing the Relational: The Archaeology of Worlds, Spirits, and Temporalities, edited by M. E. Buchanan and B. J. Skousen, pp. 115–129. University of Utah Press, Salt Lake City.

Headrick, Annabeth
2007   *The Teotihuacan Trinity: The Sociopolitical Structure of an Ancient Mesoamerican City*. University of Texas Press, Austin.

Henderson, Lucia R., and Brent Woodfill
in press Missing Persons: Animate Landscapes and Non-Human Personhood in the Maya Ritual Economy. In *"Peopling" the Americas: Animate Landscapes in New World Archaeology*, edited by Brent K. S. Woodfill and Lucia R. Henderson. Under contract with the University Press of Florida, Gainesville.

Houston, Stephen D., David Stuart, and Karl Taube
2006   *The Memory of Bones: Body, Being, and Experience among the Classic Maya*. University of Texas Press, Austin.

Houston, Stephen, Sarah Newman, Edwin Román, and Thomas Garrison
2015   *Temple of the Night Sun: A Royal Tomb at El Diablo, Guatemala*. Precolumbia Mesoweb Press, San Francisco.

Knappett, Carl
2002   Photographs, Skeuomorphs and Marionettes: Some Thoughts on Mind, Agency and Object. *Journal of Material Culture* 7(1):97–117.

Latour, Bruno
1993   *We Have Never Been Modern*. Harvard University Press, Cambridge.
2005   *Reassembling the Social: An Introduction to Actor-Network-Theory*. Oxford University Press, Oxford.

Marcus, Joyce
2020   Maya Usurpers. In *A Forest of History: The Maya after the Emergence of Divine Kingship*, edited by Travis W. Stanton and M. Kathryn Brown, pp. 49–66. University Press of Colorado, Louisville.

McAnany, Patricia A.
1995   *Living with the Ancestor: Kinship and Kingship in Ancient Maya Society*. University of Texas Press, Austin.
1998   Ancestors and the Classic Maya Built Environment. In *Function and Meaning in Classic Maya Architecture*, edited by Stephen D. Houston, pp. 271–298. Dumbarton Oaks Research Library and Collection, Washington, DC.

McAnany, Patricia A., and Shannon Plank
2001   Perspectives on Actors, Gender Roles, and Architecture at Classic Maya Courts and Households. In *Royal Courts of the Ancient Maya*, edited by Takeshi Inomata and Stephen Houston, pp. 84–129. Westview Press, Boulder.

Mueller, Melissa
2016   *Objects as Actors: Props and the Poetics of Performance in Greek Tragedy*. University of Chicago Press, Chicago.

Navarro-Farr, Olivia C., Keith Eppich, David A. Freidel, and Griselda Pérez Robles
2020   Ancient Maya Queenship: Generations of Crafting State Politics and Alliance Building from Kaanul to Waka'. In *Approaches to Monumental Landscapes of the*

Ancient Maya, edited by Brett A. Houk, Bárbara Arroyo, and Terry G. Powis, pp. 196–217. University Press of Florida, Gainesville.

Navarro-Farr, Olivia C., Mary Kate Kelly, Michelle Rich, and Griselda Pérez Robles
2020   Expanding the Canon: Lady K'abel the *Ix Kaloomte'* and the Political Narratives of Classic Maya Queens. *Feminist Anthropology* 1(1):38–55.

Navarro-Farr, Olivia, Griselda Pérez Robles, Juan Carlos Pérez Calderón, E. Menéndez Bolaños, Erin Paterson, Keith Eppich, and Mary Kelly
2021   Burial 61 at El Perú-Waka's Structure M13-1. *Latin American Antiquity* 32(1):188–200.

Owens, Erica
2007   Nonbiologic Objects as Actors. *Symbolic Interaction* 30(4):567–584.

Piehl, Jennifer
2009   *Análisis de estroncio en muestras de fauna y restos óseos humanos: Informe de los materiales exportadas en marzo 2008.* Report submitted to the Instituto de Antropología e Historia, Guatemala City.
2010   Análisis de laboratorio de los restos humanos de las operaciones 1, 3, 11 y ES. In *Proyecto Arqueológico El Perú-Waka': Informe no. 7, temporada 2009*, edited by Mary Jane Acuña and Jennifer Piehl, pp. 188–225. Fundación de Investigación Arqueológica Waka', Guatemala City.

Price, T. Douglas, Seiichi Nakamura, Shintaro Suzuki, James H. Burton, and Vera Tiesler
2014   New Isotope Data on Maya Mobility and Enclaves at Classic Copan, Honduras. *Journal of Anthropological Archaeology* 36:32–47.

Quintana, Patricia, Vera Tiesler, Mario Conde, Rudy Trejo-tzab, Catalina Bolio, J. J. Alvarado-gil, and Daniel Aguilar
2014   Spectrochemical Characterization of Red Pigments Used in Classic Period Maya Funerary Practices. *Archaeometry* 57(6):1045–1059.

Reents-Budet, Dorie, Joseph W. Ball, Ronald L. Bishop, Virginia M. Fields, and Barbara MacLeod
1994   *Painting the Maya Universe: Royal Ceramics of the Classic Period.* Duke University Press, Durham.

Reents-Budet, Dorie, Ellen E. Bell, Loa Traxler, and Ronald L. Bishop
2004   Early Classic Ceramic Offerings at Copan: A Comparison of the Hunal, Margarita, and Sub-Jaguar Tombs. In *Understanding Early Classic Copan*, edited by Ellen E. Bell, Marcello A. Canuto, and Robert J. Sharer, pp. 159–190. University of Pennsylvania Museum of Archaeology and Anthropology, Philadelphia.

Reents-Budet, Dorie, Ronald L. Bishop, M. James Blackman, Keith Eppich, Héctor L. Escobedo, David Lee, Juan Carlos Meléndez Mollinedo, Michelle Rich, and Griselda Pérez Robles
2011   La cerámica del período clásico de Waka': Las implicaciones de la composición de la pasta, la tipología arqueológica y el estilo artístico. Paper presented at the XXV Simposio de Investigaciones Arqueológicas en Guatemala, Guatemala City.

Rich, Michelle
2011   Ritual, Royalty and Classic Period Politics: The Archaeology of the Mirador Group at El Perú-Waka', Petén, Guatemala. PhD dissertation, Southern Methodist University, Dallas.

2012   Operación WK-15: Excavaciones en la Estructura P13-5. In *Proyecto Arqueológico El Perú-Waka': Informe no. 10, temporada 2012*, edited by Juan Carlos Pérez, pp. 175–198. Fundación de Investigación Arqueológica Waka', Guatemala City.

2017   Archaeology at El Perú-Waka': A Maya Ritual Resurrection Scene in Broader Perspective. *LACMA Unframed*. https://unframed.lacma.org/2017/09/21/archaeology-el-%C3%BA-waka%E2%80%99-maya-ritual-resurrection-scene-broader-perspective.

2018   An Olmec Transformation Figurine in "Ancient Bodies." *LACMA Unframed*. https://unframed.lacma.org/2018/01/09/olmec-transformation-figurine-ancient-bodies.

Rich, Michelle, and Haley Austin

2016   Excavaciones en la superficie arquitectónica de la Estructura O14-04. In *Proyecto Arqueológico El Perú-Waka': Informe no. 14, temporada 2016*, edited by Juan Carlos Pérez, pp 38–60. Proyecto Arqueológico Waka', Guatemala City.

Rich, Michelle, and Keith Eppich

2020   Statecraft in the City of the Centipede: Burials 39, 38, and Internal Alliance Building at El Perú-Waka', Guatemala. In *A Forest of History: The Maya after the Emergence of Divine Kingship*, edited by Travis W. Stanton and M. Kathryn Brown, pp. 88–106. University Press of Colorado, Louisville.

Rich, Michelle, and David A. Freidel

2010   Plate 98, Assemblage of Figurines in Burial 39, El Perú-Waka'. In *Fiery Pool: The Maya and the Mythic Sea*, edited by Daniel Finamore and Stephen D. Houston, pp. 284–287. Yale University Press, New Haven.

Rich, Michelle, David A. Freidel, and Varinia Matute

2011   WK-11A: Continuación de la investigación en la estructura *Adosada* de O14-04. In *Proyecto Arqueológico El Perú-Waka': Informe no. 9, temporada 2011*, edited by Mary Jane Acuña, pp. 5–26. Fundación de Investigación Arqueológica Waka', Guatemala City.

Rich, Michelle, David Freidel, F. Kent Reilly III, and Keith Eppich

2010   An Olmec Style Figurine from El Perú-Waka', Petén, Guatemala: A Preliminary Report. *Mexicon* 32(5):115–122.

Rich, Michelle, and Varinia Matute

2014   The Power of the Past: Crafting Meaning at a Royal Funerary Pyramid. In *Archaeology at El Perú-Waka': Ancient Maya Performances of Ritual, Memory, and Power*, edited by Olivia C. Navarro-Farr and Michelle Rich, pp. 66–84. University of Arizona Press, Tucson.

Rich, Michelle, Erin Sears, Ronald Bishop, and Dorie Reents-Budet

2019   Digging the Scene: More on the El Perú-Waka' Burial 39 Figurines. Presented at the 84th Annual Meeting of the Society for American Archaeology, Albuquerque.

Ruz Lhuillier, Alberto

1965   Tombs and Funerary Practices in the Maya Lowlands. In *Handbook of Middle American Indians*. Vol. 2, pt. 1: *Archeology of Southern Mesoamerica*, edited by Gordon Willey, pp. 441–461. University of Texas Press, Austin.

Schele, Linda, and Peter Mathews
1999   *The Code of Kings: The Language of Seven Sacred Maya Temples and Tombs.* Simon and Schuster, New York.

Scherer, Andrew K.
2015   *Mortuary Landscapes of the Classic Maya: Rituals of Body and Soul.* University of Texas Press, Austin.

Stuart, David
1998   "The Fire Enters His House": Architecture and Ritual in Classic Maya Texts. In *Function and Meaning in Classic Maya Architecture*, edited by Stephen D. Houston, pp. 373–426. Dumbarton Oaks Research Library and Collection, Washington, DC.

Taube, Karl
1992   *The Major Gods of Ancient Yucatan.* Dumbarton Oaks Research Library and Collection, Washington, DC.

2004   Structure 10L-16 and Its Early Classic Antecedents: Fire and the Evocation and Resurrection of K'inich Yax K'uk' Mo'. In *Understanding Early Classic Copan*, edited by Ellen E. Bell, Marcello A. Canuto, and Robert J. Sharer, pp. 265–296. University of Pennsylvania Museum of Archaeology and Anthropology, Philadelphia.

2005   The Symbolism of Jade in Classic Maya Religion. *Ancient Mesoamerica* 16(1):23–50.

Tedlock, Dennis
1997   *Breath on the Mirror: Mythic Voices and Visions of the Living Maya.* University of New Mexico Press, Albuquerque.

Tiesler, Vera, S. Suzuki, and J. Chi Keb
2010   Reporte final del estudio histomorfológico de los restos humanos del Sitio arqueológico de Waka' El Perú, Guatemala. In *Proyecto Arqueológico El Perú-Waka': Informe no. 7, temporada 2009*, edited by Mary Jane Acuña and Jennifer Piehl, pp. 281–304. Fundación de Investigación Arqueológica Waka', Guatemala City.

Teufel, Stefanie
2008   Marriage Diplomacy—Women at the Royal Court. In *Maya, Divine Kings of the Rain Forest*, edited by Nikolai Grube, pp. 172–173. Könemann, Cologne.

Tiesler, Vera
2020   Bodies, Introduction to bodies. In *The Maya World,* edited by Scott R. Hutson and Traci Ardren, pp. 103–127. Routledge, New York.

Vadala, Jeffrey, and Lisa Duffy
2020   Using Actor-Network Theory to Characterize the Production of Ancient Maya Caching Events at Cerro Maya (Cerros, Belize). *Journal of Archaeological Method and Theory* 28:1027–1057.

Vogt, Evon Z.
1969   *Zinacantan: A Maya Community in the Highlands of Chiapas.* Harvard University Press, Cambridge.

1970   Human Souls and Animal Spirits in Zinacantan. In *Échanges et communications: Mélanges offerts à Claude Lévi-Strauss*, pp. 1148–1167. Mouton, The Hague.

1976   *Tortillas for the Gods: A Symbolic Analysis of Zinacanteco Rituals.* University of Oklahoma Press, Norman.

Woodfill, Brent, and Lucia R. Henderson

in press a   Introduction: Animate Landscapes in New World Archaeology. In *"Peopling" the Americas: Animate Landscapes in New World Archaeology*, edited by Brent K. S. Woodfill and Lucia R. Henderson. Under contract with the University Press of Florida, Gainesville.

in press b   The Animate Landscape of the Maya: The Non-Human Personhood of Caves, Mountains, Lakes, Buildings, and Objects. In *The Oxford Handbook of the Maya*, edited by Thomas G. Garrison, Jeffrey B. Glover, and Brent K. S. Woodfill. Under contract with Oxford University Press, Oxford.

9

The Royal Palace of Waka'

A Preclassic to Terminal Classic Seat of Power

Griselda Pérez Robles, Juan Carlos Pérez,
David Freidel, and Elsa Damaris Menéndez

The Architecture of a Palace Complex

Architecture through the ages has been an effective tool to spread messages of economic and social order and to achieve social coercion. It has the ability to create functional spaces with a symbolic meaning, combined with private, semiprivate, or public uses of a daily or ritual nature, to include administrative, residential, religious, political, defensive, and popular functions like demonstrations, among others (Valdés and Fahsen 2007:42; Nelson 2004:60). The visual language of architecture deals with and includes formal compositional units, such as cornices, balustrades (or *alfardas*), niches, central stairways, stepped bases, and upper temples, among others, as well as compositional geometry that includes the systematic ordering of the structure into formal units through a network of geometry, proportion, and scale relationships (Valle et al. 2016:321).

In the Preclassic and Early Classic periods, Lowland Maya monumental buildings often had sculpted or modeled decorations in the frontal section of the stepped bodies of the pyramidal bases. They possessed crests and friezes on the façades of buildings located in front of large public squares; these were located at a considerable height for their observation from a distance (Salazar 2017:1). Later, public architecture became more complex and grander in scale, responding to the idea of the divine origin of the rulers. This sense of superiority led rulers to build stone palaces with vaulted ceilings, whose iconographic elements in the decoration repeated the acts of public ritual, even when such acts were not being performed, in such a way that reflected the royal worldview through visual images and written texts (Valdés, Valledares, and Díaz 2008:37; Miller 1998:192–194; Nelson 2004:60).

In addition to being the residence of those who held political and economic power, palaces were frequented by—and often housed a portion of—the court, a group of noble people who performed political, religious, economic, and administrative functions, as well as by those who participated in related domestic activities, such as in the preparation of food or services and storage (Nelson 2004:59; Inomata 2001:28,49; McAnany and Plank 2001:86; Harrison 2003:106, 116; Webster 2001:135; Reents-Budet 2001:213; Webster and Inomata 2004:149). It is important to remember that the economy of the "palace," to some extent, represents the economy of the state, just as the personal relationships of the ruler reflect state relationships and as the rituals performed by the royal family are state rituals. It naturally follows then that the ideology of kingship greatly influences royal architecture (Ciudad Ruíz 2001:307, 308). The palace is not the consequence of the evolution of religious institutions; instead, together with the temple, the public square, and ritual space, the palace constitutes a singular, ideological phenomenon. Its monumentality and location in the epicenter of the city are a public expression of royal power (Ciudad Ruíz 2001:334).

Groups of elevated courtyards, common in Maya cities, form palaces, which are separated from the rest of the urban space like elevated islands within the city (Quintana 2017:15; Inomata 2001:48; Webster 2001:134; Martin 2001:170). These palaces had boundary walls—converting them into private fortresses—with their façades opening outward, marking an official entrance from adjacent plazas. Many of these palaces were initially Triadic Groups. This type of complex was created to be the seat of political and religious power in a prominent area of the city (Valdés, Valledares, and Díaz 2008: 92). Within the palace complex, the space was ordered into sectors according to the basic functions that the buildings fulfilled. These various functions included housing the ruler and the royal court, reception areas, and political/administrative offices, as well as spaces for state rituals, for musicians and theater ceremonies, and for the storage of luxury products such as banners and the royal palanquin, among many others (Quintana 2017:15). This was all in addition to areas for food preparation, recreation, workshops, and possible exchange areas—perhaps the surrounding terraces served this purpose (Webster and Inomata 2004:149).

The Royal Palace Complex

Plaza 4 of Waka', at the foot of the Royal Palace Complex, is a wide, flat, and open space decorated with altars and sculpted stelae; to the north is a structure with a hieroglyphic staircase that connects it to a ball court (Figure 9.1). To the west, the elevated palace complex rises majestically. The palace itself includes two formal courtyards at the top and a series of structures, terraces, and small courtyards that flank it on the north and south sides (Lee 2004:146; Pérez Robles, Pérez, and Van Oss 2015:105). It is artificially raised between 12 and 14 meters above the surrounding terrain. Initially called the Northwest Palace Complex (Lee 2004:145), more recent research has referred to it as the Waka' Royal Palace Complex (Pérez Robles, Pérez, and Van Oss 2015).

The Royal Palace Complex is a large architectural mass, 135 meters long (north–south) and 110 meters wide (east–west), covering roughly 13,500 square meters, or 1.35 hectares, which makes it the largest architectural complex in the city (Jacobo et al. 2017:482). It is made up of 28 buildings, 7 patios, a small reservoir, 5 terraces, and 3 entrances. The two patios—Patio PC-A and Patio PC-B—are the main courtyards and are located on two different levels. The southern Patio PC-A is a semipublic area with restricted access, and is reached through Structure L12-4, which served as the eastern façade of the Royal Palace Complex that was accessed from Plaza 4 via a wide staircase. To the south of this patio are Structures L11-50 and L11-51; on the west side are Structures L11-38 and L11-49. Structure L11-41 delineates the north side of the patio and is the tallest structure here; it certainly played a prominent role in the political and ritual acts taking place in the Palace. The northern Patio PC-B is made up of Structure L11-40 to the north, which was added at the end of the Late Classic period, and Structure L11-41 to the south, which can be accessed from both courtyards. Occupying a lower-elevation open space to the east lies a small pool-sized reservoir for exclusive use by the royalty of the city, at least from the Early Classic to the Terminal Classic periods (Pérez Robles, Pérez, and Van Oss, et al. 2015:105; Pérez Robles, Pérez, Menéndez, and Couoj 2019:104). South of this is Structure L11-37, a building made up of small rooms, perhaps for ritual use, directly connected to a grandstand with balustrades; it directly overlooks the neighboring ball court (Structures L11-30 and L11-31). However, the architectural characteristics of the rooms and the lower walls evidence a clear connection with a wall that limited access to the complex from the east and north between the Early and Late Classic periods. Structures L11-42, L11-43, and L11-44 form a northern extension of the complex. The northeastern Patio PC-C is at a lower level and connects the Palace with the structure of the hieroglyphic staircase, L11-33; and Pa-

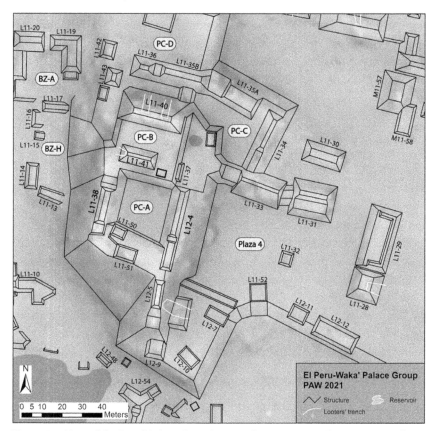

Figure 9.1. Map of the Royal Palace Complex. Map by Damien Marken, courtesy of Proyecto Arqueológico Waka'.

tio PC-C consists of Structures L11-34, L11-35, and L11-36 (Lee and Gámez 2007:127).

Archaeological evidence establishes that the Royal Palace was the center of political power during the entire time of the city's occupation. Evidence located in various sectors of the urban core dating from the Terminal Classic shows a modification or expansion of numerous constructions in the urban core, including the residential Xucub and Chok Groups, Structure M13-1, and the Royal Palace Complex itself.

We now think that the Royal Palace Complex survived Waka's historically attested military and political conflicts until its abandonment in the Terminal Classic period. Probably around 801 CE, the Palace saw extensive remodeling efforts that also took place throughout the urban core, as is evidenced by a large deposit marking lavish ceremonial and royal festivities of such an occasion. The ruling class of Waka' wielded political power from the Palace, while secondary elites engaged in similar renovation programs and architectural enlargements in their respective elite residential groups. This seems to have been a joint effort to revitalize the city, replicating the rituals that were started at the Palace. This suggests that even on the eve of the abandonment of the city, large amounts of energy and resources were invested in Waka's urban landscape.

Structure L12-4 of the Palace

Investigations started in 2003, in Structure L12-4, and have revealed an un-interrupted growth of the Royal Palace Complex from the Preclassic to the Terminal Classic periods. The Preclassic construction stage inside the Palace and behind the frontal building presents clear evidence of a series of civic-ceremonial constructions that manifest early and clear social stratification. However, it is also probable that this earliest phase of the Palace Group on its eastern side was a necropolis with both royal interment and accession func-tions like the original Tikal North Acropolis (Coe 1990; Freidel et al. 2003). We suspect that the unexplored western side of the original plaza may hold residences (Pérez Robles, Pérez, Menéndez, and Couoj 2019:244). Future tun-neling operations will elucidate this possibility.

The Preclassic Period: The Beginnings of the Power Experiment

Excavations carried out in 2017 and 2018 inside and below Structure L12-4 showed that the undulating bedrock here was modified, filled in, and leveled when the people of Waka' built the monumental plazas in the Protoclassic era (100–250 CE). This modification was present both underneath the main ac-cess grandstand of the Late Classic phase as well as below and to the west of the central room. We observed undulating and irregular bedrock in some sec-tions, while in others it was pronounced and sharp rock with serrated edges, such as the outcrops on the north slope of the Mirador hill or at the base of Structure J15-1 near the El Perú Lagoon (Pérez Robles and Pérez 2017:93,120; 2019b). The clay-fill deposits and associated ceramics indicate that at some point, perhaps at the beginning of the Late Preclassic period, the great natural platform that represents the upper part of the steep escarpment was selected for the initial construction of the Palace.

Thus, in the Late Preclassic, and perhaps a little earlier, a large upland ba-sin space of approximately 1 square kilometer on a steep escarpment, with numerous natural ponds suitable for water storage, was modified by a large and organized group of people. Their effort managed to grade the edges of the bedrock, level surfaces, and fill them with dark mud from the low-lying areas and natural ponds. Over time, these founding inhabitants laid down surfaces of stucco plaza flooring on the leveled areas, on top of which were built the public buildings that defined the design of this nascent city. We found evidence for this founding practice under the Palace Complex and under Structure M13-1 as well as in test exposures in Plazas 1 and 2 (Pérez Robles and Pérez 2019a:241). On the Preclassic floor levels, we determined that the first civic-religious buildings were raised; they were a combination of masonry platforms and superstructures of perishable materials. Most of these remain poorly defined, but they include two Late Preclassic buildings of cut masonry with stuccoed surfaces that were painted hematite red, 8 meters below the Late Classic and Terminal Classic localities of Structure L12-4. One of these, designated the Red Building, had a projecting staircase and could have been a platform of one or two stages and about seven steps. It is reminiscent of the Preclassic platforms of Group H at Uaxactun (Valdés 1994), and it may even have had masks on the sides of its stands. Through the staircase of this early royal building, mourners tunneled down from above to place a king, Burial 80, in the early fourth century CE (Figure 9.2). This was at the dawn of the Early Classic period (Pérez Robles and Pérez 2019a:242–243), when the Wak dynasty was young (Guenter 2014). Here, as in Tikal's early North Acropolis, the people of Waka' now deemed the earthly remains of rulers as the heart of religiosity.

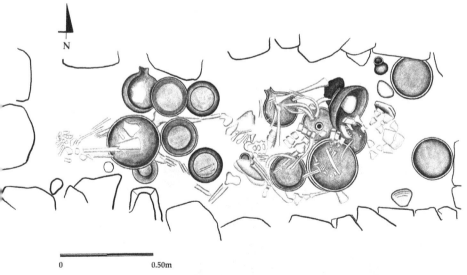

0   0.50m

Figure 9.2. Burial 80. Drawing by Juan Carlos Pérez and Griselda Pérez Robles, courtesy of Proyecto Arqueológico Waka'.

The Early Classic Period: A New Order with New Messages

From the Early Classic phase (250–550 CE), investigators identified a masonry construction with apron-molding at the base, an architectural style associated with Tikal. It is an "encasing" structure built directly on top of the Preclassic Red Building, covering it completely. The masonry construction protects the remains of a stucco mask, modeled on its west facade, that was damaged in ancient times, probably when it was terminated. Associated with the construction are two ritual deposits: one consists of fragments of a ceramic vessel containing the skeletal remains of a child, and a second contains an infant, placed in an extended dorsal decubitus position, with the skull facing west (Pérez Robles, Pérez, Menéndez, and Couoj 2019:92). Both are considered dedicatory offerings. Archaeologists have so far exposed 3.2 meters of the structure on its west façade, where the remains of a stairway to the east were discovered. The total height of the masonry construction remains unknown (Pérez Robles and Pérez 2019a:243). Until recently, it was not possible to affirm that this location constituted the possible accession building of the Early Classic Royal Palace. This was confirmed only in 2018, with the discovery of Burial 80. Both the interment and later reentry of the tomb evidence the importance of the structure and its role in the political legitimation of the Late and Terminal Classic rulers.

As in the case of Tikal's early North Acropolis, where the probable tomb of the dynastic founder King Yax Ehb Xook, Tikal Burial 85 (Martin and Grube 2008:26), has a platform over it suitable for an accession scaffold; we believe that subsequent rulers at Waka' came to power over the remains of the early fourth century king in Burial 80. He is very likely the ruler named as prophesizing on 8.14.0.0.0, 7 Ajaw (317 CE), on Stela 15, a prophecy that would be recalled by King K'inich Bahlam II on Stela 43 in 702 CE. The royal title of this man, previously nicknamed "Leaf," includes a bird over a turtle shell (Kelly, Freidel, and Navarro-Farr, this volume).

Burial 80

The Late Preclassic Palace Complex likely contained a triad of platforms on its eastern side, two of which have been partially exposed in our tunneling excavations to date. The central Preclassic platform faced west, probably toward a residential building on the western side of the complex. In terminating this set of Preclassic platforms, the Early Classic royal court built an encasing structure over the central platform, also facing west. As the founding of the dynasty itself took place in the first two centuries CE, the earlier platform likely served several generations of rulers during the Protoclassic and Early Classic periods (see Guenter 2014). Both the Preclassic central platform and the enclosure were cut into and partially destroyed in order to place the remains of a ruler from the beginning of the Early Classic (250–337 CE). Designated as Burial 80 (Figure 9.2), it contained the body of a royal individual of about 30 years of age, whose skeletal remains were profusely covered in cinnabar. Osteological analysis indicates that he had two injuries: one a healed fracture of the ring finger of his right hand, and the other a cervical vertebra that presented spina bifida pathology (Patterson 2017:346).

Originally, the mourners wrapped the body in textiles (fabric prints could be seen in fragments of the mud around the body). The total absence of the east wall of the burial chamber confirms that a reentry of the tomb occurred, perhaps during the Late Classic period, when the bones were painted with bright cinnabar red; it is at that time that the Maya deposited some artifacts and removed others, which became sacred relics. Preliminary ceramic analysis of the funerary vessels from this burial suggests these are late third or early fourth century ceramics, making this burial the earliest royal tomb in the northwest Petén (Freidel et al. in press). Thus, this ruler's death could have occurred more than half a century before the historic *entrada* of Sihyaj K'ahk' in 378 CE (see Kelly, Freidel, and Navarro-Farr, this volume).

A particularly notable find in Burial 80 is a royal crown, or *sak hunal*, almost identical to the one found in Burial 24 of Yaxuna (Suhler, Ardren, and Johnstone 1998:174; Tiesler et al. 2017). Four elongated curved elements of white coral form the crown and are accompanied by four circular shell beads, plus a pin-shaped jade bead that must have been the crown jewel, a symbol of royalty in the Late Preclassic and Protoclassic periods (Pérez Robles, Pérez, Menéndez, and Freidel 2021). In addition, under the bones of the skull, a magnificent jade boulder sculpture was found turned downward, representing the three-dimensional face of a young person with the tabular forelock ornament and prominent teeth of the Early Classic Maize God (Taube 1985). This was probably a votive head, originally placed on the king's belt or breastplate in life; it represents both the deity and the face of an ancestor (Figure 9.3). The symbolism of royalty contained in his trousseau, as well as in the main jewel as a portrait of an ancestor, reflects his role as *ajaw* (lord) in the early polity of Waka' (Schele and Freidel 1990).

At the beginning of the Early Classic period, it is probable that the audiencia and receiving throne room were located on the western edge of the Palace Complex. This was likely under Structure L11-38, the location of Burial 8, a royal tomb from the late Early Classic, and the likely burial of Lady Ikoom Sak Wayis (see Kelly, Freidel, and Navarro-Farr, this volume). This western area will be investigated in future excavations, allowing us to complete the architectural design of the earliest group on the Palace locality. In the late

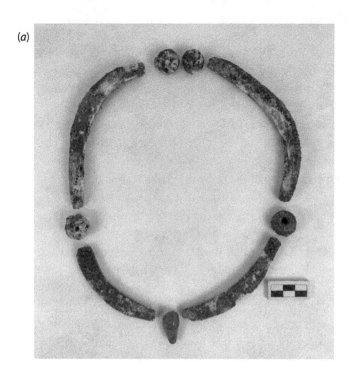

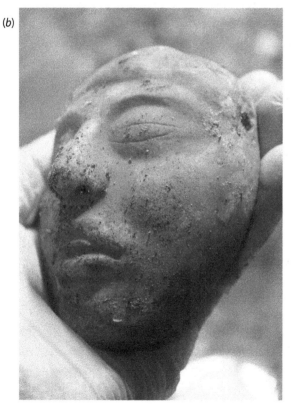

Figure 9.3. (*a*) Greenstone *sak hunal* (royal crown) from Burial 80; (*b*) jade face of the young Maize God from Burial 80. Photographs by Juan Carlos Pérez, courtesy of Proyecto Arqueológico Waka'.

sixth century, at the end of the Early Classic and beginning of the Late Classic period, the Maya interred a royal queen in the northern quarter of L11-38. She was between 30 and 40 years of age at the time of her death. Her rich grave goods included 23 vessels, more than 2,000 greenstone artifacts, more than 800 shell artifacts, obsidian, freshwater pearls, and stingray spines (Lee and Piehl 2014). According to the evidence, both her skull and femurs are absent and may have been removed as relics as part of a later reentry ritual (Lee 2004:116–118). Among the greenstone fragments were 22 rectangular plates, likely the greater part of a k'ohaw, a helmet, such as those worn by military figures, as in the case of the one also found south of the interment in the burial chamber of Lady K'abel at Burial 61 (Pérez Robles and Navarro-Farr 2013).

The Late Classic Period: The Rise of Dynastic Power

The Late Classic period (550–800 CE) was one of the most active moments in the construction of the eastern sector of the Royal Palace of Waka'. Atop a series of thin floors, corresponding to minor renovations during the Early Classic period, a solid 10-centimeter-thick floor was built, covering them. This served as the basis for the construction of the monumental façade of L12-4 and corresponds to Sub-Structure II, dated to the Late Classic period during the prolific government of K'inich Bahlam II and Ix Kaloomte' K'abel (ca. 657–702 CE). Structure L12-4 Sub II is a building of approximately 30 meters in length, composed of at least three chambers: north, central, and south. The north room was initially excavated by David Lee in 2006, while the central room was excavated in 2017; a third, as-yet unexcavated room, should be immediately south of the central one. This approximately 7-meter-high building had a richly decorated panel or frieze of human figures and deities in modeled and polychrome stucco, identified in the excavation of terminal ritual deposits inside the north and central rooms in 2006, 2016, and 2017 (Lee and Gámez 2007; Lee and Piehl 2014; Pérez Robles and Pérez 2017; Pérez Robles, Pérez, Menéndez, and Freidel 2017). The excavation of this deposit yielded modeled fragments of torsos, faces, hands, noses, headdresses, scrolls, and other polychrome ornaments that decorated the exterior molding frieze of the building. Initial analyses conducted by Lee (2006:122) suggest similarities with the façades of Structure A-3 at Ceibal (Smith 1982), the Cancuen Palace (Barrientos et al. 2002:386), Becan (Smith 1982:52), and Structure 20 at Yaxchilan (Tate 1992:188).

Below this layer of stucco, an extraordinary terminal deposit was discovered containing matrixes of earth of different colors from ritual burning, polychrome and monochrome vessels, and ceramic drums. *Unionidae* shells, bone needles, spearheads and arrowheads, figurines, whistles, snails, and animal bones completed the scene. The main focus of the ritual activity was directed toward the back (western) door, which possesses an improvised masonry altar of cut blocks directly in front of the entrance (Pérez Robles, Pérez, Menéndez, and Freidel 2017:85). Additionally, the ancient ritualists broke the Late Classic stucco floor to place two sacrificial human burials before that altar.

The central room of L12-4 Sub II has several characteristics, in addition to its location, that identify it as the structure's main room. It has two known access doors (there may be a third) opening to its terrace and a grand stairway overlooking Plaza 4 to the east. The room vault reached an interior height of 5.34 meters at the capstones. In the west wall of the room, a third door (a back door) was located that gave access to an exterior space that had a staircase of 13 stucco steps ascending south to the upper terrace of the Palace, above the level of the ornamented superior molding (Figure 9.4). The terrace, in addition to having a privileged view not only of Plaza 4, but also of Plazas 2, 3, and the fire shrine of Structure M13-1, no doubt also functioned as a theater space. This performative stage is where the rulers and courtiers revealed themselves to their people and held performances associated with the political cosmology and the dynamics of interaction between people and buildings that maintained the link with the ancestors and their descendants (McAnany 1998:271–275; Pérez Robles, Pérez, Menéndez, and Couoj 2019:245). The east terrace additionally provides a splendid setting that connects the ballcourt with the courtly group, providing a glimpse to the spectators of the activities developed at the courtly group as another mechanism of communication between the rulers and the ruled.

It is highly likely that these stucco friezes, prominently adorning the west side of L12-4, date to the late seventh century and were built during the reign of K'inich Bahlam and *Ix Kaloomte' K'abel*. They appear to have been desecrated following Waka's defeat in 743 CE. It is possible that Lady Pakal (771–790 CE), a Late Classic queen from Calakmul, may have begun the process of healing the Late Classic Palace and that she began to build what we now call the Transitional Palace (771–820 CE) from whence she and her successors ruled (Guenter 2005; Pérez Robles and Navarro-Farr 2013:3).

The Late-Terminal Classic Transition Period: Adapting to Change

Toward the beginning of the Terminal Classic (771–820 CE), a second version of L12-4 Sub I, was built (Pérez Robles, Pérez, Menéndez, and Freidel 2017:120). This remodeling is consistent with a substantial growth in other areas of the Palace, including modifications to Structure L11-41, a significant raising and leveling of Patio PA-B to incorporate Structure L11-40, a likely residential structure, as well as a remodeling of the east terrace, growing and

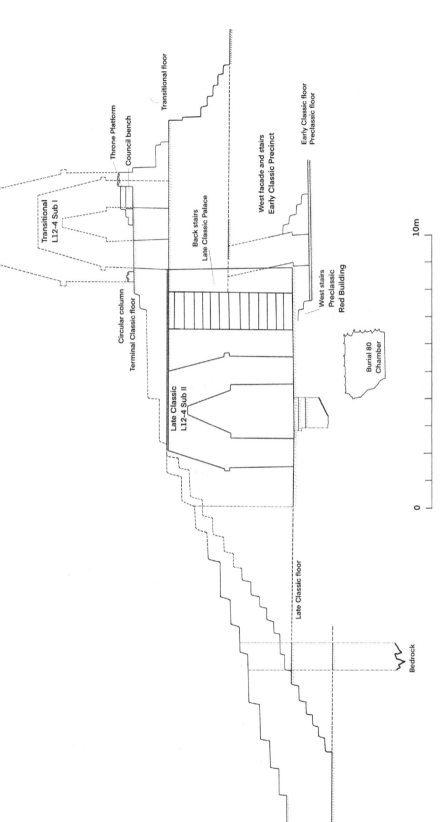

Throne Platform
Council bench
Transitional floor

Transitional
L12-4 Sub I

Back stairs
Late Classic Palace

West facade and stairs
Early Classic Precinct

Early Classic floor
Preclassic floor

Circular column
Terminal Classic floor

Late Classic
L12-4 Sub II

West stairs
Preclassic
Red Building

Burial 80
Chamber

0   10m

Late Classic floor

Bedrock

Figure 9.4. Profile of Structure L12-4. Drawing by Juan Carlos Pérez, Griselda Pérez Robles, and René Ozaeta, courtesy of Proyecto Arqueológico Waka'.

expanding the buildings of the royal residence to the north, to which more courtyards and other buildings were added for the use of the royal family and its nobles.

Recent excavations in 2021 at L12-4 partially documented the architecture of the Transitional Phase (Figure 9.4), revealing at least four rooms at the ends (two to the north and two to the south) flanking an elongated space more than 28 meters long, built with 1-meter-thick masonry walls, and penetrated by at least two doors at the ends of the east façade. There were also entrances on the north and south sides, and with likely more than three doors on the west façade connecting with Patio PC-A (Pérez Robles, Pérez, Menéndez, and Freidel 2021).

While the Transitional Palace was in use, ritualists reentered Late Classic L12-4 Sub II. As part of a large feast, possibly associated with an important and still undiscovered tomb, they sacrificed two individuals, Burials 72 and 73, whom they placed in the floor of the central room (Pérez Robles, Pérez, Menéndez, and Freidel 2017:96). This reentry is documented epigraphically on Altar 1 and associated with Stela 38, which dates to 801 CE. Its inscription narrates the epic journey of King Aj Yax Yopaat to the "heart of the turtle" for a meeting with K'inich Bahlam (Guenter 2005:379).

In the center of the room, oriented east–west, the Maya placed a carved stone head atop a longitudinal stone filling. They even stuccoed the head into place. The prominent *tau* tooth on this stone head armature suggests it was a representation of the Sun God GI (Figure 9.5). This arrangement of stones and the head of the Sun God, located on the axis on the floor of the room, is very similar to the composition of the central room of the Oropéndola building, under Structure 10L-16 from the Copan Acropolis (Agurcia and Pérez 2017). Certainly, the architectural narrative at Copan is much more elaborate and of greater dimensions, but the arrangement is practically the same: a set of stones transverse to the room, upon which rests the head of the Sun God (Pérez Robles, Pérez Calderón, and Freidel 2020). The ceramic analysis of the Waka' Palace reentry ritual deposit indicates that it dates between Tepeu II and III, within the Q'eq and Morai Complexes, at the beginning of the Terminal Classic period. For now, at least 150 vessels have been identified, not counting fragments of other recovered sherds, as part of this reentry deposit (Menéndez and Cuyán 2020).

The ancient inhabitants of Waka' had knowledge of their ancestral roots and venerated Structure L12-4 and the Royal Palace as important places to legitimize and remember past greatness and maintain the power status of their rulers (Acuña 2014; Eppich 2014; Lee and Piehl 2014; Navarro-Farr and Ar-

Figure 9.5. (a) Placement of the carved head of the Sun God GI; (b) detail of the carved stone head of Sun God GI. Photographs by Juan Carlos Pérez, courtesy of Proyecto Arqueológico Waka'.

royave 2014). Thus, as practiced in the city center, Waka' religion and politics revolved around ancestor worship, expressed in devotion and reverence to the figure of the king and his close relatives. As elsewhere in the lowland Maya world, religious symbols had political value at the state level and the elite used this complex religious form as an instrument of their power (Rivera Dorado 1995:24–25; McAnany 1998:272). This use of religious ideology is manifest in the regal ritual architecture of Waka', including Structures M13-1 and O14-04. The political-religious discourse is evident in the molded stucco ornamentation that once covered these structures. This program denoted the power of ancient rulers and priests and their ties with ancestors and gods. People could participate in public ceremonies and rituals, observe visitors and ball players from the plazas, and witness military events as well as bring tribute, offer their products, and resolve conflicts, all while observing the political speech of the architectural friezes and carved stelae. The constant presence of people in the plazas and ornate buildings was complemented during the great celebrations by extraordinary sensory experiences for sight, hearing, smelling, tasting and touching, guiding the masses in an understanding of the ideological message and their spokespersons, feeling the living city as a whole celebrate the rule of divine kingship.

It is quite probable that the ruler Aj Yax Chow Pat continued to use the Transitional Palace for a time, and he may have carried out a new remodeling, converting the great room of Structure L12-4 into three rooms, adding internal walls to create additional environments in the Palace (Pérez Robles, Pérez, Menéndez, and Freidel 2021). Evidence indicates that the upper portion of the transitional version of Structure L12-4 was dismantled at the end of its occupation, leaving only 1.25 meters of the walls standing. Around this time, dedicatory vessels were placed at the southern interior end of the structure before it was filled with a densely packed mixture of earth, lime, and stones from the same building to leave a surface that was transformed into the foundation of the Terminal Palace.

The Terminal Classic: Dynastic Decline

Far from being abandoned, Structure L12-4 and the Royal Palace, in general, were in continuous activity during the Terminal Classic period (800–1000 CE), undergoing a series of remodels and modifications that allowed the complex to continue as the seat of royal power until the abandonment of the city. The architectural evidence from this period seems to indicate that the complex underwent an important remodeling effort in practically all directions: to the south and west, small terraces were created from large, almost dry-laid stones with the intention of easily increasing the volume and height of the buildings (Pérez Robles and Pérez 2019a:246).

It is certain that the royal court experienced political difficulties and suffered significant wear and tear before the rest of Waka' society experienced the same, with significant economic, political, and social impacts being felt across the city, potentially causing the king to grant special powers, concessions, and privileges to other noble families, such as the right to elaborate and reelaborate palatial-style architecture, to erect plain monuments, and to celebrate great festivities with banquets and meetings in the manner of those of the Royal Palace (see Eppich, this volume). Terminal Classic elites in other residential compounds began to have greater access to prestigious and sumptuous goods and to direct processional celebrations such as at the Chok Group, located along the causeway connecting Plaza 2 and the Mirador Group. Granting this type of privilege allowed the current ruler, perhaps already weakened, to maintain legitimacy by sharing power among the most influential noble families, thus also allowing for the survival of a centralized government in the last years of the city. This sharing of power resulted in the elaborate rituals carried out in front of and atop Structure M13-1, where important deposits of various materials from all strata of society were discovered (Navarro-Farr 2009).

The Terminal Classic Palace evidently sought to maintain a status of grandeur, monumentality, and some degree of power-sharing. Structure L12-4 was a large open room just over 26 meters long (north–south) and 4.66 meters wide (east–west). The eastern façade was composed of solid walls, approximately 3.35 meters long at both the north and south ends, with seven circular columns between them, creating a single open interior space. The walls were 0.6 meters thick and were built with cut stone blocks, some of which were clearly reused. The spacious interior of the room was vaulted and had an elongated, 0.80 meter wide and 0.25 meter high, bench along the entire length of the northern, western, and southern walls, indicating that nobles and/or visitors had a place of honor while sharing this political space with the ruler. The axis of the building was elevated 0.50 meters, creating a central platform accessed by ascending two steps, giving added height to the location of the throne or the ruler, as the central figure of the city, in the meetings that were held there (Pérez Robles, Pérez, Menéndez, and Freidel 2021). Structure L12-4 sat on a wide platform (under which were the remains of the L12-4 Sub I), which had a 2-meter-wide front terrace and a wide staircase that extended across the entire base of the building. From Plaza 4, one could access Structure L12-4 by ascending the 13 steps of this staircase (Figure 9.4). The seven circular columns gave the feeling of openness or accessibility to this building, as part of the architectural discourse consistent with the new royal policies that indicated a profound social change.

At some point during the Terminal Classic period, the longitudinal room had a door to the south, and another to the north, in addition to those that faced west (of which we only excavated the southwestern-most door), which were accessed through narrow platforms 0.7 meters high and 0.5 meters wide. They followed a remodeling episode at an intermediate point in the Terminal Classic, when the northern and southern doors were sealed with new stucco and the council bench was installed. At the same time, the three-tiered platform was built in the center of the great hall to place the aforementioned throne at a higher level than the new bench. Rooms with thrones were used to hold diplomatic, tributary, and ceremonial receptions, among other such events (Harrison and Andrews 2004:124).

The final version of Structure L12-4 was abandoned after what appears to have been a careful cleaning, and the structure was ritually killed. Some scattered offerings and special objects were deposited to mark the abandonment of this space, which probably also corresponds to the abandonment of the entire Palace Complex. In the northwestern, southwestern, southeastern outer corners and to the rear center of Structure L12-4, sets of human and animal bones were placed with the construction fill, including at least two jaguar phalanxes as well as fragments of vessels and even a stone bark-beater. The abandonment included the dismantling of the vaulted ceiling and the upper part of the walls (Pérez Robles, Pérez, Menéndez, and Freidel 2021).

Currently there are two hypotheses about the abandonment of Structure L12-4. The first centers on the abandonment of the building, when people meticulously cleaned the great audience throne room, demolished the vault, and removed the ceiling to the level of the vault spring. The hypothesis is that they then placed the sets of bones and moved the seat of power, constructing the Structure L11-29 Popol Nah on the east side of Plaza 4, which became the new meeting place for local elites (Eppich and Van Oss 2017). The second hypothesis is that this abandonment of the building marks the precise moment of the final abandonment of the city. In both cases, it will be necessary to complete the ceramic analysis and carry out more excavations in other buildings of the Royal Palace and Plaza 4 to verify these hypotheses.

Conclusions

Undoubtedly, a momentous change occurred with the arrival of Sihyaj K'ahk' to Waka' on 3 Kan (378 CE), days before his conquest of Tikal on 11 Eb. His *entrada* impacted both the religious and political systems in the Maya Lowlands (Martin and Grube 2008; Stuart 2000). It was probably he who installed K'inich Bahlam I in Waka' in the year of his arrival. Certainly, that Waka' king was considered a valued vassal (Guenter 2005). In addition, the Teotihuacan arrival ushered in a prolific and reciprocal exchange of ideas and products from highlands of Mexico and the central zone of Petén, dominated by Tikal. Relations between Waka' and Tikal were prosperous and strong until the arrival of the first Kaan woman: Lady Ikoom, who carried the title *Sak Wayis* and was the probable wife of King Chak Tok Ich'aak (Guenter 2014; Kelly, Freidel, and Navarro-Farr, this volume). In the Late Classic, relations with Calakmul and Kaan were further strengthened with the arrival of Lady K'abel with her father, Yuknoom Ch'een the Great, who, in addition to presiding over the funeral of the dead king of Waka' around 657 CE placed his successor, K'inich Bahlam II, in power (Martin 2020). Together they governed the city, inhabiting Waka's Royal Palace. Following the death of Lady K'abel sometime between 700 and 710 CE, K'inich Bahlam II survived at least another 30 years, after which the political conflicts between Calakmul and Tikal led to the defeat of the Waka' dynasty by Tikal in 743 CE. Then a time of resilience began in Petén, with a new order in the distribution of regional political power. Though decisively defeated, the people of Waka' endured to eventually rebuild their palace and city under the tutelage of a new ruler.

A series of modifications and extensions occurred in the Royal Palace Complex after the defeat of 743 CE, when the structure built by K'inich Bahlam II and Lady K'abel was ruined. The people built a new palace between the end of the Late Classic and early Terminal Classic periods. It was located in front of Plaza 4, possibly beginning a construction boom that was shared by other sectors of the city such as found in the Chok Group and the fire shrine of M13-1. The evidence of the veneration of ancestors during the Terminal Classic period and the substantial architectural modifications that were carried out in the Royal Palace reflect the political instability of the late eighth century. Like other cities of the Maya Lowlands, this Terminal Classic crisis greatly diminished royal strength and prestige. Yet, despite the waning of royal power, large amounts of energy and resources were invested in a strong and enduring Waka' (Pérez Robles, Robles, Pérez, Menéndez, and Freidel 2021).

Elsewhere in the Maya realm, such as in Cancuen, this strategy in the face of the weakening of the royal court and the political system in general resulted in the partial opening of the palace complex. It made the civic-sacred enclosure accessible to more members of the growing nobility, incorporating them in an orderly and hierarchical way, creating new spaces so that the secondary nobility and other actors could access these privileged places (Barrientos 2015:230–231). It is very likely that the royal court experienced political difficulties and suffered significant attrition during the Terminal Classic period. The economic, political, and social repercussions within the city caused the king to grant powers, concessions, and special privileges, which enabled the current ruler not only to share power among the most important groups but also to find a new balance of the government and the city in its last years (Pérez Robles and Pérez 2019a:247). Keith Eppich argues that the city of Waka' prospered for more than two centuries after the events of the eighth century, hypothesizing that it was the royal response to the political crisis (Eppich and Van Oss 2017:130). The evidence allows the possibility of novel political arrangements and the establishment of a new, more participatory, co-governmental system whose headquarters was at Popol Nah, located east of Plaza 4 and the Royal Palace.

References

Acuña, Mary Jane
2014   Royal Alliances, Ritual Behavior, and the Abandonment of the Royal Couple Building at El Perú-Waka'. In *Archaeology at El Perú-Waka': Ancient Maya Performances of Ritual, Memory, and Power,* edited by Olivia C. Navarro-Farr and Michelle Rich, pp. 53–65. University of Arizona Press, Tucson.

Agurcia Fasquelle, Ricardo, and Juan Carlos Pérez
2017   La estructura Oropéndola en la Acrópolis de Copan. *Ciencias Espaciales* 9(2):73–106. https://doi.org/10.5377/ce.v9i2.5160.

Barrientos, Tomás
2015   El Palacio Real de Cancuen: Un análisis socio-espacial de la estructura política de las Tierras Bajas Mayas en el Siglo XVIII. In *XXVIII Simposio de Investigaciones Arqueológicas en Guatemala 2014*, edited by Bárbara Arroyo, Luis Méndez Salinas, and Lorena Paiz, pp. 223–238. Ministerio de Cultura y Deportes, Instituto de Antropología e Historia, Asociación Tikal, Guatemala City.

Barrientos, Tomás, Rudy Larios, Arthur Demarest, and Luis Fernando Luin
2002   El Palacio Real de Cancuen: Análisis preliminar de sus características y planes de investigación. In *XV Simposio de Investigaciones Arqueológicas en Guatemala, 2001*, edited by J. P. Laporte, H. Escobedo, and B. Arroyo, pp. 350–364. Museo Nacional de Arqueología y Etnología de Guatemala, Guatemala City.

Ciudad Ruíz, Andrés
2001   Los palacios residenciales del Clásico Temprano en las ciudades del sur de las Tierras Bajas Mayas. In *Reconstruyendo la ciudad Maya: El Urbanismo en las sociedades antiguas*, edited by Andrés Ciudad Ruíz, María Josefa Iglesias Ponce de León, and María del Carmen Martínez Martínez, pp. 305–340. Sociedad Española de Estudios Mayas, Madrid.

Coe, William R.
1990   *Excavations in the Great Plaza, North Terrace, and North Acropolis of Tikal.* Tikal Report No. 14. 6 vols. University Museum, University of Pennsylvania, Philadelphia.

Eppich, Keith
2014   Ritual Narratives from El Perú-Waka': Ceremonial Deposits in Non-royal, Elite Contexts. In *Archaeology at El Perú-Waka': Ancient Maya Performances of Ritual, Memory, and Power*, edited by Olivia C. Navarro-Farr and Michelle Rich, pp. 112–133. University of Arizona Press, Tucson.

Eppich, Keith, and Sarah Van Oss
2017   WK20: Excavaciones en la Plaza 4. In *Proyecto Arqueológico Waka' Informe no. 14, temporada 2016*, edited by Juan Carlos Pérez, pp. 130–160. Fundación de Investigación Arqueológica Waka', Guatemala City.

Freidel, David A., Barbara MacLeod, and Charles K. Suhler
2003   Early Classic Maya Conquest in Words and Deeds. In *Ancient Mesoamerican Warfare*, edited by M. Kat Brown and Travis W. Stanton, pp. 189–215. AltaMira Press, Walnut Creek.

Freidel, David, Olivia Navarro-Farr, Michelle Rich, Juan Carlos Meléndez, Juan Carlos Pérez, Griselda Pérez Robles, and Mary Kate Kelly
in press Mirror Conjurors of Waka'. Manuscript accepted by *Ancient Mesoamerica*.

Freidel, David, Juan Carlos Pérez, and Griselda Pérez Robles
2018   Palace of Maya Time Lords: Excavations in the Royal Acropolis at El Perú-Waka', Petén, Guatemala. *Current World Archaeology* 89. https://www.world-archaeology.com/world/south-america/palace-of-the-maya-time-lords/.

Guenter, Stanley P.
2005   Informe preliminar de la epigrafía de El Perú. In *Proyecto Arqueológico El Perú-Waka': Informe no. 2, temporada 2004*, edited by Héctor L. Escobedo and David Freidel, pp. 359–400. Fundación de Investigación Arqueológica Waka', Guatemala City.
2014   The Epigraphy of El Perú-Waka'. In *Archaeology at El Perú-Waka': Ancient Maya Performances of Ritual, Memory, and Power*, edited by Olivia C. Navarro-Farr and Michelle Rich, pp. 147–166. University of Arizona Press, Tucson.

Harrison, Peter D.
2003   Palaces of the Royal Court at Tikal. In *Maya Palaces and Elite Residences: An Interdisciplinary Approach*, edited by Jessica Joyce Christie, pp. 98–119. University of Texas Press, Austin.

Harrison, Peter D., and E. Wyllys Andrews
1998   Palaces of Tikal and Copán. In *Palaces of the Ancient New World*, edited by Susan Toby Evans and Joanne Pillsbury, pp. 113–148. Dumbarton Oaks Research Library and Collection, Washington, DC.

Inomata, Takeshi
2001   King's People: Classic Maya Courtiers in a Comparative Perspective. In *Royal Courts of the Ancient Maya, Vol. 1: Theory, Comparison, and Synthesis*, edited by Takeshi Inomata and Stephen D. Houston, pp. 27–53. Westview Press, Boulder.

Jacobo, Álvaro, Alexander Urízar, and Jaime Escobar
2017   Inventario forestal de M13-1 y la Acrópolis del sitio arqueológico El Perú. In *Proyecto Arqueológico Waka': Informe no. 15, temporada 2017*, edited by Juan Carlos Pérez, Griselda Pérez Robles, and David Freidel, pp. 461–492. Fundación de Investigación Arqueológica Waka', Guatemala City.

Lee, David
2004   WK-06: Excavaciones en la Estructura L11-38. In *Proyecto Arqueológico El Perú-Waka': Informe no. 1, temporada 2003*, edited by Héctor Escobedo and David Freidel, pp. 145–72. Fundación de Investigación Arqueológica Waka', Guatemala City.
2006   WK-06: Excavaciones en el complejo palaciego noroeste. In *Proyecto Arqueológico El Perú-Waka': Informe no. 3, temporada 2005*, edited by Héctor Escobedo and David Freidel, pp. 125–188. Fundación de Investigación Arqueológica Waka', Guatemala City.

Lee, David, and Laura Gámez
2007   WK-06: Excavaciones en el complejo palaciego noroeste: Resultados de la temporada de campo del 2006. In *Proyecto Arqueológico El Perú-Waka': Informe no. 4, temporada 2006*, Edited by Héctor Escobedo and David Freidel, pp. 125–188. Fundación de Investigación Arqueológica Waka', Guatemala City.

Lee, David F., and Jennifer C. Piehl
2014   Ritual and Remembrance at the Northwest Palace Complex, El Perú-Waka'. In *Archaeology at El Perú Perú-Waka': Ancient Maya Performances of Ritual, Memory, and Power*, edited by Olivia C. Navarro-Farr and Michelle Rich, pp. 85–101. University of Arizona Press, Tucson.

Martin, Simon
2001   Court and Realm: Architectural Signatures in the Classic Maya Southern Low-

lands. In *Royal Courts of the Ancient Maya*. Vol. 1: *Theory, Comparison, and Synthesis*, edited by Takeshi Inomata and Stephen D. Houston, pp. 168–194. Westview Press, Boulder.

2020   *Ancient Maya Politics. A Political Anthropology of the Classic Period 150–900 CE.* Cambridge University Press, New York.

Martin, Simon, and Nikolai Grube
2008   *Chronicle of the Maya Kings and Queens: Deciphering the Dynasties of the Ancient Maya*, 2nd ed. Thames and Hudson, London.

McAnany, Patricia A.
1998   Ancestors and the Classic Maya Built Environment. In *Function and Meaning in Classic Maya Architecture*, edited by Stephen D. Houston, pp. 271–298. Dumbarton Oaks Research Library and Collection, Washington, DC.

McAnany, Patricia A., and Shannon Plank
2001   Perspectives on Actors, Gender Roles, and Architecture at Classic Maya Courts and Households. In *Royal Courts of the Ancient Maya*. Vol. 1: *Theory, Comparison, and Synthesis*, edited by Takeshi Inomata and Stephen D. Houston, pp. 84–129. Westview Press, Boulder.

Menéndez, Damaris, and María de los Ángeles Cuyán
2020   Análisis del material cerámico WK-18. In *Proyecto Arqueológico Waka': Informe no. 18, temporada 2020*, edited by Juan Carlos Pérez, Griselda Pérez Robles, and Damien Marken, pp. 11–53. Fundación de Investigación Arqueológica Waka', Guatemala City.

Miller, Mary
1998   A Design for Meaning in Maya Architecture. In *Function and Meaning in Classic Maya Architecture*, edited by Stephen D. Houston, pp. 187–222. Dumbarton Oaks Research Library and Collection, Washington, DC.

Navarro-Farr, Olivia C.
2009   Ritual, Process, and Continuity in the Late to Terminal Classic Transition: Investigations at Structure M13-1 in the Ancient Maya Site of El Perú-Waka', Petén, Guatemala. PhD dissertation, Department of Anthropology, Southern Methodist University.

Navarro-Farr, Olivia, Ana Lucía Arroyave Prera, and E. Keith Eppich
2011   Interpretando los depósitos del Clásico Tardío-Terminal en la Estructura M13-1 en Waka'. In *Simposio de Arqueología XXVIII, 2010*, edited by Bárbara Arroyo, Luis Paiz, Adriana Linares, and Ana Lucía Arroyave, pp. 336–343. Museo Nacional de Arqueología y Etnología, Guatemala City.

Navarro-Farr, Olivia C., and Ana Lucía Arroyave Prera
2014   A Palimpsest Effect: The Multi-layered Meanings of Late-to-Terminal Classic Era Above-Floor Deposits at Structure M13-1. In *Archaeology at El Perú-Waka': Ancient Maya Performances of Ritual, Memory, and Power*, edited by Olivia C. Navarro-Farr and Michelle Rich, pp. 34–52. University of Arizona Press, Tucson.

Nelson, Ben A.
2004   Elite Residences in West Mexico. In *Palaces of the Ancient New World*, edited by Susan Toby Evans and Joanne Pillsbury, pp. 59–82. Dumbarton Oaks Research Library and Collection, Washington, DC.

Patterson, Erin

2017   Análisis preliminar de los restos óseos esqueléticos humanos, temporada 2017. In *Proyecto Arqueológico Waka': Informe no. 15, temporada 2017*, edited by Juan Carlos Pérez, Griselda Pérez Robles, and David Freidel, pp. 345–349. Fundación de Investigación Arqueológica Waka', Guatemala City.

Pérez Robles, Griselda, and Olivia Navarro-Farr

2013   WK01: Excavaciones en M13-1 y el descubrimiento de la Estela 44. In *Proyecto Regional Arqueológico El Perú-Waka': Informe no. 11, temporada 2013*, edited by Juan Carlos Pérez Calderón and David A. Freidel, pp. 3–26. Fundación de Investigación Arqueológica Waka', Guatemala City.

Pérez Robles, Griselda, and Juan Carlos Pérez

2017   Operación WK18, Excavaciones en la Acrópolis de Waka'. In *Proyecto Arqueológico El Perú-Waka': Informe no. 14, temporada 2016*, edited by Juan Carlos Pérez, pp. 83–126. Fundación de Investigación Arqueológica Waka', Guatemala City.

2019a   El Palacio Real de Waka': Una descripción desde la arquitectura del poder. In *II Ciclo Anual de Conferencias Arqueológicas*, edited by Mario Alfredo Ubico Calderón, Luz Midilia Marroquín Franco, and Luis Alberto Romero Rodríguez, pp. 236–249. Instituto de Investigaciones Históricas, Antropológicas y Arqueológicas, Escuela de Historia, Universidad de San Carlos de Guatemala, Guatemala City.

2019b   Operación WK25: Excavaciones en el Grupo J-15-1. In *Proyecto Arqueológico Waka': Informe no. 17, temporada 2019*, edited by Juan Carlos Pérez, Griselda Pérez, and Damien Marken, pp. 129–160. Fundación de Investigación Arqueológica Waka', Guatemala City.

Pérez Robles, Griselda, Juan Carlos Pérez, and David Freidel

2020   "Hoja" Chan Ahk: El descubrimiento de la tumba de un rey del Clásico Temprano en el Palacio Real de El Perú-Waka', Guatemala. *Anales del Museo de América* 27:76–94. Ministerio de Cultura y Deportes, Madrid.

Pérez Robles, Griselda, Juan Carlos Pérez, Damaris Menéndez, and Claver Couoj

2019   Operación WK18: La Acrópolis de Waka', el Palacio Real. In *Proyecto Arqueológico El Perú-Waka': Informe no. 16, temporada 2018*, edited by Juan Carlos Pérez, pp. 61–83. Fundación de Investigación Arqueológica Waka', Guatemala City.

Pérez Robles Griselda, Juan Carlos Pérez, Damaris Menéndez, and David Freidel

2017   Operación WK18: Excavaciones en la acrópolis y el Palacio Real de Waka'. In *Proyecto Arqueológico Waka': Informe no. 15, temporada 2017*, edited by Juan Carlos Pérez, Griselda Pérez Robles, and David Freidel pp. 84–129. Fundación de Investigación Arqueológica Waka', Guatemala City.

2021   Operación WK18: Los últimos años del edificio Palacio Real, Estructura L12-4. In *Proyecto Arqueológico Waka': Informe no. 19, temporada 2021*, edited by Juan Carlos Pérez, Griselda Pérez Robles, and Damien Marken, pp. 33–102. Fundación de Investigación Arqueológica Waka', Guatemala City.

Pérez Robles, Griselda, Juan Carlos Pérez, and Sarah Van Oss

2015   Operación WK18: Excavaciones en la acrópolis noroeste de Waka'. In *Proyecto Regional Arqueológico El Perú-Waka': Informe no. 12, temporada 2014*, edited by Juan Carlos Pérez, Griselda Pérez Robles, and David Freidel, pp. 104–119. Fundación de Investigación Arqueológica Waka', Guatemala City.

Quintana Samayoa, Oscar

2017   El noreste de el Petén: Aportes al urbanismo prehispánico. *Estudios de Cultura Maya* 49:1–23.

Reents-Budet, Dorie

2001   Classic Maya Concepts of the Royal Court: Analysis of Rendering on Pictorial Ceramics. In *Royal Courts of the Ancient Maya*. Vol. 1: *Theory, Comparison, and Synthesis*, edited by Takeshi Inomata and Stephen D. Houston, pp. 195–233. Westview Press, Boulder.

Rivera Dorado, Miguel

1995   Arquitectura, gobernantes y cosmología: Anotaciones sobre ideología Maya en los cuadernos de Oxkintok. *Revista Española de Antropología Americana* 25:23–40.

Salazar Lama, Daniel

2017   Formas de sacralizar a la figura real entre los mayas. *Journal de la Société des américanistes* 101(1–2):11–49. https://doi.org/10.4000/jsa.14397.

Schele, Linda, and David A. Freidel

1990   *A Forest of Kings: The Untold Story of the Ancient Maya*. William Morrow, New York.

Smith, A. Ledyard

1982   Mayor Architecture and Caches. In *Excavations at Seibal: Department of Petén, Guatemala*. Memoirs of the Peabody Museum of Archaeology and Ethnology, vol. 15, no. 1: Major Architecture and Caches, edited by Gordon R. Willey, pp. 1–263. Harvard University, Cambridge.

Stuart, David

2000   The Arrival of Strangers: Teotihuacan and Tollan in Classic Maya History. In *Mesoamerica's Classic Heritage: Teotihuacan to the Aztecs,* edited by D. Carrasco, L. Jones, and S. Sessions, pp. 465–513. University Press of Colorado, Niwot.

Suhler, Charles, Traci Ardren, and Dennis Johnstone

1998   The Chronology of Yaxuna: Evidence from Excavations and Ceramics. *Ancient Mesoamerica* 9:167–182.

Tate, Carolyn E.

1992   *Yaxchilan: The Design of a Maya Ceremonial City*. University of Texas Press, Austin.

Taube, Karl A.

1985   The Classic Maya Maize God: A Reappraisal. In *Fifth Palenque Round Table, 1983,* edited by Merle Greene Robertson, pp. 171–181. Pre-Columbian Art Research Institute, San Francisco.

Tiesler, Vera, Andrea Cucina, Travis W. Stanton, and David A. Freidel

2017   *Before Kukulkán: Bioarchaeology of Maya Life, Death, and Identity at Classic Period Yaxuná*. University of Arizona Press, Tucson.

Valdés, Juan Antonio

1994   El Grupo A de Uaxactún: Manifestaciones arquitectónicas y dinásticas durante el Clásico Temprano. In *I Simposio de Investigaciones Arqueológicas en Guatemala,*

1987, edited by Juan Pedro Laporte, Héctor Escobedo, and Silvia Villagrán, pp. 98–111. Museo Nacional de Arqueología y Etnología, Guatemala City.

Valdés, Juan Antonio, and Frederico Fahsen

2007 La figura humana en el arte Maya del Preclásico. In *XX Simposio de Investigaciones Arqueológicas en Guatemala, 2006*, edited by Juan Pedro Laporte, Bárbara Arroyo, and Héctor Escobedo, pp. 1160–1170. Museo Nacional de Arqueología y Etnología de Guatemala, Guatemala City.

Valdés, Juan Antonio, Marco Antonio Valladares, and José Roberto Díaz

2008 *Historia de la arquitectura prehispánica de las Tierras Bajas Mayas de Guatemala: El Preclásico (Fase I)*. Dirección General de Investigación, Instituto de Investigaciones Históricas Arqueológicas y Antropológicas, Universidad de San Carlos de Guatemala, Guatemala City.

Valle Chavarría, Lorena Gertrudis, Reina Isabel Loredo, and Carlos Berumen

2016 El Lenguaje visual como herramienta para el análisis morfológico de la arquitectura-escultura de los edificios 16, 18, 19 y 20 de El Tajín. *Revista Electrónica Nova Scentia, no. 16*, 8(1): 313–330.

Webster, David

2001 Spatial Dimensions of Maya Courtly Life: Problems and Issues. In *Royal Courts of the Ancient Maya*. Vol. 1: *Theory, Comparison, and Synthesis*, edited by Takeshi Inomata and Stephen D. Houston, pp. 130–167. Westview Press, Boulder.

Webster, David, and Takeshi Inomata

2004 Identifying Subroyal Elite Palaces at Copán and Aguateca. In *Palaces of the Ancient New World*, edited by Susan Toby Evans and Joanne Pillsbury, pp. 149–180. Dumbarton Oaks Research Library and Collection, Washington, DC.

10

Animals in the Portal

Zooarchaeological Investigations at El Perú-Waka', Structure M12-44, the Cuartito

DIANA N. FRIDBERG

> Although what we could call "waterholes," "limestone sinks," and "caves"
> have greatly differing economic uses, they are classified together and
> treated ritually much the same in the ceremonial life of Zinacantán . . . in
> the sacred geography all these *chenetik* are "openings" in the earth's crust,
> hence means of communication with the Earth Lord.
> —Evon Z. Vogt (1969:423)

This chapter presents a rich Late Classic Maya assemblage discovered in a subsurface chamber located within the urban center of Waka'. Structure M12-44, dubbed the Cuartito, produced substantial numbers of ceramics, lithics, shell, chert, and human bone; but most importantly for our purposes here, it produced an abundant and well-preserved faunal sample. The structure's unusual architecture and varied artifacts suggest its use in Late Classic ceremonial activity. This chapter describes the unique architectural and artifactual evidence found in the Cuartito and presents hypotheses regarding the nature of ritual activity at the structure. Building upon architecture, iconographic, and material analysis, I suggest that the Cuartito is a Late Classic, manmade cave used for ceremonies to access the supernatural. The associated archaeological assemblage reflects either activities that directly reference the structure's role as a supernatural portal or ceremonial refuse deposited in the space prior to its final sealing.

The Zooarchaeology of Waka'

Located in the heart of Petén, Waka' has abundant animal life. Today, the surrounding Parque Nacional Laguna del Tigre is home to some of the taxa that were most economically important and ideologically potent in ancient Maya life, such as the jaguar, scarlet macaw, and crocodile (Bestelmeyer and Alonso 2000). Biodiversity in Petén is driven by the region's physiography, warm climate, and high annual rainfall that support a variety of habitats and microhabitats—including savanna, grassland, canopied tropical forest—and a range of freshwater environments such as lakes and seasonally inundated swampland (Deevey 1978; Deevey et al. 1979; Schlesinger 2001; Sharer 1994; see also Marken and Ricker, this volume). During the city's occupation, the landscape around Waka' was subject to extensive anthropogenic changes and management. Plastered plazas, forest gardens, managed water sources, farmland, middens, and low- and high-density habitation areas created further environmental variation (Marken 2007, 2008, 2009, 2010, 2011; Marken and Ricker, this volume; Rich and Navarro-Farr 2014).

Zooarchaeology, the study of animal remains from archaeological sites, has played an important role in previous research in Petén, particularly in the southern and central areas (Emery 1997, 2003, 2004, 2008; Masson 1999a, 1999b; Moholy-Nagy 1998; Moholy-Nagy and Emery 2004; Pohl 1976, 1983, 1990; Reitz and Wing 1999). A continually growing field, Maya zooarchaeology in Petén reveals extensive and continuous, but socially and temporally variable, utilization of all classes of vertebrates (Sharpe and Emery 2015). The current faunal assemblage was collected during excavations across the city, many of which focused on the definition of architecture. Despite their ancillary role in these investigations and their often small sample size, the city's faunal remains attest to the use of a wide variety of animals in subsistence, crafting, and ritual activity. A particularly rich assemblage found in Structure M12-44 illustrates the breadth of animal utilization at Waka'. The animals it contains both attest to the variety of animal resources used in the city and, as part of a coherent package of material remains, help elucidate ritual activity there.

Background

Structure M13-1, a pyramidal temple with an attached *adosada* platform, was a major site of civic-ceremonial activity during the Classic period (see Navarro-Farr, Pérez, and Pérez Robles, this volume). East of the royal palace and forming the western edge of the city's religious-ceremonial epicenter, M13-1's elevated location in the landscape would have made it both visually prominent and ideologically potent (Navarro-Farr 2009:23). Excavations at the structure have produced abundant material evidence of Classic and Terminal Classic ritual activities, such as royal veneration and marking the passage of time (Navarro-Farr 2016; Navarro-Farr et al. 2020; see DeMarrais et al. 1996; Mock 1998). Evidence for Classic period activities at M13-1, including the burial of seventh-century Lady K'abel, suggests its use as a public stage for ritual performances honoring and reasserting the power of gods and kings (Navarro-Farr et al. 2020). The discovery of a monumental fire shrine, or *wiinte' naah*, on the western side of M13-1, which faces Plaza 2, suggests that fire rituals performed atop the building could be observed by the public (Freidel, Masson, and Rich 2017). In situ and redeposited monuments on the plaza-face of the structure suggest that the building was a vital locus for the public expression of Classic period religious and political commemoration at Waka' (Navarro-Farr, Pérez, et al. 2013).

After the ninth-century collapse of the royal court, Structure M13-1 continued to be used for commemorative activities (Navarro-Farr 2009). Excavations of material associated with terminal phase superstructure architecture revealed dense, artifact-rich deposits (Navarro-Farr 2004, 2005, 2006, 2009; Navarro-Farr and Arroyave Prera 2006, 2007, 2014; Navarro-Farr, Pérez Robles, Menéndez, et al. 2013; Navarro-Farr, Pérez Robles, and Menéndez, 2013). The diversity of these materials and their varied placement around the building indicate repeated use of M13-1 by a socioeconomically diverse population for commemorative ritual acts into the ninth and tenth centuries (Navarro-Farr 2009; Navarro-Farr and Arroyave Prera 2014). Structure M12-44 was built into a small open space just northeast of M13-1, adjacent to elite residences and not visible from Plaza 2 (Figure 10.1). In contrast to the *wiinte' naah* on the western side of M13-1, the subterranean Cuartito is in a semiprivate and restricted location. The chamber is small and rectangular, measuring 3.4 meters north–south by 2.47 meters east–west and descending to bedrock at a depth of approximately 3 meters. It was constructed with regular masonry walls and capped in antiquity with a four-sided masonry vault (Figure 10.2). Evidence for the vault shape is visible in the remaining lower courses. There is no evidence that any doors or passageways extended from within the chamber, which means that access was restricted to descent through the vault, resulting in a small, deliberately constructed masonry room descending from the surface of a semiprivate space directly associated with M13-1. Excavation of the Cuartito was performed to determine the structure's function as well as its relationship to the demonstrated ritual activities at the much larger M13-1.

Structure M12-44 was excavated over the course of two weeks during the 2012 field season and revealed complex, mixed stratigraphy. The feature was not sealed at the time of its excavation, and it was unclear whether the vault collapsed in the distant past or more recently. In addition to the collapsed vault, a fragmentary, flagstone pavement and deposits of ceramic, faunal bone,

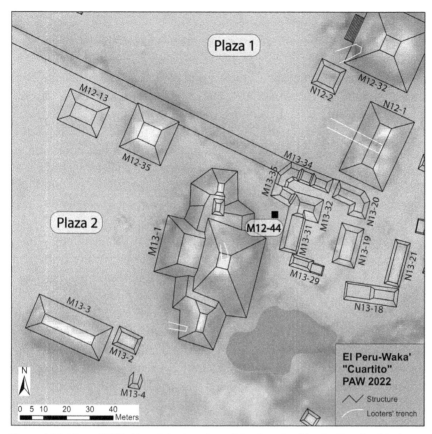

Figure 10.1. Map of M12-44 and the location of the Cuartito. Map by Damien Marken, courtesy of Proyecto Arqueológico Waka'.

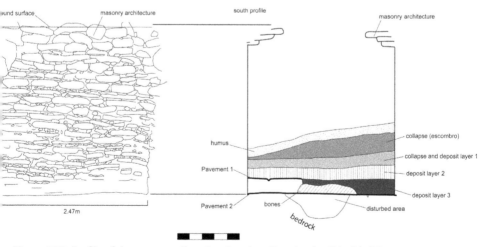

Figure 10.2. Profile of the masonry Cuartito chamber. Drawing by Griselda Pérez Robles, courtesy of Proyecto Arqueológico Waka'.

and other materials were discovered above the bedrock. This pavement consisted of cut stone blocks placed at the same depth, but in an irregular manner. It is unclear whether these blocks represent a true, intentional "paving" event. The unit was excavated in ten lots roughly corresponding to accreted humus; mixed rubble fill, including the probable remains of collapsed vault stones; a small, ashy concentration in the southwest corner; paving stones; a layer of artifact-rich deposit at the same depth as a disturbed bone bundle; material just above the bedrock; and material removed from an ancient cut in the bedrock. Fragmentary human remains extended through the layers of the deposit, suggesting the placement and later removal of a secondary burial at some point in antiquity.

The impression that emerges from this analysis is of intentional, ritualized placement of fragmentary, diverse taxa into the subterranean space of Structure M12-44. Small quantities of microfaunal remains were recovered from the flotation of bulk soil samples performed for paleoethnobotanical analysis. Faunal specimens were exported and analyzed at the zooarchaeology laboratory at Washington University in St. Louis, where each specimen was assessed for refits within its excavation lot, identified to body part and taxon, and weighed. Taxonomic identifications were made in reference to comparative skeletal material in the St. Louis and Guatemala City laboratories, material housed at the Field Museum of Natural History in Chicago, and published and unpublished photographic collections (Florida Museum of Natural History; Field Museum of Natural History, Washington University in St. Louis; and Universidad Autónoma de Yucatán) as well as reference volumes (e.g., Gilbert 1990; Gilbert et al. 1996; Hillson 1992; Olsen 1964, 1968, 1982). Natural and cultural modifications were recorded where present.

Zooarchaeological Results

A total of 1,607 fragments of vertebrate faunal material were recovered (Table 10.1). The Cuartito assemblage is notable for its taxonomic diversity. Mammalia was the most abundant class identified in all lots and in the unit overall by count (NISP = 814, 50.65% total faunal assemblage) and by weight (910.97 g, 78%). Reptiles (NISP = 146, 9.09%) and bony fish (Osteichthyes; NISP = 244, 15.18%) contributed significantly to the assemblage, with smaller quantities of amphibians (NISP = 59, 3.67%) and birds (NISP = 35, 3.67%) also present.

Overall preservation of the assemblage is very good. More than half (NISP = 828, 51.52%) of the specimens were maximally identifiable to element (i.e., humerus, femur). The remaining specimens were equally split between

Table 10.1. Taxonomic representation by lot (NISP), Structure M12-44

Taxon Lot:	396	401	406	413	418	420	425	435	446	Total
FISH, TOTAL:	**22**	**1**	**40**	**38**	**60**		**32**	**50**	**1**	**244**
Tropical gar (*Atractosteus tropicus*)		1	2		2		2	7		14
Cichlids (Cichlidae)			4							4
Bony fish, unspecified (Osteichthyes)	22		34	38	58		30	43	1	226
AMPHIBIA, TOTAL:	**1**		**10**	**7**	**16**		**24**	**1**		**59**
Frog/toad, unspecified (Order Anura)	1		7	7	12		22	1		50
Cane toad (*Rhinella marina*)			3		4		2			9
REPTILIA, TOTAL:	**60**	**20**	**39**	**7**	**4**		**10**	**5**	**1**	**146**
Turtle, unspecified	2	2	4	7	2		9	3	1	30
Iguana (Iguanidae)			3							3
Snake (Suborder Serpentes)	57	18	28		1					104
Crocodile (Order Crocodilia)								1		1
Reptile, unspecified	1	4			1		1	1		8
AVES, TOTAL:		**1**	**24**	**2**	**5**		**2**		**1**	**35**
Motmot (Momotidae)			2							2
Gamebirds (Galliformes, unspec.)			1							1
Ocellated turkey (*Meleagris ocellata*)			2						1	3
Bird, unspecified		1	19	2	5		2			29
Taxon:	396	401	406	413	418	420	425	435	446	Total
MAMMALIA, TOTAL:	**129**	**21**	**245**	**63**	**111**	**1**	**168**	**62**	**14**	**814**
Order Didelphimorphia										
American opossum (Didelphidae)	2		4		1		1	1		9
Gray four-eyed opossum (*Philander opossum*)	3									3
Order Cingulata										
Armadillo (Dasypodidae)	1		2							3
Nine-banded armadillo (*Dasypus novemcinctus*)			1							1
Order Rodentia										
Mice/rats (Muridae)		4			1			3		8
Hystricognath rodents (Infraorder Hystricognathi)			3	1	2			1		7
Central American agouti (*Dasyprocta punctata*)			6		1					7
Giant pocket gopher (*Orthogeomys* sp.)	2		4		1		1			8
Rodent, unspecified	5		12	10	19		16	4		66

(continued)

Table 10.1—Continued

Taxon:	396	401	406	413	418	420	425	435	446	Total
Order Lagomorpha										
Rabbit (Leporidae)			1							1
Order Carnivora										
Domestic dog (*Canis familiaris*)	2	2	19	4	3		17	8	4	59
Cat (Felidae)				1						1
Carnivore, unspecified					3		2			5
Order Artiodactyla										
Deer (Cervidae)	1				1					2
White-tailed deer (*Odocoileus virginianus*)	4	2	8	3				2		19
Brocket deer (*Mazama* sp.)			1							1
Peccary (Tayassuidae)	4		7							11
Artiodactyl, unspecified	1		4		1				1	7
Mammal, unspecified	104	13	173	44	78	1	131	43	9	596
NID, total:	**43**		**42**	**12**	**87**		**71**	**52**	**2**	**309**
Total	**255**	**43**	**400**	**129**	**283**	**1**	**307**	**170**	**19**	**1607**

those minimally identifiable to element (i.e., long bone shaft, rib shaft, axial fragment; NISP = 309, 24.27%) and unidentifiable fragments (NISP = 389, 24.21%). Bones in the assemblage showed minimal modification and were not highly fragmented. Rodent gnawing was minimal (NISP = 25) and mostly localized in the upper lots. Very little burning (NISP = 86) and few cut marks (NISP = 25) were present. Of the mammal remains maximally identifiable to element, 43.40% (NISP = 204) are over 50% complete (25.06% total mammal remains), and more than a third of the mammal bones maximally identifiable to element (NISP = 159, 33.82%) are over 75% complete. Because the deposit was not sealed when excavated, a degree of caution is necessary in interpreting the presence of animals that may simply have fallen into the open cavity. The amphibian remains generally displayed preservation similar to that seen in other bones in their respective lots, but because frogs and toads are commonly found in subterranean areas, both cultural and natural explanations for their presence must be considered. The completeness and white color of snake remains found in the uppermost layer suggest that it represents an intrusive individual. The snake remains found in an area of probable vault collapse display similar preservation to other bones in the lot and represent a single individual, though whether it is cultural or intrusive is unclear.

The Cuartito material is noteworthy for several reasons. It is taxonomically diverse and includes known subsistence taxa (e.g., white-tailed deer [*Odocoi-*

leus virginianus] and fish) as well as animals more likely used for decorative or ceremonial purposes (e.g., felid, crocodile [*Crocodylus* sp.]). Some taxa are represented by isolated elements; among these are a mandible and two pelvis fragments of iguana, one crocodile tooth, three dermal scutes, and one humerus corresponding to armadillo (Dasypodidae), one rabbit (Leporidae) tibia, and one molar corresponding to a large felid (Felidae, cf. puma or jaguar). A matched left and right pair of motmot (Momotidae) ulnae may be evidence of feather use. The integrity of the faunal remains suggests their protection from exposure to damaging taphonomic factors, likely due to their deposition in an enclosed space prior to the loss of the vault. The excellent level of preservation observed argues against the notion that postdepositional destruction would significantly skew taxonomic representation.

Other Materials

The Cuartito excavations produced abundant materials for analysis. In addition to the vertebrate faunal remains, 37 poorly preserved human bone fragments were collected, corresponding to a minimum of three individuals (Erin Patterson, personal communication 2012). Most of these specimens are long-bone fragments found adjacent to a cut in bedrock and interpreted as the remains of a disturbed bundle burial. Botanical remains were scarce, with most recovered samples originating in areas of high ash content. Paleoethnobotanical analysis revealed relatively large fragments of tree fruit seeds including zapote (*Pouteria* sp.), siricote (*Cordia* sp.), and hogplum (*Spondias* sp.) as well as a single maize kernel (Clarissa Cagnato, personal communication 2014). The abundance of plant remains were found in proximity to the human remains associated with the bundle. Inorganic materials from the deposit include 61 fragments of chert and 23 pieces of black and green obsidian. Artifacts suggesting ritual activity include fragments of ocher, greenstone, the head of a deer figurine, and a speleothem fragment. The removal and transport of speleothems from caves was a common practice among the ancient Maya, and speleothems continue to be used in ritual activities among modern Maya groups (Brady, Scott, et al. 1997; Brady and Prufer 2005; Peterson et al. 2005). Ceramic analysis identified types ranging from ubiquitous, coarse-paste utilitarian wares and striated water jars to palace-quality polychromes. The ceramic assemblage includes materials from the Late Classic Q'eq' Complex (ca. 550–800 CE) and the Terminal Classic Rax Complex (ca. 800–1000 CE). This was confirmed through AMS dating (Accelerator Mass Spectrometry), with selected bone material dating to the Late Classic, ca. 614–768 calibrated. During analysis, the frequencies of monochrome ceramics (blackwares and redwares) appeared to vary with the stratigraphy, but there was no statistically significant difference in the ceramic distribution in different levels. Terminal Classic indicators (i.e., Altar Orange, Danta Orange Polychrome, Poite Incised, Tres Naciones Grey, Tohil Plumbate) appeared to be more frequent in the upper strata of the deposit. Late Classic materials (i.e., Infierno Black, Nanzal Red, Tinaja Red, Carmelita Incised, Chilar Fluted) seemed to become more abundant closer to bedrock. An increase in Late Classic diagnostic sherds (approximately 2.5 meters below surface level) corresponds with the appearance of heavily eroded, palace-quality ceramics. These include a minimum of two cylinder vases of indeterminate Palmar Orange polychrome and a robust Zacatal cream polychrome bowl (Figure 10.3). The abundant presence of common, utilitarian unslipped and striated sherds contrasts sharply with the palace-quality material. The ceramic data therefore support Late Classic use with later reuse in the Terminal Classic, with significant mixing between the two.

Cosmology and M12-44

Before interpreting the artifacts of Structure M12-44, it is first necessary to interpret the unique architectural space in which they were interred. The Cuartito has two main architectural features that suggest it was constructed as a "pseudocave," or simulacrum of a natural subterranean void: it is a subsurface chamber, and it had a quadrilateral vault. The cosmology of many pre-Columbian groups is based upon a multilayered universe in which passages that pierce the earth's surface serve as conduits between the world inhabited by humans and the supernatural Underworld (Bassie-Sweet 2008; Brady and Prufer 2005; Gossen 1974; Prufer and Brady 2005; Redfield and Villa Rojas 1971; Stross 1996; Vogt 1969, 1993). Creation stories often focus on caves as origin places and as portals for the movement of spiritual forces between these realms (Redfield 1941; B. Tedlock 1982; D. Tedlock 1996; Thompson 1970; Vaillant 1962). The earth's surface is understood to be permeable, and the act of penetrating and reemerging from the earth is supernaturally charged.

In ancient Mesoamerica there is widespread evidence for the extensive incorporation of earth entries such as caves and cenotes into ritual activity. These activities vary through space and time but often incorporate concepts that reference the role of caves as portals to the Underworld. The archaeological remains of cave rituals suggest their use in accession ceremonies and lineage veneration (Bassie-Sweet 1991; Heyden 1975; Suhler et al. 1998), rites of passage (Heyden 1976), and cosmic centering (Brady and Ashmore 1999:127).

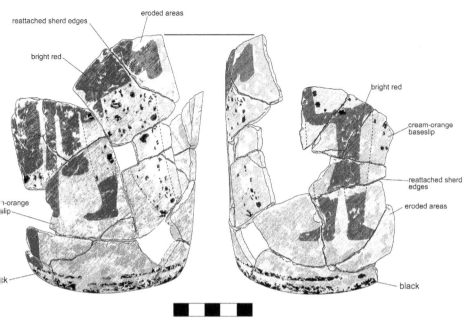

Figure 10.3. Full-figural polychrome vase from the Cuartito. Drawing by Keith Eppich, courtesy of Proyecto Arqueológico Waka'.

In multiple ancient Mesoamerican belief systems, there is a conceptual coupling between both mass above the surface and vacuity below. This duality is most explicit in regions where mountains (mass above) are themselves considered to be hollow. Caves, however, do not present the only option for piercing the surface of the earth. Caves and related topography such as sinkholes and cenotes are natural features, but subterranean spaces may also be manmade. Scholars have made the analogy that mountain is to cave as monumental architecture is to constructions below the surface, for example, tombs, cache holes, and subsurface chambers (Benson 1985; Brady and Ashmore 1999; Stuart and Houston 1994:86; Tokovinine 2013; Vogt 1981, 1992). James Brady and George Veni (1992) link such constructions specifically to caves, identifying artificial caves as an architectural form among the pre-Hispanic Maya of Highland Guatemala. They discuss several modified and constructed spaces with evidence of ritual activity and suggest that the notion of the cave as a sacred and centering location was so important to cosmology that pseudocaves were constructed at sites where none existed naturally. In other locations, such as at Waka' Structure P13-5, natural cavities in bedrock were modified and augmented with construction to create subterranean spaces that could be entered (Rich 2013; see also Freidel, this volume). The term "pseudocave" in this work and others draws the distinction between the natural world and human creations to emulate caves for ideological purposes.

David Freidel and Charles Suhler (1999) identify subsurface constructions of varying complexity as "path places" used to enact rituals that involved movement from the Underworld to the surface to the sky. They suggest that such architectural forms were important in accession rituals in which rulers were "reborn" into leadership by mimicking the descent and resurrection performed by the gods. Suhler and colleagues (1998) discuss Northern Lowland architectural forms featuring restricted-access, subsurface chambers in their analysis of Structures 6E-53 and 6E-120 at Yaxuna. The majority of examples cited, including those at Yaxuna, consist of small networks of chambers and connecting passages accessible by a "trap door" or other small entry. However, Suhler and colleagues (1998) identify the single-chambered Structure 2 at the center of Ake as a variant that potentially fulfilled the same purpose. Like the Cuartito, Ake Structure 2 is constructed of masonry with a vaulted roof, though it is round rather than rectangular (Roys and Shook 1966). In the interpretation of Suhler and colleagues (1998), these subsurface features offered places to reenact descent into and reemergence from the Underworld.

As a subsurface chamber, the Cuartito is a purposefully constructed earth entry. There is justification to think that it operated within the same semiotic framework as other natural and manmade features that pierce the surface of the earth. In Maya and broader Mesoamerican cosmology, such locations are considered to symbolize Underworld portals.

Vaulting and Quadripartite Symbolism

The quadrilateral vault further suggests that M12-44 may be interpreted as a portal. Four-part figures including quartered circles, quatrefoil, and cross motifs figure prominently in Mesoamerican iconography, including that of the Maya, from the Middle Preclassic onward (Coggins 1980; Egan 2011; Guernsey 2010). Quatrefoils and half quatrefoils are interpreted as representing the maw of the supernatural zoomorphic earth (Carrasco and Hull 2002; Joralemon 1976). They are used as fundamental orienting concepts in Maya cosmology; four-part figures are variably interpreted as representing the cardinal directions (Seler 1901–1902; Thompson 1934) and the structure of time through the solar cycle (Coggins 1980). Common interpretations of these figures connect them to the tightly coupled concepts of caves and Underworld portals (e.g., Bassie-Sweet 1991, 1996, 2008; Baudez 1996; Brady and Ashmore 1999; Freidel, Schele, and Parker 1993; Grove 1968; Guernsey 2010;

Heyden 1975; Joralemon 1976; Love and Guernsey 2007; Stone 1995, 2005; Stross 1996; Taube 1998, 2004; Vogt and Stuart 2005).

Numerous architectural manifestations of four-part symbolism have been documented in Maya culture, including the structure of quadrilateral pyramids and corbeled vault architecture (Carrasco and Hull 2002; Suhler et al. 1998). The Cuartito's squared corners and quadrilateral vault display conscious choices. When those choices are considered alongside the significant labor required to excavate a quadrilateral cavity of this size and line it with masonry, it is reasonable to assume that there are significant motives behind its design.

The isolated, subsurface room is not a common architectural form for the Classic Maya, nor is the four-sided vault as seen in M12-44 (Figure 10.2). In fact, there is no feature previously described in Maya archaeology that combines these particular features. Interpretation therefore depends on analogy to other geographic and cultural features that bear physical or conceptual similarities to the Cuartito.

Classic Period Usage of M12-44

Like the structures discussed by Suhler and colleagues (Freidel and Suhler 1999; Suhler et al. 1998), M12-44 is a deliberately constructed subsurface chamber that may have represented a portal to the Underworld and as such played a role in accession ceremonies. Its proximity to M13-1 places the Cuartito within a plausible space of royal performance. Furthermore, the placement and later removal of (likely bundled) human remains is consistent with ancestor veneration seen at other Maya cities (e.g., Chase and Chase 1996; Fitzsimmons 2006; McAnany 1995).

However, even if M12-44 was used in accession or other ceremonies to access the Underworld, the abundant faunal assemblage contained within still demands explanation. Why were these particular animals placed inside, and why are their bodies incomplete? Several ethnographically documented practices among the modern Maya offer potential insight.

Portal to the Underworld

Earth entries continue to be important ritual spaces for modern Maya communities, and ethnographic accounts suggest some continuity in both the activities performed and the sacred associations of these places. This is well documented by Evon Vogt (1969, 1993) among the Tzotzil of Zinacantán, who view the underground, hollow interior of mountains as the realm of ancestral deities and the Earth Lord, a deity with ancient roots. Communication with these figures can be achieved through activities in earth entries.

Though variable legends surround the Earth Lord, two major components of his duties and abilities featuring animals occur in ethnographic accounts. He is the lord of wild animals with whom humans must negotiate when hunting and the custodian of the animal spirit that forms part of each human soul (Vogt 1969, 1993). Offerings made to this deity within the space of earth entries (like the Cuartito) may reference both these aspects of the Earth Lord's influence.

Hunting Shrine

While the specific ritual activities performed in the Cuartito remain obscure, a potential use of the structure may be reflected in ethnohistoric accounts of hunting shrines. Appeal to supernatural figures, such as the Earth Lord, is an indispensable part of hunting rituals in Mesoamerica (Brown 2005). Bishop Diego de Landa described sixteenth-century Yucatec hunting rituals to bless future hunts and to appease the gods for the killing of animals during the hunt (Tozzer 1941:155, 162). Similar offerings to supernatural animal guardians have also been documented elsewhere in the Maya world (e.g., Redfield and Villa Rojas 1971:117–118; Thompson 1930:142, 1970:308; Villa Rojas 1945:103).

Linda Brown and her colleagues Kitty Emery and Luis Alberto Romero analyzed modern hunting shrines from the Highlands of Guatemala, where the Guardian of Animals, or Earth Lord, is first petitioned for a successful hunt and subsequently thanked (Brown 2002, 2005; Brown and Emery 2008; Brown and Romero 2002). Remains of captured animals are deposited at these sites and serve as "seeds" for the regeneration of new animal life. This belief is recorded in a myth from the Cuchumatán area in which animal bones sprout forth new creatures (La Farge 1947:50–51). The faunal assemblages from hunting shrines vary considerably in their composition and quantity of remains but bear evidence for careful curation of bones prior to their deposition. Hunting rituals are often enacted in the liminal, portal space of an earth entry.

The Cuartito assemblage is not identical to those found in hunting shrines, but it does have notable similarities. There is a general predominance of subsistence-associated animals and significant overlap with those taxa documented by Linda Brown and Kitty Emery (2008), including white-tailed deer, armadillo, peccary, agouti, opossum, brocket deer, dog, pocket gopher, felid, and turkey. The bones in the assemblage are relatively unfragmented, unmodified, and unrelated, which is consistent with conscious selection for inclusion (Brown 2005:142; Brown and Emery 2008). Unlike the shrine sites described in the literature, however, it is not an open-air site (Brown and Romero 2002:675), nor is it located in an area away from human habitation (Brown and Emery 2008:315). Complete skeletons were not deposited, as is required according to certain modern beliefs and practices (Brown and Emery 2008:313). However, consideration of this possible purpose is warranted because it is dense with remains, and observed taxonomic diversity is not unlike certain examples found in modern shrines (Brown and Emery 2008:325).

Animal Souls

A belief in animal souls may provide an alternative explanation for the deposition of animal remains within the constructed "portal" of the subsurface chamber. The concept that human souls are composed of multiple parts, one of which is animal in nature, is documented among modern Maya beliefs and has deep roots in Mesoamerican antiquity. The presence of a supernatural link between an individual human and a specific, usually nondomesticated animal, is a common theme in Mesoamerica (Dow 1986; Foster 1944; Gossen 1975; Linn 1989, Pitt-Rivers 1970; Vogt 1969; Wisdom 1940).

Epigraphers have identified the Classic period glyph *u way* (T549) as an expression for an animal spirit or co-essence. This is ethnographically documented among modern Maya groups and is referred to as *wayob* (singular *way*) (Grube and Nahm 1994; Houston and Stuart 1989). This glyph co-occurs with Classic period iconography depicting anthropomorphized or otherwise supernatural animals (Calvin 1997; Grube and Nahm 1994). The exact nature of these figures as expressed in the Classic period remains a subject of some debate due to the variability in modern Maya conceptions of *wayob* (Matteo and Manjavacas 2009). Common features of *way* spirits include their supernatural status, zoomorphic form, and textual association with an individual.

Vogt (1969, 1993) discusses the notion, held by the Tzotzil Maya of Zinacantán, that each individual has an animal that forms part of his or her soul. These spirit animals are kept in underground corrals of the Earth Lord and are tended by deified ancestors (Vogt 1969; 1993:19). The animal might be small and humble or large and powerful, depending on the social status of the individual (Vogt 1969, 1993). In the event of disrespectful behavior, these gods might punish the individual by releasing his or her spirit animal from its pen into the world, where it would be vulnerable to harm (Vogt 1969:301). Forgiveness of transgressions through offerings (including sacrifice of animals such as chickens) might allow the safe return of the animal soul (Vogt 1969:301).

The Cuartito deposit may indicate that the belief that supernatural animals of all varieties were "kept" underground extends to the Late Classic period. The notion that all individuals have an animal soul reflecting their social status greatly opens the range of potential *wayob* and may help explain the great diversity seen in the Cuartito faunal assemblage. The animals represented may be physical expressions of a diverse society's *wayob* or offerings to placate the gods who oversee the safekeeping of the community's animal souls.

Ritual Disposal

In addition to a direct appeal to the Earth Lord or another animal-associated supernatural figure, a third possibility is that the final Cuartito assemblage may represent an act of ceremonial disposal. This interpretation is supported by the incompleteness of the animal bodies (suggesting food remains rather than offerings of complete carcasses) in combination with the observed ceramic forms.

The traditional methods of preparing food in the Maya region, baking and stewing, do not tend to produce a highly visible taphonomic signature indicative of cooking (Götz 2014). The isolated and minimally modified elements of faunal skeletons found in the assemblage could therefore be the remnants of food preparation, such as for stews and tamales, where the elements themselves are disarticulated through gentle cooking rather than via mechanical separation with a bladed implement. In contrast, paleoethnobotanical identification of unusually large fragments of tree fruit seeds suggests the fruits found in the assemblage were deposited whole (Clarissa Cagnato, personal communication 2014). These fruits are usually consumed raw; if they were part of a food offering, they would likely have been deposited intact.

Palace-quality serving wares indicate consumption by the high elite. Cylinder vessels are associated with the high-status practice of cacao preparation and consumption (Ball 1983:136; Hall et al. 1990). The appearance of cylinders and other elite, Late Classic serving wares, such as plates and bowls, may be a sign of ritual consumption events or the presentation of food offerings. The lack of complete refits for serving vessels suggests that any use of the vessels for serving was performed outside the confines of the Cuartito and that the feature itself served as a place for the disposal of ritual refuse (Walker 1995; Kunen et al. 2002).

If the Cuartito assemblage is the result of the ritual deposition of prepared (and, in the case of fruits, unprepared) foods, for whom or what purpose were they intended? The associated consumption or food preparation event could be associated with any number of purposes, including honoring the Earth Lord, paying tribute to the *wayob* in his keeping, or providing a taxonomically diverse "feast" for the individual once interred in the disturbed bundle burial (Eppich et al. 2014).

Conclusion

The combined ceramic and zooarchaeological data indicate that the Cuartito was used for ritual activity during the Late Classic. The open cavity was then reused by sub-elite or commoner populations in the Terminal Classic to deposit refuse, as indicated by an abundance of coarse, utilitarian ceramic fragments. Although some amount of Terminal Classic faunal material deposition is possible, AMS provides a Late Classic date for all tested bone fragments. The upper portion of the midden deposit is similar to Terminal Classic sheet middens found elsewhere on and around M13-1, which had minimal to nonexistent faunal remains (Navarro-Farr 2009; Navarro-Farr and Arroyave Prera 2014). These factors argue that the dense, fauna-rich deposit found in lower strata is evidence for Late Classic ritual rather than for the subsequent Terminal Classic refuse disposal.

Structure M12-44 reflects the difficulties inherent in reconstructing archaeological ceremony, especially in disturbed or open contexts. The space itself is similar to pseudocaves, accession platforms, and other subsurface structures interpreted as points of access between the terrestrial world and the Underworld. Its unusual quadrilateral vault, similar to the quatrefoil motif associated with earth entries, reinforces the interpretation that the Cuartito functioned as a portal between the worlds. Yet despite these similarities, the physical structure does not have any direct archaeological or ethnographically known analog. In the absence of such repetition, interpretation of activities enacted in the structure is only suggestive.

Although in itself an unassuming architectural feature, the location of the Cuartito in the urban epicenter, coupled with its properties as a carefully manufactured hole in the earth, clearly mark it as a ritual space. The inclusion of a cave stone offers credence to the idea that this feature was interpreted at one time as a pseudocave or portal to the Underworld. The placement of faunal remains in this supernaturally charged space during the Late Classic can therefore be considered a ritually meaningful act rather than simple disposal. Regardless of whether they were the remnants of a festive meal or agents to appeal to the Earth Lord, the entry of animals into the Cuartito marked their symbolic entry into the supernatural Underworld.

References

Ball, Joseph W.
1983   Teotihuacan, the Maya, and Ceramic Interchange: A Contextual Perspective. In *Highland-Lowland Interaction in Mesoamerica: Interdisciplinary Approaches*, edited by Arthur G. Miller, pp. 125–146. Dumbarton Oaks Research Library and Collection, Washington, DC.

Bassie-Sweet, Karen
1991   *From the Mouth of the Dark Cave: Commemorative Sculpture of the Late Classic Maya.* University of Oklahoma Press, Norman.
1996   *At the Edge of the World: Caves and Late Classic Maya World View.* University of Oklahoma Press, Norman.
2008   *Maya Sacred Geography and the Creator Deities.* University of Oklahoma Press, Norman.

Baudez, Claude-François
1996   The Cross Group at Palenque. In *Eighth Palenque Round Table*, edited by Martha J. Macri and Jim McHargue, pp. 121–128. Pre-Columbian Research Institute, San Francisco.

Benson, Elizabeth P.
1985   Architecture as Metaphor. In *Fifth Palenque Round Table, 1993*, edited by Virginia M. Fields, pp. 183–188. Pre-Columbian Art Research Institute, San Francisco.

Bestelmeyer, Brandon T., and Leeanne E. Alonso, editors
2000   *A Biological Assessment of Laguna del Tigre National Park, Petén, Guatemala.* Conservation International, Center for Applied Biodiversity Science, Department of Conservation Biology, Washington, DC.

Brady, James E., and Wendy Ashmore
1999   Mountains, Caves, Water: Ideational Landscapes of the Ancient Maya. In *Archaeologies of Landscape: Contemporary Perspectives*, edited by Wendy Ashmore and A. Bernard Knapp, pp. 124–145. Blackwell, Malden, MA.

Brady, James E., Allan B. Cobb, Sergio Garza, Cesar Espinosa, and Robert Burnett
2005   An Analysis of Ancient Maya Stalactite Breakage at Balam Na Cave, Guatemala. In *Stone Houses and Earth Lords: Maya Religion in the Cave Context*, edited by Keith M. Prufer and James E. Brady, pp. 213–224. University Press of Colorado, Boulder.

Brady, James E., and Keith M. Prufer
2005   Introduction: A History of Mesoamerican Cave Interpretation. In *In the Maw of the Earth Monster: Mesoamerican Ritual Cave Use*, edited by James E. Brady and Keith M. Prufer, pp. 1–17. University of Texas Press, Austin.

Brady, James E., Ann Scott, Hector Neff, and Michael D. Glascock
1997   Speleothem Breakage, Movement, Removal, and Caching: An Aspect of Ancient Maya Cave Modification. *Geoarchaeology* 12(6):725–750.

Brady, James E., and George Veni
1992   Man-Made and Pseudo-karst Caves: The Implications of Subsurface Features within Maya Centers. *Geoarchaeology* 7(2):149–167.

Bronk Ramsey, Christopher
2009   Bayesian Analysis of Radiocarbon Dates. *Radiocarbon* 51(1):337–360.

Brown, Linda A.

2002 The Structure of Ritual Practice: An Ethnoarchaeological Exploration of Activity Areas at Rural Community Shrines in the Maya Highlands. PhD dissertation, Department of Anthropology, University of Colorado, Denver.

2005 Planting the Bones: Hunting Ceremonialism at Contemporary and Nineteenth-Century Shrines in the Guatemalan Highlands. *Latin American Antiquity* 16(2):131–146.

Brown, Linda A., and Kitty F. Emery

2008 Negotiations with the Animate Forest: Hunting Shrines in the Guatemalan Highlands. *Journal of Archaeological Method and Theory* 15(4):300–337.

Brown, Linda A., and Luis Alberto Romero

2002 Lugares sagrados para ritos de cacería. In *XV Simposio de Investigaciones Arqueológicas en Guatemala, 2001*, edited by Juan Pedro Laporte, Héctor Escobedo, and Bárbara Arroyo, pp. 771–778. Museo Nacional de Arqueología y Etnología, Guatemala City.

Calvin, Inga

1997 Where the *Wayob* Live: A Further Examination of Classic Maya Supernaturals. In *The Maya Vase Book: A Corpus of Rollout Photographs of Maya Vases*, vol. 5, edited by Barbara Kerr and Justin Kerr, pp. 868–883. Kerr Associates, New York.

Carrasco, Michael David, and Kerry Hull

2002 The Cosmogonic Symbolism of the Corbeled Vault in Maya Architecture. *Mexicon* 24(2):26–32.

Chase, Diane Z., and Arlen F. Chase

1996 Maya Multiples: Individuals, Entries, and Tombs in Structure A34 of Caracol, Belize. *Latin American Antiquity* 7(1):61–79.

Coggins, Clemency

1980 The Shape of Time: Some Political Implications of a Four-Part Figure. *American Antiquity* 45(4):727–739.

Deevey, E. S.

1978 Holocene Forests and Maya Disturbance near Quexil Lake, Petén, Guatemala. *Polskie Archiwum Hydrobiologii* 25:117–129.

Deevey, E. S., Don S. Rice, Prudence M. Rice, H. H. Vaughan, Mark Brenner, and M. S. Flannery

1979 Mayan Urbanism: Impact on a Tropical Karst Environment. *Science*, n.s., 206(4416):298–306.

DeMarrais, Elizabeth, Luis Jaime Castillo, and Timothy Earle

1996 Ideology, Materialization, and Power Strategies. *Current Anthropology* 37(1):15–31.

Dow, James

1986 Tonal and Nagual in Otomi Thought: Totemic Symbols of Caring. *Central Issues in Anthropology* 6(2):25–30.

Egan, Rachel K.

2011 New Perspectives on the Quatrefoil in Classic Maya Iconography: The Center and the Portal. Master's thesis, Department of Anthropology, University of Central Florida, Orlando.

Emery, Katherine Frances

1997   The Maya Collapse: A Zooarchaeological Investigation. PhD dissertation, Department of Anthropology, Cornell University, Ithaca, NY.

2003   The Noble Beast: Status and Differential Access to Animals in the Maya World. *World Archaeology* 34(1):498–515.

2004   Maya Zooarchaeology: New Directions in Method and Theory. In *Maya Zooarchaeology: New Directions in Theory and Method*, edited by K. Emery, pp. 1–100. Cotsen Institute of Archaeology Press, Los Angeles.

2008   A Zooarchaeological Test for Dietary Resource Depression at the End of the Classic Period in the Petexbatun, Guatemala. *Human Ecology* 36:617–634.

Eppich, Keith E.

2011   Lineage and State at El Perú-Waka': Ceramic and Architectural Perspectives. PhD dissertation, Department of Anthropology, Southern Methodist University, Dallas.

Eppich, Keith, Olivia Navarro-Farr, Griselda Pérez Robles, and Michelle Rich

2014   Un banquete para honrar a los muertos: Cerámica funeraria real de la ciudad Maya Clásica de El Perú-Waka', Guatemala. Paper presented at the XXVIII Simposio de Investigaciones Arqueológicas en Guatemala, Guatemala City.

Fitzsimmons, James L.

2006   Classic Maya Tomb Re-entry. In *Jaws of the Underworld: Life, Death, and Rebirth among the Ancient Maya: 7th European Maya Conference, The British Museum, London, November 2002*, edited by P. R. Colas, G. Le Fort, and B. L. Persson, pp. 33–40. Acta Mesoamericana. Verlag Anton Saurwein, Markt Schwaben, Germany.

Foster, George

1944   Nagualism in Mexico and Guatemala. *Acta Americana* 2:85–103.

Freidel, David, Héctor Escobedo, David Lee, Stanley Guenter, and Juan Carlos Meléndez

2007   El Perú y la ruta terrestre de la Dinastía Kan hacia el Altiplano. In *XX Simposio de Investigaciones Arqueológicas en Guatemala, 2006*, edited by Juan Pedro Laporte, Bárbara Arroyo, and Héctor Mejía, pp. 59–76. Ministerio de Cultura y Deportes, Instituto de Antropología e Historia, Guatemala City.

Freidel, David A., and Linda Schele

1988   Symbol and Power: A History of the Lowland Maya Cosmogram. In *Maya Iconography*, edited by Elizabeth P. Benson and Gillett G. Griffin, pp. 44–94. Princeton University Press, Princeton.

Freidel, David, Linda Schele, and Joy Parker

1993   *Maya Cosmos: Three Thousand Years on the Shaman's Path*. Quill, New York.

Freidel, David, and Charles Suhler

1999   The Path of Life: Toward a Functional Analysis of Ancient Maya Architecture. In *Mesoamerican Architecture as a Cultural Symbol*, edited by Jeffrey K. Kowalski, pp. 250–273. Oxford University Press, New York.

Freidel, David A., Marilyn A. Masson, and Michelle Rich

2017   Imagining a Complex Maya Political Economy: Counting Tokens and Currencies in Image, Text and the Archaeological Record. *Cambridge Archaeological Journal* 27(1):29–54.

Gilbert, B. Miles

1990   *Mammalian Osteology*. Missouri Archaeological Society, Columbia.

Gilbert, B. Miles, Larry D. Martin, and Howard G. Savage

1996   *Avian Osteology*. Missouri Archaeological Society, Columbia.

Gossen, Gary H.

1974   *Chamulas in the World of the Sun: Time and Space in a Maya Oral Tradition*. Harvard University Press, Cambridge.

1975   Animal Souls and Human Destiny in Chamula. *Man*, n.s., 10(3):448–461.

Götz, Christopher M.

2014   La alimentación de los Mayas prehispánicos vista desde la zooarqueología. *Anales de Antropología* 48(1):167–199.

Grove, David C.

1968   Chalcatzingo, Morelos, Mexico: A Reappraisal of the Olmec Rock Carvings. *American Antiquity* 33(4):486–491.

Grube, Nikolai, and Werner Nahm

1994   A Census of Xibalba: A Complete Inventory of *Way* Characters on Maya Ceramics. In *The Maya Vase Book: A Corpus of Rollout Photographs of Maya Vases*, vol. 4, edited by B. Kerr and J. Kerr, pp. 686–715. Kerr Associates, New York.

Guernsey, Julia

2010   A Consideration of the Quatrefoil Motif in Preclassic Mesoamerica. *Res: Anthropology and Aesthetics* 57/58:75–96.

Hall, Grant D., Stanley M. Tarka Jr., W. Jeffrey Hurst, David Stuart, and Richard E. W. Adams

1990   Cacao Residues in Ancient Maya Vessels from Rio Azul, Guatemala. *American Antiquity* 55(1):138–143. https://doi.org/10.2307/281499.

Heyden, Doris

1975   An Interpretation of the Cave Underneath the Pyramid of the Sun in Teotihuacan, Mexico. *American Antiquity* 40(2):131–147.

1976   Los ritos de paso en las cuevas. *Boletín del Instituto Nacional de Antropología e Historia* 2(19):17–26.

Hillson, Simon

1992   *Mammal Bones and Teeth: An Introductory Guide to Methods of Identification*. Institute of Archaeology, University College London, London.

Houston, Stephen D., and David Stuart

1989   *The way Glyph: Evidence for "Co-essences" among the Classic Maya*. Center for Maya Research.

Joralemon, Peter D.

1976   The Olmec Dragon: A Study in Pre-Columbian Iconography. In *Origins of Religious Art and Iconography in Preclassic Mesoamerica*, edited by Henry B. Nicholson, pp. 27–71. UCLA Latin American Center Publications, Los Angeles.

Kunen, Julie L., Mary Jo Galindo, and Erin Chase

2002   Pits and Bones: Identifying Maya Ritual Behavior in the Archaeological Record. *Ancient Mesoamerica* 13(2):197–211.

La Farge, Oliver
1947   *Santa Eulalia: The Religion of a Cuchumatán Indian Town*. University of Chicago Press, Chicago.

Law, I. A., R. A. Housely, Norman Hammond, and R. E. M. Hedges
1991   Cuello: Resolving the Chronology through Direct Dating of Conserved and Low-Collagen Bone by AMS. *Radiocarbon* 33(3):303–315.

Linn, Priscilla Rachun
1989   Souls and Selves in Chamula: A Thought on Individuals, Fatalism, and Denial. In *Ethnographic Encounters in Southern Mesoamerica: Essays in Honor of Evon Zartman Vogt, Jr.*, edited by Victoria R. Bricker and Gary H. Gossen, pp. 251–262. University of Texas Press, Austin.

Love, Michael, and Julia Guernsey
2007   Monument 3 from La Blanca, Guatemala: A Middle Preclassic Earthen Sculpture and Its Ritual Associations. *Antiquity* 81(314):920–932.

Marken, Damien B.
2007   Reconocimiento del transecto norte y el periferia de El Perú. In *Proyecto Arqueológico El Perú-Waka': Informe no. 4, temporada 2006*, edited by Héctor L. Escobedo and David A. Freidel, pp. 387–396. Fundación de Investigación Arqueológica Waka', Guatemala City.

2008   Reconocimiento regional de El Perú-Waka', 2007: Investigando los patrones de asentamiento en el sector sur del Parque Nacional Laguna del Tigre. In *Proyecto Arqueológico El Perú-Waka': Informe no. 5, temporada 2007*, edited by Héctor L. Escobedo, Juan Carlos Meléndez, and David A. Freidel, pp. 5–72. Fundación de Investigación Arqueológica Waka', Guatemala City.

2009   Reconocimiento regional 2008 en El Perú: Investigación sobre los patrones de asentamiento al sur del Parque Nacional Laguna del Tigre. In *Proyecto Arqueológico El Perú-Waka': Informe no. 6, temporada 2008*, edited by David A. Freidel and Juan Carlos Meléndez, pp. 145–246. Fundación de Investigación Arqueológica Waka', Guatemala City.

2010   Reconocimiento regional 2009 en El Perú: Investigación sobre los patrones de asentamiento al sur del Parque Nacional Laguna del Tigre. In *Proyecto Arqueológico El Perú-Waka': Informe no. 7, temporada 2009*, edited by David A. Freidel, Jennifer Piehl, and Mary Jane Acuña, pp. 127–187. Fundación de Investigación Arqueológica Waka', Guatemala City.

2011   City and State: Urbanism, Rural Settlement, and Polity in the Classic Maya Lowlands. PhD dissertation, Department of Anthropology, Southern Methodist University, Dallas.

Masson, Marilyn A.
1999a   Animal Resource Manipulation in Ritual and Domestic Contexts at Postclassic Maya Communities. *World Archaeology* 31(1):93–120.

1999b   Postclassic Maya Communities at Progreso Lagoon and Laguna Seca, Northern Belize. *Journal of Field Archaeology* 26(3):285–306.

Matteo, Sebastian, and Asier Rodríguez Manjavacas
2009   La instrumentalización del way según las escenas de los vasos pintados. *Península* 4(1):17–31.

McAnany, Patricia A.
1995   *Living with the Ancestors: Kinship and Kingship in Ancient Maya Society.* University of Texas Press, Austin.

Mock, Shirley Boteler, editor
1998   *The Sowing and the Dawning: Termination, Dedication, and Transformation in the Archaeological and Ethnographic Record of Mesoamerica.* University of New Mexico Press, Albuquerque.

Moholy-Nagy, Hattula
1998   A Preliminary Report of the Use of Vertebrate Animals at Tikal, Guatemala. In *Anatomía de una civilización: Aproximaciones interdisciplinarias a la cultura Maya*, edited by Andrés Ciudad Ruíz, pp. 115–130. Sociedad Español de Estudios Mayas, Madrid.

Moholy-Nagy, Hattula, and Katherine F. Emery
2004   Vertebrates in Tikal Burials and Caches. In *Maya Zooarchaeology: New Directions in Theory and Method*, edited by K. Emery, pp. 193–205. Cotsen Institute of Archaeology Press, Los Angeles.

Navarro-Farr, Olivia C.
2004   WK-01: Excavaciones en la Estructura M13-1. In *Proyecto Arqueológico El Perú-Waka': Informe no. 1, temporada 2003*, edited by Héctor L. Escobedo and David Freidel, pp. 13–42. Fundación de Investigación Arqueológica Waka', Guatemala City.

2005   WK-01: Excavaciones en la Estructura M13-1, segunda temporada. In *Proyecto Arqueológico El Perú-Waka': Informe no. 2, temporada 2004*, edited by Héctor L. Escobedo and David Freidel, pp. 5–36. Fundación de Investigación Arqueológica Waka', Guatemala City.

2006   WK-01: Excavaciones en la Estructura M13-1, tercera temporada. In *Proyecto Arqueológico El Perú-Waka': Informe no. 1, temporada 2003*, edited by Héctor L. Escobedo and David A. Freidel, pp. 15–67. Fundación de Investigación Arqueológica Waka', Guatemala City.

2009   Ritual, Process, and Continuity in the Late to Terminal Classic Transition: Investigations at Structure M13-1 in the Ancient Maya Site of El Perú-Waka', Petén, Guatemala. PhD dissertation, Department of Anthropology, Southern Methodist University, Dallas.

2016   Dynamic Transitions at El Peru-Waka': Late Terminal Classic Ritual Repurposing of a Monumental Shrine. In *Ritual, Violence, and the Fall of Classic Maya Kings*, edited by Gyles Iannone, Brett A. Houk, and Sonja A. Schwake, pp. 243–269. University Press of Florida, Gainesville.

Navarro-Farr, Olivia C., and Ana Lucía Arroyave Prera
2006   Un final macabro: La terminación ritual de la Estructura M13-1 de El Perú-Waka'. In *XX Simpósio de Investigaciones Arqueológicas en Guatemala*, edited by Juan Pedro Laporte, Bárbara Arroyo and Héctor Mejía, pp. 583–594. Museo Nacional de Arqueología e Etnología, Guatemala.

2007   WK-01: Excavaciones en la Estructura M13-1, cuarta temporada. In *Proyecto Arqueológico El Perú-Waka': Informe no. 4, temporada 2006*, edited by Héctor L.

Escobedo and David Freidel, pp. 7–88. Fundación de Investigación Arqueológica Waka', Guatemala City.

2014   A Palimpsest Effect: The Multi-layered Meanings of Late-to-Terminal Classic Era, Above-Floor Deposits at Structure M13-1. In *Archaeology at El Perú-Waka': Ancient Maya Performances of Ritual, Memory, and Power*, edited by Olivia C. Navarro-Farr and Michelle Rich, pp. 34–52. University of Arizona Press, Tucson.

Navarro-Farr, Olivia C., Mary Kate Kelly, Michelle Rich, and Griselda Pérez Robles

2020   Expanding the Canon: Lady K'abel the *Ix Kaloomte'* and the Political Narratives of Classic Maya Queens. *Feminist Anthropology* 1(1): 38–55.

Navarro-Farr, Olivia, Griselda Pérez Robles, and Damaris Menéndez Bolaños

2013   Operación WK-1: Excavaciones en la Estructura M13-1. In *Proyecto Regional Arqueológico El Perú-Waka': Informe no. 10, temporada 2012*, edited by Juan Carlos Pérez Calderón, pp. 3–91. Fundación de Investigación Arqueológica Waka', Guatemala City.

Navarro-Farr, Olivia, Griselda Pérez Robles, Damaris Menéndez, Francisco Castañeda, and Juan Carlos Pérez

2013   Staying Power: Ritual Dynamics of Pre-Abandonment Political and Symbolic Agency at Classic Maya El Perú-Waka'. Paper presented at the 78th Annual Meeting of the Society for American Archaeology, Honolulu, Hawaii.

Olsen, Stanley J.

1964   *Mammal Remains from Archaeological Sites: Part 1: Southeastern and Southwestern United States*. Harvard University Press, Cambridge.

1968   *Fish, Amphibian, and Reptile Remains from Archaeological Sites*. Harvard University Press, Cambridge.

1982   *An Osteology of Some Maya Mammals*. Peabody Museum of Archaeology and Ethnology, Harvard University, Cambridge.

Pérez Robles, Griselda, and Ana Lucía Arroyave

2008   Tipología cerámica preliminar de El Perú. In *Proyecto Arqueológico El Perú-Waka': Informe no. 5, temporada 2007*, edited by Héctor L. Escobedo, Juan Carlos Meléndez, and David Freidel, pp. 207–260. Fundación de Investigación Arqueológica Waka', Guatemala City.

Pestle, William J., and Michael Colvard

2012   Bone Collagen Preservation in the Tropics: A Case Study from Ancient Puerto Rico. *Journal of Archaeological Science* 39(7):2079–2090.

Peterson, Polly A., Patricia A. McAnany, and Allan B. Cobb

2005   De-fanging the Earth Monster: Speleothem Transport to Surface Sites in the Sibun Valley. In *Stone Houses and Earth Lords: Maya Religion in the Cave Context*, edited by Keith M. Prufer and James E. Brady, pp. 225–247. University Press of Colorado, Boulder.

Pitt-Rivers, Julian

1970   Spiritual Power in Central America: The Naguals of Chiapas. In *Witchcraft Confessions and Accusations*, edited by M. Douglas, pp. 183–206. Tavistock Publications, London.

Pohl, Mary D.

1976   Ethnozoology of the Maya: An Analysis of Fauna from Five Sites in Petén, Guatemala. PhD dissertation, Department of Anthropology, Harvard University, Cambridge.

1983   Maya Ritual Faunas: Vertebrate Remains from Burials, Caches, Caves, and Cenotes in the Maya Lowlands. In *Civilization in the Ancient Americas*, edited by R. Leventhal and A. Kolata, pp. 55–103. University of New Mexico Press, Albuquerque.

1990   The Ethnozoology of the Maya: Faunal Remains from Five Sites in the Petén, Guatemala. In *Excavations at Seibal, Guatemala*, edited by G. R. Willey, pp. 144–174. Harvard University Press, Cambridge.

Prufer, Keith M., and James E Brady

2005   Introduction: Religion and Role of Caves in Lowland Maya Archaeology. In *Stone Houses and Earth Lords: Maya Religion in the Cave Context*, edited by Keith M. Prufer and James E. Brady, pp. 1–24. University Press of Colorado, Boulder.

Redfield, Robert

1941   *The Folk Culture of Yucatan*. University of Chicago Press, Chicago.

Redfield, Robert, and Alfonso Villa Rojas

1971   *Chan Kom: A Maya Village*. Abridged ed. University of Chicago Press, Chicago.

Reimer, Paula J., Edouard Bard, Alex Bayliss, J. Warren Beck, Paul G. Blackwell, Christopher Bronk Ramsey, Caitlin E. Buck, et al.

2013   IntCal13 and Marine13 Radiocarbon Age Calibration Curves 0–50,000 Years Cal BP. *Radiocarbon* 55(4):1869–1887.

Reitz, Elizabeth J., and Elizabeth S. Wing

1999   *Zooarchaeology*. Cambridge Manuals in Archaeology. Cambridge University Press, New York.

Rich, Michelle

2013   Operación WK15: Excavaciones en la Estructura P13-5. In *Proyecto Regional Arqueológico El Perú-Waka': Informe no. 10, temporada 2012*, edited by Juan Carlos Pérez Calderón and David Freidel, pp. 172–174. Fundación de Investigación Arqueológica Waka', Guatemala City.

Rich, Michelle, and Olivia C. Navarro-Farr

2014   Introduction: Ritual, Memory, and Power among the Maya and at Classic Period El Perú-Waka'. In *Archaeology at El Perú-Waka': Ancient Maya Performances of Ritual, Memory, and Power*, edited by Olivia C. Navarro-Farr and Michelle Rich, pp. 3–17. University of Arizona Press, Tucson.

Roys, Lawrence, and Edwin M. Shook

1966   Preliminary Report on the Ruins of Ake, Yucatan. *Memoirs of the Society for American Archaeology* 20:1–54. https://www.jstor.org/stable/i25146690.

Schlesinger, Victoria

2001   *Animals and Plants of the Ancient Maya: A Guide*. University of Texas Press, Austin.

Sharer, Robert J.

1994   *The Ancient Maya*. 5th ed. Stanford University Press, Stanford.

Seler, Eduard

1901–1902   *Codex Fejervary Mayer*. Edinburgh University Press, Edinburgh.

Sharpe, Ashley E., and Kitty F. Emery
2015   Differential Animal Use within Three Late Classic Maya States: Implications for Politics and Trade. *Journal of Anthropological Archaeology* 40:280–301.

Stone, Andrea J.
1995   *Images from the Underworld: Naj Tunich and the Tradition of Maya Cave Painting*. University of Texas Press, Austin.
2005   Scribes and Caves in the Maya Lowlands. In *Stone Houses and Earth Lords: Maya Religion in the Cave Context*, edited by Keith M. Prufer and James E. Brady, pp. 135–147. University Press of Colorado, Boulder.

Stross, Brian
1996   The Mesoamerican Cosmic Portal: An Early Zapotec Example. *Res: Anthropology and Aesthetics* 29/30:82–101.

Stuart, David, and Stephen D. Houston
1994   *Classic Maya Place Names*. Studies in Pre-Columbian Art and Archaeology 33. Dumbarton Oaks Research Library and Collection, Washington, DC.

Suhler, Charles K., David A. Freidel, and Traci Ardren
1998   Northern Maya Architecture, Ritual, and Cosmology. In *Anatomía de una civilización: Aproximaciones interdisciplinarias a la cultura Maya*, edited by Andrés Ciudad Ruíz, Maria Y. Fernández Marquínez, Jose M. García Campillo, Maria J. Iglesias Ponce de León, Alfonso Lacadena García-Gallo, and L. T. Sanz Castro, pp. 253–274. Sociedad Española de Estudios Mayas, Madrid.

Taube, Karl
1998   The Jade Hearth: Centrality, Rulership, and the Classic Maya Temple. In *Function and Meaning in Classic Maya Architecture*, edited by Stephen D. Houston, pp. 427–478. Dumbarton Oaks Research Library and Collection, Washington, DC.
2004   Flower Mountain: Concepts of Life, Beauty, and Paradise among the Classic Maya. *Res: Anthropology and Aesthetics* 45:69–98.

Tedlock, Barbara
1982   *Time and the Highland Maya*. Rev. ed. University of New Mexico Press, Albuquerque.

Tedlock, Dennis
1996   *Popol Vuh: The Mayan Book of the Dawn of Life*. Translated by Dennis Tedlock. Simon and Schuster, New York.

Thompson, J. Eric
1930   Ethnology of the Mayas of Southern and Central British Honduras. *Publications of the Field Museum of Natural History. Anthropological Series* 17(2):27–213.
1934   *Sky Bearers, Colors and Directions in Maya and Mexican Religion*. Carnegie Institution of Washington, Washington, DC.
1970   *Maya History and Religion*. University of Oklahoma Press, Norman.

Tokovinine, Alexandre
2013   *Place and Identity in Classic Maya Narratives*. Dumbarton Oaks Research Library and Collection, Washington, DC.

Tozzer, Alfred M.
1941   *Landa's Relación de las Cosas de Yucatan: A Translation*. Peabody Museum of American Archaeology and Ethnology, Harvard University, Cambridge.

Vaillant, George C.
1962   *Aztecs of Mexico: Origin, Rise, and Fall of the Aztec Nation.* Doubleday and Company, Garden City.

Villa Rojas, Alfonso
1945   *The Maya of East Central Quintana Roo.* Carnegie Institution of Washington, Washington, DC.

Vogt, Evon Z.
1969   *Zinacantán: A Maya Community in the Highlands of Chiapas.* Belknap Press of Harvard University Press, Cambridge.
1970   *The Zinacantecos of Mexico: A Modern Maya Way of Life.* Holt, Rinehart and Winston, New York.
1981   Some Aspects of the Sacred Geography of Highland Chiapas. In *Mesoamerican Sites and World-Views*, edited by Elizabeth P. Benson, pp. 119–142. Dumbarton Oaks Research Library and Collection, Washington, DC.
1992   The Persistence of Maya Tradition in Zinacantán. In *The Ancient Americas: Art from Sacred Landscapes*, edited by Robert F. Townsend, pp. 60–69. Art Institute of Chicago, Chicago.
1993   *Tortillas for the Gods: A Symbolic Analysis of Zinacanteco Rituals.* University of Oklahoma Press, Norman.

Vogt, Evon Z., and David Stuart
2005   Some Notes on Ritual Caves among the Ancient and Modern Maya. In *In the Maw of the Earth Monster: Mesoamerican Ritual Cave Use*, edited by James E. Brady and Keith M. Prufer, pp. 155–185. University of Texas Press, Austin.

Walker, William H.
1995   Ceremonial Trash? In *Expanding Archaeology*, edited by James M. Skibo, William H. Walker, and A. E. Nielsen, pp. 67–79. University of Utah Press, Salt Lake City.

Wisdom, Charles
1940   *The Chorti Indians of Guatemala.* University of Chicago Press, Chicago.

11

World-Making

Turtle Mountain and the Oracle of Waka'

DAVID FREIDEL

Introduction: The Oracle of Turtle Mountain

The Maya have always contemplated the past and prophesized about the future and they continue to do so. This is demonstrated in glyphic texts of the Classic period and affirmed in the codices and books of Chilam Balam in the Postclassic and early Colonial periods. In the Classic period, there is also reason to believe there were oracles (Zender 2004:210–221; Martin 2020:91). In this chapter, I propose that the first documented *kaloomte'*, Sihyaj K'ahk', did not "arrive" (Guenter 2006) on pilgrimage, bringing a sacred object (Martin 2020:122–123) and taking command of El Perú-Waka' eight days before he conquered Tikal in 378 CE, just because it was on his way from the west (Stuart 2000:480). This account, as related on Stela 15, is more a religious and political declaration than an itinerary (Stuart 2014; Kelly, Freidel, and Navarro-Farr, this volume). I suggest instead that Sihyaj K'ahk' went to Waka' to seek out affirmation of the prophecy that he would establish dominion in the Maya world, from Turtle Mountain and its goddess, *Ix Uh*, Lady Moon, later probably Three Moon like the rebus of the Great Goddess of Teotihuacan (Milbrath 1995; Kelly et al. in press). I suggest that Sihyaj K'ahk' received that affirmation, and he certainly also conquered Tikal's king—as implied on Tikal Stela 31 (Stuart 2000; Martin and Grube 2000). And in the course of these dramatic events, Sihyaj K'ahk' also elevated the oracle of Waka' to the status of world-maker. As a consequence, command of Waka', Turtle Mountain, and the Wiinte' Naah (fire shrine) at its center, became an enduring ambition of the aspiring hegemons of the core area of the Maya Lowlands. Verifiably, at least twice more, great rulers would stand on Turtle Mountain and receive the approval of its oracle: once in 556 CE, when K'ahk' Ti' Chi'ch ruled Kaan; and

Figure 11.1. Upper segments of Stela 30 showing the headdress with cartouched *Wak Ajaw* epithet. Photograph by Philip Hofstetter, courtesy of Proyecto Arqueológico Waka'.

again around 656 CE, when Yuhknoom Ch'een II did. In both these instances, the oracle of Turtle Mountain was a queen: Ikoom Sak Wayis in the sixth century and Lady K'abel in the seventh. Rulers of Waka', vassals to changing great powers through centuries of warfare, raised more than fifty carved stone stelae of impressive size. All of them were violently brought down or desecrated in antiquity by conquerors ambitious to erase the past and establish control of the future through the oracle and its temples (Figure 11.1). The people of Waka' repeatedly gathered their broken stelae and reset the fragments as altars or in their shrines. Their mountain endured, and their oracle outlasted all the rulers who fought for its blessings and attention.

Founding Turtle Mountain

The Mirador hill at Waka' rises 45 meters above the ambient level of the city, itself some 100 meters above the nearby Río San Pedro. The viewshed needs to be calculated, but one can observe the Sierra Lacandon to the west. This promontory, when terraformed and crowned by pyramids and temples, was a clear landmark declaring entry from the west on the Río San Pedro Mártir into terrain of the Central Karstic Uplands. Established in the Late Preclassic period, river and floodtide canoe routes connected Waka' and its landmark hilltop shrines to the El Mirador realm to the east and the lowlands to the west (Acuña and Chiriboga 2019).

Late Preclassic inhabitants lived along the shore of the Río San Juan and established the Mirador hill as an in-line triad of sacred localities trending from southwest to northeast. This in-line triad marked the hill with the three belt stars of the constellation Orion as the great turtle (Schele, in Freidel, Schele, and Parker 1993).

Sponsored by the Fundación de Patrimonio Cultural y Natural Maya (PACUNAM), a lidar survey of Waka' confirmed the terraforming of the hill as observed by Michelle Rich and others in 2001 during exploration of the site (Figure 11.2). Large rough boulders and coarse walls define massive terraces and smaller features along the south, west, and north sides. A wide stairway on the northwestern end of the hill provides access to the summit localities and the southwestern locality in particular. At its foot, that stairway gives way to a formal causeway crossing a reservoir framing the northwestern side of the hill, rising over a ridge called the Chok Group, home to the Late and Terminal Classic priesthood and the "Last Palace," and continuing to the southern end of Structure M13-1, the main temple of the city (Eppich, this volume). Test excavations on the causeway linking the hill to the city temple, and on a second causeway linking Structure O14-04 to Structure O14-02, both yielded Late Preclassic ceramics (Marken and Ricker, this volume). A formal offering on the plaza of the southwestern summit locality dated to the Late Preclassic. Thus, Turtle Mountain was a Late Preclassic sacred landmark in the Maya world. Griselda Pérez Robles (2004) discovered buried Terminal Preclassic platforms made of fine masonry with formal apron moldings in Plaza 2, fronting the city temple. It is likely that the original temple in the M13-1 locality dates to the Preclassic period.

The Great Turtle and Royal Power

Linda Schele (Freidel, Schele, and Parker 1993:66–94) outlined the Classic creation story and the role of the great turtle as embodied in the in-line triadic

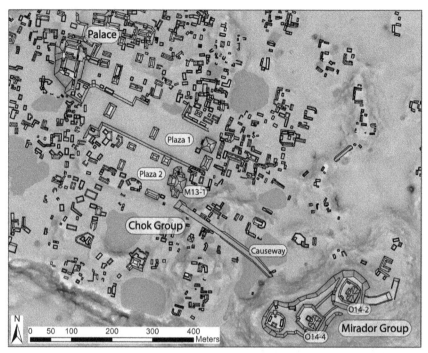

Figure 11.2. El Perú-Waka' urban core, showing Turtle Mountain (Mirador Group), the causeway, the Chok Group, and the Wiinte' Naah (Structure M13-1). Map by Damien Marken, courtesy of Proyecto Arqueológico Waka'.

belt stars of Orion. It is a story that takes hold in the Preclassic period. The Maya Maize God is resurrected out of a cosmic turtle as a representation of the Earth (Taube 1985). The Late Preclassic west wall mural of the Pinturas shrine at San Bartolo depicts the Maize God dancing inside the turtle having dived into the waters of death, and it depicts the Maize God as an infant on the other side of the turtle (Taube et al. 2010; Saturno 2009). The scene occurs above a sky band, in the heavens like the belt stars of Orion. At El Achiotal, up the Río San Juan from Waka', the Late Preclassic royal mortuary bundle house is a turtle effigy, with the head of the turtle emerging from a dais fronting the doorway (Acuña 2013; Freidel n.d.). The association of the turtle with the Wak realm is tangible. The altar depicting the Wak ruler K'inich Bahlam II in the heart of the turtle still rests in front of the palace acropolis and, as discussed below, on the major k'atun celebration of 9.13.0.0.0, he is depicted standing on the turtle on El Perú-Waka' Stela 33 (Freidel, Schele, and Parker 1993:Figure 4.27).

In 2012, Michelle Rich excavated Structure P13-5, a platform containing a vaulted subsurface chamber at the northeastern end of the Mirador hill.

Figure 11.3. Gullet of turtle mountain. Photograph by Michelle Rich, courtesy of Proyecto Arqueológico Waka'.

Her investigation showed that the platform was built over elaborate flowstone formations suggesting that it was originally a spring coming out of the rock shelter immediately to the southwest of it (Rich 2013). Ceramics indicate that this locality was in use from the beginning of the Early Classic, if not earlier. The vaulted chamber, thought to be a looted tomb when investigated by the project in 2001, was a subsurface performance chamber accessed by an ornate vaulted stairway "gullet" (Figure 11.3). I suggest that this fossil spring and subsurface chamber are the head and mouth of Turtle Mountain. The association of this mountain with royal power is affirmed by the discovery of tombs and offerings in the central summit locality, Structure O14-04. The main pyramid of Structure O14-04 dates to the Early Classic and has an apsidal plan. That unusual design suggests the carapace of a turtle, just as the great mosaic maw and "cave" penetrates the heart of the Terminal Classic Pirámide del Adivino, the famously apsidal pyramid of Uxmal, showing a Turtle Mountain as a living being.

Karl Taube's (2018a [1989]) argument that the turtle embodies the world floating on the primordial sea and, at least in the Classic to Postclassic period, time itself in the *k'atun*, is relevant to identifying the oracular function of the masters and mistresses of Turtle Mountain at Waka'. The circular form of the turtle carapace and the *k'atun* wheel turtle, as discovered at Mayapán, is presaged by the Esperanza phase vessel from Kaminaljuyu depicting the quadripartite turtle surrounded by a circle of dots resembling the astronomical crosses and circles at Uaxactun, Teotihuacan, and in the Alta Verapaz (Taube 1988; Kidder, Jennings, and Shook 1946:Figure 71 a and b) and as first discussed by Aveni (Aveni and Hartung 1979). I suggest an association with the ceramic divining bowls as discussed by Taube (2018b [1992]). They are also decorated with lines and dots representing casting tokens and prophecy, essential features of oracles in the Maya world (Freidel, Pérez et al. in press; Freidel, Masson, and Rich 2016; Freidel and Rich 2015). In the Contact period, the goddess Ix Chel had a famous oracle on Cozumel Island (Freidel and Sabloff 1981), and as patron of sorcerers and prophets, she blessed their "little spider" casting tokens (Tozzer 1941; Freidel and Schele 1988).

The interior of the subsurface sanctuary in Structure P13-5 has a smooth, vertical end wall made entirely of yellow crystalline calcite (Figure 11.4). A large white "snake" of flowstone emerges from the top of this faux doorway and crawls across the roof of the chamber. It seems likely that the head of Turtle Mountain was a place of royal performance not only of entering and emerging from the world in the symbolic cycle of death and resurrection (an Early Classic individual, likely a sacrifice, was cached in the northwestern end of this ritual platform) but also of association with the oracle of Turtle Mountain and the Fire Shrine.

Waka Oracles and Their Instruments

Contemporary Maya peoples have oracles (Astor-Aguilera 2002) such as those of the "talking crosses" of the Chan Santa Cruz of Quintana Roo, with clear evidence of continuity in form and function of such communicating objects, such as quadripartite crosses (Freidel, Schele, and Parker 1993). The oracle of the Moon Goddess, Ix Chel, on Cozumel underscored the power of the feminine divine in the pre-Columbian Maya world (Freidel 1975).

The Moon Goddess is prominent in the triad of patron gods at Waka'. She is foregrounded in the left-side text of El Perú-Waka' Stela 51, which on the front has a probable depiction of a currently anonymous Wak dynasty king (Kelly, Freidel, and Navarro-Farr, this volume). Her name may be given as Three Moon on El Perú-Waka' Stela 44 (Kelly, Freidel, and Navarro-Farr,

Figure 11.4. Interior of the subsurface chamber showing the yellow calcite portal into Turtle Mountain. Photograph by Michelle Rich, courtesy of Proyecto Arqueológico Waka'.

this volume). The king on Stela 51 wears on his middle the upturned crescent of Waka' oracles identified as the profile mirror bowl (Kelly, Freidel, and Navarro-Farr, this volume). The oracles of Waka' may have been associated with this goddess as embodied in Turtle Mountain even before the arrival of Sihyaj K'ahk'. But in light of the evidence that the Moon Goddess is central to the cult of the Wiinte' Naah after the arrival of Sihyaj K'ahk' in 378 CE, it is likely that he underscored the correspondence of the Maya Goddess with the Teotihuacan Goddess as two world-making mountain deities. Returning to the opening argument here: at Waka', the salient communicating objects are mirrors and divining plates/bowls used in conjunction with casting tokens (Freidel, Masson, and Rich 2016; Navarro-Farr, Pérez Robles, Pérez Calderón, et al. 2021; Freidel, Navarro-Farr, Rich, et al. in press). The principal deity of the oracle was the Moon Goddess, but she had a powerful guardian in Akan Yaxaj, the Wasp Fly Death God Groaner, another patron god of the realm (Kelly, Freidel and Navarro-Farr, this volume).

The earliest material evidence of the oracle of Turtle Mountain is a cist tomb, Burial 25, in front of Structure O14-04, the central temple on that mountain. Rich and Eppich (this volume) make a compelling case that the elderly woman from this burial was likely a queen and perhaps a shaman. I would say that they are right, and that this is the oracle of her time, the mid-

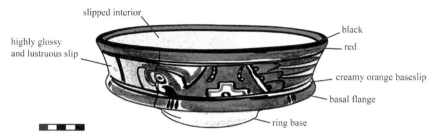

Figure 11.5. Macaw plate with Mountain Bird deity of the dowager queen oracle. El Perú-Waka' Burial 25. Drawing by Keith Eppich, courtesy of Proyecto Arqueológico Waka'.

fourth century. As Rich and Eppich describe, she was interred with a *Spondylus* shell on her head, possibly a diadem. At Calakmul, a coeval ruler in Tomb 1 of Structure 3 (Folan et al. 1995) was also buried with a *Spondylus* diadem near his skull (Juan Carlos Meléndez, personal communication 2022). The Burial 25 woman had a large jade bead placed in her mouth, the seat of her spirit and source of her prophetic words (Taube 2005). She had a water jar, symbol of the divine midwife and goddess Chak Chel (Taube 1994). Finally, she had a large polychrome dish decorated with two scarlet macaws (Figure 11.5). Each of these macaws has a stepped mountain in its body, representing the hill, I suggest, on which they flew. This hill motif, *almena*, is especially found adorning Teotihuacan-style temples in Early Classic depictions and, indeed, it functions as a logograph for temple or building (García-Des Lauriers 2017:Figure 1; Domencici 2023). This logograph has a small black outlined circle within it, perhaps a mirror. Each of the painted macaws has three prominent red tail feathers. This resonates with the three feather-flames on the Stela 51 profile bowl.

The Burial 25 vessel is a fire bowl representing, in my hypothesis, the Fire Shrine *Wiinte' Naah*, a divining instrument such as can be discerned in the possession of later oracles. As mentioned by Kelly, Freidel, and Navarro-Farr (this volume), a mirror bowl covers the mouth of a face inside an animate mountain in the Late Preclassic Structure H X Sub. 3 in Group H of Uaxactun. The mirror bowl was already an instrument of the lowland Maya before the *entrada* of Sihyaj K'ahk' (Schele and Freidel 1990:Figure 4.7). Indeed, it is likely that La Venta Altar 5 depicts an Olmec oracle emerging from just such a mirror bowl (Drucker 1952:177, and Figure 52).

The earliest epigraphic evidence of the oracle at Waka' dates from the fourth century, the era of the *entrada* of Sihyaj K'ahk' and the New Order in the Maya Lowlands he established (Martin and Grube 2000). El Perú-Waka' Stela 15 declares in monumental history the arrival of the *kaloomte'* at a place qualified as the *wiinte'*? (Guenter 2006), or with a mirror qualified as a *wiinte' naah* mirror. The partially eroded logograph in question following Wiinte' is an oval cartouche and not a glyph for *naah*, or house. In light of the identification of a mirror bowl on the abdomen of the individual portrayed on Stela 51 (Kelly, Freidel, and Navarro-Farr, this volume), I suggest that this logograph depicts a mirror of the *wiinte' naah* goddess of Teotihuacan, brought to establish her presence as the Moon Goddess at Turtle Mountain with its fiery scarlet macaws.

Stela 15 was dedicated in 416 CE, a year after the dedication of Tikal Marcador (Laporte and Fialko 1995; Schele and Freidel 1990). I now think that the feather-rimmed cartouches on top of the Marcador were mirrors, such as those that surmounted Aztec standards, in continuity with Teotihuacan practice as argued by Headrick (2003). Such mirrors were capable of conjuring powerful deities like the Feathered Serpent of Teotihuacan, as related in the text of the Marcador. The Marcador mirror cartouches contain two names. On one side is the name Spearthrower Owl, king and sovereign lord of Sihyaj K'ahk', perhaps a king of Teotihuacan (Stuart 2000, Freidel, Escobedo and Guenter 2007) and certainly a lord of Tikal as declared on Stela 51 (Kelly, Freidel, and Navarro-Farr, this volume). On the other side is the profile basin and an in-line triad of dots. I follow Susan Milbrath (1995) in identifying this as the Moon Goddess of Teotihuacan. The logograph on Stela 15 then, in my view, celebrates the installation of the mirror of Sihyaj K'ahk' in the Wiinte' Naah there. The arrival is framed in history, with the side cartouches conveying the *k'atun* divining and prophecy of previous kings of Waka' extending back to 317 CE. The oracle priesthood of Waka', in accepting the arrival of Sihyaj K'ahk' and the mirror bowl, very likely abandoned the ruler in power and the oracle of that time in favor of the *kaloomte'*. K'inich Bahlam I of Waka', vassal to Sihyaj K'ahk' in this model, was put in power soon after the arrival of the Teotihuacan lord, analogous to the replacement of Tikal king Chak Took Ich'aak I by Yax Nuun Ahiin I. The continued celebration of these momentous events in carved stelae history through the fourth century supports such a scenario.

El Perú-Waka' Stela 51 depicts a king dressed as a Teotihuacano celebrating the great *k'atun* divination and prophecy of 9.0.0.0.0 in 435 CE (Kelly, Freidel, and Navarro-Farr, this volume). The Stela 51 individual wears the netted mirror bowl of the Goddess of Teotihuacan in her guise as spider woman on his abdomen (see Taube 1983, 2018b [1992]). The bowl has five Teotihuacan style flames/feathers on it, three forming an in-line triad, echoing the triad of dots accompanying the bowl in the name of the Teotihuacan Goddess, as proposed by Freidel, Sugiyama, and Sugiyama (2024) on the girdle of the Tepantitla

Mural, and two on the rim defining the feather rim of the mirror. We propose that like the inverted basin on the abdomen of the Tepantitla Mural depiction of the Goddess, this mirror bowl is the womb of the Goddess here birthing fire instead of water. If this is the case, then the fiery mirror bowl is a rebus for "Fire Born," the name Sihyaj K'ahk'. The speculative implication of this is that the Stela 15 text can be glossed as Sihyaj K'ahk' arriving on 3 Kan, January 8, 378 CE, with the Wiinte'? object, the mirror, and performing as the oracle, prophesizing that he would conquer Tikal.

Further archaeological evidence of the oracles comes from Burial 8 from the sixth century, the time of the first historically attested takeover of Waka' by the Kaan regime. In the case of Burial 8, a queen was interred directly under the floor of what we discern to have been the Early Classic audiencia room of the palace, and the evidence is in a retrospective reentry tableau arrangement dating to the late eighth or early ninth centuries (Lee and Piehl 2014; Pérez Robles et al., this volume). The reentry of the tomb may have been part of a series of reentries and leave-takings in that era. The skull and femora were removed from the individual, very likely as relics; materials on the stone dais had been rearranged; and new offerings had been placed in the tomb to join the original late sixth-century ones. The individual was clearly royal: the late worshippers had placed a greenstone royal diadem jewel in the cleft between the dais and the west wall of the chamber. The original offerings included a large cylinder tripod vessel with a knobbed lid and a large chunk of copal inside. I have suggested that this is a kind of "white soul flower/seed cache vessel" (Freidel and Guenter 2006). The principal feature of the tableau arrangement on the dais in Burial 8 is a large red basin turned upside down over the abdomen of the queen. This basin covered the intact and relatively undisturbed hands of the woman, which were accompanied by three distinctive jade jewels carved as the symbol *Ik*. The word means wind and breath in ancient Mayan and is particularly associated with jade jewels conveying those ideas and spirit (Taube 2005). A fourth tubular bead with *Ik* carved on it was placed directly south and "below" the basin. As mentioned, the name of the Teotihuacan Goddess embodied in the Moon Pyramid and associated with the Moon, feminine divine, and water, was denoted in the motif on the abdomen of the Tepantitla Mural, among others: the in-line triad of three dots over the upturned crescent bowl/basin taken by other scholars to be an abbreviation of the name of the Storm God (Nielsen and Helmke 2017). On the Tepantitla Mural, shells flow out with yellow liquid. I take these shells to be divining tokens, along with white shell beads and incised shell plaques that might have symbolized tally sticks such as used by diviners and scribes (Tokovinine 2020; Freidel, Masson, and Rich 2016). These shells were concentrated around the hands underneath the basin. On the prospect that my identification is correct, the tableau on the dais retrospectively declares the queen to have been the Moon Goddess and, perforce, the oracle. The great queen of the sixth century was Ix Ikoom Sak Wayis, and she is likely the interred individual as well as this oracle.

The mid-sixth century was a dramatic time in the history of lowland Maya civilization. It now appears that King K'ahk' Ti' Chi'ch' of Kaan led the conquest of Tikal in 562 CE according to a new reading of Caracol Altar 21 by Sergei Vepretski (Martin 2020:248). This Kaan ruler was overlord of Waka' in 556 CE, when he supervised the accession of Wa'oom Uchab Ahk; therefore, he was commanding Turtle Mountain and the Fire Shrine *Wiinte' Naah*. The new oracle at the time of the accession was Ix Ikoom Sak Wayis, who had buried her husband in Structure M12-32. Between her and her overlord, they would have prophesized that he would conquer Tikal, just like Sihyaj K'ahk', and that he would preside over hegemony in the core Maya world, just like the first *kaloomte'*. K'ahk' Ti' Chi'ch' evidently acceded to the status of *kaloomte'* of Kaan at Dzibanche in 554 CE (Martin and Beliaev 2018:5) two years before the death of Chak Tok Ich'aak of Waka' in 556 CE and the accession of the young prince. He performed as overlord at Waka' in conjunction with the likely queen regent Ix Ikoom Sak Wayis. Stela 44, in my interpretation, served as a victory monument for the conquest of Tikal, revenge for the death of the Wak king in 556 CE, and brought Chak Took Ich'aak of Wak into the celebration as conjurer of the gods of Turtle Mountain and the Fire Shrine *Wiinte' Naah* of Sihyaj K'ahk'. The planting at the same time of the lower fragment of Stela 51 into the plaster floor of the plaza fronting Structure M13-1 Sub II built by Ix Ikoom honored the burial of Lady K'abel in her tomb cut through the stairway of M13-1 Sub II. On Stela 51, there is an in-line triad of fire feathers on the mirror bowl that is related to the name of the Goddess. This may have inspired the name Three Moon on Stela 44, which Ikoom originally may have planted north of Stela 51's position on a special low platform of its own (Freidel and Navarro-Farr 2024).

The next oracles I can discern in the research record are the mid-seventh-century ruler in Burial 39 and this person's contemporary in Burial 38 in Structure M13-12 of the Chok Group. Both individuals lived in the seventh century and likely passed away in the middle of it (Rich and Eppich 2020, this volume). In both cases, the physical remains were degraded, and the identification of sex is no longer possible. Added to the ambiguity of gender is the exceptional prospect that the royal oracle might be accompanied by a companion who functioned as a divining priest and ritual specialist—although such sages may be referenced by the turtle epithets on Stela 51 (Kelly, Freidel, and Navarro-Farr, this volume). Burial 39 is described in detail by Rich and Eppich (this volume), and this ruler (king or queen) was surely the oracle. Buried inside a cut through the final Early Classic phase of the *adosada* frontal platform of the central temple of Turtle Mountain, Structure O14-04, the *adosada* was covered by a seventh-century masonry shrine that contained the head of a larger-than-life sized stucco image of a goggle-eyed and buccal-masked Teotihuacano. This is very likely Sihyaj K'ahk', given his depiction on Stela 16. The interred had a series of offering bundles to the north of the head containing casting tokens; a giant cowrie amulet; carved bone scribal sticks for writing on wax, wet plaster, or leather-hard ceramic; paints; a square slate-backed iron-ore mosaic mirror; and an Olmec-style heirloom figurine. The individual had a large plate suitable for divining on its abdomen, decorated with a painted image of the Sun God GI, the dawning sun that brings the rains (Stuart 2005).

The figurine assemblage at the foot of the deceased (Rich, Freidel, et al. 2010) includes a kneeling king sprouting foliage from his head and being prayed over by a magical deer. I have taken the kneeling king to represent the interred and the deer to be the *wahy* spirit companion of the young queen standing next to him, Lady K'abel (see Rich, Bishop, et al. [2020] for evidence that the principal figurines were made at Calakmul; Navarro-Farr, Pérez, and Pérez Robles, this volume). Lady K'abel was the next great oracle of Waka' following her arrival from Calakmul. However, if the interred royal person was a woman and if the mother of her husband, King K'inich Bahlam II, was another Kaan woman, and if the deceased king is buried somewhere else, then I would suggest that the old woman shaman, who is in fact the central focus of the figurine assemblage, is the oracle and dowager queen and that the king being prayed over could be K'inich Bahlam II being transformed into a divine ruler. This seated personage is singing (or howling), eyes wide open. Her body is full of life-giving cinnabar, and she is surrounded by dwarfs and other assistants, some with effigy writing mirror tablets and styli. She has a sketched face under her left breast, and traces of upright ears suggest that this is the rabbit who accompanies the Moon Goddess in the genre of Jaina figurines. A conjuring dwarf carries an effigy conch trumpet and wears a deer headdress, an allusion again to the deer *wahy* of Kaan rulers. If this is the stranger, the dowager queen, she likely would also have been a princess bride of Kaan, and she would have had the deer *wahy* companion of her people. Lady K'abel on Stela 34 in 692 CE at the height of her powers is portrayed with a dwarf; she is the only Wak ruler to have such a companion on a stela, and he (the dwarf) has a turtle name. It could be that Lady K'abel's predecessor also had dwarfs. If the old shaman is the oracle dowager queen, she might be commemorated in the figurine assemblage arranged as her "place," south of her body. Man or woman, this royal was in life the oracle of Turtle Mountain. Lady K'abel as a young woman is depicted carrying her divining plate as a battle shield in the figurine assemblage (Freidel and Rich 2015), so she was already the oracle's successor in this scene. It seems likely to me that she, in collaboration with her father, the Kaan king Yuhknoom Ch'een II standing next to her in the figurine scene, declared that Kaan would again conquer Tikal. The king did so in 657 CE, the same year that his vassal K'inich Bahlam II, named after Sihyaj K'ahk's vassal, planted Stela 1 in front of Structure O14-04. The prophetic power of the oracle of Turtle Mountain was again made manifest to the Maya world.

As mentioned, Lady K'abel was the great oracle of Turtle Mountain and the Fire Shrine *Wiinte' Naah* in the latter half of the seventh century. El Perú-Waka' Stela 34's text in 692 CE relates that she "arrived" at Waka', but the date of her inauguration of power is lost. Martin (2020:184) suggests that it was perhaps not long before 677 CE, but we would place her entry twenty-five years earlier, at the beginning of her husband K'inich Bahlam II's reign (ca. 651 CE). That she "arrived" makes her like in kind to the first historically great oracle, Sihyaj K'ahk'. Like him, she was declared *kaloomte'* on Stela 34. In that stela portrait, the queen stands on a mask of the Principal Bird Deity, the solar avatar of the creator oracle Itzam. The bird wears a profile mirror bowl and an upright mirror on its brow (Figure 11.6).

On Stela 34, she wears a battle shield on her left arm, like the divining plate shield she wore in the Burial 39 figurine portrait and the divining plate on her left arm in her tomb, Burial 61 (Navarro-Farr, Pérez, and Pérez Robles, this volume). Her husband, on his companion monument Stela 33, stands on a turtle marked with the St. Andrews cross indicating its cosmic centrality (Figure 11.7).

K'inich Bahlam II personifies *witz*, the water spray serpent perhaps emblazoned on the scutate lid of the main offering vessel in Burial 24, fronting Structure O14-04 and dating from the time of Sihyaj K'ahk'. The effort to sustain parallels between the New Order hegemony of Sihyaj K'ahk' and the fragile hegemony forged by Kaan is palpable in these monuments. I am proposing that the prophecy of the oracle of Turtle Mountain and the Fire Shrine *Wiinte' Naah* of Sihyaj K'ahk' was vital to that effort.

In 695 CE, King Yuhknoom Yich'aak K'ahk' experienced disastrous defeat in battle at the hands of Tikal king Jasaw Chan K'awiil. The Kaan ruler escaped through La Corona, 30 kilometers north of Waka' (Stuart 2012). He was dead within two years and replaced by the last significant Kaan king, Yuhknoom Took K'awiil. That king reinforced the alliance with Waka'. El Perú-Waka' Stela 7, a very large monument now in broken pieces in front of Structure M13-1,

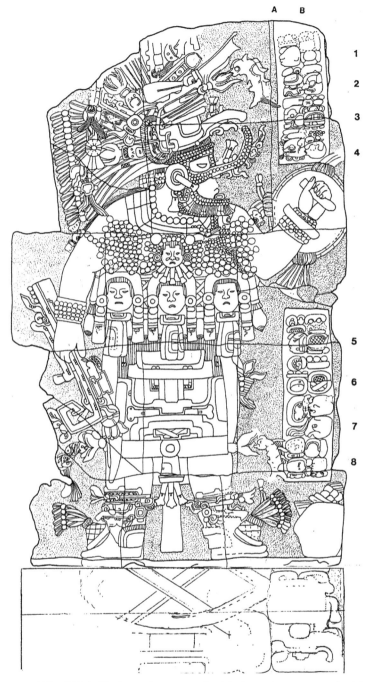

Figure 11.6. El Perú-Waka' Stela 34, showing Lady K'abel standing on a mask of the Principal Bird Deity, the solar avatar of the creator oracle Itzam, on the occasion of the 9.13.0.0.0 prophecy. The bird wears a profile mirror bowl and an upright mirror on its brow. Drawing by John Montgomery, side texts by Kevin Brown, and compiled by Phillip Wanyerka.

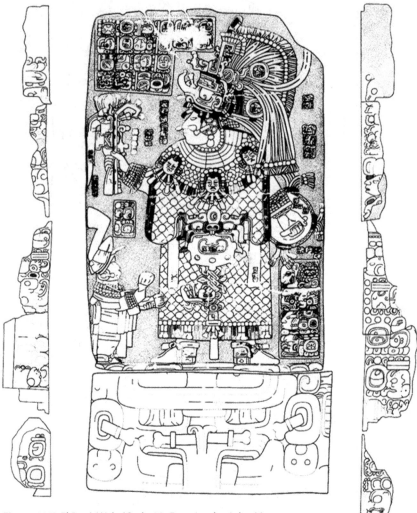

Figure 11.7. El Perú-Waka' Stela 33. Drawing by John Montgomery, compiled by Phil Wanyerka.

depicts a king dancing with a large back-rack; it is the dance of the Maize God in alliance. The eroded text includes a Kaan emblem glyph. Stela 7 is flanked by Stela 6, depicting an eroded Late Classic queen, very likely Lady K'abel; and Stela 8 and very likely the bottom half of Stela 43 offer another portrayal of K'inich Bahlam II (Navarro-Farr, Eppich, et al. 2020:203–206). Stela 43 gives the accession of Yuhknoom Took K'awiil and K'inich Bahlam II, who celebrated his connection to Ix Ikoom Sak Wayis. K'inich Bahlam II identified Ix Ikoom as the ruler who performed a period-ending prophecy in 573 CE—as recorded on Stela 43 and as discussed above (Kelly 2019; Kelly, Freidel, and

Figure 11.8. Lady K'abel's divining plate, Burial 61. Drawing by René Ozeata, courtesy of Proyecto Arqueológico Waka'.

Navarro-Farr, this volume). While it is plausible that K'inich Bahlam II descended from Ix Ikoom, it is also likely that she was the builder of Structure M13-1 Sub II (Freidel and Navarro-Farr 2024). This is the Wiinte' Naah, in front of which these three stelae (6, 7 and 8) were probably originally planted in 702 CE on the occasion of the *lajuntun* (the 10-year halfway celebration of the 20-year *k'atun*). Later, they were replanted in front of M13-1, the Fire Shrine built by K'inich Bahlam II after he buried Lady K'abel in the stairway of M13-1 Sub II.

Lady K'abel's tomb is the subject of Navarro-Farr's chapter (this volume) and other publications (Navarro-Farr, Eppich, et al. 2020; Navarro-Farr, Pérez Robles, Pérez Calderón, et al. 2021). As mentioned earlier, Lady K'abel had a great divining plate over her left arm like the one carried by her figurine portrait in Burial 39 (Figure 11.8). This plate had three sets of three personified red flame-feathers on the outer rim, echoing the mirror bowl name of Sihyaj K'ahk' on Stela 51, in addition to painted whorl tokens and liquid marking.

In death she stood on the place of the Vision Serpent plate (Van Oss and Navarro-Farr, this volume). Her conjuring mirror bore an image of a giant centipede, the symbol of the Wak dynasty and the city. There is no doubt that she was the greatest oracle since Ix Ikoom and, like Ix Ikoom, an agent of the imperial ambitions of Kaan. Between them, I think these queens solidified the role of the queen of the realm as oracle of Turtle Mountain. Olivia Navarro-Farr, Griselda Pérez Robles, and Damaris Menéndez Bolaños (2013) discovered a remarkable stucco head, presumably from the last façade of the Fire Shrine, repurposed in a niche shrine on the south side of the main temple building and the focus of Terminal Classic fire offerings. I thought this beautiful face was an image of the Maize God, but excavations on the surface above the last monumental hearth of the Fire Shrine revealed the torso and head of that god taken from the façade and left as part of a final offering. So, I now regard this head as another portrait of Lady K'abel, serene and majestic in her role, and remembered forever by her people.

The last clear successor in the dynastic line of Waka' is King Bahlam Tz'am. The Kaan king Yuhknoom Took K'awiil supervised his accession, and it is clear that Bahlam Tz'am was loyal to the Kaan to his last breath. He was conquered and probably sacrificed by the Tikal king Yik'in Chan K'awiil in 743 CE. Certainly, an image of Akan Yaxaj, the death god aegis of the Moon Goddess of Turtle Mountain, was captured in this war. A now-broken stela once portrayed both Bahlam Tz'am and his Kaan queen, a stela so grand that Ian Graham (1988) thought it was two different monuments. This queen's name is lost to history, but the signatures of courtier carvers on the monument leave no doubt that she was a Kaan princess like Lady K'abel before her. She was probably the oracle, but she must have presided over the great defeat of Waka' and probably the sacking of the city of Turtle Mountain. With the collapse of Kaan, the victors in Tikal strove to completely replace Turtle Mountain: they built Tikal Temple IV, the greatest of their own mountain effigies and one of the largest Classic Maya pyramids, celebrating the transformation of the Waka' Akan Yaxaj into a Tikal god. It may be more than coincidence that the two massive basal platforms of Temple IV are stacked rectangles with rounded corners like an effigy turtle carapace (Morales et al. 2008). Pilgrims and the devout of the realm continued to worship at the Fire Shrine *Wiinte' Naah*, building fragments of monuments into it, concentrating them elsewhere on the plaza, and leaving modest offerings. The priesthood of the Chok Group continued services to the oracle while a greatly diminished royal court presided at the Palace. Elsewhere in the Classic world, people repudiated the old dynasties. At Waka', they remembered as history passed into legend.

Concluding Thoughts

With ongoing fieldwork, laboratory research, and analysis, the complex and substantial record of the past at Waka' will continue to be subject to evolving interpretations. There is always a risk of regarding the past at one's own place of research as being particularly important to understanding the larger society of which it was a part. But as Joyce Marcus (1983) pointed out in the last Wenner-Gren meeting at Castle Berg Wartenstein, size is only one way to gauge the importance of an ancient city. Some were important because they were sacred cult centers. The patterns in evidence, archaeological and historical, that I have touched on here, trend toward regarding Turtle Mountain and the Fire Shrine *Wiinte' Naah* of Waka' as a place of signs and wonders whose role in the region was defined by a shared perception of ephemeral powers shaping historical events. We will continue to approach that past with respect for those who made it and for those who embrace it as their inheritance.

References

Acuña, Mary Jane
2013   Art, Ideology, and Politics at El Achiotal: A Late Preclassic Frontier Site in Northwestern Petén, Guatemala. *All Theses and Dissertations (ETDs)*, 1192. https://doi.org/10.7936/K7125QMW.
Acuña, Mary Jane, and Carlos R. Chiriboga
2019   Water and the Preclassic Maya at El Tintal, Petén, Guatemala. *Open Rivers: Rethinking Water, Place and Community* 14:147–166.
Astor-Aguilera, Miguel A.
2010   *The Maya World of Communicating Objects: Quadripartite Crosses, Trees, and Stones.* University of New Mexico Press, Albuquerque.
Aveni, Anthony, and Horst Hartung
1979   The Cross Petroglyph: An Ancient Mesoamerican Astronomical Calendrical Symbol. *Indiana* 6:37–54.
Berlo, Janet C.
1992   Icons and Ideologies at Teotihuacan: The Great Goddess Reconsidered. In *Art, Ideology, and the City of Teotihuacan*, edited by Janet C. Berlo, pp. 129–168. Dumbarton Oaks Research Library and Collection, Washington, DC.
Brady, James E.
1989   An Investigation of Maya Ritual Cave Use with Special Reference to Naj Tunich, Peten, Guatemala. PhD dissertation, University of California, Los Angeles.
Chinchilla Mazariegos, Oswaldo
2017   *Art and Myth of the Ancient Maya.* Yale University Press, New Haven.
Domenici, Davide
2023   "The Writing System of Teotihuacan: An Overview." In *Western Mesoamerican Calendars and Writing Systems* [Proceedings of the Copenhagen Roundtable], edited by Mikkel Bøg Clemmensen and Christophe Helmke, pp. 1–24. Archaeopress Pre-Columbian Archaeology, Oxford. https://archive.org/details/mikkel-bog-clemmensen-christophe-helmke-eds.-western-mesoamerican-calendars-and-writing-systems-2023/mode/2up.

Drucker, Philip
1952   La Venta, Tabasco: A Study of Olmec Ceramics and Art. *Bureau of American Eth-nology Bulletin* 153: 1–257. https://repository.si.edu/handle/10088/15448.
Folan, William J., Joyce Marcus, Sophia Pincemin, Maria del Rosario Dominguez Carras-co, Laraine Fletcher, and Abel Morales López
1995   Calakmul: New Data from an Ancient Maya Capital in Campeche, Mexico. *Latin American Antiquity* 6(4):310–334.
Freidel, David A.
1975   The Ix Chel Shrine and Other Temples of Talking Idols. In *Changing Pre-Columbian Commercial Systems: The 1972–1973 Seasons at Cozumel, Mexico*, edited by Jer-emy A. Sabloff and William L. Rathje, pp. 107–113. Monograph No. 3. Peabody Museum of Archaeology and Ethnology, Harvard University, Cambridge.
n.d.   Kingship, Kinship, and Community: Excavating the Foundations of Classic Maya Alliance and Conflict. In *Faces of Rulership in the Maya Region*, edited by Patricia McAnany and Marilyn Masson. Dumbarton Oaks Research Library and Collec-tion and Cambridge University Press.
Freidel, David, Héctor L. Escobedo, and Stanley P. Guenter
2007   A Crossroads of Conquerors: Waka' and Gordon Willey's "Rehearsal for the Col-lapse" Hypothesis. In *Gordon R. Willey and American Archaeology: Contemporary Perspectives*, edited by Jeremy A. Sabloff and William Fash, pp. 1287–208. Univer-sity of Oklahoma Press, Norman.
Freidel, David A., Héctor L. Escobedo, and Juan Carlos Meléndez
2013   Mountains of Memories, Structure M12-32 at El Perú. In *Millenary Maya Societ-ies: Past Crises and Resilience*, edited by M. Charlotte Arnauld and Alain Breton, pp. 235–247. Mesoweb Publications, San Francisco.
Freidel, David A., and Stanley Guenter
2006   Soul Bundle Caches, Tombs, and Cenotaphs: Creating the Places of Resurrection and Accession in Maya Kingship. In *Sacred Bindings of the Cosmos: Ritual Acts of Bundling and Wrapping in Mesoamerica*, edited by Julia Guernsey and F. Kent Reilly, pp. 59–79. Boundary End Archaeology Research Center, Barnardsville, VA.
Freidel, David, Barbara MacLeod, and Charles Suhler
2003   Early Classic Maya Conquest in Words and Deeds. In *Ancient Mesoamerican Warfare*, edited by M. Kathryn Brown and Travis Stanton, pp. 189–215. Altamira Press, Walnut Creek, CA.
Freidel, David A., Marilyn A. Masson, and Michelle E. Rich
2016   Imagining a Complex Maya Political Economy: Counting Tokens and Currencies in Images, Texts, and the Archaeological Record. *Cambridge Archaeological Jour-nal* 27(1):29–54.
Freidel, David A., and Olivia C. Navarro-Farr
2024   Stelae, Spirits, Desecration, and Devotion: The Fate of Some Time Lords in the Maya Lowlands. In *Materialization of Time in the Ancient Maya World: Mythic History and Ritual Order*, edited by David A. Freidel, Arlen F. Chase, Anne S. Dowd, and Jerry Murdock, 149–183. University Press of Florida, Gainesville.

Freidel, David A., Olivia C. Navarro-Farr, Michelle Rich, Juan Carlos Meléndez, Juan Carlos Pérez, Griselda Pérez, and Mary Kate Kelly
in press "Mirror Conjurors of Waka', Guatemala." In "Recent Research on Iron Ore Mirrors in Mesoamerica and Central America," edited by Matthieu Ménager, Silvia Salgado, and David Freidel, special issue, *Ancient Mesoamerica*.

Freidel, David, Juan Carlos Pérez, Griselda Pérez Robles, Olivia Navarro-Farr, and Michelle Rich
in press Birthing Gods: Queen K'abel's Mirrors, Plates, Writing Tablets. In "Recent Research on Iron Ore Mirrors in Mesoamerica and Central America," edited by Matthieu Ménager, Silvia Salgado, and David Freidel, special issue, *Ancient Mesoamerica*.

Freidel, David, and Michelle Rich
2015 Pecked Circles and Divining Boards, Calculating Instruments in Ancient Mesoamerica. In *Cosmology, Calendars, and Horizon-Based Astronomy in Ancient Mesoamerica*, edited by Anne Dowd and Susan Milbrath, pp. 249–264. University Press of Colorado, Boulder.
2018 Maya Sacred Play: The View from El Perú-Waka'. In *Ritual, Play and Belief in Evolution and Early Human Societies*, edited by Colin Renfrew, Iain Morley, and Michael Boyd, pp. 101–115. Cambridge University Press, Cambridge.

Freidel, David A., and Jeremy A. Sabloff
1984 *Cozumel: Late Maya Settlement Patterns*. Academic Press, New York.

Freidel, David A., and Linda Schele
1988 Kingship in the Late Preclassic Lowlands: The Instruments and Places of Ritual Power. *American Anthropologist* 90(3):547–567.

Freidel, David A., Linda Schele, and Joy Parker
1993 *Maya Cosmos: Three Thousand Years on the Shaman's Path*. William Morrow, New York.

Freidel, David A., Saburo Sugiyama, and Nawa Sugiyama
2024 Teotihuacan as the Tree of Time and the Maya Stela Cult. In *The Materialization of Time in the Ancient Maya World: Mythic History and Ritual Order*, edited by David A. Freidel, Arlen F. Chase, Anne S. Dowd, and Jerry Murdock, pp. 433–459. University Press of Florida, Gainesville.

Freidel, David A., and Charles K. Suhler
1999 The Path of Life: Toward a Functional Analysis of Ancient Maya Architecture. In *Mesoamerican Architecture as a Cultural Symbol*, edited by Jeff Karl Kowalski, pp. 250–275. Oxford University Press, Oxford.

García-Des Lauriers, Claudia
2017 The Regalia of Sacred War: Costume and Militarism at Teotihuacan. *Americae: European Journal of Americanist Archaeology* 2:83–98. http://www.mae.u-paris10 .fr/americae-dossiers/americae-dossier-teotihuacan/the-regalia-of-sacred-war -costume-and-militarism-at-teotihuacan/

Graham, Ian
1988 Homeless Hieroglyphs. *Antiquity* 62(234):122–126. https://doi.org/10.1017/ S0003598X00073609.

Guenter, Stanley Paul

2006   Informe preliminar de la epigraphia de El Perú. In *Proyecto Arqueológico El Perú-Waka': Informe no. 3, temporada 2005*, edited by Héctor L. Escobedo and David Freidel, pp. 359–399. Fundación de Investigación Arqueológica Waka', Guatemala City.

2014   The Epigraphy of El Perú-Waka'. In *Archaeology at El Perú-Waka': Ancient Maya Performances of Ritual, Memory, and Power*, edited by Olivia C. Navarro-Farr and Michelle Rich, pp. 147–166. University of Arizona Press, Tucson.

Headrick, Annabeth

2003   Seeing through Sahagun: Observations on a Mesoamerican Staff of Office. *Mesoamerican Voices* 1:23–40.

Jones, Christopher, and Linton Satterthwaite

1982   *The Monuments and Inscriptions of Tikal—The Carved Stone Monuments: Tikal Report 33A*. University of Pennsylvania, Philadelphia. https://doi.org/10.9783/9781934536377.

Kelly, Mary Kate

2019   Epigraphic Documentation during the 2019 Field Season at the Site of El Perú-Waka'. Manuscript.

Kelly, Mary Kate, Olivia C. Navarro-Farr, David A. Freidel, Juan Carlos Pérez Calderón, and Griselda Pérez Robles

in press Waka' Stela 44 and the Early Classic Kaan Hegemony. Manuscript accepted by *Ancient Mesoamerica*.

Kidder, Alfred V., Jesse D, Jennings, and Edwin M. Shook

1946   *Excavations at Kaminaljuyu, Guatemala*. Publication 561. Carnegie Institution of Washington, Washington, DC.

Kubler, George

1985   Pre-Columbian Pilgrimages in Mesoamerica. In *Fourth Palenque Round Table, 1980*, edited by Elizabeth P. Benson, pp. 313–316. Pre-Columbian Art Research Institute, San Francisco.

Laporte, Juan Pedro, and Vilma Fialko

1995   Un reencuentro con Mundo Perdido, Tikal, Guatemala. *Ancient Mesoamerica* 6:41–94.

Lee, David F., and Jennifer C. Piehl

2014   Ritual and Remembrance at the Northwest Palace Complex, El Perú-Waka'. In *Archaeology at El Perú-Waka': Ancient Maya Performances of Ritual, Memory, and Power*, edited by Olivia C. Navarro-Farr and Michelle Rich, pp. 85–101. University of Arizona Press, Tucson.

Marcus, Joyce

1983   On the Nature of the Mesoamerican City. In *Prehistoric Settlement Patterns: Essays in Honor of Gordon R. Willey*, edited by Evon Vogt and Richard Leventhal, pp. 195–242. University of New Mexico Press and the Peabody Museum of Archaeology and Ethnology, Harvard University, Cambridge.

Martin, Simon

2020   *Ancient Maya Politics, A Political Anthropology of the Classic Period 150–900 CE*. Cambridge University Press, Cambridge.

Martin, Simon, and Dmitri Beliaev
2017   K'ahk'Ti' Ch'ich': A New Snake King from the Early Classic Period. *PARI Journal* 17(3):1–7.
Martin, Simon, and Nikolai Grube
2000   *Chronicle of the Maya Kings and Queens: Deciphering the Dynasties of the Ancient Maya.* Thames and Hudson, New York.
Meléndez, Juan Carlos
2014   Contextualizing Burial 37 from El Perú-Waka', Petén, Guatemala. Master's thesis, Department of Anthropology, Washington University, St. Louis.
2019   A Contextual and Technological Study of Ancient Maya Greenstone Mosaic Masks. PhD dissertation, Department of Anthropology, Washington University, St. Louis.
Milbrath, Susan
1995   Gender and Roles of Lunar Deities in Postclassic Central Mexico and Their Correlations with the Maya Area. *Estudios de Cultura Nahuatl* 39:45–93.
Miller, Arthur G.
1982   *On the Edge of the Sea: Mural Painting at Tancah-Tulum, Quintana Roo, Mexico.* Dumbarton Oaks Research Library and Collection, Washington, DC.
Morales, Tirso, Benito Burgos, Miguel Acosta, Sergio Pinelo, Marco Tulio Castellanos, Leopoldo González, Francisco Castañeda, Edy Barrios, and Rudy Larios y Cruz Jau
2008   Trabajos realizados por la unidad de Arqueología del Parque Nacional Tikal, 2006–2007. In *XXI Simposio de Arqueología en Guatemala, 2007*, edited by Juan Pedro Laporte, Bárbara Arroyo, and Héctor Mejía, pp. 413–436. Museo Nacional de Arqueología y Etnología, Guatemala City.
Navarro-Farr, Olivia C., Keith Eppich, David Freidel, and Griselda Pérez Robles
2020   Ancient Maya Queenship: Generations of Crafting State Politics and Alliance Building from Kaanul to Waka'. In *Approaches to Monumental Landscapes of the Ancient Maya*, edited by Brett A. Houk, Bárbara Arroyo, and Terry G. Powis, pp. 196–217. University Press of Florida, Gainesville.
Navarro-Farr, Olivia C., Griselda Pérez Robles, and Damaris Menéndez Bolaños
2013   WK-01: Excavaciones en la Estructura M13-1. In *Proyecto Arqueologico El Perú-Waka': Informe no. 10, temporada 2012*, edited by Juan Carlos Pérez, pp. 12–100. Fundación de Investigación Arqueológica Waka', Guatemala City.
Navarro-Farr, Olivia C., Griselda Pérez Robles, Juan Carlos Pérez Calderón, Elsa Damaris Menéndez Bolaños, Erin E. Patterson, Keith Eppich, and Mary Kate Kelly
2021   Burial 61 at El Perú-Waka's Structure M13-1. *Latin American Antiquity* 32(1):188–199.
Nielsen, Jesper, and Christophe Helmke
2017   The Storm God: Lord of Rain and Ravage. In *Teotihuacan: City of Water, City of Fire*, edited by Matthew H. Robb, pp. 138–143. Fine Arts Museums of San Francisco and University of California Press, Oakland.
Ortiz C., Ponciano, and Maria del Carmen Rodríguez
1999   Olmec Ritual Behavior at El Manati: A Sacred Space. In *Social Patterns in Pre-*

Classic Mesoamerica, edited by David C. Grove and Rosemary A. Joyce, pp. 225–254. Dumbarton Oaks Research Library and Collection, Washington, DC.

Pasztory, Esther
1976   *The Murals of Tepantitla, Teotihuacan*. Garland Press, New York.

Patel, Shankari
2005   Pilgrimage and Caves on Cozumel. In *Stone Houses and Earth Lords: Maya Religion in the Cave Context*, edited by Keith M. Prufer and James E. Brady, pp. 91–115. University Press of Colorado, Boulder.

Prager, Christian M.
2004   A Classic Maya Vessel from the Calakmul Region in the Museum zu Allerheiligen, Schaffhausen, Switzerland. *Human Mosaic* 35(1):31–40.

Pérez Robles, Griselda
2004   Excavaciones de sondeo en las Plazas 1, 2, 3 y 4. In *Proyecto Arqueólogico El Perú-Waka', Informe no. 1, temporada 2003*, edited by Héctor Escobedo and David Freidel, pp. 257–282. Fundación de Investigación Arqueológica Waka', Guatemala City.

Pérez Robles, Griselda, Juan Carlos Pérez, and David Freidel
2021   "Hoja" Chan Ahk: El descubrimiento de la tumba de un rey del Clásico Temprano en el Palacio Real de El Perú-Waka', Guatemala. *Annales del Museo de America* 27:76–94.

Pohl, John M. D.
1999   The Lintel Paintings of Mitla and the Function of the Mitla Palaces. In *Mesoamerican Architecture as a Cultural Symbol*, edited by Jeff Karl Kowalski, pp. 176–197. Oxford University Press, New York.

Rice, Prudence M.
2007   *Maya Calendar Origins: Monuments, Mythistory, and the Materialization of Time*. University of Texas Press, Austin.

Rich, Michelle E.
2013   Operación WK-15: Excavaciones en la Estructura P13-5. In *Proyecto Regional Arqueológico El Perú-Waka', Informe no. 10, temporada 2012*, edited by Juan Carlos Pérez, pp. 175–198. Fundación de Investigación Arqueológica Waka', Guatemala City.

Rich, Michelle, Ronald L. Bishop, and Dorie Reents-Budet
2020   Digging the Scene: More on the El Perú-Waka' Burial 39 Figurines. Paper presented at the Society for American Archaeology annual meeting, Albuquerque, New Mexico.

Rich, Michelle, and Keith Eppich
2020   Statecraft in the City of the Centipede: Burials 39, 38, and Internal Alliance Building at El Perú-Waka', Guatemala. In *A Forest of History: The Maya after the Emergence of Divine Kingship*, edited by Travis W. Stanton and M. Kathryn Brown, pp. 88–106. University Press of Colorado, Boulder.

Rich, Michelle, David Freidel, F. Kent Reilly III, and Keith Eppich
2010   An Olmec-Style Figurine from El Perú-Waka', Petén, Guatemala: A Preliminary Report. *Mexicon* 17(5):115–122.

Robb, Mathew H.

2017   The Water Goddess. In *Teotihuacan: City of Water, City of Fire*, edited by Mathew H. Robb, pp. 154–157. Fine Arts Museums of San Francisco and University of California Press, Oakland.

Saturno, William A.

2009   Centering the King: Maya Creation and Legitimization at San Bartolo. In *The Art of Urbanism: How Mesoamerican Kingdoms Represented Themselves in Architecture and Imagery*, edited by William L. Fash and Leonardo López Luján, pp. 111–134. Dumbarton Oaks Research Library and Collection, Washington, DC.

Schele, Linda, and David A. Freidel

1990   *A Forest of Kings: The Untold Story of the Ancient Maya*. William Morrow, New York.

Smith A. Ledyard

1950   *Excavations at Uaxactun, Guatemala 1931–1937*. Publication 588. Carnegie Institution of Washington, Washington, DC.

Stone, Andrea J.

1995   *Images from the Underworld: Naj Tunich and the Tradition of Maya Cave Painting*. University of Texas Press, Austin.

Stuart, David

2000   The Arrival of Strangers: Teotihuacan and Tollan in Classic Maya History. In *Mesoamerica's Classic Heritage: Teotihuacan to the Aztecs*, edited by D. Carrasco, L. Jones, and S. Sessions, pp. 465–513. University Press of Colorado, Niwot.

2005   *The Inscriptions from Temple XIX at Palenque: A Commentary*. Pre-Columbian Art Research Institute, San Francisco.

2011   *The Order of Days: The Maya World and the Truth about 2012*. Crown Publishing Group, a division of Random House, New York.

2012   Notes on a New Text from La Corona. *Maya Decipherment*, June 30. https://decipherment.wordpress.com/2012/06/30/.

2014   Naachtun's Stela 24 and the Entrada of 378. In *Maya Decipherment: Ideas on Ancient Maya Writing and Iconography* (blog), May 12, 2014. Electronic document, https://decipherment.wordpress.com/2014/05/12/naachtuns-stela-24-and-the-entrada-of-378/

Stuart, David, Marcello Canuto, Tomás Barrientos, and Alejandro Gonzales

2018   A Preliminary Analysis of Altar 5 from La Corona. *PARI Journal* 19(2):1–15.

Sugiyama, Nawa

2014   Animals and Sacred Mountains: How Ritualized Performances Materialized State-Ideologies as Teotihuacan, Mexico. PhD dissertation, Department of Anthropology, Harvard University, Cambridge.

Sugiyama, Saburo

2005   *Human Sacrifice, Militarism, and Rulership: Materialization of State Ideology at the Feathered Serpent Pyramid, Teotihuacan*. Cambridge University Press, Cambridge.

2017   Teotihuacan: Planned City with Cosmic Pyramids. In *Teotihuacan: City of Water, City of Fire*, edited by Matthew H. Robb, pp. 28–37. Fine Arts Museums of San Francisco and University of California Press, Oakland.

Sugiyama, Saburo, and Leonardo López Luján
2007   Dedicatory Burial/Offering Complexes at the Moon Pyramid, Teotihuacan: A Preliminary Report of 1998–2005 Explorations. *Ancient Mesoamerica* 18(1):127–146.

Taube, Karl A.
1983   The Teotihuacan Spider Woman. *Journal of Latin American Lore* 9(2):107–189.
1985   The Classic Maya Maize God: A Reappraisal. In *Fifth Palenque Round Table, 1983*, edited by Merle Greene Robertson, pp. 171–181. Pre-Columbian Art Research Institute, San Francisco.
1988   The Iconography of Mirrors at Classic Teotihuacan. Paper presented at the symposium Art, Polity, and the City of Teotihuacan, Dumbarton Oaks Research Library and Collection, Washington, DC.
2018a [1989]   A Prehispanic Katun Wheel. In *Studies in Ancient Mesoamerican Art and Architecture: Selected Works by Karl Andreas Taube*, pp. 108–117. Precolumbia Mesoweb Press, San Francisco.
2018b [1992]   The Iconography of Mirrors at Teotihuacan. In *Studies in Ancient Mesoamerican Art and Architecture: Selected Works by Karl Andreas Taube*, pp. 204–225. Precolumbia Mesoweb Press, San Francisco.
1994   The Birth Vase: Natal Imagery in Ancient Maya Myth and Ritual. In *The Maya Vase Book*, vol. 4, edited by Barbara Kerr and Justin Kerr, pp. 650–685. Kerr Associates, New York.
2005   The Symbolism of Jade in Classic Maya Religion. *Ancient Mesoamerica* 16:23–50.

Taube, Karl A., William Saturno, David Stuart, and Heather Hurst
2010   *The Murals of San Bartolo, El Petén, Guatemala. Part 2: The West Wall.* Ancient America 10. Center for Ancient American Studies, Barnardsville, VA.

Tiesler, Vera, Andrea Cucina, Travis Stanton, and David Freidel
2017   *Before Kukulcan, Bioarchaeology of Life, Death, and Identity at Classic Period Yaxuna, Yucatan, Mexico.* University of Arizona Press, Tucson.

Tokovinine, Alexandre
2020   Bundling the Sticks: A Case for Classic Maya Tallies. In *The Real Business of Ancient Maya Economies: From Farmers' Fields to Royal Realms*, edited by Marilyn Masson, David A. Freidel, and Arthur Demarest, pp. 276–295. University Press of Florida, Gainesville.

Tozzer, Alfred M.
1941   *Landa's "Relación de las cosas de Yucatán": A Translation.* Papers of the Peabody Museum of American Archaeology, Vol. 18. Harvard University, Cambridge.

Zender, Marc
2004   A Study of Classic Maya Priesthood. PhD dissertation, University of Calgary.

CONTRIBUTORS

Keith Eppich is professor in the Department of History, Geography, and Anthropology at TJC–The College of East Texas. He is coeditor of *Breath and Smoke: Tobacco Use among the Maya*.

David Freidel is professor of anthropology emeritus at Washington University. He is directing research at the royal capital of El Perú-Waka'. Recent publications include *Excavations at Yaxuná, Yucatán, Mexico* with his colleagues Travis Stanton, Charles K. Suhler, Traci Ardren, James N. Ambrosino, Justin M. Shaw, and Sharon Bennett, and he is the coeditor, with Arlen F. Chase and Anne S. Dowd, of *Maya E-Groups: Calendars, Astronomy, and Urbanism in the Early Lowlands*.

Diana N. Fridberg is a freelance researcher who served as the project zooarchaeologist for the Waka' Archaeological Project from 2009 to 2017. She is currently based in Baltimore, Maryland.

Mary Kate Kelly is the project epigrapher for the Waka' Archaeological Project, and sessional instructor at Mount Royal University. She received her PhD in linguistic anthropology in 2022 from Tulane University.

Damien B. Marken is associate professor in the Department of Anthropology, Criminal Justice, and Sociology at Commonwealth University of Pennsylvania and codirector of the Waka' Archaeological Project. A National Geographic Society grantee and Explorers Club Fellow, he is the coeditor, with James Fitzsimmons, of *Palenque: Recent Investigation at the Classic Maya Center* and *Classic Maya Polities of the Southern Lowlands*; and the coeditor, with M. Charlotte Arnauld, of *Building an Archaeology of Maya Urbanism: Planning and Flexibility in the American Tropics*.

Elsa Damaris Menéndez received her *licentiatura* in archaeology from San Carlos University in Guatemala and her masters in prehistory and rock art from the Universida de Trás os Montes do Alto Douro in Portugal. She has extensive fieldwork and laboratory experience and has worked on a number of projects in Guatemala, at sites such as El Perú-Waka', Uaxactun, San Bartolo, and El Zotz, and in Portugal.

Olivia C. Navarro-Farr is associate professor of anthropology and archaeology at the College of Wooster and codirector of the Waka' Archaeological Project. She is coeditor (with Michelle Rich) of *Archaeology at El Perú-Waka': Performances of Ritual, Memory, and Power*, and she has led investigations at El Perú-Waka's primary civic-ceremonial structure (M13–1) since 2003. Her recent research has been supported by the Alphawood Foundation.

Erin E. Patterson is the project osteologist for the Waka' and La Corona Archaeological Projects. She recently earned a PhD in anthropology from Tulane University. Her dissertation research focused on assessing health and diet using osteological indicators and stable isotopes.

Juan Carlos Pérez is codirector of the Waka' Archaeological Project and previously served as Director of Prehispanic and Colonial Monuments, Director General of Cultural and Natural Heritage, and Vice Minister of Cultural and Natural Heritage for the government of Guatemala. He has published on topics such as forensic anthropology, colonial archaeology, the Maya Lowlands, and cultural heritage management, among others.

Griselda Pérez Robles obtained her *licenciatura* from San Carlos University analyzing Preclassic ceramics from the site of Piedras Negras, Guatemala. She has worked at El Perú-Waka' since 2003. She has also completed a master's degree in the conservation of architecture from San Carlos University and is the former director of the Prehispanic and Colonial Monuments Department in Guatemala.

Michelle Rich is the Ellen and Harry S. Parker III Assistant Curator of Indigenous American Art at the Dallas Museum of Art. Rich coedited *Archaeology at El Perú-Waka': Ancient Maya Performances of Ritual, Memory, and Power* (with Olivia Navarro-Farr). A former National Science Foundation Graduate Research Fellow, she was the venue curator for *Spirit Lodge: Mississippian Art from Spiro* and edited the 360-page, color-illustrated volume *The Arts of the Ancient Americas at the Dallas Museum of Art*.

Matthew C. Ricker is assistant professor of soil science in the Department of Crop and Soil Sciences at North Carolina State University. He has authored 21 peer-reviewed articles that quantify how humans and climate change impact soil formation in a variety of unique ecosystems.

Sarah Van Oss began working with the Proyecto Arqueológico Waka' as an undergraduate at the College of Wooster, where her undergraduate thesis focused on iconographic material from the site. She has been involved in field and laboratory investigations in various capacities since then. She is now a PhD student in anthropology at Tulane University where she continues to study the archaeology of Waka' for her dissertation research.

INDEX

Page numbers followed by *f* and *t* indicate figures and tables.

Maya Studies

Edited by Diane Z. Chase and Arlen F. Chase

Salt: White Gold of the Ancient Maya, by Heather McKillop (2002)

Archaeology and Ethnohistory of Iximché, by C. Roger Nance, Stephen L. Whittington, and Barbara E. Borg (2003)

The Ancient Maya of the Belize Valley: Half a Century of Archaeological Research, edited by James F. Garber (2004; first paperback edition, 2011)

Unconquered Lacandon Maya: Ethnohistory and Archaeology of Indigenous Culture Change, by Joel W. Palka (2005)

Chocolate in Mesoamerica: A Cultural History of Cacao, edited by Cameron L. McNeil (2006; first paperback edition, 2009)

Maya Christians and Their Churches in Sixteenth-Century Belize, by Elizabeth Graham (2011; first paperback edition, 2020)

Chan: An Ancient Maya Farming Community, edited by Cynthia Robin (2012; first paperback edition, 2013)

Motul de San José: Politics, History, and Economy in a Classic Maya Polity, edited by Antonia E. Foias and Kitty F. Emery (2012; first paperback edition, 2015)

Ancient Maya Pottery: Classification, Analysis, and Interpretation, edited by James John Aimers (2013; first paperback edition, 2014)

Ancient Maya Political Dynamics, by Antonia E. Foias (2013; first paperback edition, 2014)

Ritual, Violence, and the Fall of the Classic Maya Kings, edited by Gyles Iannone, Brett A. Houk, and Sonja A. Schwake (2016; first paperback edition, 2018)

Perspectives on the Ancient Maya of Chetumal Bay, edited by Debra S. Walker (2016)

Maya E Groups: Calendars, Astronomy, and Urbanism in the Early Lowlands, edited by David A. Freidel, Arlen F. Chase, Anne S. Dowd, and Jerry Murdock (2017; first paperback edition, 2020)

War Owl Falling: Innovation, Creativity, and Culture Change in Ancient Maya Society, by Markus Eberl (2017)

Pathways to Complexity: A View from the Maya Lowlands, edited by M. Kathryn Brown and George J. Bey III (2018; first paperback edition, 2021)

Water, Cacao, and the Early Maya of Chocolá, by Jonathan Kaplan and Federico Paredes Umaña (2018)

Maya Salt Works, by Heather McKillop (2019)

The Market for Mesoamerica: Reflections on the Sale of Pre-Columbian Antiquities, edited by Cara G. Tremain and Donna Yates (2019; first paperback edition, 2023)

Migrations in Late Mesoamerica, edited by Christopher S. Beekman (2019)

Approaches to Monumental Landscapes of the Ancient Maya, edited by Brett A. Houk, Bárbara Arroyo, and Terry G. Powis (2020)

The Real Business of Ancient Maya Economies: From Farmers' Fields to Rulers' Realms, edited by Marilyn A. Masson, David A. Freidel, and Arthur A. Demarest (2020)

Maya Kingship: Rupture and Transformation from Classic to Postclassic Times, edited by Tsubasa Okoshi, Arlen F. Chase, Philippe Nondédéo, and M. Charlotte Arnauld (2020)

Lacandón Maya in the Twenty-First Century: Indigenous Knowledge and Conservation in Mexico's Tropical Rainforest, by James D. Nations (2023)

The Materialization of Time in the Ancient Maya World: Mythic History and Ritual Order, edited by David A. Freidel, Arlen F. Chase, Anne S. Dowd, and Jerry Murdock (2024)

El Perú-Waka': New Archaeological Perspectives on the Kingdom of the Centipede, edited by Keith Eppich, Damien B. Marken, and David Freidel (2024)